INHERITING
THE WAR

ALSO BY LAREN McCLUNG

Between Here and Monkey Mountain: Poems

INHERITING
THE WAR

Poetry and Prose
by Descendants of Vietnam
Veterans and Refugees

Edited by LAREN McCLUNG

W. W. Norton & Company
Independent Publishers Since 1923
New York | London

For information about special discounts for bulk purchases,
please contact W. W. Norton Special Sales at
specialsales@wwnorton.com or 800-233-4830

Manufacturing by Quad Graphics Fairfield
Book design by Abbate Design
Production manager: Lauren Abbate

ISBN: 978-0-393-35428-7 (pbk.)

W. W. Norton & Company, Inc., 500 Fifth Avenue,
New York, N.Y. 10110
www.wwnorton.com

W. W. Norton & Company Ltd., 15 Carlisle Street,
London W1D 3BS

1 2 3 4 5 6 7 8 9 0

for those who saw the war,
& the next generations

&

for Andrea, Katie, Linda, & Pop

CONTENTS

INHERITING
THE WAR

FOREWORD

YUSEF KOMUNYAKAA

They have left a pool
made of father, mother, and child.
Let us look
in it,
look for our own blood and bones,
look for them in the mud of Vietnam . . .

—**PABLO NERUDA** (from "In Vietnam,"
translated by Ilan Stavans)

As I reflect, it seems as if I'm transposed, standing in the atmosphere of a memory—a feeling, a place. I can see the room. I can hear a voice. Usually I'm listening acutely. In this memory, time is sequential. I am standing in the living room where my great-uncle is asleep and I hear him sob and cry out. This is not the first time I hear him this way. But in this memory, I am six or seven, and, only the way a child can, I ask, "What you crying 'bout, Uncle Jesse?"

He rises, sits on the edge of the couch, takes my hand, and says, "I was on a death detail overseas. Soldiers were droppin' like flies. We cut trenches in the ice. I learned what dog tags are good for: I put one into the mouth of each dead soldier and the other dog tag in a canvas bag, and we pushed the dead into ditches till we come back to dig 'em up." Then he rolls a cigarette from his red can of Prince Albert.

My great-uncle Jesse was a veteran of World War I. He fought under the French flag because at the time the US military was segregated. This image of him digging up corpses from the trenches recurred in my psyche; it had already begun to direct my childhood play where one fights imaginary wars. But perhaps this knowing also created a real sense of reflection—at only six or seven, I wasn't eager to pretend to be dead. I knew something about the truth of war. "I learned how to dig graves and gamble. That's all I learned," he'd say. And "you know, I need to go back to France."

The man never stopped talking in his sleep.

Mama Mary, my maternal grandmother, had one rule. Whenever he knocked on her front door, he'd pause at the threshold, and she would say, "Wait here, Jesse." She'd return, holding out with both hands a white handkerchief, and he would place his .38 Smith & Wesson Special onto it, and she would wrap the pistol and place it into the chifforobe in her bedroom, lock it, and put the key into her apron pocket.

This ritual between them taught me the rules of inclusion and ways to negotiate a space. Such rituals create the illusion that we are in control of the larger world and its mysteries. Here was this man who had carried the gun as part of his identity, and he was handing it over to my grandmother as if handing over his role as a man, as a soldier; instead, now, he could relax; he could be a brother, an uncle. He could momentarily undo the rituals of war that had shaped him when he was seventeen.

In childhood, I had not become aware that I was internalizing these rituals, but I vividly remember each action, each image. I grew up with framed photographs of soldiers displayed on ornate shelves and tables in living rooms of small Southern houses. They were presented in the same way sports trophies are displayed—with pride and ceremony. The war had come home in multitudinous disguises and changed faces. I encountered these images of men dressed in World War II uniforms—men in my family and community—on display without any real dialogue about it. Four of my great-uncles had been in that war overseas.

When I was a boy, my mother and I would peer into a viewfinder and gaze at images of distant places, natural landscapes from around the world—Japan and Mexico, illuminated caves and deserts, a whole menagerie of animals. But it seemed as if the only people I knew that had travelled away from Bogalusa were those individuals who had been in war.

Years later, when I entered the US Army stationed in Chu Lai with the Americal Division, I fully understood war was indeed a life and death matter. However, what began to visit me were echoes of Southern religious culture. Thou Shalt Not Kill. And yet there was also a sense of belonging to a fraternal order, to a symbolic community; to be a full-fledged American, this is expected. Perhaps this need to be fully initiated was even cultural or racial.

But whatever one witnessed in battle became a silence carried within. Soldiers are always dreaming themselves into the future as a way of getting beyond this, of moving forward. As a man, I sometimes think back to the fragments of Uncle Jesse's experience, and I realize that those closest are left merely to imagination as a means of understanding.

After I returned from Vietnam, Uncle Jesse took the .38 from under his suit coat, placed it on the white handkerchief, and he and his sister knew it would be the last time they'd go through their ritual. He had been diagnosed with incurable lung cancer, and he had returned to my grandmother's to die. That was love and duty, but she wouldn't buy him any cheap wine or fifths of whiskey. What he witnessed in war still defined him. He still talked in his sleep, and in retrospect I believe his graphic details were an antiwar statement. Also, he spoke of a daughter in France, and this was news to his sister.

Mama Mary called me one day.

"He's worrying me to death, begging for whiskey," she said. "He knows he can't drink under my roof."

A long, agonizing silence hung between us.

"Son, what do you think?"

"Mama, give Uncle Jesse the Old Crow."

"I knew you'd know what to do—all this war business."

Whenever I travel back across the years, it has become a balm—even with my acute memory of his psychic pain—to remember Uncle Jesse, his pocketsful of silver dimes for children in the neighborhood, and his ritual of refuge in his sister's house.

Yet I hadn't found my own refuge. I didn't wish anyone to know I had served in Vietnam. I wanted to forget that time, even in a cultural landscape where the institution of war was so apparent. But the echoes of war can traverse or circumnavigate borders of the mind and flesh.

Now, as I read through the works in this collection, I think back to 1990, to when I journeyed back to Vietnam. Kevin Bowen had called me from the William Joiner Center for the Study of War and Social Consequences at the University of Massachusetts in Boston and said, "Yusef, do you want to go back to Vietnam for a visit?" It wasn't something I had to think about. "When?" I asked.

I arrived in Bangkok two days behind schedule, after three or four detours on Northwest Airlines, my luggage lost, but I hadn't thrown my hands up and said, "To hell with this." The others had taken bets if I'd abort my trip. I flew to Vietnam early the next morning with poets and writers Kevin Bowen, Philip Caputo, W. D. Ehrhart, Larry Heinemann, David Hunt, Larry Rottmann, and Bruce Weigl. We were headed to Hanoi for a conference with members of the Vietnamese Writers' Union.

It had been 20 years, and I never dreamt of walking the streets of Hanoi. My mind played back images of my childhood friend Andrew Johnson who had been killed. I didn't know how it would feel to be there, or how I, once "the enemy," would be received. Still, the day before I traveled, a dud ammunition fired years earlier exploded when struck by a farmer's plow in a rice paddy, maiming him and his three children. And yet, the Vietnamese welcomed us and we engaged in a dialogue. We listened to their stories and they listened to ours.

After one of our joint sessions, I introduced myself to Nguy Nga, a local short story writer, and asked, "If you could do something you never did before, what would it be?"

I don't know where the question came from.

"Teenager," he said.

"Huh?"

"I never been a teenager."

"Oh," I said.

It was a punch in the gut.

I had survived by contrasting my teenage years—swimming in the creek, fishing, fighting and making up, dreaming of distant places, kissing among the trees—with adult realities. I still can't imagine not having been a teenager.

Today, I have no doubt that—across time and place—we soldiers have carried home echoes of our war. Yes, we carry with us the pathos, and our loved ones often inherit the caustic baggage. Some spend a lifetime attempting to make sense out of the distant, protracted silence and detachment where bridges seldom exist. *Inheriting the War*, however, is a poignant anthology that connects voices from the next generation that traverse numerous borders. This compendium of experiences and impressions is a lived forum of feelings. It is also a conduit that moves toward understanding, to a place of negotiation through simple speech. All the "search and destroy missions" have been left behind, and a new territory of reconciliation emerges on the horizon. *Inheriting the War* brings people together; voices speak to each other. And, in this sense, a natural pragmatism is the underpinning of this anthology where each poem, short story, excerpt of fiction and nonfiction, serves as a bridge in psychological time and space. This is the stuff of supreme caring. Sometimes, when we speak of ourselves we are also telling each other's stories.

Perhaps the closing paragraph of Neil L. Jamieson's *Understanding Vietnam* aligns with the task this anthology accomplishes:

> Americans or Vietnamese of all political persuasions and all generations and all walks of life must work to expand the sense of "we" and diminish the sense of "they." If we cannot humanize those whose destinies have impinged upon our own, if we cannot increase empathy and vanquish self-righteousness, if we cannot expand our moral imaginations to discern and accept the pattern that connects us all in a common human condition, then we shall all continue to have lost the war in Vietnam. . . .

What Jamieson says about armies and nations, this anthology says about loved ones—fathers, mothers, wives, and children. The chronicles of proverbial silence, along with exile, dislocation, unrequited rage, alcoholism and drug addiction, PTS, Agent Orange, it is all addressed here. These pages underscore a needful, unselfish dialogue. Sometimes spoken through crafted metaphor, sometimes straight on, each unique work in *Inheriting the War* embraces a collective that aims to engage through some daring and passionate truths calibrated by bravery.

THE LOST PILOT

For my father, 1922–1944

Your face did not rot
like the others—the co-pilot,
for example, I saw him

yesterday. His face is corn-
mush: his wife and daughter,
the poor ignorant people, stare

as if he will compose soon.
He was more wronged than Job.
But your face did not rot

like the others—it grew dark,
and hard like ebony;
the features progressed in their

distinction. If I could cajole
you to come back for an evening,
down from your compulsive

orbiting, I would touch you,
read your face as Dallas,
your hoodlum gunner, now,

with the blistered eyes, reads
his braille editions. I would
touch your face as a disinterested

scholar touches an original page.
However frightening, I would
discover you, and I would not

turn you in; I would not make
you face your wife, or Dallas,
or the co-pilot, Jim. You

could return to your crazy
orbiting, and I would not try
to fully understand what

it means to you. All I know
is this: when I see you,
as I have seen you at least

once every year of my life,
spin across the wilds of the sky
like a tiny, African god,
I feel dead. I feel as if I were
the residue of a stranger's life,
that I should pursue you.
My head cocked toward the sky,
I cannot get off the ground,
and, you, passing over again,
fast, perfect, and unwilling
to tell me that you are doing
well, or that it was mistake
that placed you in that world,
and me in this; or that misfortune
placed these worlds in us.
                    —James Tate

INTRODUCTION

James Tate's poem "The Lost Pilot," published in 1967 when he was 24 years old, provides one framework—or tradition—to begin this conversation. Through an act of imagination and through a life of questions and research, the son attempts to assemble his own identity by recovering the fragments of his father, a World War II pilot. In the year the poem was written, Tate had become older than his father at the time of his death. In a *Paris Review* interview with poet Charles Simic, Tate, who was born during his father's deployment, said he had spent much of his life piecing together his father's disappearance: "I was never given straight answers as a child. I was told that my father was never found. . . . I have since utterly verified that he is in a military graveyard near Liege. . . . Was he killed in the crash? Did he parachute out? I don't know." For Tate, the loss of his father and the brutality of war have instilled these questions and have charged him with the relentless task of unearthing the past.

When one inherits the residue of a parent's experience of war— whether a momentary disruption in time and place, the phantom weight of a weapon or the stench of a village in flames, the perpetual suffering of exile—one also inherits an abstraction, maybe in the form of total silence, or in the form of a family history told and retold at the dinner table. But the said and unsaid leave only impressions. What descendants of war witness may persist in the body of the parent, though much is left to the imagination and to a perpetual search.

It is through a dialog with the past that one begins the work of reconstruction; thus, this collection conjures pasts—personal and historical. Pursuit becomes a motif throughout the collection: adult sons and daughters travel across temporal landscapes, or even across oceans, to retrace their parent's footsteps. Poet Gardner McFall, in her poem "On the Line," writes of an actual and metaphorical search for her father, a Navy pilot who disappeared during a mission: "I am traveling fast, propelled / by you, doing what I must, / ready to answer for it." Karen Russell goes underground through the Cu Chi tunnels and writes that she'd hoped "the tunnels might be a literal portal, a way to enter the deep grammar of [her] dad's past." Brian Ma writes of his own journey to Vietnam, "I came for a reason / but his prison is a school now, / my family's house a pharmacy." The search is an attempt at creating dimension. Adam Karlin also follows in his father's footsteps, though he does not find the war in Vietnam, but rather a place where, yes, once the war existed, along with the landscapes, and a people, and a culture that can be traced back nearly four millennium—one that survives, and, in fact, flourishes. Through pursuit, Karlin transforms the once mythical place, defined by the limits of his imagination, into a real one. He writes, "The moment wasn't perfect. But it was real, I thought, and so is Vietnam, which I am maybe seeing for the first time, through its own joss stick smoke and rituals and land and sea and sky." Sadly, the Western experience of Vietnam has been perceived as little more than a theme-park for war, a monument to recent history.

The first American troops were deployed to Vietnam just over 50 years ago in March of 1965, shortly after the departure of the French. This arrival was expected: in fact, there was a saying—leave one grave open for the first American. Over the next ten years, the conflict escalated (along with guerrilla tactics and the use of the most aggressive machinery, technology, and chemical warfare of the time) until it officially ended with the fall of Saigon (known in Vietnam as "Liberation Day") in April 1975 when the last flights of soldiers—American and South Vietnamese Army—and civilians evacuated, and when those Vietnamese who could escaped on boats they navigated by the stars across tumultuous waters for refugee camps in the Philippines, Malaysia, Hong Kong, Indonesia, Singapore, and Thailand (many were later granted access to the United States, Australia, Canada, France, and elsewhere).

Yet, there are 58,307 names on the Vietnam War Memorial in Washington, DC—the reflective black granite a metaphorical portal into an underworld where the dead wander and the war persists. Vietnam veterans who stare into the granite see their own faces in the cemetery stone in the year where they will find the names of their comrades. We must mourn our dead. We must recover them. But what we seldom hear of are the millions of unnamed casualties—more than 2.5 million Vietnamese: 1.1 million North Vietnamese soldiers, approximately 250,000 South Vietnamese Army soldiers, and 2 million civilians; more than 500 Australian soldiers; and 3,000 South Korean soldiers. We seldom hear of those soldiers—American and Vietnamese—and civilians who have died due to illnesses related to exposure to Agent Orange, or to other war-related injuries, since the end of the war. How do we reflect on these casualties? How can we, now, 50 years after the war, removed from the tension of our political past, understand the larger truth—that we all endure the aftershocks.

For those who survived, the course of their lives was altered for generations to come. This collection is not intended as a history of the Vietnam War, nor as a political statement about that war, but an account of its complicated aftermath. Yes, the descendants of these soldiers—career military personnel and draftees, and from the many perspectives—American, South Vietnamese, Vietnamese, Australian, Khmer, Hmong, Laotian—have sometimes retold war stories. But more importantly, the collection conveys the way war has entered into the imagination of this generation, and the tremendous work that these writers have enacted to understand. It has come into our houses and has kept us awake at night trying to bridge the clinical distance of history. It has provoked us to interrogate the past until the unknowable becomes a vivid landscape, until the ghosts have names and faces, until the boats stop swaying. It has asked us to reckon with many kinds of grief the war has given us.

But what do the children of war inherit? The question is political but also deeply personal. The word *inheritance* is a conceptual term, but also a biological and social one. In war, soldiers—from all sides—experience, witness, and perform acts of violence; they face the perplexing reality of mortality on a daily basis, and, then, if they survive, return to live their lives. But realities such as reintegration or relocation can be deeply affecting. Studies report that the families of war veterans, especially children, may suffer post-traumatic stress, anxiety, and depression. These struggles are not merely psychological, but—in the deep connection between brain and body—physiological. Over the last several years, researchers have studied this long-term physiological inheritance. For decades now, research has shown that the offspring of a parent exposed to Agent Orange is four times more likely to suffer biological effects, including birth defects, cancer, and other illnesses. (In the US, such individuals are often denied claims by Veterans Affairs and their illnesses remain unacknowledged; in Vietnam, the effect of chemical warfare is even more drastic as the toxin polluted the land, food supply, and water.)

In this way, the correlation between the parent's body chemistry and the genetic health of the offspring seems apparent. But, also, the body houses emotion, and the emotional and nervous systems indeed translate into the physical. Recent research has begun to examine how even trauma may be inherited from a parent. In a TED-X statement, Tori Egherman recounts these studies. She reflects on laboratory research by neuroscientist Isabelle Mansuy and her colleagues at the University of Zurich in Switzerland who have demonstrated that trauma is a trait that can be passed on to offspring. She reports:

> [T]he offspring of mice who experienced high levels of trauma experienced high levels of stress and depression. . . . The scientists showed that the stress and depression were passed on genetically, rather than socially, by injecting sperm into mice who had not undergone trauma.

She connects this research to the "children of survivors" by citing author and science editor Virginia Hughes:

> People who were traumatized during the Khmer Rouge genocide in Cambodia tended to have children with depression and anxiety, for example, and children of Australian veterans of the Vietnam War have higher rates of suicide than the general population.

Understanding that a parent's experience of trauma could appear socially, or biologically through genetic expression in their children, leaves a great deal to think about.

Whether through a genetic inheritance, or through a social one, in the imagination, and sometimes in the body, the history of a parent converges with one's own personal history. Carl Jung, in *Dreams*, teaches us, "Return to childhood is always the return to father and mother, to the whole burden of the psychic non-ego as represented by the parents, with its long and momentous history. Regression spells disintegration into our historical and hereditary determinants, and it's only with the greatest effort that we can free ourselves from their embrace." These "historical and hereditary determinants" are recursive factors that become the basis for one's identity—or else we spend our lives attempting to exorcise them. It is evident in this collection that this terrain of childhood has been carried into the adult psyche, and that history has compelled us.

In obvious ways, and across cultures, this is a collection about fathers. Throughout modern psychology, the father is often a source of myth, but the father who has seen war, who has performed acts of violence, heroism, or survival, is in many ways inaccessible, a mystery to us, and he may enact the power dynamics of war or military ritual in the household. One may spend one's life in pursuit of him, or engulfed in the empathetic attempt at understanding, but may only find a labyrinth of the past or an inscrutable distance of power. This distance becomes a motif in the collection: Tom Bissell asks, "Can God create a boulder so large that even he cannot move it? Similarly, could a child ever feel bigger than his parents? I was not thinking of size. Rather, could a child feel *existentially* bigger?" Teresa Mei Chuc writes of meeting her father: "He was like an Egyptian cat: skinny, foraging, stern. He was impenetrable. He didn't smile; he didn't run up to swoop me into his arms. He was a stranger coming to live with us." David Ellis writes: "He was a bit of a stranger to me, one that I tried to unstrange by snooping through his stuff." Here we begin to recognize that the process of discovering is an attempt at making the father *real*—perhaps to see the past with clarity, or attempt to understand as adults what was confusing as children.

While the father is an expected character in the narrative of war, perhaps more importantly, both implicitly and explicitly, the experiences of women during wartime are portrayed. The poet Nguyen Phan Que Mai, born in a village in North Vietnam in 1973 and raised in the Mekong Delta in the South of Vietnam, conveys the experience of women who work the earth with their hands, and who know the deep emotional suffering of war: pregnant women who survive bombings, or women who call out for their dead children or husbands. Through the rendering of these lyrical narratives and through a careful reconstruction of her own lineage, Nguyen Phan Que Mai creates a portrait of woman that is both fractured and resilient. Of her own mother, who gave birth during wartime, she writes: "To protect me from those storms, my mother spread her wings." This Vietnamese poet's verse resonates with Vietnamese American poet Cathy Linh Che, whose poem "Split" relays the story of her mother, as a young woman in a village in Vietnam, and her encounter with US Marines who want a cutting of her hair: "With scissor-fingers, / they snip the air, / repeat *cut*, // point at their helmets / and then at her hair." Che asks, "What does she say / to her mother / to make her so afraid?" After encountering the troops, Che's mother is sent away from her nameless village never to return. These writers convey only a glimpse at the experience of their mothers during war, but one begins to see a reality often overlooked.

In many ways, as revealed through their detailed renderings, these authors have performed great acts of listening, but also acts of bearing witness to the weight of silence in the household. This is true of war in the family dynamic—where one learns whether to ask, or not to ask, especially in a culture that had moralized the role of the soldier. Tom Bissell writes: "There were two types of Vietnam veterans: those who talked about the war and those who did not talk about it." Many of the US veterans were among a small percentage of Americans who actually deployed to war. This feeling of otherness was only magnified by the pressures of reintegrating into a hostile public from a war deemed unethical. Yet, despite the silence often carried into the household, the language of war was indoctrinated. As Ada Limón writes in "Listen": "When you live with a veteran, the language of war becomes a natural thing." Perhaps for Vietnamese Americans the relationship to silence is even more complicated; perhaps there are two simultaneous realities—one that exists within the Vietnamese American community, and another when engaging in the larger society. In the former there is a sense of shared history, where the refugees share an understanding of what the other has survived; perhaps this constructs a mutual understanding, even in the unsaid. Yet, integration poses another barrier, one that often carries the stigma of silence. In "The Good Immigrant Student," Bich Minh Nguyen conveys this struggle as she relays her experience as a Vietnamese student in a Midwestern public school; she writes, "I was nearly silent, deadly shy, and wholly obedient. My greatest fear was being called on, or in any way standing out more than I already did in the class that was, except for me and one black student, dough-white."

In *Inheriting the War*, accounts of witness are told from the descendant's point of view; they deliver another kind of war story—one that asks us to discard the romanticized view of war, and to seek a more truthful, long-term depiction—one of brutality, suffering, and even forgiveness. Here, the history of family converges with history itself, and these authors, who have internalized these histories, whose lives have been shaped by conflict and survival, ask for a listener. In doing so, they subvert the dehumanized depictions of the other.

The psychology of otherness is intended to keep us from seeing one another as human. In a chapter titled "Images of the Enemy" in his 1959 philosophical memoir *The Warriors: Reflections on Men in Battle*, published during the Vietnam War, professor and World War II veteran J. Glenn Gray conveys that the use of the definite article "the" constructs a psychological war tactic: "not 'an' enemy or 'our' enemy," but 'the' enemy" (134). He suggests that the construct implies a "unified, concrete universal" (134). He writes, "By designating him with the definite article, it is made to appear that he is single and his reality consists in hostility to us. Thus do the moral absolutisms of warfare develop through the medium of language, and, all unconsciously, we surrender reason to the emotional contagion of the communal" (134). This generalization strips the individual of personhood, autonomy, and humanity. The language of the military dehumanizes. It objectifies. It desecrates personhood and poses the greatest danger to that which makes us human.

But, in these pages, the concept of "the enemy" is extended, not merely in reference to "the other side" as enemy, but to their children, often called "children of the enemy." In his astounding work of scholarship *Children of the Enemy: Oral Histories of Vietnamese Amerasians and Their Mothers*, Steven DeBonis depicts the realities of Amerasians in the United States, in the refugee camps, and in Vietnam. In his introduction he conveys the complex reality these individuals endure. He writes, "In most of these Amerasians, the genes of their fathers predominated; there was little of Vietnam in their looks. Freckle-faced girls, lanky young black men, blonds, red heads" (3). He illustrates this stigma: "Outsiders in the land of their birth, fatherless children in a culture where identity flows from the father, Amerasians were generally considered fair game for abuse. The taunts *My lai* and *con lai*, suffered by almost all Amerasians, and *My den* by those of black descent, carry stronger negative connotations then their approximate English equivalents: 'Amerasian,' 'half-breed,' and 'black Amerasian' " (5). Black Amerasians, he reports, feel that they've faced more severe abuse than whites: he quotes the mother of one black Amerasian girl: "Vietnamese say, 'You go back to America, you dirty American, go back.' They say like that many times to my daughter, 'cause she is black. My son is white, not so many problems' " (5). DeBonis reports on abandoned or orphaned children and others abused and ostracized by their parents; Amerasians who suffer bullying, depression, or who perform self-mutilation: "Cigarette burns and razor slashes on the arms and legs, and occasionally the torso are common among both males and females. Also not unusual among men is the lopping off of a part of a digit, generally the pinky, occasionally the index finger" (6). Such accounts of cruelty and brutality, delivered in the most intimate form as oral histories, recur throughout his study.

Inheriting the War begins with a poem by Quan Barry titled "child of the enemy" that explores this complex identity. Barry writes: "the floating world carved its shame / on the dark meat of my face." Barry's work is a meditation on the convergence of identity one individual embodies right here in the United States. And later in the collection, in "Motherland," Amy Phan delivers the story of Huan, a black Amerasian man rescued during Operation Baby Lift, who returns to his homeland. Often through innuendo, gesture, or the character's reflection, Phan's work illustrates the difficult racial experience of the character in both cultures. These works, and others, present the experience of identity as a result of a culture that has adopted this brutal mindset.

Indeed, objectification through language as conceptual warfare extends beyond the military and far beyond the war-zone; in fact, such language is used to devalue the other in everyday interaction. t.k. lê conveys this in "Part of Memory Is Forgetting" when, at happy hour, white co-workers talk about the Vietnamese American writer as the "Viet Cong": "I listened to her laugh echo in the bar. It was as if something about my face was a riddle, a joke, and Viet Cong was the punchline." It's important to reflect here. This is not happening 40 years ago. This is now.

Perhaps this reduction of the other—the veteran at home, the refugee, and the cultures abroad—is a by-product of the cleansing of history— revisions and erasures. This erasure of the other as human is an attempt at justifying brutality. Names of battle and military lingo persevere while the personal is written out. Critic John Berger explains this revision as one that constructs distance in his essay "Hiroshima" when he writes that human stories have been torn out of the pages of history. He argues, "Of course, the facts are there in textbooks. It may even be that the children learn the dates. But what these facts mean . . . has now been torn out. It has been a systematic, slow and thorough process of suppression and elimination" (*The Sense of Sight* 291).

If an official history silences, literature cultivates a space where those voices torn out of the pages of history survive to reinstate themselves. In *A Journey with Two Maps*, poet Eavan Boland writes "the rift between the past and history [is] real; but it [is] not simple"; she continues, "In those shadows, in the past, I was well aware that injustices and griefs had happened without any hope of the saving grace of elegy or expression—those things which an official history can count on. Silence [is] a condition of the past" (13). I once asked her to clarify what she means by this "rift." She said that *the past* and *history* are not the same thing. History has been edited into an official document of the winners—it says little of the pasts of everyday people. Poetry is one way of telling those untold stories.

The language of war turns the other into an object—the language of literature humanizes. Through the narratives of others we can more clearly see the world, and in them, we see ourselves. These narratives subvert the clinical accounts delivered in history books. They complicate the glorification of war delivered by Hollywood as near propaganda. These narratives ask more than to listen to the politician, the historian, or even the soldier, but to the soldier's family. They ask us not only to listen to those who are on "our" side of history, but to a communion of voices that together create a multidimensional history, whether through the vivid depiction of landscape or psyche. As Grace Paley writes: "Now the dead and the living are telling us about the war. No matter whose side they're on, they tell the truth" (Paley, *Just As I Thought*, "Everybody Is Telling the Truth" 73).

In Tom Bissell's book *The Father of All Things*, he includes several oral histories that he conducted. One of them is an encounter with a Vietnamese woman who tells him:

> Mostly I remember bombs falling, airplanes coming. I remember always moving. My father was political. He was a farmer, then he was a VC. My mother was not political. My brother was not political. We were poor. We were chased out of our home many times. Sometimes by the VC when my father was gone, sometimes by the bombs.
>
> I remember as a little girl not believing I would survive. I remember thinking, "Tomorrow, I will die." Can you imagine? Later when I went to the United States to study, many professors asked me, "Why do you want to come here? Don't you hate Americans?" I said, "Behind the soldiers, behind the governments, there are always hearts, families, memories, childhoods, pasts." (355–356)

She says that she started to read short stories by American authors about the war, but that she could not recognize her own experience in those accounts: "That was not my war. My war was my mother crying, my brother crying, always moving" (356).

Many authors in this collection, across cultural borders, were also living during the war. Their accounts here sometimes convey the experience of war as a child, or reflect on the immediacy of war in their families. These accounts, both Western and Vietnamese, transcend politics. With time having passed now, we can begin to listen to those most vulnerable— others like us, everyday citizens—with understanding.

A nd now more than ever it is necessary to listen to these refugee narratives. The stories of those whose families fled on boats to arrive in refugee camps can provide a truthful gaze into the reality of refugees today fleeing war-torn nations and other countries emblazoned in conflict. In his essay "The Stories They Carried," Andrew Lam delivers insight. The title is an allusion to the acclaimed novel *The Things They Carried*, written by Vietnam veteran Tim O'Brien, except Lam directs the reader's focus not on the soldiers, but rather on the Vietnamese refugees. In 1991, 16 years after the end of the war, Lam spent six months living and working as a Vietnamese interpreter in Whitehead, a refugee detention center in Hong Kong known for "riots and gang fights and mass protests and a handful of self-immolations." Many of these detainees were rejected for political asylum and were to be sent back to Vietnam. He writes, "There were eleven people, mostly women, who disemboweled themselves in protest of being forced back." During his time there he reported on the gruesome accounts of these Vietnamese refugees, including children born in the camp who have never known life outside of the barbed and chicken-wire fences. He lets the people tell their own accounts, through his translation, to deliver to the reader a detailed reality of the circumstances. Through Lam's work, and through many other writers here who convey their own experience as refugees in Western culture, in the aftermath of a war 50 years past now, we may have some clarity on the continuing refugee crises in the face of war.

T hrough each deeply personal individual narrative, and through a rendering of the imagination, these writers restore empathy to those who suffer the psychological and everyday erosions of war. Yet it is through the collective body of work that one discovers a many-sided truth in order to, as Berger urges, "reinsert those events . . . back into living consciousness" (*The Sense of Sight* 287). But the work of the collective is not merely to leave an imprint of experience. Rather, sociological imagination calls for an act of empathy; listening, imagining, researching, and excavating history—personal and cultural—becomes the work of transformation. I've often said that telling implies a listener, and that, perhaps, being heard is the first step toward healing. In this way, the collection of voices here aims to reveal that the individuals, both soldier and civilian, women and children, all equal from all sides, suffer. And more importantly, we must recover—as individuals, as families, as a nation, and as human beings who share in this history.

In *The Other*, Ryszard Kapuściński teaches us: "just as a bad childhood leaves its mark on the whole of a person's later life, so a bad historical memory has an effect on later relations between societies." In this light, there is work to be done. During the war effort, the United States sprayed 5.5 million acres of land with Agent Orange. The toxin, which sickened Western veterans as well as Vietnamese and civilians with lifelong, life-threatening, or fatal illnesses and cancers, continues to pollute the landscape. In 2008, the United States proposed a program to begin restoring the land in Da Nang, but the *New York Times* reported, "Many here have not hesitated to call the American program too little—it addresses only the one site—and very late." Vietnamese-born artist Binh Danh, who teaches at Stanford University, addresses this environmental inheritance in his photographic series *Immortality: The Remnants of the Vietnam and American War*. He makes use of photosynthesis in his photographic process by recording war images onto tropical leaves using chlorophyll and light. In an artist statement he writes: "The images of war are part of the leaves, and live inside and outside of them. The leaves express the continuum of war. They contain the residue of the Vietnam War: bombs, blood, sweat, tears, and metals. The dead have been incorporated into the landscape of Vietnam during the cycles of birth, life, and death; through the recycling and transformation of materials, and the creation of new materials. As matter is neither created nor destroyed, but only transformed, the remnants of the Vietnam and American War live on forever in the Vietnamese landscape." In this moment, with awareness that human interference has damaged the environment, almost irreparably, it is our responsibility to do all we can to restore the land for the health of the people and the planet.

Further, one must realize that to this day there are casualties of the Vietnam American War. In September 2016, brothers Done (10 years old) and Pone (9 years old) were killed when they "struck an unexploded device while digging for crickets in Nongbua village . . . some 250 km southeast of Lao capital Vientiane," according to the *Vientiane Times*. In Laos, the United States dropped more than 2 million tons of ordnance. According to the National Regulatory Authority, there have been 20,000 victims of the war in Laos alone since the war ended in 1975—and almost 300 casualties annually for the last decade, many of whom are children. And in Vietnam and Cambodia there are claims that, since the end of the war, more than 100,000 civilians have been killed by unexploded ordnance.

While the United States has been working to make reparations, and in fact is now engaged in trade and tourism with Vietnam, US veterans have been invited back—but the Vietnamese Diaspora in many ways still experiences severance and dislocation. And those refugee families, many of whom identify as American, still feel divided from their motherland. On March 10, 2015, at Poets House in New York City, the poet and peace activist Nguyen Phan Que Mai read with her translator, Vietnam veteran and Pulitzer Prize–nominated poet Bruce Weigl. During a discussion, she spoke of mending the relationship between the United States and Vietnam. As she welcomed Americans to visit her country, Vietnamese American poet Paul Tran addressed another, more complicated question. What of the relationship between the Vietnamese Diaspora and Vietnam? Tran's question highlights the anxiety of the former generation in regards to their homeland—an anxiety that is shared by this generation. Yet those descendants of the former South Vietnam are now traveling, many for the first time, to their parents' homeland. This discussion publicly recognizing the rift between Vietnam and her Diaspora is an important one, and perhaps the beginning of a real initiative toward reconciliation.

The work collected here, while confronting histories and eulogizing pasts, is an attempt at transformation. The poems and narratives depict only a sliver of the larger experience. In regards to history, the truth is manifold, and through this collective of voices these writers direct us both backwards and forwards: the aftermath of war crosses borders of generation and culture. In many ways this is new territory, as writers of this generation are still emerging; thus, there are voices not yet represented here—missing are works by descendants of women veterans and nurses; there are few writers living in Vietnam represented in these pages; and there are many other writers of this community who are not included within the confines of this collection. So let this be a continuum. Let this conversation extend beyond these pages, beyond even literature, into action, policy, and acts of empathetic listening.

QUAN BARRY is the author of the novel *She Weeps Each Time You're Born* as well as four poetry books published by the University of Pittsburgh Press (*Asylum*, *Controvertibles*, *Water Puppets*, and *Loose Strife*). Barry is Professor of English at the University of Wisconsin–Madison.

FROM "CHILD OF THE ENEMY"

> I've seen thousands of Amerasians, and I have two Amerasian
> [children] of my own. Amerasians are willful and stubborn.
> They have serious identity problems. They have no discipline.
> Down the street at the Floating Hotel you'll find Amerasian
> prostitutes plying their mother's trade. I think there's a racial
> thing here, something genetic.
>
> —*An American ex-soldier as quoted in* Vietnamerica

I. NIGHT TERROR

It started when I was four.
Vacation. Door Country. Wisconsin.
The alewives rippling on the rocks
like a flock of birds, the sudden knowledge
growing like a toll. Then
I couldn't have articulated it, but I knew.
It wasn't the beached fish that frightened me.
It was the ones that got away
under the wreck of water. The ones that survived
by fleeing, kin left rotting on the shore.

II. TWENTY YEARS LATER

Someone who had been there
(and now incidentally is serving
a natural life sentence)

told you it wasn't all
about killing. Don't ever believe
you weren't conceived in love.

You take his word for it
like an imago splitting the shell,
each wet wing a voice

purged and steeling.

III. CHILD OF THE ENEMY

a.

I was born with a twelfth hole. Instantly
the floating world carved its shame
on the dark meat of my face. A love child, child of perfidy, allegiance
     split like a door.
I was born a traitor in the month of Cancer, the white phosphorus
pungent, knowing.

b.

1973. The rice winnows out like shrapnel. Before it's over
there are fifty thousand new hostilities, each birthed face inimical
as our fathers stealing home.

c.

Think of the places women dilate. Beds. Barns. Saigon streets.
No good Samaritan comes forward and only the moon like a platoon
treacherously approaching, its extended hand like a speculum, the
     better
to illuminate, disgrace.

d.

Or more importantly
the places women leave. An unsuspecting caretaker. The bacterial streets.
Or
perhaps the unspeakable pitch into burlap
and water. A gulf off the South China Sea where another sinking form
is anyone's guess.

e.

That time Tet fell in the year of the snake. As in reptilian. As in
no turning back. As in when I became
a child of containment. As in how like a monetary policy

I was loosed to an existence feral as a raised bayonet. As in
what the serpent might say: knowledge for knowledge's sake
is both industrial and complex.

f.

At birth
I was swaddled
in a blanket. Pink
wool. Threadbare.
Like everything else
moth-eaten.
Man-made.

g.

Before the last vertical bird lifted like a gurney out of April
and twenty years clotted to a tumor brilliant as a stuck fish
and the dreams began in which you saw yourself as the killer
of trees, before the army finally said it was something in the water
and orange came to be the cloak of mourning, tell me soldier:
who taught you to love like a man, you with nowhere to go
but tacitly free?

TOM BISSELL was born in Escanaba, Michigan, in 1974. After graduating from Michigan State University, he worked briefly as a Peace Corps volunteer in Uzbekistan and then as a book editor in New York City. He is the author of *Chasing the Sea*; *God Lives in St. Petersburg*, winner of the Rome Prize; *The Father of All Things*, a hybrid work of history and memoir about his father and the Vietnam War and finalist for the *Los Angeles Times* Book Prize and the Kiriyama Prize; and *Extra Lives*. He has lived in Michigan, Uzbekistan, New York, Saigon, Rome, Las Vegas, Estonia, and currently resides in Portland, Oregon, and teaches fiction writing at Portland State University.

FROM *THE FATHER OF ALL THINGS*

> My father, it was your sad image,
> so often come, that urged me to these thresholds.
> My ships are moored on the Tyrrhenian.
> O father, let me hold your right hand fast,
> do not withdraw from my embrace.
>
> —*Virgil*, The Aeneid

I

While sitting next to my father on the All Nippon Airways flight from Tokyo to Ho Chi Minh City, I finally grasped what had been bothering me. It was not the odorlessness of the processed cabin air, or the tidally sustained roar of the engines, or even the handful of tranquilizers I had gobbled. What bothered me was the increasingly unsettling sensation of simply being beside my father. Somehow he made me feel physically diminished. Perhaps fathers could not help but make their sons feel smaller. What was a father if not the one man who would always wield power over his son? One did not have to love (or even like) one's father to sense this essential inequality. I loved my father very much, but I was suddenly a little too reminded of him, which is to say, a little afraid.

I studied the hairy hands that held open the Vietnam guidebook I had bought for him: thick fingers, big knuckles, huge glossy nails. I then regarded my father's head. It seemed something out of a circus tent. I could not even look at it all at once. His round, wet eyes, Kilimanjaran nose, lost-cavern nostrils, and geological chin dimple belonged to separate facial ecosystems. The westernmost edge of the United States' mainland was eleven hours behind us, and his striking physiognomy occurred to me now because during the previous leg of our trip I had been seated one row ahead of my father, not next to him. I had also tired of the book I had brought aboard and was actively searching for something to think about, since, while flying, if I was not vigilant, my thoughts tended toward the macabre, such as, for example, the imminence of my own death.

Maybe all I really felt was simple filial humility. I recalled the famous schoolyard question: Can God create a boulder so large that even he cannot move it? Similarly, could a child ever feel bigger than his parents? I was not thinking of size. Rather, could a child feel *existentially* bigger? I did not believe so. I doubted it. And with that the various sleep aids I had ingested began, once again, to bring on the ugly process of manufactured sleep: eyelids as heavy as anchors, mind blown out like a candle, head in free-fall . . . .My nose smooshed hard against my father's shoulder. I sparked upright.

My father adjusted himself in his seat, still reading. Then, in an instructive singsong voice: "If you sleep now you're going to spend the first few days completely jet-lagged."

Moments before our first flight this morning, I had taken an Ativan, an antianxiety medication. I took another Ativan right after we lifted off. A few hours later I took another. In Tokyo's airport I washed down another with a Diet Coke. I had taken a Sominex about an hour ago. I had also drunk a Sapporo. None of this was so I could sleep. The odds of my falling asleep on an airplane were cosmologically long. The reason I had taken the pills was to relax.

I was now touching my head with fascination. "I think my hair has lost its curl."

My father looked over at me and asked, almost fondly, "How can anyone who travels as much as you be so afraid of flying? It's ridiculous."

"*Of course* it's ridiculous. *All* pathological fear is ridiculous. It's not as though I'm afraid of much. Flying, sharks, snakes. The classics."

My father shook his head, the overhead light igniting around his head a dandruffy nebula. Thankfully, he changed the subject. "Do you know that today is the Marine Corps's two-hundred-and-twenty-eighth anniversary?"

"No kidding?"

A single nod. "November tenth."

"Are you thinking this is a good omen or a bad omen?"

"I'm not thinking anything. I just thought it was a neat coincidence."

He returned to his reading. I stared out my window at a moon so close and bright I could count the dark wrinkles around its craters. Flying to Vietnam on the 228th anniversary of the United States Marine Corps: "a neat coincidence," indeed. While growing up, I had associated nearly everything about my father with the Marine Corps and Vietnam.

There were two types of Vietnam veterans: those who talked about the war and those who did not talk about it. My father talked about the war, though, if anything, this only deepened the abyss between us. I had learned something from discussions with those who had veteran fathers. This was that our fathers seemed remote because the war itself was impossibly remote. Chances were, the war had happened pre-you, before you had come to grasp the sheer accident of your own placement in time, before you recognized that the reality of yourself—your bedroom, your dolls and comic books—had nothing to do with the reality of your father. This strange, lost war, simultaneously real and unimaginable, forced us to confront the past before we had any idea of what the past really was. The war made us think theoretically before we had the vocabulary to do so. Despite its remoteness, the war's aftereffects were inescapably intimate. At every meal Vietnam sat down, invisibly, with our families.

Inspired, I pulled out my handheld tape recorder. "Hold on. I'd like to get some stuff down." I pushed the plastic brick toward my father's mouth.

His dubious eyes took their time traveling from me to the tape recorder before they returned to his guidebook. "All right."

"I don't think we've ever really talked about why you joined the Marines. Why *did* you join the Marines?"

He did not look up and spoke very softly. "I'd always wanted to be a

Marine, so I enlisted after I graduated from college. It was that simple. I couldn't get any other job."

"But you went to Georgetown. You couldn't get a job after Georgetown?"

"Do you plan on letting me read?"

"You can read in a minute. Let's get this down."

"What was your question?"

"Georgetown. You couldn't get a job."

He sighed and looked straight ahead. "Well, there was a huge recession then. I suppose I could have worked in a department store or something. But I liked the Marines. I enlisted, and once they found out I could spell 'college' they sent me to Officer Candidates School."

"You did this knowing Vietnam was coming."

"We all knew it was coming. Keep in mind we did not train for Europe or the desert or mountain warfare. We did not go to northern California. We went to the swamps of Virginia. We knew exactly where we were going. Our drill instructors told us. Our officers told us. 'We are headed for Vietnam. You and me, brother.'"

"Did it ever bother you that Johno and I didn't join the Marines?"

His face scrunched thoughtfully. "I don't know if I would say it *bothered* me . . . .It could have been something for me to feel some pride in, yeah. I don't know." Back to reading.

"Let me ask you about these Marine Corps commercials they have nowadays . . ."

He looked tired. "Which commercials?"

"The one with the knight defeating an evil sorcerer, getting hit by lightning, and turning into a Marine. Or the one with the guy fighting a magma monster in a volcano, getting hit by lightning, and turning into a Marine."

His hand moved in an oblique, conjuring manner. "I've seen them."

"But have you ever seen Soviet propaganda? One major difference is that Soviet propaganda had some connection, however deranged, to reality. Is being a Marine *at all* like fighting sorcerers?" No response. "Doesn't seeing those commercials bother you, as a Marine?"

"Absolutely not."

"Come on. You don't find it a little bit weird?"

"It's an honorable career."

"That's not what we're talking about."

He held out a flattened hand, palm up. "What is a Marine's job? A Marine is a professional soldier, trained to kill. He's not trained to do anything else except kill, sustain himself in a horrible situation, do whatever good he can, and accomplish what he's told to do by his superiors. Or her superiors. Like it or not, that's a Marine's job. It's not always right, or correct, but that's what Marines are sworn to do."

At this he retreated back into his guidebook. I decided I would leave him alone, switched off the recorder, and watched our bunned and kerchiefed Japanese stewardesses wander up and down the 777's plastic corridors. Finally I was left staring into the blank shallows of the television screen mounted in the seat before me.

As a boy, I dreaded those evenings my father had had too much to drink, stole into my bedroom, woke me up, and for an hour at a time would try to explain to me, his ten-year-old son, why the decisions he had made—decisions, he would mercilessly remind himself, that had gotten his best friends killed—were the only decisions he could have made. Other nights, he would remember fondly the various women he had courted in Vietnam, of which there seemed an extraordinary number, given over my still-unformed imagination to bizarre thoughts of myself as an Asian boy. With my school friends I would tell elaborate stories about my father. How he had single-handedly fought off an entire company of "gooners." The day he had gotten lost rafting down a river and survived a waterfall plunge. The time he had been multiply shot and how a kind black soldier had dragged him to safety. Some were true; most were not. The war had not ended for him, and soon it was alive in me.

Sometimes it felt as though Vietnam was all my father and I had ever talked about; sometimes it felt as though we had never really talked about it. Oddly, the Vietnam War had given me much for which to be thankful, such as the fact that my father's friend and fellow Vietnam veteran Philip

Caputo ultimately became my literary mentor. My father makes a brief appearance in Caputo's *A Rumor of War*, which is commonly regarded as one of the finest memoirs of the conflict and was the first Vietnam book to become a major bestseller. When in *A Rumor of War* Caputo learns of the death of his and my father's friend Walter Levy, who survived all of two weeks in Vietnam, he remembers a night in Georgetown when he, Levy, and some others went to a bar "to drink and look at girls and pretend we were still civilians." And then this: "We sat down and filled the glasses, all of us laughing, probably at something Jack Bissell said. Was Bissell there that night? He must have been, because we were all laughing very hard and Bissell was always funny." I still remember the first time I read that sentence—I was twelve, thirteen—and how my heart had convulsed. Here was the man of whom I had never had as much as a glimpse. Here was the man whose life had not yet been hewn by so much death, whom I did not find in bluish, 2 a.m. darkness drinking wine and watching *Gettysburg* or *Platoon* for the fortieth time. In *A Rumor of War* I saw the still-normal man my father could have become, a man with average sadnesses.

I used to stare at his famed purple heart ("the dumb medal," he always called it) and, next to it, a photo of him taken during his training at Quantico: BISSELL stenciled across his left breast, friendly Virginia greenery hovering behind him, my smirking father looking a little like a young Harrison Ford, holding his rifle, his eyes unaccountably soft. How I had wanted to find that man. A dinner with a magazine editor, during which we were supposed to come up with ideas I might write about, led me to talking about my father and, inevitably, about Vietnam. The magazine editor, having regarded my earlier ideas as "terrible," looked at me, leaned back, and said, "*That's* what you should write about." I was almost thirty years old, my father just past sixty. It staggered me, suddenly, how little relative time we still had left together. I knew that if I wanted to find the unknown part of my father I would have to do it soon, in Vietnam, where he had been made and unmade, killed and resurrected. Months ago I told my father over the phone that a magazine was willing to send us to Vietnam. He was quiet, as quiet as I had ever heard him. "Gosh," he said.

Now, on the plane, the Japanese captain made the announcement that we were "making our final approach" into Ho Chi Minh City, his English pronunciation that of a man whose tongue had been injected with codeine.

My father's head tilted at a doglike angle. "What did he say?"

"I think he said we're 'baking our final perch.'"

"I thought he said we were 'making our finer porch.'"

We laughed, and then my father's large hand clamped down on my knee. He squeezed too hard and for too long. "You okay?" I asked him.

He nodded, then smiled. "Nervous."

"Well, I'm nervous, too, if that makes you feel better."

He thought about this far longer than I had intended, which was not at all. "That does not make me feel better."

STAR BLACK was born in Coronado, California, and raised in Washington, DC, and Hawaii. Her father graduated from West Point and served in the US Army for 31 years, with three tours of duty in South Viet Nam. She visited the country, briefly, six months after the Tet Offensive, while working as a sound girl for a Swiss television company filming a news story on the safety of Saigon. She is the author of *Guide to Bali*, a travel book published in 1970, four books of sonnets, including *Balefire*, a book of double sestinas, *Double Time*, and a collection of free verse, *October for Idas*. She has received grants from The Fund for Poetry and the New York Foundation for the Arts.

TO A WAR CORRESPONDENT

I am here, and shells are quaking over the cracked city,
taking, randomly, its besieged citizenry, one by two by
three, as they, ripped by shrapnel, enter swift mounds
crowding the rubble. I am here, among "fair trails" and

sea salt, thinking of you amidst burials and howitzers,
and how, when you return, there will only be small talk,

strange T.V. channels, vapid parties, and how you will see
everyone scrambling in weird, uninviting careers that

mean nothing pertinent to honor or belief but seem
like flaxen fish aswim within a turquoise aquarium,
quirky and mesmerizing to those who have time for
them, and how the social pages will appear so crazy,

sports events so distant, how you'll pray to be swept
back, out of irrelevance, to hell's urgent significance.

RECOLLECTION

The verified random green,
its mossbacked canisters and C-rations
its spiky bamboo
hacked from pulsant jungles,

rumbles like a helicopter,
above the mind,
zinging fire into shut-eye,
wambling like a diseased wasp,

its intruding scrievings
locked within. The blade's buzz,
its "Friendly" wallop,
I've heard it—the medevac, the dead—

seen the memorial's enwreathing green
placed upon the stone-deaf.

LILY KATHERINE BOWEN received her MFA in poetry from The New School. Her work has previously been published in *Best American Poetry Blog* and in Clemson University's *The Chronicle*. Her graduate thesis focuses on her relationship with her father, a poet and Vietnam War veteran, and the lasting emotional and physical consequences of the war that she observed through his experience. She received a BA in English from Clemson University in May 2015, where she was the recipient of the Undergraduate Creative Writing Award in Poetry.

LANTERNS

A slight breeze bends paper lanterns
and we are swaying
on a swanky rooftop bar
in downtown Saigon.

"This is where the officers stayed,"
my father whispers as
waiters bring us drinks.
"No place for us soldiers."

Reaching for my mother's hand
he guides her to the dance floor,
I take photos and imagine
my father—

twenty-one again,
shy and unfaded,
his Irish skin tanned
from long days in the jungle,

my mother, brother, and I
intangible—
the lanterns sway again,
an earthquake in Laos.

FALLING

Before I left I watched him—
sinking into a stupor of draught Guinness
and old whiskey.

I assumed it was one of those nights—
sleep robbed by unforgiving ghosts,
extracting his cranial walls

like leeches, once inebriated off
his freckled legs in the jungle. His fall
had rejuvenated the flashbacks and

lately it seemed like every night
was one of *those* nights—
my mother holding him upstairs,

old boyfriends asking me what's wrong,
smiling and telling them to kiss me.
Waking up before dawn,

because I didn't want his apologies.
Running until the sweat collided with tears,
dripping down abandoned streets at sunrise.

I imagine that's how he felt too.
Abandoned. Maybe he wished no one ever
found him, only ten am when his skull

crashed into icy, black concrete.
Blood splattering, with it releasing,
oozing, every beautiful word

from his right hemisphere—words that
painted the parking garage walls
red like the pasta sauce

thrown in the kitchen sink, because
he can't do anything right.
And he took to his bedroom to dull

the pounding like a pan against
the metal. Over and over, like gunfire,
surrendering to his battered brain,

persuading pills down a liquored throat,
down like the spaghetti we were meant to enjoy
at the dining room table. As a family.

EMILY BRANDT is the author of three chapbooks. Her poems have appeared in *The Recluse, The Offing, Lit Hub,* the *Wall Street Journal,* and other journals. She's been in residence at Saltonstall Arts Colony and a Fellow at Poets House. Emily is an editor of *No, Dear* and at VIDA. She earned her MFA from New York University, where she facilitated the Veterans Writing Workshop for veterans of the wars in Iraq and Afghanistan. Her father, Richard H., a USAF veteran of the Viet Nam war, served with the 6th TCS, 3rd MAS, and 732nd MAS.

We must know what materials are needed to build airplanes.

—*from "Air World Map by American Airlines, Inc"*
(1944)

from *Air Age*

PETROLEUM

Kick dirt from your boots and get
up on the bus now, survival
camp is closing in.

You startle, lie,   *it's fun*
it's neat.   They drop
you off   they drop   you off

a knife and string and matches. You
survive. What else to do?

Today you play   mock torture.
They oil ropes.

        You scratch your hands, your thumbs
and plunge into the water drum. They slide
slick ropes like snakes   they rope your body   bolt

but no way out. Remember this. The ropes a drill
in case you're caught. And then you're off to war.

KAPOK

Downy fluff from seed pods of kapok
makes sound-deadening material that insulated
airplanes, sometimes cushioned cockpit seats.

Forest of kapok trees, in Khmer, is *Prey Nokor*, later called
Saigon. My father might have crouched behind these trees
in '68. The trunks and branches crowded
with large, simple thorns. The leaves like palms.
The pods, the size of soda cans, grow hundreds
to a tree. Their fibers light, buoyant,
resilient, highly flammable, resistant to water.

His favorite drink was root beer. My three sisters, star-eyed
in '82, gulped A&W in the yard
and when an airplane crossed, they'd stretch tan
arms and hold up cans in an unheard toast.

CORK

There's only the cork bobbing in the sink where water soaks plates
greased by meat. Think where the wing joins to the airplane's body.
Think the passing air. Coat anything in this grease and it would burn
but the cork trees would be renewed in time for harvest.
At the holiday table you told us about a soldier you knew
who slit his wrists. Cork can be harvested a dozen times
before the death of the tree. It forms the fairings that smooth the
    surface
so the plane can sail. Even the tip of the wing, so far from the body,
must be streamlined, must be corked. You told us about a buddy

shot down, VC imprisoned seven years. He came home to a wife
who had left him for dead so he died by his hand. The bark
of the cork oak deadens vibrations in the walls of the plane.
Your bark. What has been cut from you a dozen times Dad?
Sometimes you sit so still.

ASH

It's not a climbing tree. Strong but elastic,
it is for bent parts: wingtip bows or door jambs,
your knuckles, your brow. You climbed
through clouds, dead soldiers in your cabin. You climbed

clouds with flight attendants stirring your coffee, calling
you Captain, serving you the pinkest steaks,
extra coffee in winter when ice sleets wings.
You circled airports in snowstorms. You pulled

in the driveway with cusswords on your lips and arctic gear
in the trunk. In case of? You hid beneath your plane
when you heard Vietnamese. You bought a boat,
yelled for us to keep our goddamned arms in when you docked

as if the water could hold our floating limbs. If a small cry
comes from under my door jamb, will you bend to hear?

SILK

In the attic boxed in mothballs, no silkworms cocoon,
no white mulberry leaves, rather, an *áo dài* from Lam Dong
and a taffeta gown in violet, for bleached-cotton mom.
Miles
of silk thread coil the wires of aircraft electrical units. Radio waltzes
spool the air-traffic commands that fold around you, your switches

around you on your workshop floor, scrubbed cat food
cans, lengths of twine, blunted nails in coffee cans,
wall sockets, brushes in their packages, locks in their packages,
a wood plane, zip ties and bungie cords,
spools—

And upstairs, in your study so overfilled
you've moved out, under boating magazines
is your pile: pages of ball gowns clipped,

cut and glued so the skirts flare fuller.
Each one turns figure-eights
beneath the weight of men's things.

CATHY LINH CHE is the author of the poetry collection *Split* (Alice James Books), winner of the Kundiman Poetry Prize, the Norma Farber First Book Award from the Poetry Society of America, and the Best Poetry Book Award from the Association of Asian American Studies. Her father was a soldier in the South Vietnamese Army for eight years and a helicopter mechanic in the Air Force for four additional years. Her mother also grew up in Viet Nam during the war. They both escaped on a boat in 1975 and ended up in a refugee camp in the Philippines for 11 months before being sponsored to the United States.

SPLIT

I see my mother at thirteen
in a village so small,
it's never given a name.

Monsoon season drying up—
steam lifting in full-bodied waves.
She chops corn for the hogs,

her hair dipping to the small of her back
as if dipped in black
and polished to a shine.

She wears a side-part
that splits her hair
into two uneven planes.

They come to watch her,
Americans, Marines, just boys,
eighteen or nineteen.

With scissor-fingers,
they snip the air,
repeat *cut*,

point at their helmets
and then at her hair.
All they want is a small lock.

What does she say
to her mother
to make her so afraid?

Days later
she will be sent away
to the city for safekeeping.

She will return home
only once to be given away
to my father.

Her hair
was dark, washed,
and uncut.

LOS ANGELES, MANILA, ĐÀ NẴNG

California drought withering the basins,
the hills ready to ignite. Oh, stupid ways

I've loved and unraveled myself.
I, a parched field, and not a spit of rain.

I announced to a room of strangers,
I've never loved anyone more.

Now he and I no longer speak.
Outside: Manila, 40 years after my parents' first arrival.

I deplane where they debarked.
At customs, I am given a sheet warning of MERS—

in '75, my parents received fishermen's lunches,
a bottle of fish sauce. They couldn't enter

until they were vaccinated. My mother, 22,
newly emptied of a stillborn daughter.

In Đà Nẵng, my cousin has become unrecognizable
after my four year absence. His teeth, at 21,

have begun to rot. His face swollen over.
I want to shield him from his terrible life.

Tazed at 15 by the cops until he pissed himself.
So beaten in the mental institution, that family had to

bring him home. His mother always near tears
when I ask, How are you doing?

You want to know what survivorhood looks like?
It's not romantic. The corn drying huskless

in the front yard. The ducks chasing each other in the back.
The thick arms of a woman who will carry bricks

for the rest of her life. The plainness with which
she speaks of hardship. The bricks aren't a metaphor

for the weight she carries.
Ánh, which means light, is sick, and cannot work,

but instead goes wandering the neighborhood,
eating other people's food, bloating

his mother's unpayable debts.
What pleasure can be found here,

even if the love is palpable?
My mother stopped crying years ago.

What's the use, she says, of all this leaking.
Enough to fill a drainage ditch, a reservoir?

No, just enough to wet a pillow.
What a waste of time, me pining after

a man who no longer feels for me.
Today, I would give it up. Trade mine

for theirs. They tell me that they are not hungry.
Happy is their toil. My uncles and their

browned skins, not a pinch of fat anywhere.
They work the fields and swallow

beer after beer, getting sentimental.
Whose birds have come to roost, whose pigs in the muck?

Their dog has just birthed four new pups.
Despite ourselves, time moves on.

I walked lover's lane with my cousin.

The heart-lights reflected on the river's black.
The locks clustered and dangling.

I should have left our names on that bridge.
My name, the names of my family, written there.

TERESA MEI CHUC was born in Saigon, Vietnam, and immigrated to the United States under political asylum with her mother and brother shortly after the Vietnam War, while her father, who had served in the Army of the Republic of Vietnam (ARVN) during the war, remained in a Vietcong "reeducation" camp for nine years. Teresa is the author of two full-length collections of poetry, *Red Thread* (Fithian Press, 2012) and *Keeper of the Winds* (FootHills Publishing, 2014) and a recent chapbook, *How One Loses Notes and Sounds* (Word Palace Press, 2016). She is a graduate of the Masters in Fine Arts in Creative Writing program at Goddard College in Plainfield, Vermont, and teaches literature and writing at a public high school in Los Angeles.

from *Year of the Hare*

HOANG LIEN SON REEDUCATION CAMP

Baba was a military captain in the ministry of law for the Republic of Vietnam. The Vietcong communists wanted to "re-educate" him.

On June 5, 1975, Baba reported to the Vietcong. Mama lost all contact with Baba for one year, then she was able to find out where they had taken him.

If Baba worked hard in the labor camp, every one or two years they let him read the letters Mama sent. Before he could read them, the letters were inspected by the Vietcong—they were not to be criticized in the letters.

Baba and about one thousand other prisoners worked in a forest in North Vietnam. They built a house for themselves with bamboo that they gathered in the forest. All the prisoners lived in this house and each one slept in a space about the length of his body. Every day, seven days a week, the prisoners dug holes, chopped bamboo and trees, built houses, and cooked for the Vietcong. In cold, windy weather, they walked barefoot up the mountains to find bamboo, trudging miles from mountain to mountain until their feet were bleeding and the soles were pink, red, and swollen, the exposed flesh scraping against rocks and branches. Due to the difficulty of finding the bamboo sticks, the weight of the sticks, and the weak, emaciated state of the prisoners, each one of them was usually only able to carry one bamboo back to camp each day.

They had no rest. Baba, like the other prisoners, wasn't given any meat or rice to eat. They gave him two meals a day, one in the afternoon and one at night. One meal would consist of fifty corn kernels, and Baba counted as he held each one between his thumb and index finger, slowly placing it on his tongue, savoring each bite. The meals alternated between corn kernels and small pieces of yucca root.

The prisoners were always hungry, always thinking about food, but after eating they felt even more hungry. At night, they chewed in their sleep and dreamt of eating.

One day, Baba fell down a mountain that was about three stories high because he was too tired and his feet collapsed under his own weight. He rolled down and lay there at the bottom like a sack of rice. His foot was injured and he couldn't walk. For a week, Baba wrapped his foot in heated lemon leaves and salt. He got better and continued to work.

If prisoners didn't follow the rules, they were forced to work more hours, deprived of food, beaten, tortured, put in isolation, or sentenced to death, depending on the seriousness of the offense. The Vietcong said to Baba and the other prisoners, "We don't need a bullet to kill you, 'cause you are not worth a bullet. We'll let you live like this to die day by day. You have to work for us, then you die."

Baba couldn't think about Mama, Brother, or me. If he did, he couldn't survive. He would break down. He would want to kill the people keeping him in prison or kill himself. He didn't think about anything at all. He told himself, "Don't feel, don't think, just survive."

Every couple of months, the prisoners were given weed to smoke. When someone was put in reeducation camp, there was no sentence; you could stay your whole life. They released you when they wanted to.

SNAPSHOTS OF EARLY CHILDHOOD

When I was three years old, I was still drinking from a bottle and sucking my index finger. Mama was praying to Buddha and gave up eating beef in the hopes that it would contribute to our reunion with Baba.

In Saigon, Mama had worked for ten years as a telephone operator in an American trading company, so she knew some English. Mama studied data entry for eight months and got a job at Bank of America. She worked nights for a year, and I remember waking up crying to Grandma. I continued sucking my finger in kindergarten until Uncle put chili pepper on my finger to get me to stop.

Mama, Brother, Grandma, and I lived with Aunt, Uncle, and their four sons in a faded yellow house on Allen Avenue in Pasadena until they moved to Missouri and we rented an apartment a couple of streets over on Parkwood. Shortly after that, Mama, Brother, Grandma, and I moved to a small house on Oak Avenue. The house was divided into two parts, and our neighbor Joe had two cats, Shadow, a black and white cat, and Snowy, a white cat with one blue eye and one yellow eye. Snowy's tail had been cut off by a kid and he always ran away from us. At that house, I met my first love—the garden.

Life was grass, bugs, flowers, and trees. I could eat bananas all day and climb the avocado tree or the plum tree, which was alternately full of flowers and fruits and naked, its branches clawing the sky. I would pick a plum, tear its skin with my teeth, and let its juice and flesh flood my mouth. I loved the fig tree, loved the fruits that bloodied the ground, loved sinking my teeth into the red, seedy meat.

The grass was great for flips, cartwheels and fights with my brother.

My sky was green. I would track down butterflies and follow them around. I developed a hobby of catching butterflies by their wings, but I never kept any of them. I was collecting spiders and would go around the garden, looking under leaves, in the cracks of the walls, under the rusting table, in corners, anywhere I could find a spider and put it in a jar. I had ten different spiders in a jar spinning ten different kinds of webs.

My brother and I would make villages out of branches and leaves from the avocado tree, dig up a trail around it, and pour water into the winding trench to make a stream.

I loved bananas so much. I was nine years old when I heard that Baba was coming. Baba was finally coming home! I always wanted a baba; the other kids had one, but I didn't. I was thinking, "What should I give him? It should be something really special." I decided to bring him a banana.

Mama got us ready and we drove to the airport in our yellow Datsun. I was holding the yellow banana and while I rode in the car, I felt something changing; I felt myself changing. Someone was coming to live with us. I thought about what I'd longed for for so long—a papa like the ones who picked up my friends from school. The ones with the faces that lit up when they saw my friends, the ones who hugged and smiled. A papa that swooped up his little daughter as if he held the world in his hands.

We waited at the airport and Baba got off the plane. I saw him and I started to cry; I cried and cried because I was scared. I saw my baba for the first time and I was scared that he'd be living with us. He was like an Egyptian cat: skinny, foraging, stern. He was impenetrable. He didn't smile; he didn't run up to swoop me into his arms. He was a stranger coming to live with us. I kept the banana, I kept crying in the car on our way home. Mama said, "See, your daughter is so glad to see you, she can't stop crying." I ate the banana.

MY FIRST DINNER WITH BABA

It was my first dinner with Baba after we picked him up from the airport. Grandma, Mama, Brother were there. We were sitting down for our first dinner together in nine years. We had rice, mixed vegetables and meat dishes, a typical Chinese dinner. Everyone had a pair of chopsticks. My brother and I had to "call" everyone before we could eat. "Ah Maa (paternal grandma) sik fan (eat meal), Ah Ba (papa) sik fan, Ah Ma (mama) sik fan." Before anyone could touch the food, we waited for Grandma to eat first. We all picked up our chopsticks, ready to eat. I held my chopsticks and Baba started to yell at me. I was scared; I was confused.

He said that I couldn't use my left hand anymore; otherwise, he would punish me, and that I was bad because I was using my left hand. He said he wouldn't love me anymore if I did. His screaming paralyzed me; no one had ever screamed at me like that before. I began to cry. I didn't know how to use my right hand; I had never used it before for eating or writing and I didn't understand Baba. Mama had never punished me before for using my left hand. I did as he said because I thought he was going to beat me or kill me if I didn't. I knew my life was going to be different from then on. I wished he'd never come.

A KNIFE

I was sitting on the floor behind the leaves of a potted plant, doing my homework. Baba was in the next room, in the kitchen. He was busy cooking; I could hear the clanging of dishes and pots and see the smoke that carried the aroma of food into the living room. Then a knife flew past my face, on the left side, missing it by an inch. Baba had seen me using my left hand and didn't like it. I thought that I could never forgive him. He could've killed me. Fear and anger became a constant reality. I lived with Baba, but pretended that he didn't exist. Otherwise, I couldn't have survived.

THE HORSE STANCE

I was in elementary school. Baba had promised me that he would take me to some kind of event. The day before the event, while in the car, I reminded Baba that he had promised to take me to school that evening.

He said, "Well, no, I'm not taking you." I asked pleadingly, "But why?" He replied, "I'm just not taking you."

I was upset that Baba broke his promise and I had been looking forward to going. We got to our driveway and I got out to push open the gate so that the car could go in. I pushed the gate a bit harder than usual and Baba got mad at me for showing anger toward him. So I had to "chol houng hay" which literally means "sit in the air" also known as "the horse stance," a kind of Chinese punishment. My back had to be straight and not leaning against anything, I had to hold my ears with my hands, and my thighs had to be parallel to the floor. I had to sit as if I was sitting on a chair, except there was no chair. Five minutes of doing this and I couldn't stand it anymore: my thighs tightened up and I felt like the house was falling down on me. Baba put a stick across my thighs as I was sweating and sitting in the air and said if the stick dropped, then he would hit me. No one in the house could stop him; no one wanted to stop him. I was crying and Baba said that I had to stop crying or else he'd hit me. I felt like I was dying; I was shaking, sweating, crying, and my heart was broken. For two hours, Baba made me sit in the air with my back straight and a stick across my thighs. Finally, Grandma begged him to let me go. He let me go. I went to the bathroom and cried. I cried loudly, gasping for breath. Baba heard me crying and told me to stop. I couldn't stop, I couldn't stop it. He said that I had to go back to being punished. So, I went back to *chol houng hay*. It was one of the worst days of my life.

RED

Baba refused to wear anything that was the color red. He said that it was a good thing that mama's car wasn't red; otherwise, he would've repainted it. He said he hated red because he said it was the color of communism.

BABA

When Baba was in Hoang Lien Son "Reeducation" Camp, his fellow inmates died of hunger, sickness, beatings. If someone attempted to escape and was caught, they would get one year in solitary confinement or the death penalty. Some were bludgeoned to death in front of the other prisoners. Some prisoners were hung upside down from the ceiling and beaten as they swung, and if they screamed in pain they were beaten some more. As punishment, prisoners were tied up in excruciating positions, shackled, and placed in small boxes where their tied-up legs became gangrenous and had to be chopped off. Prisoners were punished for "reactionary statements," forced to work more hours and deprived of their small ration of food. Prisoners died during interrogation. There was a list of rules they had to memorize and follow.

BRANDON COURTNEY is a veteran of the United States Navy, and the author of *The Grief Muscles* and *Rooms for Rent in the Burning City*, as well as of the chapbooks *Inadequate Grave* and *Improvised Devices*. Another full-length collection is forthcoming from Yes Yes Books. His poetry appears or is forthcoming in *Best New Poets*, *Tin House*, *Guernica*, *Memorious*, *The Progressive*, and *American Literary Review*.

PROMETHEUS
for Neal D. Courtney, Cambodia, 1969–70

Years before his bedridden blindness,
        my sobriety,
there was day-tripping
                through the National Mall's
gazing pool—The Three Soldiers—
an embossed flask
        clanging
against my father's belt buckle.
He poured shot after shot
of off-brand bourbon into cut glass,

chain-smoked Chesterfields, rolled spliffs,
                offering me a swallow,

a medicinal hit,
       from the same ashen hand
that formed his fist
that christened drywall,
my mother's lip.
       Fever wasn't the only thing to break
in Cambodia,
in roadside ditches dark
           as umbilical blood.
There was the slug fired from the angel end
of his rifle,
ripping through eucalyptus leaves.
There was him,

left in tourniquet grass
to shepherd home our dead.
       Now when he sits
on the steps and tells me of the world's
       original fire,
how black wasps carouselled
the tongues of bloated bison,
           I believe him.
No maggot went unfed.

YEAR WITHOUT DUSTING

There's softness
to the photograph's
     image after a year

without dusting:
my father
in his uniform,
     the picture

hanging in the hallway,
        crooked,
a single nail

pulling from the drywall.
It held the weight
        mother couldn't.

        He told her once
that after a month
in Vietnam, warm

water from the shower
was enough
        to make

the soldiers' cocks hard.
Now, spring storm,
        the sky coming apart

in a thousand places
has knocked the power
        from its lines; my wife

warms water on the stove,
tests the temperature
        against her wrist.

She pours pot after pot
into the tub,
pours blood-warm
        water over me.

ACHILLES, VETERANS' HOSPITAL (PHILADELPHIA, PENNSYLVANIA)

Because his pain's no longer phantom,
he traces two fingers along the scar
where surgeons went looking for a lion,
opened the bone cage of his chest.

He waits in the emergency room's
borrowed light for orderlies to drag
his corpse behind the wheelchair's shadow,
knowing doctors will make peace

with his parts. His greaves have been
replaced with gauze, cuirass for paper
gown, mitra for colostomy bag.
He knows how an august father could perch

on his son's shoulders, grip the wick
of his neck, as they both flee the burning city.

LINH DINH was born in Saigon in 1963. He is the author of two collections of stories, *Fake House* (2000) and *Blood and Soap* (2004); five books of poems, *All Around What Empties Out* (2003), *American Tatts* (2005), *Borderless Bodies* (2006), *Jam Alerts* (2007), and *Some Kind of Cheese Orgy* (2009); a novel about Vietnam, *Love Like Hate* (2010); and a nonfiction account of a declining USA, *Postcards from the End of America* (2017). Linh Dinh is also the editor of the anthologies *Night, Again: Contemporary Fiction from Vietnam* (1996) and *The Deluge: New Vietnamese Poetry* (2013). He has also published widely in Vietnamese.

VIET CONG UNIVERSITY

When I tell people I went to VCU, they usually ask, "Viet Cong University?"

"No, Virginia Commonwealth."

Talking of Viet Cong Universities: when a squadron of Viet Cong took over the ARVN officers' club at Tan Son Nhat Airport on April 30, 1975, they opened a fridge and saw twenty cans of coke. Noticing a tab on each can, their officer, a man whose face resembled a backhanded fist, explained: "Hand grenades. A special kind. That's why they're being kept in this cold box."

The Viet Cong took one of the grenades outside and flung it against a burnt out jeep. It clanked off the side but did not explode. A black, fizzing liquid oozed out.

"Chemical weapon," the officer explained, "like Agent Orange."

A mangy dog came by to lap up the black, fizzing liquid. He was still seen to be alive a week later.

PRISONER WITH A DICTIONARY

And so a young man was thrown into prison and found in his otherwise empty cell a foreign dictionary. It was always dark in there and he couldn't even tell if it was a dictionary at first. He was not an intellectual type and had never even owned a dictionary in his life. He was far from stupid, however, but had an ironic turn of mind that could squeeze out a joke from most tragic situations. He could also be very witty around certain women. In any case, he did not know what to do with this nearly worthless book but to use it as a stool and as a pillow. Periodically he also tore out pages from it to wipe himself. Soon, however, out of sheer boredom, he decided to look at this dictionary. His eyes had adjusted to the dim light by now and he could make out all the words with relative ease in that eternal twilight. Although he was not familiar with the foreign language, and did not even know what language it was, he suddenly felt challenged to learn it. His main virtue, and the main curse of his life, was the ability to follow through on any course of action once he had set his mind to it. This book represented the last problem, the only problem, he would ever solve. The prisoner began by picking out words at random and scrutinizing their definitions. Of course, each definition was made up of words entirely unknown to him. Undeterred, he would look up all the words in the definition, which led him to even more unfathomable words. To define "man," for example, the prisoner had to look up not only "human" and "person" but also "opposable" and "thumb." To define "thumb," he had to look up not only "short" and "digit" but also "thick" and "of" and "a" and "the." To define "the," he had to look up "that" and "a" (again) and "person" (again) and "thing" and "group." Being alone in his cell night and day, without any distraction, allowed the prisoner to concentrate with such vigor that soon he could retain and cross index hundreds of definitions in his head. The dictionary had well over a thousand pages but the prisoner was determined to memorize every definition on the page. He cringed at the thought that he had once torn out pages to wipe himself. These pages now represented to him gaps in his eventual knowledge. Because they were gone forever he would never be able to learn *all* of the words in that particular language. Still, it was with an elation bordering on madness that he woke up each morning, eager to eat up more words. Like many people, he equated the acquisition of a vast vocabulary with knowledge, even with wisdom, and so he could feel his stature growing by the day, if not by the second. Although he did not know what the words meant, what they referred to in real life, he reasoned that he *understood* these words because he knew their definitions. And because he was living inside this language all the time, like a fetus thriving inside a womb, there were times when he felt sure he could guess at the general implications of a word, whether it was a plant or an animal, for example, or whether it indicated something positive or negative. But his guesses were always wrong, of course. Because "bladder" sounded somehow vast and nebulous to the prisoner, he thought that it must have something to do with the outdoors, most likely the weather, a gust of wind or a torrential rain or a bolt of lightning. "Father," with its forlorn, exasperated tone, made the prisoner think of something dead and putrid: a corpse or a heap of garbage. He guessed that "homicide" was a flower. He thought "July" meant "August." The prisoner was also justifiably proud of his pronunciation, which was remarkably crisp and confident, the stresses more often than not falling on the right syllables. If he were to speak on the phone, the prisoner could almost be mistaken for a native speaker, albeit one of the lower class. But if the prisoner was convinced he was gaining a new language he was also surely losing one because he had, by this time, forgotten nearly all the words of his native language. By this time he could no longer name any part of the anatomy, even the most basic, hand, nose, face, mouth, etc., and so his own body was becoming vague, impersonal, unreal. Although he was surrounded by filth, he could no longer conjure up the word "filth." The only word that came readily to his tongue, automatically, unbidden, was "prison" because that was the last thing he thought of each night, and the first thing he thought of each morning. His dreams had become entirely devoid of conversations or thoughts. Often they were just a series of images or abstract patches of colors. Sometimes they were also made up entirely of sounds, a cacophony of his own voice reciting bits of definitions. Even in his worst nightmare, he could no longer shout out "mother!" in his own language. But this loss never bothered him, he barely noticed it, because he was convinced he was remaking himself anew. As he was being squeezed out of the world, the only world he had a right to belong in, he thought he was entering a new universe. Perhaps by purging himself of his native language, the prisoner was unconsciously trying to get rid of his horrible past, because, frankly, there was not a single word of his native tongue that did not evoke, for the prisoner, some horrible experience or humiliation. Perhaps he could sense that his native tongue was the very *author* of his horrible life. But these are only conjectures, we do not know for sure. In any case nights and days the prisoner shouted out definitions to himself.

If one were to press one's ear against the thick iron door at midnight, one would hear, for example: "an animal with a long, thin tail that commonly infests buildings." Or "a deep and tender feeling for an arch enemy." Or "a shuddering fear and disgust accompanied by much self-loathing." With so many strange words and definitions accumulating, surely some profound knowledge, some revelation, was at hand? What is a revelation, after all, but the hard-earned result of an exceptional mind working at peak capacity? The prisoner was thankful to be given a chance to concentrate unmolested for such a continuous length of time. He felt himself victorious: condemned to an empty cell, he had been robbed of the world, but through a heroic act of will, he had remade the universe. He had (nearly) everything because he had (nearly) all the words of an entire language. But the truth is the prisoner had regained nothing. He only thought that way, of course, because he had to think that way. After decades of unceasing mental exertion, the only fruit of the prisoner's remarkable labor, the only word he ever acquired for sure, was "dictionary," simply because it was printed on the cover of a book he knew for sure was a dictionary. For even as he ran across the definition for "prisoner," and was memorizing it by heart, he didn't even know that he was only reading about himself.

DAVID ELLIS lives in New York City where he writes and teaches. He is a recipient of the Hearst Prize for Poetry and has had fiction appear in *The Bridge* and *Sandscript Art and Literary Magazine*. His father spent 1965 flying combat missions over Viet Nam in Huey gunship helicopters, an experience he's kept locked away until recently. "Aphasia" recounts the desire from both son and father to enter the darker conversations about war and one's inner demons, while finding more success in kindling connections through indirect means.

APHASIA

We were warned repeatedly not to touch the paper lunch bags hanging in the trees, warned by teachers, neighborhood parents, segments on the local news, and the ugly contents of the bags themselves.

Inside: two blackened figs, shriveled to leathery Jivaro heads. I make that connection to shrunken human heads now, 35 years on, with their rough-sewn stitching across eyes and mouths, but even then, in grade school and limited knowledge of darker practices, I saw the little blackened blobs as unsettling and enticing, testicular sacks, made even more ominous and intriguing with the knowledge they were poisoned. In 1970s and early '80s California, Big Agra of the Central Valley, and its exploitative *Grapes of Wrath* existence, was under mortal threat from a tiny, nearly invisible, Mediterranean fruit fly. The rotting and poisoned bait sitting in the open sacks strung up in the trees, meant for the flies, and all the warnings around it was too great of a temptation for all of us kids who made a playground of the fig orchards.

I spent my pre-teen years as a latchkey kid. After school I walked the few short blocks of modest, cookie-cutter tract homes that edged acres of fig orchards to our house, a virtually indistinguishable brick and stucco job. Most of the diffuse edges of Fresno during that time seemed like little more than an oversized farm town. Our little corner of the city, Fig Garden, was a quiet place to grow up, seemingly tucked safely away in God's pocket. Of a certain kind of god, or pocket, anyway. Many winter mornings were blanketed in thick, pea-soup fog; summer days were similarly blanketed in a heavy smog and haze that drifted up from L.A. It was a place easy to lose perspective, like the entirety of the world was merely a pill bottle stuffed and muffled by a protective cotton ball. Running along the subdivisions of houses was an eerie shielding band of fig orchards. Rows upon rows of gnarled, runty fig trees—branches, roots, and bark knotted and warted—surrounded our neighborhood like stands of wizened hags set up as sentinels when fog or smog drifted through. This place suited my quiet and safe family, insulated in our own silence and separated from the dark, cultivated wood.

I had hours to myself every day after school. My mother worked as a social worker in a neighboring county. My dad worked as a pilot for the Border Patrol, up in the sky scanning the surrounding miles and miles of farms for undocumented pickers who ran when *La Migra* showed up. His main job was, simply, to radio down where the migrant farmers ran to as agents on the ground attempted to round the workers up. My older brother was busy with high school, sports, and friends across town. I

liked having the house to myself. I could watch whatever I wanted on
TV, sneak as many Chips Ahoy as I dared, and I didn't have to talk with
anyone, except when I left the house and my friends and I headed into
the orchards to play.

Being home alone presented the usual temptations to poke around.
Both my parents were quiet, but my mom—trained as a clinician—often
tried to break the silence with probing questions or with stiff inquiries
that seemed gleaned from a workbook. My dad, on the other hand, didn't
make those efforts. He worked long and odd hours, napped on the couch
often when he was home, and was sometimes sent off on months' long
assignments as a government pilot. "Detail" is what my mom called it. He
was a bit of a stranger to me, one that I tried to unstrange by snooping
through his stuff.

Secreted up on a shelf in his closet, hidden under some t-shirts, were
three cardboard cigar boxes. To my eight-year-old mind, these boxes held
relics of a nearly spiritual kind and had a drawing power greater than
lunch sacks of poisoned fruit hung in knotted trees. As I examined them,
the objects found in the cigar boxes took form as nebulous constellations,
but, just as quickly, whatever inchoate image growing out of my hap-
hazard curation disintegrated. The inability to make sense of anything
only underlined that the value of the objects must be otherworldly. There
were two rattlesnake tails, some arrowheads, rusty pocketknives, brightly
colored and intricately patterned foreign bills, and the like. A few Army
patches, insignia, and ribbon bars were interspersed with other odds and
ends. There was a small movie reel that I unwound once in the harsh
light of the single bulb dangling in the closet. I slipped the slim frames
through my hands a few inches from my face: black and white, a woman
and a man standing near a bed in what looked like a motel room, both
of them dressed smartly—he, a tight suit and skinny black tie, she a pale
dress with a fur cape hanging over the shoulders—then sitting on the
bed talking, a cigarette is lit and passed back and forth. Part of me won-
dered if the man was my dad, it was hard to tell, though it clearly wasn't
my mom in the frames. I unspooled yards and yards of film, gathering
around my feet in a blooming tangle, before it turned out to be a dirty
picture. I was surprised and not surprised: baffled that two people, look-
ing bored, then slouched in those stretches of unwound film, could end

up so shockingly and clinically naked. The lack of discernible causation unnerved me, as if any conversation could take such a foul turn. Yet, I must have suspected. Why else peel through the reel?

In another box, there were more insignia and bars from his army uniform, dog tags, a few more scattered patches, some spent bullet shells. And, what seemed most precious of all to me, a hard-case jewelry box lined in white satin. Within it, pinned to a satin cushion, was a ribbon and pendant of George Washington in profile: my dad's Purple Heart. I'm not sure how at eight years old I knew that there was something special about this thing, or even what it was, really, but I intuited immediately that it had something to do with war and bravery. Yet, its being hidden away with other bits and pieces, among things that a small boy like me might keep, along with the film reel, told me that there was a pride splintered with shame. And, I knew, that I could never ask anyone about it.

I've come to believe, from pop-culture and Studs Terkel, I guess, that there is a long heritage of silence from combat veterans, what I've heard to be a foundational tenet of the reputed Warrior Code of Honor. To talk openly about combat can be seen as a breach of trust, or at least evidence that whoever is telling the tales didn't see any real action. This is conjecture on my part; the war that people my age served in, the first Iraq war, I observed on CNN from the safety of couches in the TV lounge of my dorm, and it hasn't gotten any more personal than that since then. My dad is likely the only "warrior" I've known and isn't an exception to the Code. He spent his year in Viet Nam, 1965, as a combat helicopter pilot, and until recently I've known almost nothing about his time there. He's taciturn by nature—at about 12 years old his mom gave him the silent treatment for two days just so he could see what it felt like—and maybe nurture, too. At 15, in 1958, my dad's dad, after months of debilitating depression, shot himself to death with my dad's squirrel-hunting rifle. The sonic blast of the shot, the thump of the body, and the screams of his mother spilling out as she attempted to fit the shattered skull and brain matter back together all happened just a room away from where my father lay in bed. In an era when depression, especially suicide, was taboo, the event was called an accident and rarely referenced again. It must have seemed perfectly suitable for my dad to keep a lid on his experiences in Viet Nam. In fact, I can't recall a single conversation that I ever had with him when I was growing up, about anything, let alone war or suicide. He wasn't cold, just distant. We exchanged words, and he certainly told me what to do frequently and, on occasion, explained how the world worked in his estimation. At bedtime, he hugged me and said that he loved me when I said good night, and I felt that he did. Still, I don't recall any sort of back and forth.

We talk now, whether it is on the phone or in person, and it is much better, but rarely is it much of a conversation. Now that he's older, you might say elderly at 73, he's become a bit of a talker, taciturn turned inside out, but not much of a listener. He's happy to report on the weather or what is wrong with the world—especially anything connected with the Democratic party—but the war stories have remained locked away.

Yet, as a kid, I knew that my dad had been in Viet Nam and that he had been a helicopter pilot there, even though I can't pinpoint how I came to know any of this. It never came from his mouth. Or my mother's, that I know of. In addition to the clutch of treasures hidden away in the cigar boxes, there were a few other obvious clues around our low-slung suburban house: plaques from his combat unit hung up in the dark and narrow hallway that led to the bedrooms, a sliver of wood onto which a rocket tail-fin had been mounted, along with a cryptic engraving, sat prominently in the family room. Then there were less obvious clues, at least for me: a statue of fat Buddha perched on the bookshelf by the encyclopedias; a black lacquer painting of a quaint Asian sea-side village, composed of a few simple brush strokes indicating villagers donning conical *lon la* hats, water buckets balanced on long poles slung over their shoulders, the whole scene faintly lit by a watery moon; a silken silvery-blue kimono tucked in my mom's bureau. Souvenirs of Indochina. Perhaps it was my older brother who told me about Dad and Viet Nam. At four years my senior, for better or worse, he was often a source of knowledge and myth. I suspect, rather, that I'd simply pieced together that our familial silence, Indochine bric a brac, and the generalized cultural angst of the lost police action in Viet Nam were bound up in ways that even I could see at that young age.

As I handled the pieces in the hush of the closet my dad seemed only farther away. The objects themselves, though, held their own totemic power for something I didn't understand. Not in the realm of bread as the body of Christ, more slant wise, objects as vacuum, collections of vacancy, anti-matter with mass.

In the same closet, I found slides and a slide projector buried in a crumbling cardboard box. During my first forays, I merely held the slides up to the single naked bulb dangling in the closet the same way I did the dirty picture, taking in what seemed like x-rays of soldiers, luminous and diaphanous figures glowing in white, very difficult to make out. In later trips, I dug out the whole operation and projected the slides onto the fake wood-paneling of the living room. In the whir and quiet of the fan in the projector, slide after slide after slide loudly clicked by of men in flight suits, soldiers standing next to helicopters, men by tents, quonset huts, jeeps, men gathered in front of palm trees, crowded city streets teeming with Vietnamese. Never my dad. Looking back now, I can figure it out. He was the one taking the photos, of course, but as a kid all these slides pointed to the same thing I knew of him as a father, his ghostlike qualities. He was there, but not there.

The mind of an eight-year-old can be powerfully computational. It knows a limited world to some degree, yet can tell that the world is much, much larger than that limited understanding. As adults we get used to pressing up against the thresholds of our knowledge and, often, shy away from what we don't know. Children, at least me as a kid, don't recognize that limitation. I believed knowledge to be finite, like a mapped out world, merely a place I hadn't been to but could easily journey toward with patience and persistence. I kept digging. I found reel-to-reel tape recordings, and a tape player, dark green and smelling strongly of early-era plastics, what I imagine heated Vaseline to smell like, a scent that somehow deepened the secrecy of what I was hunting in my expeditions into the closet, like some half-living fossil exhumed from a plastinized earth.

The tapes were labeled and were all from my dad's war stint. They were messages to his mom and to his wife, and theirs to him. I tried to play them, but it was difficult to understand the words. Many of the tapes were distorted and warped from age, but long moments of semi-clarity emerged too, though the voices could seem like those on newscasts altered to protect anonymity. I heard my grandma, her voice brighter than what I was used to, but slowed during the playback, recounting her fears. She had not lost anyone to war yet: not her husband to WWI or WWII, not her eldest child to Korea, so she felt she was statistically fated to lose her youngest to Viet Nam. Her fear was bound into the tape, occasionally wailing like a hired mourner. I heard my mother, her Texas accent stronger than it was once we were living in California. She said she missed my dad, but had trouble recalling what he looked like and how that saddened her. I heard my dad, giving brief, stilted updates about the weather. All these disembodied voices coming from a weak little speaker, stretched and pulled long and low, hung in the air around me as I computed some sort of picture of so much I didn't know of the world and the people I loved, images that failed to coalesce entirely, more like fun-house mirror faces bubbling through my mind. In the distortions crept the shame that I sensed; the shame of juxtaposition of dirty movies and Purple Hearts tucked under t-shirts and my shame for sneaking to fill in the gaps of someone I lived with but didn't know very well. I knew my digging was a violation. I felt, too, that there was a deeper violation that I couldn't attach words to at the time, only a sense of dread, one of another juxtaposition: a record of my dad's voice pressed into tape that called up so little for me while the oily scent and the heat emitted off the laboring old tape player offered a type of companionship. It touched upon, even if lightly and vaguely, the erotic charge of spying, of scrolling through film frames to find a woman with a beehive hairdo suddenly sprawled out nude on a motel bed, of peeking inside a brown paper sack and finding what looked like dried up dog's balls, fearful, too, that the real reason I was so curious about the sacks of poisoned figs was that I wanted to eat them and that the real reason I rummaged through my dad's most private things is that I wanted to be caught, hoping that any anger that could emerge from my dad would prove something to me.

My parents have been retired for many years now, having buried their parents, several friends, and some of their siblings. Nostalgia reigns. They've moved to the hinterlands of central Texas and have few hobbies beyond church going and keeping track of cable news and the Weather Channel. My dad has taken up with a local group, a band of former military pilots that gather once a month or so in a small conference room of an area motel to have lunch and listen to a presentation about some aspect of military aviation history. These talks are given by invited guests or by selected members. Afterwards, they sit around and shoot the shit over pie and coffee. My dad has invited me along to a few of these luncheons—they seem to coincide with my trips out to see them. At first it seemed like it was just another attempt to convince me of the hero worship of the military and veterans that has been a deep, and vocal part of my parents' worldview since 9/11. But, I soon figured out it was my dad's way of opening up to me. He clearly felt the chasm between us too.

The pilots come from every branch of the military, and, from what I can tell, all of them have been in combat. They are all old. Some flew in WWII, some in Korea and Viet Nam. My dad might be the only heli-copter pilot. They've become friendly, I suppose, the band of ex-pilots, but none of them knew each other till they saw an ad in the local paper and decided that spending the afternoon over a fifteen-dollar-a-head buffet in a motel banquet room sounded like a pretty good idea.

After they shuffle through the buffet, minding that their windbreak-ers don't dip into the ranch dressing, they get down to the business of catching up on ailments and bits of news, pulling out business cards, receipts, or newspaper clippings jammed into a shirt breast pocket along with a reading glasses case. Eventually, they recount flying tales while in the service. They like to interrupt each other to ask questions about type of aircraft and other technical aspects, which they dutifully report. Many of the conversations I've heard remain in the realm of facts, mili-tary branch, where stationed, when, what aircraft. A few stories broach combat missions, but also only factually. Whenever a story comes close to anything very hairy, touching even glancingly upon some emotion, the talk often turns to war policy, or some other diversion. One WWII pilot spoke of flying patrol over Japanese islands during the Occupation, sup-posedly a time of peace. On a new route he suddenly came under attack from the ground. Bullets pierced his plane in several spots. At this point in the story, the old man said something like, "ho golly!" and lifted his cap off with a big grin. "Did I think my goose was cooked!" These patrol mis-sions took place nearly two years after the treaty had been signed. Despite that, this was the first incident of gunfire of many that then repeated from the same location. Later, it turned out, a Japanese soldier in the area was captured. He was a pilot that had crashed, hiding, not knowing the war was over, shooting at American planes whenever they went overhead. The old men gathered round the table listening to this story simply nodded, took a sip of coffee, pulled on the brims of their caps, chuckled a bit while shaking their heads, then talked about the necessity of dropping the A-bomb. One man asked about the plane he flew and "what the Jap flew," skirting what I wanted to know, what I think anyone would want to know who hasn't been in that position. What is that moment like when bullets flip through the thin skin of a plane hurtling through the air? What do you say to yourself or the guy on the ground shooting at you? How many years does it take before you can feel that no one is shooting anymore, or that you don't have to keep the plane of yourself aloft? Within a few conversational beats they somehow moved onto the aircraft used in the Iraqi invasion.

At one of these ex-fliers meetings I attended, the speaker for the day was a member who had also been self-publishing mystery novels for years. He had joined a writer's group through a writing class at the local satellite campus of an Austin junior college, and he had the writing group bug, and the drive to capture stories. He proposed that the group write out their war experiences so they could be gathered in book form that they would publish together, as the presenter said, "to record the history for friends, family, and others before it is lost."

The men were game. The press of old age was in a lot of the faces nodding "yep." The idea was that it was time to get these stories scratched onto paper before there was no one left to do the scratching. My dad was moved to contribute and started right away. In fact, though he didn't say what he was up to, he spent much of the rest of my short visit at the computer, seemingly vomiting up words. A few weeks later when I was back home in New York he sent me an email asking for advice about how to shape and edit what he came up with before he sent it along to the group. A natural favor to ask of me as a college writing teacher. It was titled, simply, "My War," and ran to nearly 50 single-spaced pages. At 42 years old I was finally getting the stories that he'd been carrying around for years. Like me, his story didn't start in the moment—his year in Viet Nam—but first with a preface that meandered through a thrilling and beautifully rendered encounter with a mountain lion while on foot as a Border Patrol agent in south Texas, the place where he gathered the tails of rattle snakes and found old Indian arrowheads as he scoured the desert for undocumented migrants. Then he sketched out the history of his dad as an airplane mechanic, and then his own childhood as a partly orphaned farmhand, punctuated with philosophical reflections on how war shapes and has shaped people and our country more than any other source other than God. These were fascinating stories to me, to hear my dad spilling out reminiscences about people I wished I knew better (him, my aunts and uncles, my grandma, the grandfather I never met) but the more I read, the more distant the war seemed. As more and more little stories and background filled paragraphs and pages, he was becoming a smaller and smaller speck within them, even as they were about him. It was difficult to read without getting the sense of a man in avoidance, slowly stalking his prey, tacking left and right, but never directly approaching.

Flight school takes up more than half of the narrative, then comes a section heading simply titled "War Stories." He starts with his arrival in Bien Hoa airbase, but then backtracks into a history of the Viet Nam war and, to him, misguided war policy conducted by Kennedy and Johnson, finally righted by Nixon, but then frittered away after his resignation. Yet, behind all of this deflection I can feel him straining to reveal, to cut down to the marrow, only to slip past whatever it is that is sitting there.

The most revealing sentence about the war is not about the war at all, but about a childhood nightmare unrelated to his combat experience, when, as a five-year-old saturated in anti-Japanese propaganda of WWII, he dreamed of menacing Japanese fighter pilots attacking his home. He called it the most vivid and frightening nightmare of his life, except for one other. He recreates the image of a snarling pilot, taking aim at him and his family. As I read pointy-toothed demons filled my mind, images my dad declares as imprinted in his memory, images he can conjure at will or sometimes still faces against his will as he sleeps. He then calls it again the most frightening nightmare of his life, except for one other. The other, he says succinctly, is a recurring dream about the war in Viet Nam. That is the depth of the description of the dream he ranks as more terrifying than a propaganda-induced, demonic-fiend out to slaughter him and his family. The rest of his war stories come out like the tales of the old guys at the fliers' club lunches, mostly emotionless facts or ginned-up hulla-balloos as masquerade for brushes with death. And, I'm left to wonder what my dad means by saying that war shapes a person and a country more than anything besides God. What is that shape?

Whatever that answer is, the question of what it would mean to me as an editor—not a middle-aged son reading the packed away thoughts of his dad's service years—seemed moot. I was rooting through the depths of the closet again, this time with permission, but the taint of violation bubbled up.

In the mid-sixties my folks married after a courtship of three months. They met in a small Texas town at a dance, possibly in a bar, that was thrown in honor of graduation from flight school; both my parents are a bit cagey about it now. My mom was at a women's college at a nearby city, so she and her classmates were invited as a busload of blind dates for the Army boys. My dad was then shipped off to Viet Nam, the reason behind the haste if you don't consider what must have been a gut-tearing tale of love at first sight, since I know my mom and dad aren't anything if not deliberate and sober individuals, more than doubly so as a couple. It is utterly inconceivable to me that the same man who checks the tires, oil, and belts on the minivan before heading into town asked my mom to marry him after a couple of weeks. Who was this man who had the emotional wherewithal and open, loving heart to fall for my mom and to have her fall for him in such a short time? If that year after their brief courtship hollowed him out, which is what I think my dad unintention-ally means by being shaped by war, then what was there beforehand? It could be that my mother drew up something from him, and the courtship was a brief moment of filling in that was rapidly deflated by the war.

There is a story that he gives a little more space in "My War," seem-ingly as emotionless as the other ones, but the details invite a fuller imag-ining. For a time, my dad flew Army helicopters off of a Navy ship, the USS *Tortuga*. Mostly, he was on the *Tortuga* as a "slick" pilot, that is, to do personnel or material transport when needed, but there was the occa-sional assault mission.

As he flew back to the *Tortuga* after a sortie my dad's chopper, a Huey Gunship, took enemy fire from below. A bullet came up through the floor, travelled through his thigh, and then grazed his face. He flew on towards the ship, but the chopper, too, had been damaged and it eventually pitched into the water within a few hundred yards of the *Tortuga*, or as my dad says, lightly, he took a swim in the South China Sea. Fortunately the bay they were anchored in was not extremely deep, since the helicopter sank rapidly to the sea floor. The body of the helicopter was twisted from the collision with the water. One of the large doors could not open, and the other was wedged into sand. Seemingly trapped, my dad kicked out a window just large enough to squeeze through.

Almost.

He became stuck about halfway through, around the waist, that is, as all the excess fabric of the flight suit gathered, corklike, and he could move no further. I can imagine this moment in no other way except to see him frantically trying to free himself, kicking legs and arms, pounding on the window frame, tugging at the flight suit. From all the jostling, the big door loosed, the one my dad was not stuck in, and slowly slid open. I guess this ironic insult from the fates gave my dad just enough to get out of the little window, tearing the flight suit along the way. It is easy for me to imagine this scene since I've seen movies where cars have flown off piers into the drink. I can see the harried struggle painfully slowed by the thickness of water, bubbles of released breath, hair floating like a sea creature. Though I'm sure my dad's hair was Army buzz cut I picture it longer, trailing the movements of his head. Because I've seen movies, I can hear the bubbles, how they become the only sound inside the blanket of water, how their pitch increases as they rise as if the bubbles were running across the keys of a piano on their way to the surface, how the noise of underwater air is as suffocating to the ears as the water itself is to the lungs. In my non-film influenced imagination I hear the bending and twisting of metal, but I can only picture my dad as part of a movie in my mind so that grinding of steel is absent as I work through the scene in my head. Exhausted, oxygen depleted, bleeding, finally free he floated and swam weakly towards what he took for the light of the sun. It was. As he surfaced, there were already teams of rescue pontoons in the water circling the bubbling above the wreck. It is easy to imagine this scene for other reasons too. Despite his life of near silence with me, replaced with a near silencing *of* me in later life, I can picture my dad struggle with all his being to fight for his life, but not merely for himself. He may not have ever said this, and he might even be unable to form the words, but I do have absolute clarity about one thing about him. He did not fight to stay alive for himself. He fought for his newlywed, for the promise of his unborn children, for his mother, for his fellow soldiers, for his country, and for his God, for a conviction of rightness that cuts through anything and everything else. He fought to give his children a quiet home, a home safely tucked away at the suburban edge of protective fig orchards standing sentinel, where a few cigar boxes can harbor a few tokens of darker elements of people and the world they live in, gathered under t-shirts at the back of a high shelf in a small closet.

I sent back very few notes on my dad's write up for the book that his fliers club will be putting out. I only corrected typos and made a few line-edit suggestions, despite my usual habit with my students' work to spill a lot of ink on the page with comments and suggestions of structure and cuts. My students must get tired of me writing "more here" on their work, coupled with some challenging question meant to get them to dig deeper and unpack a potent insight rather than gliding over the surface of it. From the perspective of a writing teacher, my dad's work lacks coherency and explicit depth. Yet, I saw any fix I could suggest as eliding what was there. The inability to cut to the marrow is the story. The inability to speak aloud the shape of what one has become, or how one has carved into unknown lives and families thousands of miles away and four decades past, takes on its own shape, even as it shifts. I said little back to my dad, which I hope he didn't take as an offense, though I'm not sure I'll ever know. I said that the writing was particularly beautiful and vivid when he described encountering a mountain lion on a high ridge overlooking the Rio Grande as a Border Patrol agent, and that the conflicting feelings of awe and fright that he captured in his telling of that event were palpable. I said that I felt like I was there, that I was him for a moment. I said, too, that his war stories told me something similar. What I left unsaid was not that I felt like I was there, but I still felt like I was him for a moment: running away from something so deeply a part of myself that it becomes running toward another thing entirely.

One can't know how he will react when he faces imminent death, like my dad did—shot, sunk, and trapped at the bottom of the sea—but I feel, with pale shame, a shame I would like to stash away, hidden from myself and others, that I might not have fought like he did to stay alive. I see myself wanting to violate, filled with a desire to dig until even the valor of fighting, for whatever reason or cause, is a darkened and shriveled fruit made into bait and poison. I see myself breathing the water, hoping death would come quickly.

HEINZ INSU FENKL is an author, editor, translator, folklorist, and professor of creative writing at the State University of New York, New Paltz. His fiction includes *Memories of My Ghost Brother*, which was a Barnes and Noble "Discover Great New Writers" selection in 1996 and a PEN/Hemingway finalist in 1997. His most recent short story, "Five Arrows," was published in *The New Yorker*. *Skull Water*, a sequel to *Memories of My Ghost Brother*, will be published by Graywolf Press in 2017. He is currently working on an experimental memoir, *The Monkeypuzzle Tree*, about his father's experiences as a military advisor with the Montagnards in Vietnam in the late 1960s.

FROM *MEMORIES OF MY GHOST BROTHER*

The day of my father's return from his first tour of duty in Vietnam, Mahmi and I waited at the U.S. military airport in Kimpo for seven hours. We had arrived early in the morning. We had taken an Arirang taxi from Pupyong to Kimpo airbase, expecting to wait only an hour or two for his out-processing after he came off the flight, but the plane was late and our wait became a daylong vigil. I did not know what my mother was thinking, whether she was imagining the flight shot out of the sky, or whether she doubted the Korea House translator's reading of my father's letter and imagined we had come on the wrong day. If we were not there to meet him, there was no way my father would be able to find us unless he wrote to her again from his new post in Korea. As the day drew on and the pleasant warmth of the morning became the blinding heat of noon, and then as the shadows lengthened where we waited outside, in the shade of a deuce-and-a-half truck, I tried to remember my father's face. He had only been gone for a year, but without a picture I could only imagine him in the vaguest way. The short yellow hair, the square face, the plumped skin, the slightly downturned eyes, the sharp beaked nose.

I remembered my father as an MP in the First Cavalry Division. On his shoulder he wore the shield-shaped golden patch with the diagonal black stripe and horse-head silhouette. He would dab my cheeks with shaving cream while I crept around him and splashed the dirty water in the wash basin. When I learned to talk, I said *"Aboji myondo"* each time he shaved, and he tried to teach me the English: "Daddy, shave." I could never make the strange words, but I learned games quickly. I would imitate his shaving by using a dull knife, or play cowboy, making him snort and rear up to make the horse noise while I clung to his back. I would stop him, patting his short, yellow bristles, and motion for him to graze on the dry leaves I had strewn on the floor. I learned how to unlace his low-quarter shoes so I could use one lace as reins and the other as a whip. We would play until the sweat poured from his body, filling the room with his strange animal smell. I remembered the smell of yellow Dial soap, the gritty texture of Colgate tooth powder, the cold sting of Mennen Skin Bracer, the warm and wet lather of Old Spice shaving soap he brushed on my face with the two-tone bristles of a shaving brush. I remembered the odd musk of the foot powder he rubbed between his toes and dumped into his green wool socks and into his black combat boots, the sweet mildewy smell of damp leather, the pleasant bit of Black Kiwi shoe polish. I could remember all these things, but I could not picture his face. I could see his gap-toothed smile when he removed his false teeth. I could see the blue and green flash of his eyes, the plumpness of the back of his hand when he grasped a pen to write, but I could not remember his face. I had only pieces of my father.

"Mahmi," I said. "Do you think Daeri's face has changed?"

"His skin might be a bit burnt," she said. "Maybe he's lost a little flesh because of his hard life in Vietnam, but why would he look any different?"

"I don't know. What if I don't recognize him?"

"You'll recognize him."

"Do you think he'll remember me?"

"Of course! He's been thinking only of you for that whole year. You're his son." Though she tried to keep pale, Mahmi's skin was burnt quite dark by the summer sun. In her beehive hair and her white polyester *wan-*

pisu, she was darker than me. Her skin was dark even for a Korean, and sometimes people said she had the skin of a *sangnom*, a commoner. "Do you remember the last time you saw him?" she asked.

"It was with the beggars," I said. "He gave them money and he said I shouldn't make fun."

"That's right." Mahmi looked suddenly worried, and I knew she was thinking of the wounded veterans with pieces of their bodies missing.

"Why didn't he tell me he was going?" I said. Then I saw my father in the distance through the waves of heat rippling over the tarmac, and he looked smaller than I remembered. Other yellow-haired soldiers had come out before him, and I had been afraid to confuse one of them for him, but there was no mistaking when my father emerged from the terminal building—the fresh-cropped crew cut that made his hair bristle straight up like a brush, the fleshy square shape of his face. He was leaner and darker, burnt by the tropical sun and wasted by bouts of malaria. He was wearing his short-sleeved summer khakis, with his bars of decorations and the coiled blue Infantry braid around one shoulder, but he walked differently—methodically, with a step more cautious than I remembered, a step more suited for someone in camouflage fatigues. His ice-blue eyes had a distant look to them—or had they sunk subtly back in their sockets?

Mahmi did not immediately run to him as I had expected. She gave me a quick glance, and I charged forward, sprinting until I grew suddenly self-conscious just in front of my father and came to an awkward stop to look sheepishly up at him. He stepped up to me and lifted me into his hug. He patted and rubbed the top of my head as he let me down on my mother's approach. When she reached him he kissed her. That was the first and only time I saw them kiss.

We rode back to Pupyong in another Arirang taxi. I sat in the front seat with the window open so I didn't hear what they talked about in the back. We drove off the good pavement of the airbase and out into the winding dirt road through the several villages that skirted the other army posts along the bus route to ASCOM. I sat sweating in the vinyl seat, watching the meter click up nickel by nickel as we rattled on in the heat.

In the evening I bathed after my father, standing in a wash basin full of soapy water as he scrubbed me with a rough washcloth and poured cold water over me to rinse me clean. Emo cooked a steak, which Mahmi had gotten the day before and kept under a block of ice. My father was happy but uneasy. Even when he pierced the top of his Falstaff beer with the can opener, making that cold *crack-hissss* sound that used to make him smile, he seemed preoccupied by something.

I do not remember what he talked about that first night. I do not remember if the dinner was pleasant or if he had brought lavish gifts for everyone. I remember being shocked at the contrast between his burnt forearms and the paper-white flesh of his armpits. I remember thinking the damp curls of hair in his underarms were the color of the hairs around an ox's nostrils. I remember how his feet filled the entire wash basin and how the room became pungent with the familiar odor of his sweat. In his duffel bag he had brought back all the cigarettes he had not smoked or traded from his C-rations, the packets of acrid coffee, the packets of toilet paper, salt, sugar, pepper, and cream, the metal can openers, the white plastic spoons—things that we would use every day in the house. He had brought my mother a red Vietnamese costume called an *ao dai*; he had brought fresh green wool socks for Hyongbu, grease pencils and yellow wooden pencils for Yongsu and Haesuni, and a leather wallet from my grandmother for me to hang around my neck. He asked me about school and I told him that I enjoyed it. I left out all the important things.

———

"What did you do in Vietnam, Daddy?"

We were at the edge of the parade field at Yong-san 8th Army Head-quarters, just under the flagpole, and my father had put me astride the howitzer to take a quick picture. They fired deafening blanks out of the howitzer each day when the flag came down, and everything stopped to listen to the bugler play the sad taps music. The dark green barrel was hot under my thigh.

"You're sitting on top of the Zam-Zammah!" said my father.

"Zam-Zammah!" I shouted.

"Thy father was a pastry cook!"

The shutter of my father's borrowed camera clicked and I quickly swung my leg over and leaped down. "What's a pastry cook?"

"Oh, that's someone who makes doughnuts and cakes. Like *ttok*."

"You're not a *ttok* man, Daddy. What you do in Vietnam? You kill lotsa' number ten VC?"

"I was a red bull on a green field," he said quietly, still talking some sort of riddle I didn't understand.

"How come you not say?"

"I was on an Advisory Team near a place called Nha Trang," he said. "I helped people called Montagnards fight the Vietcong. You'd like the Montagnards, Booby. They're like Indians."

"They got Indians in Vietnam? Make fire with sticks? Wow!" I took my father's sunburnt hand, and he led me across the street, past the Main Library, to the Snack Bar. I heard a raspy metallic sound and looked back over my shoulder at the parade field, suddenly expecting to see people ice skating the way they did when the field was flooded in winter. It was nothing, just a sound like the sound of a blade on ice, but it made me shiver.

My father was quiet. He had seemed happier since he returned from Vietnam, but he was also distant, as if a part of him had not made it back. I had seen my share of limp, black body bags and rigid aluminum coffins on AFKN television, and I imagined he had left something like that—some feeling that hurt like the sight of those containers—back in the highlands outside Nha Trang.

My father treated me to an early turkey dinner at the special buffet that afternoon. He wanted me to have the dark and white meat, but I found the sliced turkey loaf neater and less like a dead animal—more palatable under the lumpy gravy and the dark red cranberry sauce. I had never learned how to handle a full set of western silverware, and today was my lesson on how to eat European-style, keeping the fork in my left hand, the knife always in the right. My father corrected me and told me anecdotes while I sawed at the turkey with the dull knife and struggled to use the fork in its upside-down position without letting the food slip off.

"I used to go swimming out on Nha Trang beach," he said. "The water was so blue it was like looking up at the sky, and for lunch I used to eat a green dragon fruit."

"Green dragon? Like dinosaur?"

"Like a cactus—you know, like you see in the cowboy movies. Green dragon fruit tastes really good."

"Can I have one, Daddy?"

"You come to 'Nam with me sometime, Booby." He tapped on his false front teeth. "One time I lost my partial plate when I went to the *benjo*. I dropped it in there and it was night, so I couldn't find it later even with a flashlight. In the morning I went out without my partial, and the Montagnards thought it was funny. I said, 'See, me Montagnard, too.' The chiefs got a real kick out of it. They file down their front teeth and they all smoke cigars, even the little kids your age."

I made a face to show him I didn't like cigars.

"Don't spill that. Pull your elbows in. That's right, and sit straight."

After I corrected my posture, my father took some change out of his pocket and put it on the table. "How about some chocolate cake?" he said. "Then we catch the bus home."

"Okay!"

The cake, I learned, was not to be eaten with a knife and fork, but simply cut apart with the fork itself. The crumbs could be compressed down and squeezed between the tines if you wanted to get them without touching them with your fingers. My father pronounced that I had made good progress, and we went down to the bus station where he bought his usual copy of *The Stars and Stripes*. On the bus we sat near the back, with the window open so he could smoke one of his pungent cigars even though the Korean women sitting around us grimaced and complained. He ignored them, but he knew what they were saying, and he actually enjoyed annoying them. He told me more about Vietnam as the bus droned on and I settled against his side, half drowsing.

"We used to go on patrol," he said. "We'd hump our gear up into the highlands and watch the big planes spraying the defoliants. Long clouds of it would come down. Agent Orange. It was beautiful. In a few days everything would be dead. Not a blade of grass for Charlie to hide under. And we used to take Bangalore torpedoes—they're long tubes packed with plastic explosives—we used them to blow up bunkers and patches of barbed wire. We'd go out to the Montagnards and stick the Bangalores down into the roots of their big trees and blow a few of them. When the trees fell over the Montagnard kids and women would run into the crater or to the roots that stuck out at the bottom of the trunk and catch all the stunned rats. That was a delicacy for them—a special food. They really liked us *taksan* for getting them those rats."

I fell asleep to the sound of my father's voice telling me something about a monkey and a shotgun. The pictures he took that day never came out.

My father stayed in Korea for eleven months after his return. Forty-eight weekends, and he came home on half of them. With the few three-day passes and holidays, he was home for less than fifty days before he left again. My mother and I visited him only once up in Camp Casey where he was stationed near Wijong-bu, and he wasn't at all happy to see us. He told my mother later that having his men see his Korean wife undermined his authority. We never visited again.

While my father was on leave for my birthday in January of 1968, the U.S.S. Pueblo, an electronic spy ship, was captured off the coast of North Korea, and all over the country, the military went on alert. My father went back up to his unit early after hearing the news on his transistor radio. Later that month, during the Vietnamese New Year's celebration of Tet, the NVA and the Vietcong simultaneously attacked over a hundred towns, cities, and military installations all over Vietnam. It was the bloodiest offensive of the war. The outpost where my father had served near Nha Trang was overrun, and many of his friends were among the Killed-in-Action. The mood among the GIs in Korea became thick and black, full of hate for Asian people and tense with the fear that the North Koreans might invade. The GIs were afraid to stay in Korea, but even more afraid that they might be shipped to Cam Ranh Bay to join some counteroffensive against the North Vietnamese. Houseboys and prostitutes were beaten more frequently; there were more fights in the clubs. The Korean army stayed on alert and continued to mobilize more men to send to Vietnam. There was constant news about the White Horse Division, the Tiger Division, and the Blue Dragon Brigade.

I don't think my father ever considered our house his home that year. We were just the family that kept him occupied when he wasn't working. Korea and Vietnam were both countries divided along their middle by a Demilitarized Zone, with Communists in the north and pro-American governments in the south. Both countries had Buddhists and Catholics and Animists, they farmed wet rice, they plowed fields with oxen, they were populated by people with yellow skin. When he took me to the Snack Bar that day to teach me how to use a knife and fork, he had said something about "The Great Game" when he sent me to buy my own slice of cake. "Heinz," he said to me, "What old man is going to teach you the important things while I'm off in The Great Game?" What was the "The Great Game," I had thought back then. Was my father, like my mother playing two slot machines, but one was Korea and the other Vietnam?

I think now that what he wanted was retribution. And that is why he volunteered for Vietnam again and left before the summer of 1968. And because I had not read the blue book he had given me, I wouldn't know what he meant by "The Great Game" or "Zam-Zammah" or bulls on green fields for another twenty years.

———

Black hourglass against a field of red. Seventh Division—Bayonet. An Indian head in a feathered headdress superimposed on a white star. A field of black. Second Infantry Division. A black horsehead silhouette, like a chess knight, above a diagonal black slash across a shield of gold. The First Calvary Division. In his German accent, he called it "The First Calf." These were the totemic symbols of my father, his military insignia. The four cardinal points in green, which the Germans in World War II had called "The Devil's Cross." Fourth Mechanized Infantry Division. A white sword pointing upright between two yellow batwing doors against a field of blood. The Vietnam campaign. Golden chevrons, a white long rifle against a blue star, oak-leaf clusters, a cross of iron for excellent marksmanship. Symbols of power. Totems of the clan that kills people whose skin is the color of mine. Indelible.

NICK FLYNN is the author of four books of poetry: *Some Ether* (2000), *Blind Huber* (2002), *The Captain Asks for a Show of Hand*s (2011), and *My Feelings* (2015), as well as a play, *Alice Invents a Little Game and Alice Always Wins*. He has received fellowships from, among other organizations, the Guggenheim Foundation and the Library of Congress. His creative and critical works have appeared in *The New Yorker*, the *Paris Review*, and the *New York Times Book Review*. He is also the author of three memoirs: *The Reenactments*; *The Ticking Is the Bomb* (2010), which the *Los Angeles Times* called a "disquieting masterpiece"; and *Another Bullshit Night in Suck City* (2005), which won the PEN/Martha Albrand Award, was shortlisted for France's Prix Femina, and has been translated into fifteen languages. He teaches at the University of Houston and spends the rest of the year in (or near) Brooklyn.

PRACTICAL JOKE

(1971) Travis, just back from Vietnam, is renovating the house next door. The war's an unending muddle. My mother bakes a blueberry pie, puts it in the window to cool, invites him over for a piece. Thirty-one, divorced ten years now, she makes a good pie. Travis is twenty-one and still looks like a Marine—his USMC tattoo, his fatigues—albeit freaky, bright-eyed, his hair going wild. Not a hippie, but drifting toward hippiedom. Trigger-hippie, you might call him, as he's armed to the teeth, having smuggled out his M-16 and various sidearms. They begin seeing each other and, as per usual, he begins renovating our house. My mother likes a man who's good with his hands. Skipping school one day, I'm lingering around the house alone when he pulls into the driveway, lets himself in to work on a dead outlet. I hide in my closet, hear him talk to my dog as he works, and what he says sounds insane. He tells my dog that in 'Nam he ate better-looking dogs, that over there a dog would never get so fat, that all dogs knew enough to run the other way from him instead of rolling on their backs, waiting for the knife to slip in. He tells my dog about the villages he burned and the people he killed and that not all of them were soldiers. About bulldozing a tunnel and later finding out it was filled with kids. Through the cracked door I can see him holding my dog's ears and crying and I don't dare breathe. A few months later my mother stands me

in the kitchen to tell me she's going to marry him. That's a mistake, I say. She nods that she knows but says she'll marry him just the same, and she does, and they're happy, for a while. He's fun to have around in a frenzied sort of way. If we want to go fishing he takes us down to the Harbor, tells us to wait on the loading dock and goes off to hot-wire someone else's boat. We go out for the afternoon, catch a few fish, and he drops us off again. We knew the boat was stolen, even though he said it was his friend's. We knew there'd be trouble if we were caught but we went anyway. His impunity thrills me, I mistake it for fearlessness, though years later he will admit to being afraid all the time. When he decides to put an addition on the house he takes me down to the lumberyard and I see how he pays for a couple sheets of plywood and a few two-by-fours, how he takes the slip out to the yard and backs up to a stack of plywood and has me get on the other side of it so we can load the whole pile onto his truck, until the springs sag. We jump into the cab and he slams it into drive and with the first jerk forward all the plywood slides out onto the ground. We get out and reload it, his entire body now coiled energy, waving off an offer of help from the guy who works there. That weekend we double the size of my mother's cottage, the second and last house she'd buy, all of us and a few of his friends furiously hammering, desperate to finish quickly because Travis never bothered to get a permit. The last thing we do that Sunday night is paint the whole thing yellow, so it will blend in with the rest of the house. It will take two years to get around to shingling it, and only then when the yellow is peeling off in sheets.

In Vietnam he'd been a mine-sweeper, the guy who cleared the path, made it safe to put your foot down. Usually he was good at it, but sometimes he'd screw up, and when he did someone was blown to pieces. After being in-country for a year he signed on for another hitch, but caught some shrapnel a few months into it and was shipped home. In the States he became a color guard in Washington, standing at white-gloved attention at high-level events. But he landed back in the "world" with a short fuse, and when a car full of hippies honked at him at a traffic light that had turned from red to green Travis got out and pistol-whipped the driver, pulled him right through the car's window. Half an hour later, when the police found him, he was in a fast-food joint eating a burger, having forgotten what he'd done. He got off, but then Kent State happened and they ordered him into the basement of the Pentagon, "full combat gear, the whole nine yards." He refused. He knew he'd be sent to college campuses, and was terrified that he'd have to kill more kids. They locked him up in Bethesda for six months, shot him full of thorazine, gave him honorable discharge, cut him loose. A few months later he was at our dinner table.

I liked to play what were called "practical jokes." I had a spoon with a hinge, a dribble glass, a severed rubber hand. I'd leave booby traps around our house, usually a piece of thread strung across a doorway as a tripwire, one end tied to a broom or the racks from the oven, anything that would fall and make a racket. I don't think I knew that Travis had spent his time in Vietnam checking for tripwires—I don't know if knowing would have stopped me. I would set the trap and maybe it would catch someone and maybe it wouldn't. One night Travis took the racks and tucked them between my bottom sheet and the mattress. I came in later that night and crawled into bed. Why I didn't notice the racks right off I can't say, but hours later I awoke from dreams of torture.

Mid-afternoon, one Saturday Travis comes home after digging clams with a buddy. Leaning on pitchforks knee-deep at low tide, they'd each managed to kill a case of beer before noon. He dumps the clams in the sink and tells my brother and me to circle around, he wants to show us his photo album. For the first few pages he's a teenager, cocky beside hot rods, girls sitting on the hoods, one with her arm draped over his shoulders. The next page shows him at boot camp, Parris Island—crewcut, sudden adult. The next show Vietnamese women dancing topless on tables, and on the next page a village is on fire. Corpses next, pages of corpses, bodies along a dirt road, a face with no eyes. As the stories of what he'd done unreel from inside him, my brother stands up and walks into his room, back to his wall of science fiction. I look at the photos, at Travis, look in his eyes as he speaks, somehow I'd learn to do that, like a tree learns how to swallow barbed wire.

Years later, when I track him down, he shows me another photo, one I hadn't seen or don't remember—him on a dusty road outside Da Nang, a peace sign dangling from his neck. The reason he signed up for a second hitch, he tells me, was so that he could go into villages ahead of his unit, ostensibly to check for landmines and booby traps, but once there he'd warn the villagers to run, because if they didn't he knew there was a good chance they'd be killed by his advancing soldiers. Then he set off a couple rounds of C-4, radio in that it was still hot, smoke a joint, watch the villagers flee.

T he night he showed us his photo album, after the house went quiet, I crept into the kitchen for a glass of water, the sink still full of sea clams, forgotten. Under the fluorescent hum they'd opened their shells and were waving their feet, each as thick as a long forearm. A box of snakes, some draped onto the countertop, some trying to pull themselves out.

FROM *THE TICKING IS THE BOMB*

THE FRUIT OF MY DEEDS

Thich Nhat Hanh gave a dharma talk about a Vietnam vet, an ex-soldier who came to him, unable to sleep. After seeing a buddy killed, this soldier had put rat poison in some sandwiches and left them outside and watched as some children ate them—and since that day what he did has been slowly tearing him apart. *You have only two choices,* Thich Nhat Hanh told the soldier—*continue destroying yourself, or find a way to help five other children. These are your only choices.*

Thich Nhat Hanh always has a contingent of Vietnam vets at his retreats, at least at the ones he holds in America. As the years pass, more and more are from our subsequent wars. I first met some of these vets nearly twenty years ago, and the time I spent with them convinced me to track down Travis, my stepfather, whom I hadn't heard from in years. Travis had served in Vietnam from 1968 to 1970 as a combat Marine— my mother got together with him soon after he got back stateside. They stayed together for four or five tumultuous years, and then they split up.

The years Travis lived with us I never called him my stepfather. He was more of a wild older brother, just a guy who was around for a few years, who taught me how to bang a nail, how to build an addition without pulling a permit, how to "borrow" a stranger's boat to go fishing—then he was gone. When I found him, all those years later, in upstate Vermont, I wanted to ask him two questions: how did he meet my mother, and how did he find out she had died? I'd brought a video camera to film his answers, telling him, telling myself, that I was making a documentary film—the home movie we never had. Later, I would seek out my mother's other boyfriends, ask them the same two questions. What surprised me about Travis was that he felt responsible for her death in some way. He thought she'd used his gun, which I don't even think is true—my mother had her own gun.

———

(1999) Four years after Travis and I reconnected, a filmmaker tracked me down (she'd seen my home movie), and asked if Travis and I would be interested in flying to Vietnam to be part of her documentary film— three combat veterans and three of their children, the vets returning to the scene, their children along to bear witness. The conceit of her film was to examine if war trauma was passed on through generations.

Travis turned fifty on a train from Ho Chi Minh City to Na Trang.

Three weeks into it we spent a day filming a single stretch of road outside Da Nang, where Travis had been stationed. Each night, Travis told us, this dirt road was destroyed by "the gooks," and during the day the Americans would hire the locals to rebuild it. Travis knew, everyone knew, that it was likely that the same ones who destroyed it then rebuilt it the next day. This went on for months. It was, for Travis, as if Sisyphus had to hire someone else to push his rock, thereby denying himself even that pleasure. The day we were filming, Travis spent a long time trying to find the spot he'd spent so many days on thirty years earlier, the exact stretch of road that had been blown up so many times. He spoke with the other vets, pointed to the line of mountains in the distance, tried to line up a photograph of his younger self, standing on that road, with the line of mountains today. While Travis was being interviewed I stood under an umbrella, trying to protect myself from the merciless sun, watching farmers work the rice paddies on either side of the road. Each shoot of rice, once it reached a certain height, had to be transplanted by hand—the bent-over farmers were doing that this day. Travis needed to stand upon the same piece of road he'd stood upon so many years earlier. *Maybe we'd bombed the line of mountain beyond recognition*, José offered—*it happens*. Travis finally had to accept that it wasn't exactly as he remembered. As we drove back to Da Nang we passed small mounds of rice piled along the edge of the road, drying in the sun. Some of the rice got caught up in our tailwind as we passed, rose up in the air, then settled back down to earth.

That night, over dinner, the director announced that the next morning we were to visit the site of the My Lai massacre. It was the first we'd heard of it. The other two vets were not happy about this, and threatened to leave the film if they were forced to go. *No one will be forced to do anything*, the director insisted. The other vets said they'd spent their lives living down My Lai, being called baby-killers by strangers, and this was not why they'd agreed to be part of the film. Travis looked at them. *This is what we all did*, he said. *This is what they meant when they ordered us to clear a village—these guys just got caught*. Travis asked me what I thought. I told him I thought we should go, but that it was up to him.

The next morning the bus pulled up in front of the site of the massacre, which is now a museum, a sacred site. Travis and I walked in together, the camerawoman walking backward in front of us. The other vets and their children remained on the bus. The museum is a small building with framed photographs on the walls, most of the photographs from the *New York Times* or other American newspapers. I remembered seeing a lot of the same photographs when they were first in the *Boston Globe*. At some point Travis told the camerawoman to shut off the camera, that he didn't want to be filmed. Then he walked slowly away from us, talking softly to the translator.

The trip back to Vietnam had been difficult for Travis. He'd only been on an airplane twice in his life—once when he was seventeen and enlisted in the Marines, and again three weeks before this moment. His first days back in-country he couldn't even look a Vietnamese person in the eye, especially anyone in authority, for they all wore the uniforms of the Vietcong. Even the "mama-sans," he couldn't look at them. He told the director a day before we left America that he was planning to bring a small sidearm with him, for "protection." *A gun?* she asked, incredulous. She called me and asked if I thought he was serious. *As far as I know,* I said. She called him back—*Travis, you can't bring a gun with you to Vietnam.*

Fuck it, he said. *I'll buy one over there.*

So Travis and I spent the first few days in Saigon (Ho Chi Minh City) searching the markets for a gun, or even a big knife, but in the end he settled for a bag of marijuana and a massage.

Outside the My Lai museum building is an open field, with small plaques marking the sites of what happened—a spot where some huts stood, a well where a baby was thrown down, the ditch the women and children were herded into. A woman, maybe in her forties, was seated on the grass, her legs folded under her, weeding the lawn very slowly, one stalk at a time. Travis watched her for a while. From a distance I watched Travis watching her. It was as if she was meditating on each blade, considering whether to uproot it (*And now it seems to me the beautiful uncut hair of graves*). I found out later the translator whispered into Travis's ear that the woman had been a child at the time of the massacre, and had survived by hiding beneath the body of her dead mother. Travis nodded, asked if he could speak with her. The translator went to the woman, knelt down, spoke some words, looked back at Travis, gestured for him to come. I watched Travis walk up, say something for the translator to translate. I watched him kneel down before this woman, still seated on the grass, take her hand, kiss it, ask her to forgive him, to forgive America.

TRAVIS REDUX

(2007) I spend a day driving route 100 north, the entire length of Vermont, to see Travis—a few years without a face-to-face have slipped past again. I made the trip to ask him about torture, I told myself, but now, sitting across from him, it seems enough to simply catch up. *Sue was with a guy for a while,* Travis tells me—*he'd been in Iraq, came back with a short fuse.* Sue is his daughter. *It must be hard,* I say. *If they were there for a reason it might be different,* Travis mutters. Twelve years ago, when we first reconnected, we'd talked about the first invasion of Iraq, about how he went off the rails—breaking into his estranged wife's apartment, standing at the kitchen stove, burning her clothes item by item on the open flame, until he noticed the blue lights swirling outside. He kicked out a window, crawled on his belly to his truck, outran the cops for a hundred miles. The next morning, once he'd sobered up, a cop knocked on his door—they all knew him—so he turned himself in. The judge went easy, sentenced him to group therapy for vets with posttraumatic stress at the V.A.

A few years later, when we went to Vietnam together, it seemed he'd righted himself—no new stories of run-ins with the law, a jewel-like cabin in the woods he was building for his new girlfriend, his house a little less chaotic. We went to lunch with his kids.

And now, eight years later and three years into another war, I ask him how he's faring. He goes to bed early these days, he tells me, wakes up at three or four, watches the news for an hour or two, then goes to breakfast at Flo's. The other workers—carpenters and plumbers, electricians and mechanics—push some tables together, talk about the war. *Did you know that in Camp Lejune* (a Marine Corps base in North Carolina), *five out of seven wells were contaminated, and the government knew, for five years, and still let the army wives and children drink from them?* I shake my head, but I'm not surprised. The Walter Reed Army Medical Center is in the news these days, paint peeling from the ceilings, roaches in the food, soldiers with head injuries wandering from building to building like an army of zombies, looking for help. We talk about how soup kitchens are set up on bases now, run by church groups, how the rate of suicide among military personnel is the highest it's ever been. Travis is remarkably well informed—*The corporations are getting all the money,* he says, *just like always.* When the war started he went off the rails again, got another DUI, lost his license for eighteen months, got caught driving on a suspended, and ended up spending ten days in lockup, just as the bombs were falling on Baghdad. I bring up Abu Ghraib. *Seems like things got out of control on the night shift,* he says. I tell him about the memos from the White House, about Charles Graner getting high marks for the work he was doing, about how the photos were cropped so that we couldn't see the CIA spooks and the private contractors just outside of the frames. He shakes his head, but it doesn't surprise him. *We look so bad now,* he says. *Invading Iraq was like opening Pandora's box, now no one knows how to stuff everything back in.* We talk about our trip to Vietnam, about My Lai. I tell him that the moment he kissed that survivor's hand and asked her forgiveness was one of the most beautiful things I'd ever witnessed—utterly transformative. I tell him that the same guy who released the My Lai photographs released the Abu Ghraib photographs. Travis shakes his head.

Here for a purpose, he mutters.

Memorabilia from our trip to Vietnam hangs on his walls—a wood-block print of a water buffalo, a straw hat.

Inez is pregnant, I tell him.

Get ready, he smiles.

TERRANCE HAYES is the author of *How to Be Drawn* (Penguin Books, 2015), a finalist for both the National Book Award and the National Book Critics Circle Award; *Lighthead* (Penguin, 2010), which won the National Book Award for Poetry; *Wind in a Box* (Penguin, 2006); *Hip Logic* (Penguin, 2002), which won the 2001 National Poetry Series and was a finalist for the *Los Angeles Times* Book Award; and *Muscular Music* (Tia Chucha Press, 1999), winner of the Kate Tufts Discovery Award. His honors include a Whiting Writers' Award and fellowships from the MacArthur Foundation, the National Endowment for the Arts, and the Guggenheim Foundation. He was elected chancellor of the Academy of American Poets in 2017.

THE LONG SHADOW OF WAR

> Now I see what there is in a name, a word, liquid, sane, unruly, musical, self-sufficient.
>
> —*Walt Whitman*

When I met my biological father, Earthell "Butch" Tyler, Jr., for the first time in February 2004, he did not begin by telling me the year he was born. He did not open his wallet to show me pictures of his children or siblings. A small 40-year-old picture of his father was the only thing he carried. He placed it on the table before me, a worn black-and-white photograph only a little bigger than a stamp. Peering into it I saw a head the size of a thumbprint, so faded I could barely make out the man's features. He told me my grandfather was a war hero. Sergeant Earthell Tyler, Sr., had been killed saving his men's lives in Vietnam. "There are medals to prove it," Butch said. A Purple Heart and a Bronze Star. He promised to find them and show me. When he moved into his own place, he'd hang them on his wall. Butch lived with his girlfriend, Ronnie. He and his son, she and her two children, stayed in her two bedroom apartment. I'd traveled 500 miles from Pittsburgh, Pennsylvania, the place I lived, to Columbia, South Carolina, the place where I was born, to meet him. I'd driven from the house of James L. Hayes, the man who'd raised me, to find Butch Tyler, the man whose blood ran through me.

I could already hear myself boasting that I came from two generations of soldiers—even if the soldiers, Earthell Tyler, Sr., and James L. Hayes, were not related to one another. It was the kind of family mythology I'd come looking for. For a moment I thought James L. Hayes, retired Sergeant 1st Class of the United States Army, would be proud to know my grandfather was a war hero. But I was not brave enough to talk about this with him, hadn't even told him I wanted to find my real father. I was afraid it would hurt him to hear me, his son, utter the words "real father." Words both true and untrue. The evening I met Butch, I left James Hayes before his big-screen television still wearing his correctional officer uniform, his badge and buttons polished bright as mirrors. Ten years after retiring from the Army, he remained a soldier to the bone; still dutiful, stoic. What I was going to do didn't concern him, I told myself. I thought I could learn a few biological details, a few stories about the Tyler in my blood, and then quietly return.

"I don't want anything. I only want to look into your face," I'd said to Butch when I spoke to him on the phone for the first time. His voice was warm, already familiar, saying he wanted to meet me as soon as possible. That evening I followed the address he gave me to a run-down neighborhood some people called "The Hole." Outside I passed by boys playing basketball at a makeshift hoop in the darkness. They paused for what seemed too long when I stepped from my mother's Volvo. No streetlights or porch lights burned at the row houses' narrow doors. Though it was February, it was hot. I was nervous and sweating in the long black coat I'd worn against the thick snows of Pittsburgh.

Before his sister, Maimie, told him about me, Butch had no idea I walked the earth. My mother kept her pregnancy from him, kept my father's name from her husband, and tried for most of my life to keep Butch from me, too. Maybe she'd only told me the truth a year earlier in 2003 because I'd caught her off guard. We were in the midst of a family crisis: my younger brother was going to war in Iraq, planning to marry an ex-girlfriend before leaving. When I asked him why he couldn't marry her when he got back, he said he just wanted to leave something behind. He feared he might not return, and I laughed at the idea, as cruel or in as much denial as anyone who has never gone to war.

Foolishly, I thought I understood military life. In Columbia, it was nearly inescapable, as it was home to Fort Jackson, the largest and most active basic combat training center of the United States Army. Several times a week my family moved between the base—shopping at the commissary and PX—and the city, as if the worlds were identical. We lived in a neighborhood where other black military families posed as ordinary middle class citizens. We frequented malls and restaurants where young privates moved among us more like well-behaved exchange students than soldiers in training. It never occurred to me that any of them could be sent off to war, which existed only in history books and Hollywood movies. No one I knew had died for his country.

My father served for more than 20 years and never saw combat, enlisting during the cooling years of Vietnam and retiring at the beginning of the first Gulf War. It was one of America's longest periods of peace. I asked him once whether he was afraid he'd be sent to Vietnam when he enlisted. "I thought I'd have to go to Nam," he said. "But you know where I come from, going to fight in Vietnam would have been a step up."

In our family's oldest photo album, there is a photo book picture of James L. Hayes the day he left Florida for Ft. Jackson. In a picture the same size as the one Butch showed me, he grins like a boy on his way to college. His gold tooth and small afro suggest none of the buzz cut discipline awaiting him. His fist is raised in the gesture of Black Power, as if that was what the military held for him: pride, power. "At the Miami Airport getting ready to go to Fort Jackson for Basic and A.I.T." is written on the back below the date "November 24, 1971." I had been born seven days earlier in the state he was headed for. I can't even say for sure how he met my mother after arriving there. No one talked about those years in our family, I think, because the story of my birth was bound to them. But I grew old enough to wonder why my younger brother was named James L. Hayes, the 2nd, and not me. I overheard the stories they told their friends, who marveled at my height: to some they said it came from James' side of the family; to others my mother's side. Even with these slow recognitions, I considered James L. Hayes my father. The word father had nothing to do with blood.

But when I was 18, in the midst of a quarrel, I told my mother what

I knew. The truth flashed between us, and a moment later we were both calling him my father. We didn't talk about it again.

At 25, I found a Polaroid of my mother at 16 in the same album that held the picture of James L. Hayes. Scribbled on the back in her handwriting was: "Butch, Bubby, and Me at El Matador Bay somewhere dancing around. We had a boss time! February 19, 1971." I had seen the photo before, but never thought of it as anything more than an image of my mother and two friends. When I realized the date was almost nine months to the day before my birth, November 18, 1971, the tall, handsome boy with his arms around her came into focus.

Still, it was seven years before I had the courage to confront my mother about the image. In the midst of talking on the phone about war and my brother, I asked her if Butch, the boy in the picture, was my father. She stuttered, quieted. Then said with a sigh of relief, "I thought I'd have to take that secret to my grave."

After keeping the truth locked up for so long, my mother told me everything. Within the week she'd contacted Butch's sister, Maimie, the only Tyler she'd been in contact with since his mother, Miss Rebecca, died in 1999. Maimie said the family had broken up since the funeral. "Maybe you'll be a reason for all of us to come together again," she said. She hadn't heard from Butch in two years, but she'd do whatever it took to find him, she told me.

It took nearly a year. When she called with a phone number, she told me Butch had been sort of wandering from place to place, woman to woman since his divorce. She insisted he was a good man. He had dropped out of school to help raise his brothers and sisters, but he was smart. "I bet he'll want to read your poetry," she said.

"Lord, he look just like you!" Butch's girlfriend Ronnie exclaimed when she opened the door. I stepped into a small room that was spare enough to suggest hardship, spruced up enough to suggest affection. Half a dozen empty Crown Royal whiskey bottles lined up like museum vases along the top of the kitchen cabinet. Chatter and R&B music murmured behind a door at the end of a short hall. Ronnie sat on the couch before an old floor-model television, half pretending she wasn't interested in what was about to happen. At the other side of the room Butch drank a tall can of beer at a small table.

"Come here and let me look at you," he said, gesturing through a gauze of smoke. He stubbed his cigarette and pulled a crumpled pack out of his short-sleeved work shirt's pocket. Maimie had told me he had a job fixing air conditioners, that he'd always been good with his hands. He had the long-muscled arms of an athlete, but deep creases lined his face. His eyes were bloodshot with exhaustion and drinking, his slow movements almost graceful. "You definitely got the Tyler head," he said when I sat across from him. I did as he did, looking for the ways we were alike. Almost without wanting to, I compared him to James L. Hayes. He slouched where my father sat upright even in his sleep. "You got the Tyler head," he said again, suddenly palming my head. Something like tenderness entered his face. Butch was loose where my father was careful; he was like a wisp of smoke, my father a length of rope.

"My son Earthell Number Three got his momma head, but his little brother, Rashad, your little brother, Rashad, he got our head," Butch said, calling for Earthell Number Three to come out and meet his brother. A handsome, lanky 20- or 21-year-old emerged from the back room talking on a cell phone. He wore a basketball jersey, loose jeans, and a ball cap.

"What up, big brother," he said in a deep voice somewhere between nonchalant and friendly, as he put his long arms around me. "Nothing. Talking with my big brother," he said into the phone. Maybe it didn't surprise him that his father might have a son he didn't know about. Ronnie asked us to stand side by side. I'm six foot five inches and Earthell Three was an inch or two taller. Butch stood grinning at us, an inch or two shorter than me.

"Damn y'all tall," Ronnie said. "He definitely your son, Butch," she added as if to settle the matter once and for all.

"You want me to pick up some more beer, Pop?" Earthell Three asked, looking, I thought, for a good way to back out of the room. He still held the phone to his ear.

"Hell yeah, Baby!" Butch exclaimed grabbing the boy's shoulder as he looked at me. "Earthell is my partner!" The boy's smile seemed too mature, more like his father's caretaker than his partner. Maybe he was there instead of with his mother and brother in order to look after Butch.

"Your Daddy likes to drink too much," Ronnie said. She said it with ease: "your daddy." I'd arrived in my mother's Volvo, an emblem of the most stuck-up members of the black middle class. Mid-week, I'd flown from Pittsburgh to Columbia. I was a college English professor, a poet. Standing in the middle of the spare living room, I felt like I wore the wrong skin. But still, they'd welcomed me in.

Butch said, "I'm proud of you, son."

And it embarrassed me.

For months after that visit when I tried to remember what Butch looked like, I could recall nothing but a version of my own face; when I thought about the photograph of Earthell Tyler, Sr., I could recall nothing but a shadow. Often I returned to the photograph I had of Butch and my mother. In it they clutched each other at the waist, a young smiling couple. The thick veins looping Butch's hands and forearms were like my own. I believed I saw myself in the shape of his ears, his brows, and thin lips. I studied my mother's handwriting, the message that had been waiting for my eyes even before I was born: February 19, 1971. The date was nearly six years after Butch's father had died in Vietnam, November 17, 1965, and almost nine months to the day before my birth, November 18, 1971.

Butch smiled when I told him about the picture. "I remember that night. I got so drunk your momma had to drive. She didn't even have her license yet," he said.   .

I knew this story. The story my mother revealed to explain why she'd never told anyone Butch was my father. I waited to see how he'd finish it.

He continued, "Your Momma's always been a little crazy, but I really loved her back then. She was my first love, and I think I was hers." He took a drag from his cigarette, thinking. "That's why I can't figure out why the hell she ain't tell me about you?" He half-asked, half-fussed. He seemed to have no idea anything wrong might have happened that night.

"I don't know. You'll have to ask her," I said, looking away from him.

My mother told me they'd fought in the hotel. "I guess nowadays they call it rape . . . ," she said, almost sighing, as if she were still trying to figure out what happened after all these years. "I was too embarrassed to tell anybody I was pregnant. Definitely not him and his mother. When she died, it was the thing I regretted most."

I remember Miss Rebecca. She was a tall, serious woman my mother and I visited when I was a boy. Something like respectful fear or fearful respect emanated from my mother in this woman's presence. Maybe she was waiting for the moment Miss Rebecca truly saw me. Waiting to tell everything. We'd sit quietly for hours in her den. There might have been portraits of people who looked like me around her room: her sons, daughters and grandchildren, her deceased husband. They never spoke of them. They never spoke of me. My mother told me babysitting for Miss Rebecca was her first job.

Having now told me things she thought she'd take to her grave, my mother talked, as she rarely did, about what it was like for her growing up. She, her sister, and two brothers were raised by a single mother in one of Columbia's first government projects. Before moving there they'd lived in a tiny tin-roofed house with her grandmother and two uncles. Her own father lived in New Jersey with his wife and legitimate children. She only saw him a few times before he died. She remembered when Butch's father died in the war. "I remember the money Miss Rebecca got after his death," she said. "I would sit on my steps across the street from their house and watch all those kids opening sodas, and then leaving the half-full cans on the porch. I wanted to be part of their family." Then, as if she'd forgotten what she told me about Butch, she reminisced fondly about him. How he was the first boy tall enough to touch the ceiling when they were in school together. How all the other girls wanted him.

I felt like a coward for not asking Butch if what my mother told me was true. Or maybe I felt it would be wrong to accuse him. But, really, it was why I'd come. Had I been born as a result of rape? What did that say about who I was, about the kind of blood that made me? I had to see the man to know the truth, and sitting across from him I still didn't understand. I strained to see the person he might have been beneath who he seemed to be. I thought of the boy in the photograph. He looked incapable of violence. I know that's a foolish thing to say. Maybe he looked drunk. Maybe he drank because his father drank? Maybe he drank because his father was dead? Everything riddled with "maybes," and who could answer these questions? All I knew of my past was that my grandfather had died a Vietnam war hero. Everything I tried to understand about Butch was tied to this fact.

Nearly two years later in January 2006, I spoke with Butch in person for only the third time. I wanted to know more about my blood, my grandfather, our history. What was his earliest memory of his father? Could he describe the last time he'd seen him; what did he remember about the day he learned his father was dead? I wanted to know how losing Earthell Tyler changed the family.

Butch had moved between two or three places since I'd last seen him. He was renting a room now in a motel off the highway and had a new construction job out of town during the week. He no longer lived with Ronnie, kicked out because of his drinking, but he asked me to meet him at her place. I hoped to catch him before he was drunk.

"My daddy didn't give a fuck!" Butch said, half slouched at the table, a beer in hand, a cigarette between his lips. I knew there should have only been the two of us for the interview, but I could tell he didn't want me to see where he lived. We sat drinking with Ronnie and her best friend, Brenda. Ronnie's 10-year-old son watched two older boys play a video game, their taunt and laughter blending with the sound of "What's Going On," Marvin Gaye calling "Brother, Brother, Brother . . . " from a tiny CD radio. I propped a tape recorder in the middle of the table, hoping Butch's voice would cut through the noise. He was talking to me, but he was talking to Ronnie as well, half-boasting, half-testifying when I asked him his earliest memory of his father.

"You know what, he didn't give a fuck," Butch said to the room. "When he came back home and Mother had all those children you know what he said? 'How y'all doing?'"

The boys playing the video game let out a snatch of laughter.

"Don't use that kind of language on the tape!" Brenda said, Ronnie nodding.

"It's alright," I said, beginning to realize how tricky this interview might be for me to moderate, how difficult for Butch to recall any details. "You mean he was easy going?" I asked.

"Yeah, he didn't give a fuck," Butch said.

"Was it that he didn't give a fuck, or was it that he was easy going?" I asked. "There's a difference."

"He was easy going," Butch said, beginning to soften. "He was like me. When he came home—he didn't come home that much—when he came home, everybody would say, 'Earthell's home! The man!'"

"He was in Korea, too, right?" I asked only a little surprised at how suddenly Butch opened up. He could be, at times, the most forthcoming man I'd ever met. Gentle and charming. When I mentioned I wanted to interview him about his father, he seemed ready to tell me every story right there over the phone. When he said his father had served in Korea, it changed my idea of the kind of man I'd thought his father might have been. Not a soldier green going to war in Vietnam, but someone experienced, a career soldier. Now I wanted to know if he'd told his son any stories about the Army—about being a black man in the Army.

"Yeah, he served a year in Korea. But he was never home. He never was. You know why? My momma wasn't about that. She could have been with him; I could have been with him. Every time he left, we could have went with him. But she wouldn't do it. She wasn't willing to leave home," he said.

"Cause she was a strong woman," Brenda said, but Butch was paying no attention, speaking almost to himself. Ronnie looked lovingly from Butch's face to mine. Maybe she'd heard some of it before, but I suspect she'd never seen Butch reminiscing this deeply.

"Before he went to Vietnam he came home. For a minute. He was never there. He came home in a VW. He had a red Volkswagen. He came home. . . . He said, 'Well, I'm going to Vietnam.' I think he knew he wasn't coming back. Me, my momma, my oldest brother, Darrel, and one of Pop's drinking partners—cause Pop liked to drink, too—one of his drinking partners drove us to Alabama. And he was going to leave

Alabama and go to Vietnam. Before that he came home. And he left the VW to Darrel. Now Darrel wasn't his son! When they got married, mother already had Darrel. He left his red Volkswagen to Darrel because he was the oldest. Whose he was didn't matter to him. Cause that's how my daddy was. Darrel was a Tyler and that's just how he looked at it. After that he went to Vietnam. If he had made it back, he would have retired. But he didn't make it back, and he died trying to save somebody else."

"Do you know what happened? Who he saved, how he died?" I asked.

"Well, they sent us the Purple Heart and the Bronze Star. I saw the official papers that said Sergeant Earthell Tyler did such and such and such. That's why they awarded him the Bronze Star."

"You could probably get that information from the government," Brenda said. "You're a journalist, I bet they'd give that information to you."

"He's his grandson, he's family," Ronnie added. "They have to give him that information."

But I'm not a journalist, I'm a poet. I'm not good at asking questions; I'm good at making things up. What I wanted to know Butch couldn't tell me. I had not gone to Washington to see his father's name etched into the black stone, but I'd seen it online: Panel 3 East, Row 96. The only "Earthell" among the 58,022 names, he had been easy to find. "Earthell" sounded both strange and familiar to me—grand and simple at the same time—the kind of name that required a nickname. He might have been called "Slim" or even "Bullethead," nicknames I had growing up. He could have been the original "Butch." (I never thought to ask Butch how he came by the name.) In the army they might simply have called him "Tyler" or "Sarge." Among websites dedicated to veterans, I found slim details of his life: E5, US Army, age 35, married, Delta company, 2nd Battalion, 7th Calvary, born July 22, 1930, died November 17, 1965, cause of death: small arms fire.

It was online that I learned he was among those killed during three days of fighting in the Battle of la Drang, the first major battle between the United States Army and the People's Army of Vietnam (PAVN). I had not heard of the battle until I saw his name associated with it, but detailed accounts filled many websites. On the Army's website, I learned that it was one of the first times in which U.S. forces combined air mobility and air artillery. There were almost no roads into the area, but the new airmobile tactics allowed soldiers on their way to battle and soldiers wounded and killed to be transported to landing zones by Huey helicopters. It was also the battle in which the PAVN and Viet Cong forces learned they could undermine the air strikes by fighting at very close range. They would later refine this tactic, calling it "getting between the enemy and his belt." Some websites featured animated maps and diagrams, reducing the battle and landing zones to the kinds of lines and arrows you might find in a football coach's playbook. On one there was even a war game, complete with military figurines and a gameboard for sale. The battle had acquired mythic proportions in the 40-plus years since it happened.

At wikipedia.org, the yellow-haired Lieutenant Colonel Hal Moore is mentioned in relation to the yellow-haired Lieutenant Colonel George Armstrong Custer, who commanded the same unit, the 7th Calvary, in 1876 at the Battle of Little Big Horn. As with Little Big Horn, American forces underestimated the enemy and faced them in perilously unfamiliar terrain. On lzxray.com, the la Drang campaign is described as two fights between November 14 and November 17: the first at Landing Zone X-ray where 450 American soldiers clashed and fought back over 2,000 PAVN forces; the second near the smaller Landing Zone Albany, while the exhausted soldiers of 2nd Battalion, 7th Calvary, took a break in the tall grass of a clearing. I wondered if my grandfather was among the ambushed soldiers. According to a synopsis on the website, the fighting was "a wild melee, a shoot-out, with gunfighters killing not only the enemy but sometimes their friends just a few feet away." Online I read how the Landing Zone Albany battle lasted through the day and night, descending into hand-to-hand combat. Sergeant Tyler was among more than 155 killed and 126 wounded on November 17, the deadliest day for American forces during the entire Vietnam War. What had he done to earn the medals? I searched for his name on the sites by and for veterans, web pages memorializing little-known fallen soldiers. There were ardent testimonies and words like "Hero," "Honor," "Sacrifice" floating against backdrops of American flags and photos of young men, but on the rare occasion Earthell Tyler was mentioned, it was only a name listed among the dead. Big or small, war or warrior, steeped in tragedy and pride, every website pitched with nostalgia, but none told me what I wanted to know.

I knew Earthell Tyler was a man whose head was shaped like mine, but I didn't know who he was: prankster or preacher, did he sing out loud or to himself, was he thinking of his fellow soldiers or his family in the moments before his death?

"What did she do when she found out he was gone? When she found out he'd been killed?" I asked.

"I'll never forget that day. A taxi-cab driver brought the telegram to the house. I'll never forget that day," Butch said as he lit another cigarette. "I was right there. I was surprised she broke down like she did. I didn't really think she loved my daddy. But uh, I was surprised that she broke down and she cried."

"How old were you?" I asked, already imagining a boy shocked to see his mother crying for the first time. Maybe initially more shocked by the sight of her weeping than at the news of his father's death. I could see Rebecca Tyler now, a big woman with a face like that of my daughter, and I could hear the immense sound of her weeping. And the softness of it.

"I was 11 or 12. I remember when the taxi-cab driver brought the telegram," Butch said.

"I need details," I said, hoping to coax him into a deeper story, something better than my imagination. "Was it a weekend? Were you coming home from school? Were you watching cartoons? Was your mother at work?"

"I think I was at work," he said, laughing. "I've been working ever since I was 12. I had a job changing tires."

"You were pretty much taking care of the family while he was gone?"

"Yeah, my great-uncle got me a job changing tires," he said, and I saw him kneeling at a car in 1965, a boy whose body was trained already in the habits of labor. Except it occurred to me that he was working even before his father died. He hadn't gotten a job to take his dead father's place as breadwinner like some character in a Charles Dickens novel. What I was thinking when I came to speak with Butch was too easy. I thought if he'd never lost his father, he might never have lost his family. I thought he would never have started drinking, might have learned to love my mother the right way.

"So you didn't think they loved each other?" I asked, realizing the story I expected to hear about Earthell Tyler, Sr., also wasn't simple. I imagined the words he'd written home to his wife, pictured him as the kind of man who had a deep, almost foolish capacity for love—a man capable of loving even a country or a woman that might not love him back. Such a man would believe anyone could be changed by his love: a country that did not see his race as equal could change if he devoted his life to protecting it; a woman could change by his devotion and give the same back.

"When they married, they were in love," Butch said. "Mother met my daddy when they were teenagers. She'd already had Darrel. They were young. Daddy was in the Army. I think the problem was when she didn't want to go where he had to go. She just wasn't leaving her family to go to Europe or overseas or Germany—all them places he was going. She said, 'I just can't do that, baby. I'm so sorry.' So he went by himself. Which was a problem. You can't leave your woman like that. That creates some problems."

Ronnie and Brenda and I, we all nodded. His story reminded me of my own. Like Earthell Tyler, Sr., James L. Hayes was a career military man. And like Miss Rebecca, my mother chose to stay in Columbia the years he was stationed on military bases inside and outside the country. Called to Germany when I was eight, he did not live in Columbia again "full time" until retirement 14 years later. It was during those years I first remember meeting Miss Rebecca. Maybe at some point during a visit, my mother asked Miss Rebecca whether she should take the family abroad with James. Perhaps Miss Rebecca told her not to follow him, said it was better to raise children around their blood. Maybe Miss Rebecca told my mother staying was the best way to have a stable family. Except none of it happened that way. As Butch said, leaving your woman behind created some problems. Problems for the woman and the man; troubles for the family.

There was a little rush of movement. The boys left the room, done with their video game; Brenda rose to leave. More than an hour had passed, but Butch and I were still where we'd started. "But you know what," he continued, "I'll say this much about him. He wasn't even in the United States, and she was having babies. And she named every damn one of them Tyler. And you know what he said? Nothing. When he would come home—before he died he came back to the United States— you know what he said? Nothing. But I be the only Earthell Tyler, Jr., baby! My daddy was the only man she ever married. I ain't no bastard. I ain't worried about it. My father was genuine."

He stood up, smiling and sang, "You know what I'm saying, baby?" He leaned over to palm my head. "That's why you who you are! You got Tyler blood in you. You ain't no bastard, baby. You be legit." He swaggered, staggered into the kitchen for more beer.

I'd been thinking about the idea of legitimacy. Butch was one of eight or nine children—I never really got a clear number—all of them scattered now across the city. He had not seen most of them since his mother's funeral six years earlier. His emphasis on legit, genuine, made me wonder if he grew up believing he was more legitimate than any of his siblings. He had been the only one born into a genuine family: a mother and a father who were married. Except his siblings might have seen more of their fathers than he did of his own. . . . As one of the oldest children, he might have seen those men about his mother's house before and after his father died. I wondered if he called any of them father; if he ever wanted to call any of them father. I didn't think of myself as illegitimate even when I knew James L. Hayes wasn't my biological father. I didn't want to find someone to replace him. I didn't want a new name, but I wanted to know my family history. Maybe Butch knew what I'd come looking for. He wanted to give me something to be proud of, and the only thing he could offer was his father's story.

James L. Hayes had wanted to provide me something else. A man who talked little of the past, he wanted to present his family a future to be proud of. An only child, he'd been born to a 14-year-old girl in Pompano Beach, Florida. He did not discuss the circumstances of his conception, but my mother told me his father had been an older man at the time, that he'd never known him. He grew up shuffled between relatives. My mother said he never bothered looking for his father, how poor and virtually parentless he'd been. He joined the Army as soon as he was old enough to enlist. Perhaps meeting a young woman with a small child when he arrived in Columbia reminded him of his own story. They married in 1974, and, a year later, my brother was born in Fort Bragg, North Carolina. We moved often at first, living in military housing among other young soldiers and their families, but when my father was stationed in Germany, my mother moved back to her hometown, my brother and me in tow.

During the decades my father didn't live with us, he remained for me that same hero he'd been when I was eight: an artist whose half-finished, paint-by-numbers portrait of John F. Kennedy awaited him in the hallway, a music lover who left his Curtis Mayfield and Roberta Flack records behind for me, and above all a true soldier, a man of honor. He once collared a young private for strolling through an amusement park with his uniform's shirt untucked. I watched with a mix of fear and awe as the white boy straightened himself up, and then saluted my father. I remember my mother smiling broadly at the scene. In many ways, he was always attentive and responsible during those years, forwarding her money for bills, sending my brother and me clothes and souvenirs from abroad (gaudy mugs from Germany when I was in fourth grade; a jogging suit with my name stitched across the pocket from Korea in eighth grade), but he was mostly a husky, long-distance voice whose main refrain was "listen to your mother." He was her weapon. "I'm going to call your daddy" was a phrase much like "I'm going to call the cops." He was too far away to ever do anything, but her threat stilled me. As the man of the house in his absence, I wanted his respect. I never wanted to let him down.

By the time he retired and moved back to Columbia, though, the myths had clouded over. I wished the white boy he cornered at the amusement park had said, "I'm just here having a good time, man. Relax!" I was in my early 20s, measuring my idea of manhood against James L. Hayes. For a long time, I didn't think about how those years had affected my little brother. Just four when we moved to South Carolina without our father, he was 18, about to move from home, when he retired. I doubt he remembered a time when we all lived together in the house. We spent summers, and often when our parents fought, weekends, in military quarters during the years he was stationed in Fort McClellan, Alabama. Our mother almost always stayed behind in Columbia. I remember the tanks and jets perched around the base like bland oversized toys, the distant camouflaged men. To me, the military was a world of stale rituals and mindless regulations. It took my father from his family, and I assumed my brother harbored the same resentment for military life. Then he enlisted. Ironically, the Army sent him to Fort Bragg, North Carolina, his birthplace two decades earlier.

It broke my father's heart. "The military is no place for a black man," he told my brother. It shocked me to hear such a thing from someone who'd spent nearly half his life in the Army. In the same album where I'd found the photo of Butch and my mother, a newspaper clipping showed James L. Hayes receiving an award for his stellar recruiting record. I don't believe he lied to the poor black boys he talked into joining the Army. He had wanted to offer them the same kind of escape from poverty or rootlessness, the same kinds of opportunities the Army gave him. He believed his own sons wouldn't need to escape anything. "You're going to college," he often told us, but never said how he would make it happen. There was no money, no knowledge of grants and fellowships. When I graduated from high school, I went on a basketball scholarship. I wouldn't have gone to college otherwise. Four years later, my brother was offered some partial academic grants, but not a full scholarship. He tried paying his way through for a few semesters, but eventually decided—without discussing it with anyone in the family—that the best way to pay for school was the military. It's a familiar story: when he arrived after returning from Iraq, he had a handful of college credits, but no degrees. He had a new wife and bad knees.

Like my father, I was broken-hearted when my brother entered the military. Perhaps even more so when he retired without fulfilling his dreams. I feared the military might make him into a dumb machine, that he would be ruined by learning to act without asking. But mostly I dreaded he'd have more in common with our father—with his father—than I did; that James L. Hayes would have more respect for the son who'd been a soldier. Some days I watched them, James L. Hayes, the first and second, standing side by side at the grill. I wondered how much of who my brother was had to do with blood. They gestured and laughed as if they were the same person, possessing the same mix of gentleness and toughness, the same wide smile, the same devotion to our family.

I believe our father returned home after retirement because of this devotion, which is a world like love, to his family. Or his devotion to the idea of family. I want to say blind commitment to one's family is as dangerous as blind commitment to one's nation; that sometimes it is more courageous to question or even abandon that which one loves, but I'm not sure that's what I believe. Was Earthell Tyler, Sr. blind? Was following an order the cause of his death? Was he, like my brother and father, a man devoted to words like "duty" and "honor," to ideas that could be held, but never touched?

"Tell me something you remember about your father," I asked Butch when the room quieted—just Ronnie, him, and me drinking and smoking: the CD player still playing music from the 1970s in the corner.

"I wasn't that close to him. I never really knew him," Butch said, lighting another cigarette, calm enough to seem sober.

"But you wanted to know him," I said.

"I really did. My mom wasn't too close to him either. But he just wasn't there."

"Do you remember him making people laugh? Was he shy, was he serious?"

"He was serious. But on the other hand, he was like me. He wasn't the kind of guy to kick the door in and shoot you for fucking his woman. He wasn't like that. He was a good guy. He died trying to save the life of one of the guys in his platoon. That's how he was."

"You never thought about going in the Army?"

"I went in the Army," Butch said.

"You did? What happened? How old were you when you went in?"

"I was 18. And I had three kids. I had twins and a little girl, and I went in the Army because I was trying to make it better for us. Everybody in my family was in the military. Your Uncle Walter, your Auntie Vickie. She was a lieutenant."

I thought of Fort Jackson's shadow looming over Columbia. It covered so much territory that we all seemed destined to pass through its gates. The military was an escape for black people, and during Vietnam,

America's Army was more integrated than ever before. It meant something that Earthell Tyler was a sergeant, an E5; that the men he served and those who served him were black and white. It meant something that later James L. Hayes, who retired as an E9, would serve and be served in the same way. The leadership roles in the military have never been racially equal, but maybe in the midst of the Civil Rights Movement, the Army was a model for race relations in America. Not because there was no racism, but because blacks and whites were willing or forced to crawl on their bellies together. Maybe the military was, and is, one of the few places minorities can ascend through service.

I did not ask Butch why he thought his father enlisted. All I could think about was his mention of three kids. "Where are these people?" I asked. "How many damn brothers and sisters do I have?"

Butch let out an embarrassed laugh.

"You know how many children your daddy got?" Ronnie said. "Seven."

"I went in the Army for them," Butch continued. "I was going to marry my children's mother. Her name was Ella Mae. But it didn't work out. I hated the Army. And I think the Army hated me, too."

I couldn't imagine Butch in the Army. If he had gone in to be the kind of man his father had been, what did it mean to fail? Had he not succeeded at being a soldier or had he refused to be one? Some black men seize upon the promises of America and some turn from them. Some embrace America for its rags-to-riches myths and others spurn this country because of its racist history. But I should not speak as if the choices we make are that simple. Often these feelings—compliance or resistance, calm or outcry—exist within the same man.

I was calculating numbers in my head: Butch's three children by a woman named Ella Mae had to be just a few years younger than me; then came Earthell the Third, who was 21; Rashad who was 16; I was the oldest. It didn't add up to seven. I felt a web of siblings spreading around me and realized I might be related to half the people in Columbia. It was something I'd considered many times in the years before finding Butch.

"Did your father have any brothers and sisters?" I asked.

"It was just him and his sister. There's a preacher in Denmark, South Carolina, right now. His name is Earthell Tyler. My daddy's sister named her first born son after her brother," he said.

"What's her name?"

"I never met her. There are a lot of people I work with from Denmark, where he was born. There's a whole bunch of Tylers. The whole town is Tylers. But my daddy's uncle raised him and his sister here in Columbia. Uncle Johnny raised them. And every time I would see him—he was a deacon in the church, he raised my daddy—every time he would see me, he would say, 'Oh My God,' and kiss me on the forehead." Butch demonstrated by leaning to kiss me in the middle of my forehead. I could feel the wetness he left there like a small splatter of rain.

"Y'all gonna make me cry," Ronnie said over her beer. She was already crying.

"He loved my daddy just like that. He raised my daddy and his sister. That's all I know," he said, leaning back in his chair. "I don't know their momma, and I don't know their daddy. I know our people from Denmark. Every time he would see me, look at that head, 'That's Earthell!' and he would kiss me. . . . He used to kiss me. You come from a long line of men that love people. Alright. You come from a long line of loving men. Ain't nothing wrong with loving. That don't make you a punk. That makes you a man."

During the flight back to Pittsburgh, I thought of the interview and how I'd failed at it, but beyond that I mulled over what happened after leaving Ronnie's apartment. I followed Butch's swerving old pickup truck to his ex-wife's place. She lived surprisingly close, but he'd been there so rarely we got lost two or three times before pulling onto a road dark enough to seem the right place. A few minutes later we stood on the unlit porch with Rashad Tyler: tall, quiet, 16, my little brother; the one Butch said was like me. Like us.

What is that aura some boys have just before they grow into men? Vulnerability? Openness? It was in Rashad, and it reminded me of the little brother I'd grown up with. It's the type of goodness that makes certain boys perfect soldiers; makes them dutiful, faithful. It's the kind of spirit often broken or dulled with age.

"He think I don't love him," Butch joked, palming his son's do-ragged head. I could tell the boy smiled, but I couldn't make out his features in the darkness. As we got ready to leave I gave him my phone number, told him to call if he ever needed anything. We'd been there only 10 or 15 minutes. As Butch and I stepped from the shadows of the porch into the late, half-lit evening, Rashad asked, shyly, "You gone come see me, Daddy?"

It was the bond the three of us had in common: wanting to see and be seen by our father. Thinking about it on the plane home, I had to put my hand over my eyes. "Hell yeah, I'll see you, baby," Butch assured him.

It was nothing any of us believed.

———

When a father is lost, the ones he leaves behind have to make everything up. The man must be set firmly upon the branch of a family tree even if he seemed to speak little or have no history. Raised by his Uncle Johnny in Columbia, kin to the black people in Denmark, let us make the father of Sergeant Earthell Tyler, Sr., a farmer; let us make his mother a tall, brown woman with a love for gardening. Let the thing that separated the parents from their son and daughter, the crime against them or the crime they committed, the nature of the bad luck that befell them—let it remain a mystery.

When a soldier dies, especially in war, his loved ones make things up. Even the past—which is not the same thing as history. The cool and generous spirit of the deceased; how he sent not only his family, but his sister and Uncle Johnny, money; how whosever child his wife bore while he was away became a member of his family. One must make up the secrets the wife never learned and the secrets the wife never shared. One must imagine the letters that arrived decorated with hearts. One must create the litany of promises and fantasies the man and woman could not keep.

When a loved one is lost, the people left behind have to make up everything. I would like to make up my grandfather's future: imagine it beyond the years of service and medals of honor, far into the ensuing years. He might have worked as a postman or a prison guard. I imagine the way the bones of his huge fingers would begin to ache and give off, even 40 years after the war, a vague gunpowder scent. If, in his 80s, he suffered some ailment that caused him to shrivel or dull, if he walked humped with a walking cane or did not walk at all, I would be the one driving him to his doctor, clutching his arm at the car door, lifting him up.

———

After I returned to Pittsburgh, while browsing a bookstore, I found, incredibly, my grandfather's name in a book about the war, Lieutenant Colonel Hal Moore's *We Were Soldiers Once. . . And Young: La Drang the Battle That Changed Vietnam*. James H. Shadden recounts the battle: "Men were wounded and dead" and among the last six alive were Sergeant Earthell Tyler:

> Tyler gave the only order I heard during the entire fight: Try and pull back before they finish us off. After one of the men was killed the remaining five [men] proceeded to pull back but snipers were still in the trees. Soon I was hit in the right shoulder, which for a time rendered it useless. Tyler was hit in the neck about the same time; he died about an arms length of me, begging for the medic, Specialist 4 William Pleasant, who was already dead. . . . The last words Tyler ever spoke were: I'm dying.

I say not "begging for the medic," but asking. Maybe demanding. He led them through the jungle's foliage of noise, through the bullets and bodies of the enemy falling from the trees. He led them until the trail vanished into the brush, the only one to say, "Try and pull back," when he saw the limbs of men and trees gouged by bullets. I imagined him in death doing something unbelievable, that he'd jumped on a grenade to save his platoon, sacrificing himself.

And reading the story and hearing the stories Butch told me, I still imagine him a hero, though not the kind the Army had in mind. This man is my history. He and I, we see the blood on the deep green leaves, and we think the blood smells like gunpowder. We are not supposed to be there leading black and white boys down into the dirt. We are not supposed to be there with an ache blooming our neck, spreading up to our ears and down into our body. We think calmly: I am almost unborn. I have made love to a woman and left her with a son who looks like me. I am not begging for the medic, I am asking if he is alright. I have a son who bears my name as if it were a long shadow, a glorious light. I am not dying.

JENNIFER JEAN is the author of a chapbook, *In the War* (2010), and a full-length collection, *The Fool* (2013). She is the poetry editor of *The Mom Egg Review*, managing editor of *Talking Writing* magazine, and co-director of Morning Garden Artists Retreats. She teaches Free2Write poetry workshops to sex-trafficking survivors—many of whom suffer from PTSD. Her father, who she has barely known, was diagnosed with schizophrenia and PTSD following his soldiering in Vietnam.

IN THE WAR

I.

When I was twelve I willed the soldiers home.

All the men were bright and rank
and frayed—and blood
flowed from their hearts unbound.

They'd died of shrapnel or honor,
toxin or friendly
fire. These spirits named and numbered
deaths by your side, dad, deaths
by your hand,
during the eon of your two tours.

Still, I could not understand the conflict—
Viet Nam.

I needed endless intel, and your men
to be my men and in their camo
loom above me at the school library,
echo the barbed text in murmurs,
lead me through warfare and weather, through white
lies in letters home. They helped me
find the hills and huts

you conquered
by chance, in wonderment, by force.

II.

It was easy, dad,
to believe in you because you lived

a wizened parallel half-life
across town—in Hollywood, forever
in-country—
drinking your days away
for my sake, maybe

desperate to fill my absence.

In those days I'd curl
on a chair in my living room, cool and away
from the scorch
of a San Fernando Valley summer cig alert.

Fully giddy, my spirit would crouch
and conspire with those red
and flesh and black
and blue fellow combatants.

We soldiers
then launched standard mission procedure: *Prisoner of war!*

they whispered, *You are one of us.*
Or, *You must*
suit up. When he departs, you will be the only one
who can save him.
This was what I had always wanted!

To know your jungle just enough to pull you
out with pincers, to pull you out
whole and mewling
and at my unformed mercy.

III.

When I turned eighteen, they said, *It's time*

for search and rescue. So, I gathered my self
away from my solid, still form on the chair—
my spirit stood with them,
as tall and square boned.

Then, a grunt named Joe, just like you
dad, took my lucent hand and bade me leap
through the carpet, then the concrete,
till we struck soil and traveled southwest,
bypassing pearlescent grubs essential for decomposition.

Soon, we launched out of earth,
through the hardwood lobby floor of the Hastings Hotel—
one of Hollywood's un-retrofitted relics
housing hookers, actors, and castaways
in its dull efficiencies.

I arrived unarmed,
hoping the troll recon said was you was not
you. This troll seemed busy,
bloated, and badly hunched. Like me,

he had audible words for invincible invisible companions.
His hair was pomaded black,
long, magnetic. I let go of Joe,
set my sights on that scurrying thing and spoke
with what turned out to be your smooth voice
in my stiff mouth. Oh, you were lovely
if I looked away and only listened:

You are not mine,
the troll that was you whispered distinctly.

Swiftly, my own
invincible invisible companions scattered
like one body
hit hard by a betty bomb.

IV.

The Hastings Hotel door seemed to swallow
you—you left me
to find my way out of a lobby existence
again. On tenterhooks,

I ordered my grunts to stay
the course, and they clambered to me,
out from behind potted plastic plants
and from under scuffed ottomans. They wrenched me
down through the floor and the fault lines,
then up into a disfigured barroom
serving you the thick liquids of our Azor ancestry.

Our entire lineage drank through you—
I could see in you our kin layered atop one another,
numbing their own petty crimes,
their *saudade*.

What he does for the Azor kin corrupts
their trust in him—their hometown hero,
the soldiers reported, as I eyed the hoards
of thick haired pearl hunters and stocky fishwives
attached to you,
their infant eyes gaping.

Their eyes flashing
like drumfire through the pattern on my living-room carpet

back in the Valley where I woke
from the barroom visitation to spy my
beloved platoon.
I asked them if I was doomed
to be a crowded bar. They said, *When your father dies*
the ancestors must possess you.

Understand, little soldier—
they will not be able to help themselves.

I understood
that eventually you would acknowledge me—
you would live among their ranks
and I would order Abstinence and Attention
and possibly the dressing of all wounds.

ADAM KARLIN was born in Washington, DC, and raised in rural southern Maryland. His father, Wayne Karlin, served in the United States Marine Corps in Vietnam and is professor of Languages and Literature at College of Southern Maryland. Adam has worked as a journalist and travel writer in Asia, Africa, Australia, and North America, including stints as a desk editor at *The Vientiane Times* (Laos) and *The Nation* (Thailand). His writing has appeared in the BBC, *World Hum*, *The Christian Science Monitor*, and *The Lens*, among other publications, and he has written almost 60 guidebooks for Lonely Planet. He currently lives in New Orleans with his wife and daughter.

HOW I DIDN'T FIND MY FATHER'S WAR IN VIETNAM

When I went to Vietnam searching out the battlefields of my father, I wanted it to be another time, all the time. Sometimes I wanted it to be the past. Sometimes I was sick of the past. But whatever the present was, it prickled my skin like hot needles.

Anything modern made my mind lapse into a made-up nostalgia for what I call "film Vietnam." In a Saigon bar I wanted heat thick enough to boil and bubble the beer, like the beef-rich globules of fat that refract across a good bowl of pho. The heat would be thick and orange. It wouldn't just sit in the canopy of the bar ceiling (*You use the word canopy my mind interrupted because every description of Vietnam has to include some reference to triple-canopy jungle. But this isn't the jungle. It's a bar for lonely Australian civil engineers*) but be pushed around with a dusty cough by a slowly *whump whump whumping* ceiling fan made of rattan or teak or some other exotic wood-y noun. But there was no slow fan.

It was freezing; an air conditioner was set to full blast. Outside the night was sticky enough to inspire Graham Greene to spill prose about post-colonial ennui and lost love, but in here the air had an arctic bite. A boon for the engineers, who had done stints in the Persian Gulf and were used to switching out exterior heat for interior chill, but bumpkiss for my fantasy.

Plus, in my old school dreams the Doors would probably play, but

Coldplay was on the sound system. Coldplay and the Corrs. 2002 was buzzkilling my Vietnam bar scene trope.

I was a college senior, awash in waves of Humanities departments and sick of them. I was done deconstructing. Wanted something sincere and solid. To be a writer. Not just a writer, but a travel writer. A trip to Vietnam seemed like a good step along both paths. Go to another country and search for . . . what, exactly? Well, my dad had fought in the Vietnam War, but "searching for my father" sounded a cliché away from a Hallmark card. That said, quests for paternal identity are a time honored way of Becoming A Writer (even if, my College Degree whispered to me, I was not searching for a past but re-appropriating the present from another past experience.

[*Shut your post-modern mouth*, my mind snapped]).

But the College Degree was right: Vietnam wasn't my past. It was my father's. And I already knew my father well, could know him better by sitting with him over a cup of coffee back in Maryland or reading one of his own books—dad was already a writer—as opposed to dodging in and out of bars in Vietnam.

But that wasn't as romantic. Plus the travel writer part required, well, travel. My present self wants to tell younger self: fine, go. Just don't spend too much time in those bars. You'll get to know them later in life. You'll be intimately acquainted with Southeast Asian Nightlife Joint 1.0: vaguely bamboo chic décor, Tiger beer in frosty mugs, English football on TV, karaoke. A few Singaporean businessmen roaring at each other. Dusting of young Vietnamese, giggling at their nouveau riche-ness. Local Chinese, red-faced, puffy and loud. Tired Australian expatriates. The usual crop of hippie-chic backpackers.

I'm pretty sure the bar was named the Blue Gecko. "Blue" and a reptile definitely featured prominently. Par for the course for Southeast Asian backpacker bars.

Bars in Saigon. And Hue. And Hoi An. And Nha Trang. And Da Lat. And Hanoi. Did they all count towards the identity quest? Dad wasn't in Hanoi during the war, obviously, and a part of me felt like seeing that city was eluding my purpose; I went to find my father's war, not sightseeing. Sightseeing made me a tourist, and in my self-importance, I wanted to feel larger than that.

But in Vietnam, being a tourist and being seeker of the past, spe-cifically the past generations' wars, are often the same. The Vietnamese know foreigners come to their home suffused with images of, as they call it, the American War. A war with its own soundtrack (CCR, the Animals, Jimi Hendrix) and celebrities (Charlie Sheen, Tom Hanks), an entire set of cultural signifiers set to "All Along the Watchtower." India promises spirituality; Italy cuisine; Egypt the pyramids and Vietnam, often enough, the war: marketed, prepackaged and sold to thousands of true seekers.

The cynicism—mine or the marketers or both—wore me down. I went from the DMZ to the Mekong Delta to the Central Highlands, a litany of "War Tours." Asking: what am I looking for in Vietnam? More specifically: *when* was I looking for? Nha Trang, Part A: a beach town overwhelmed with pink-faced Russian tourists who tossed endless reserves of money and insults at locals. Part B: the hometown of Mr. Nguyen, family friend, who fled as a boat person to the Philippines and smuggled himself to America to become a NASA engineer. Was Da Nang pocked with dust and Chinese construction equipment and fore-men? Or was it the port where dad first landed in Vietnam? Were the Cu Chi tunnels a network of underground passages used by the Viet Cong to attack American infrastructure, or a theme park where tourists could empty AK-47 clips into paper targets? Pencil in: C) All of the above.

You could even get laughs and franchising out of the war. In the "DMZ Bar" in Hue, where backpackers watched Premier League foot-ball while rocking to Fogarty belting "It Ain't Me" (one Swedish twenty-something proudly showed me how much the soundtrack in the bar synched with "Battlefield: Vietnam," his new first person shooter video game), I watched a Dutch and French tourist reenact a scene from *Rambo*. Using the live end of a flickering light bulb, they pretended to give each other electroshock torture. Their friends laughed. The Vietnamese bar staff laughed. I laughed. Roughly 40 years earlier, in this same city, roughly 6,000 Vietnamese were tortured in a similar manner before they were shot or buried alive by re-conquering Viet Cong and North Viet-namese during the Tet Offensive.

If the war was far enough from me to laugh at a crude parody of its atrocities, it seemed almost as distant to the Vietnamese. Publicly, Vietnam wears the war, its David moment against a geopolitical Goliath, proudly on its sleeve. Scan a Vietnamese newspaper on a national holiday: the state-certified line gushes victory, victory, victory, memorializes the cause, as well as wars of resistance against the French and Chinese. Vietnam is free. Vietnam is independent. Vietnam is often defined, essentially, in negative terms: not American, not French, not Chinese.

Which begs the question: what, then, is Vietnam? Sixty percent of its population was born after 1975. If officialdom uses the war as a propaganda crutch, they also encouraged the practical attitude on the street: "Everything-is-over-the-past-is-the-past-so-let's-do-business." Outside of the afore-mentioned tourist sector and Communist party iconography, the war is distant to daily life, unless you were one of those unlucky enough to lose a limb or a family member or a friend, and to be fair, millions are in that demographic. But most young Vietnamese—which is to say, most Vietnamese—don't bear those bad memories. Even those blacklisted Southerners whose family members fought on the side of the Americans are more concerned about escaping history than remembering it. Vietnamese aren't apathetic to their nation's history of resistance struggles. But the ones I met who were under 40 seemed aware of those conflicts as a dim source of feel-good nationalism, and nothing more— the way many Americans perceive their own formative history.

I was noticing all of this, trying to figure out how the Vietnamese saw the war, because all my ways of looking for it seemed to prevent me from seeing the country as it was. Vietnam was not becoming a magical travel catharsis. I'm a member of the *Eat Pray Love* generation, conditioned to expect growth from a journey, which itself is a fairly presumptuous word to describe what was, in many ways, a three week vacation. But I was selfishly indignant at being denied what was my right as an American—to turn a country into a melodramatic chapter of my own story.

In a way, this was how America treated the nation of Vietnam during the Cold War: stage prop in a geopolitical drama. Vietnam was never its own country with its own people with their own history. It was a peg the US was going to hammer into the circle-shaped hole of the Cold War Communist-Containment Foreign Policy Playset. The problem was: Vietnam wasn't circle-shaped. It was Vietnam-shaped. Robert

McNamara was unhappy with his toy when all his hammering didn't reshape it into his vision.

I bashed away in a similarly futile manner. I wanted to be inspired by Vietnam, while ignoring that the Vietnam *War* I sought, as opposed to Vietnam the country, was a font of pain and loss. The lessons of the war stemmed from trauma, and there was an uncomfortable conflict voyeurism to seeking the aftermath of that trauma out.

But writing doesn't have to come from trauma. It can also come from experience. I had been experiencing the country of Vietnam while I had been looking for its wars. Ever since I arrived, those two ideas, war and nation, bore the same name and the same identity. They were inseparable in my head, even though they were separate in reality.

The tension between war and place had driven my trip. I wanted to split them, but doing so ultimately happened, ironically, by bringing the two Vietnams together, in a way personal to my father and I, but—I hoped—respectful of Vietnam.

I was staying in Hoi An, about an hour from Marble Mountain, the location of one of my dad's major airbases. I rented a motorbike and drove to the mountain and climbed it: fists of granite and sharp rocks, cracks of sunlight slanting through cave ceilings, handfuls of sharp, shrubby grass. Here and there, embedded in the mountain, bullet holes and Buddhist shrines. An old lady with betel-blackened teeth approached me and thrust a bundle of joss sticks in my hands. She indicated I should bring it to the top of the mountain. I thought: I came here because of my dad, but "here" is Vietnamese. Follow the rules.

I cradled the incense. A stony scrabble later and I was on top of the mountain, where I lit the bundle, wedged it between porous rocks, daggersharp pumice. Blue smoke curled out in lost ribbons. I said a prayer to Jim Childers, a helicopter gunner who switched missions with my dad and was subsequently killed. My father touches his name every time he visits the black wall in Washington DC.

All around, highways tangling, clipped asphalt yarn in green checkerboards of rice paddies and dark knives of jungle. In the distance, a cornhued lip of sand and the flushed ocean kissing the sky. The blue smoke of the joss sticks vapored over the mountain, carrying my prayers away from a beautiful moment—but not an epiphany. Because the moment wasn't perfect. The wind blew the joss sticks about. Loud Irish tourists interrupted my solitude, cursing the heat and the climb. My own ankle was swelling from slipping and sliding on rocks.

The moment wasn't perfect. But it was real, I thought, and so is Vietnam, which I am maybe seeing for the first time, through its own joss stick smoke and rituals and land and sea and sky. This was now, in Vietnam. I clattered down the mountain to my motorbike, kicked it into gear, and went home.

ELMO KEEP is an Australian writer and journalist in America, published with *Matter, The Awl, Vice, The Verge, The International New York Times, The Rumpus, The Lifted Brow, The Best Australian Science Writing 2015,* and many others. In her 10 years of writing and reporting, Elmo's work has taken her around Australia, to London, Paris, Latin America, Greenland, through the Northwest Passage, across 28 US states, and to Vietnam, where she retraced her father's steps where he served in counterintelligence during the war in Saigon and Long Tan.

THE BOOK I DIDN'T WRITE

I didn't write the book because the thought of it made me feel vaguely ill at all times. Even when I wasn't thinking about it directly I was thinking about it. None of the thoughts were good.

I didn't write the book because it was a book about betrayal that could only be facilitated by my betrayal of other people, many of whom had already been betrayed. This wouldn't have been a clever metatextual commentary on the nature of betrayal; it would have just been really quite mean of me, and sad.

I didn't write the book because I thought that in the end it would not be interesting. Every day I wondered who would care about the story. There are only so many books that each of us can read in a lifetime; why would this book be one of them? The enterprise of writing—or not writing—the book took on the tenor of the absurd in my mind because it would have hurt no small number of people, and for me to dig around in their lives to turn them into Characters with a Point To Make was not a moral calculus which would ever come out with me in the black.

I had gotten as far as an epigraph:

We are who we pretend to be, so we must be careful about who we pretend to be.

This was also a problem. In this one sentence, Kurt Vonnegut had elegantly expressed everything I'd hoped I might say in an entire book.

There were also roughly forty thousand words, written over two years, mostly useless, arranged into folders that I liked to move around. One day I dragged them over to the little trash icon and they disappeared with that noise meant to mimic crunching up paper.

The book was about secrets—the personal, complicated kind—about what constituted love, and what did not. But the secrets were not mine to tell. I thought a lot about their corrosive nature, and how so much could have been avoided if only people hadn't kept secrets. But I could not resolve the conflict of a story that was not mine. So the secrets stay buried.

Sometimes I thought I imagined the voice of my father, who has been dead for ten years, imploring me to just not do this, *please*, though he would have never said "please." I could tell you that for certain; what else he would say, I have no idea. My father was a complete stranger to me, even though I had known him for all of my life. The whole point of the book was that I might be able to find out who he was, if I could just uncover enough evidence, enough facts, stir enough ghosts.

My father was not a good man; he was what an objective reader might call a terrible person. This presents what is known as the unsympathetic lead. It also presents what will be familiar to all children of narcissists—a great deal of various awfulness that will haunt you in a seemingly unending number of ways for most of your life, until you decide that you are going to actively undo it.

My father stole people's money, was prone to flights of unhinged fabrications—mostly concerning his self-professed genius—and frequently unleashed truly terrifying maelstroms of pure, animalistic, verbal rage. He meddled in other people's affairs because he was bored and vindictive; when not doing this, he shut himself in a room during the day and slept for hours, then roamed the house all night. It was like living with a caged bear that was also responsible for ensuring your welfare, such as it was. By the end of his life at sixty-four he had alienated everybody he knew. He died alone and broke in a rooming house, and that is kind of poetic, but it's also something that, when I think about it, makes me feel like a plastic container crumpled in on itself.

I spent my advance to get copies of his financials and academic transcripts and military records, which I tried to divine like runes, but which stubbornly refused to reveal intelligible patterns. I tracked down people from his past and somewhat traumatized them with the truth of his nature. I came to think that, in the amateur's assessment, my father was quite possibly a sociopath: He was profoundly gifted at lying and charming and bilking others while, at home, he was a slovenly, profane, inexpressibly miserable figure of terror. Those two versions of himself never crossed paths with each other.

I traveled to Vietnam to try and retrace his steps at the Rex Hotel in Saigon, where he would have received his briefings to take back to the field. There's a bar on the roof where the press would gather to do more drinking than reporting. I sat and looked over the city as giant Christmas lights were strung across a department store and carol snippets hung, disjointed, in the hot, thick air. It was hard to imagine how things would have looked back then, not least because what had been the so-certainly-threatening Communist scourge was obscured now by boutique, luxury shopping that felt like walking the streets of Soho. My father had never talked about this time in his life with me. He never really talked about any part of his life in an authentic way, but this part—the tail end of the first decade of the war—least of all.

I rode on the rickety bus to the sweating, dust-ridden Cu Chi tunnels where, after being given a sobering history of the war by an elderly Vietnamese man—who up until he had no choice except to fight, had been training in the seminary—tourists excitedly mounted the decommissioned tank and posed for photographs, brandishing the turret's machine gun. I went further through the jungle to the firing range. When I pulled the trigger of an M16, I thought I was going to vomit. Next to the range is a gift shop staffed by people forced to listen to every deafening round being fired for ten hours a day. A heavily pregnant dog lied on the cold concrete floor of the shop; I patted her absently while drinking a couple of cans of one-dollar beer, one after another, to erase the sensation of the gun from my hands.

I puttered along the Mekong, lying in a hammock on the bow of a small boat for hours, until we arrived at a tiny fishing village at the end of a tiny estuary. At the village on the water, while the sun beat down on our necks and we dangled our feet in the river, we wordlessly ate charred, barely dead fish we folded into rice paper with cold noodles, fragrant, fresh mint and chopped chilis so hot I felt the heat on the outside of my face. Back in the dense, steaming city I daydreamed, briefly, of buying a motorcycle, abandoning the book I wasn't writing, and living on cups of strong Vietnamese coffee and piping hot pho forever.

I kept thinking of what the book was about: What would it say? What was its point? Why did it *exist*? People would ask me and I would say that it was about choices. Choices and their consequence. They would look at me like they didn't understand.

The book would have been about power—power in institutions, of social structures. Of wars and who wielded them. Of personal agency and people with none. I thought that I could impose a structure of order upon chaotic personal histories and reckon things right. The book would have been about memory. How memory is porous, fallible, tensile, illusory. It would have been a book of fiction even if it were, in the reportorial sense, true.

I thought that the book might be about becoming, perhaps mine. I thought that if I looked hard enough into the past that something would be revealed. I thought it might have been a cleansing fire. But it wasn't; it was a yoke. I had been seduced by the idea of being a writer, a writer of books. I imagined the book might advance my career, legitimize my tinkering. That isn't a reason to write a book.

The book would have ended up on a shelf labeled *Sad and Torturous Family Histories*. Or, *Read These Books and Feel Great About Your Own Parents!* For a book that was meant to be about how these experiences did not come to define me, in the end, the process of explaining that had taken over almost all of my interior; it was like getting a flu shot only to come down with a bout so debilitating it put you in the hospital.

I lurked an email list I had been added to after my father died by someone who had served in his battalion. They would write to each other with news of their grandchildren's graduations, and of commemorative group outings and increasingly of notices of those on the list who had died as well. There were barely any of them left alive now. I read their messages, keeping them all, for years. I was never quite able to invade their decades' old web of careful connections, to disturb it, to dirty it up. So I watched as the years passed and their numbers thinned and their annual get-togethers grew increasingly more sedate. It was like witnessing a once mighty machine winding down. Where would my father ever have fit in to this? I didn't have it, that sliver of ice.

We aren't who we can't pretend to be.

ANDREW LAM is an editor and writer at New America Media and the author of *Perfume Dreams: Reflections on the Vietnamese Diaspora*, a memoir that won a Pen Open Book Award, and a book of essays, *East Eats West: Writing in Two Hemispheres*. His latest book is *Birds of Paradise Lost*, a collection of short stories. Lam has contributed stories and essays to numerous journals and newspapers and magazines. He is working on a novel.

THE STORIES THEY CARRIED
December 1994

The image once gripped us—a small boat crowded with Vietnamese refugees bobbing on a vast, merciless sea. From its mast a ragged SOS flag flew while its equally ragged passengers waved thin arms at passing ships. "Help Us. We Love Freedom," their sign said. "We Love USA!"

Once during the cold war, we couldn't get enough of their stories. Today, as the refugee crisis has become a pandemic, the charm Americans felt at the asylum seeker's naïve enthusiasm for our country has turned into resignation and fear. The thirty-five thousand boat people of Southeast Asia now being sent back to Vietnam have no place in our New World Order narrative.

But stories are all that the refugees possess—all that stand between their freedom and forced repatriation.

In the summer of 1991, as a cub reporter, I found myself with access to a refugee detention center called Whitehead at the western edge of Hong Kong. Journalists were, by and large, barred from entry to this place known for riots and gang fights and mass protests and a handful of self-immolations. There were eleven people, mostly women, who disemboweled themselves in protest of being forced back. The place, divided into sections, is built like a maximum security prison. Barbed wire on top of five-meter-high chicken wire fences.

I got lucky. For several weeks I visited Whitehead (as well as several other refugee centers) as a Vietnamese interpreter for two human rights lawyers. The lawyers represented pro bono a few refugees whose cases, they felt, were strong enough to fight repatriation. No one among the Hong Kong authorities knew I was a journalist.

But the refugees knew. The moment I entered the camp, I was swamped. News traveled fast. A journalist got in. He speaks Vietnamese. Talk to him. Tell him your stories.

In many sections I visited I was called a "hero." Several women called me their "savior." I was neither. I was hoping for a story or two. I was sympathetic and hoping, in my own way, to help. I was willing to listen to their stories. And by listening, I was the only source of communication they had with the outside world.

Everyone I met wanted to tell me his or her story. The boat people wanted to convey the injustice they had suffered, first under communist hands and now from Hong Kong authorities in conjunction with the UNHCR—United Nations High Commission on Refugees—who screened them out and deemed them economic refugees ineligible for asylum. Many were called liars when they told of communist atrocities, of oppression back home. In the late eighties, many came from North Vietnam—supposedly the winning side—and forced the international community, in tandem with the UNHCR, to reconsider their asylum policy. They produced the Comprehensive Plan of Action in 1989, which had two key points. The first was to screen all arrivals—to Hong Kong as well as to other ports of asylum—to determine whether the boat people were genuine refugees or, according to the UN Convention, ineligible "economic refugees." The second point was more controversial, entailing the repatriation of those who failed the screening back to their home countries. For the first time since the war ended, Vietnamese boat people were being repatriated en masse.

It was, of course, much easier for the power that be to not listen, to label them economic refugees and ship them back, a bunch of liars stripped of their stories at the end of history. The few thousand people in Whitehead Detention Center were all waiting to be sent back. There were apparently two categories, "voluntary repatriates" and "involuntary repatriates."

"Either way," so one man told me, "all of us are condemned prisoners."

Such certainly will soon be the fate of Diep Tran, a forty-six-year-old former lieutenant in the South Vietnamese Army I met in Section 4. Caught while trying to escape in 1979, he was tortured and sent to a reeducation camp while his wife was forced to live with a communist cadre to prevent her family from being blacklisted and sent to the New Economic Zone.

When he and his son finally did reach Hong Kong, he was denied refugee status because he lacked the $3,000 cash demanded by a screening official, he said. In protest, his son, Anh Huy, committed self-immolation in front of the UNHCR official. Tran showed me his son's photos. One is of a smiling teenager. The other is a picture of a burnt, bloodied corpse flanked by grim-looking Vietnamese men.

When he showed me the pictures, Tran's eyes welled up with tears. "I didn't expect him to do this. I didn't escape so that my son would die right in front of my eyes."

In another section, Section 8, considered the most unruly of all eleven sections in Whitehead, thirty-eight-year-old Dai Nguyen pulled off his T-shirt and showed me the scars on his back. The scars described years of cruelty in a reeducation camp. But they failed to convince the screening officer of his political past. "I have no papers with me. No one told me that I had to have proof besides what I carry on my back." He was waiting to be repatriated. On top of the barrack, someone had torn up a piece of tin and painted a picture of Lady Liberty holding her torch. Hanging on the wall of another was a sign written in blood: "Freedom Or Death."

In that same barrack, a teenager had tattooed Lady Liberty's face onto his own chest, using ink from a pen, a needle, and a little mirror.

Huong Nguyen, 43, a haggard-looking woman, spent ten years as a forced laborer in the New Economic Zone clearing jungle and watching her fellow laborers get blown to bits by land mines. She was pregnant and had a one-year-old child. Her husband, a South Vietnamese lieutenant, had been killed while trying to escape a reeducation camp. She had tried to escape in 1985 with her sons but wound up separated from them. In the end, the sons arrived in Hong Kong before the cutoff date of June 16, 1988, after which all arrivals had to be screened to qualify as political refugees. Although her sons arrived in time, she came on a different boat and was screened out.

Lam A Lu was a Montagnard tribesman who fought for the United States and was sent to hard labor camp where he was tortured before he escaped. Hong Kong authorities judged his story a lie and denied him asylum, despite the seven bullet wounds in his body.

If A Lu and Tran—both meeting the criteria required of political asylum seekers—were rejected, their fellow detainees wondered in despair, who could get accepted? Certainly not the Buddhist monk in Section 6 who fled Vietnam because he was forbidden to perform ceremonies in the rural area; nor the Catholic nun who was punished for singing Catholic songs. And certainly not a number of men and women who had worked for the US armed forces as interpreters or office workers during the war.

The stories are endless, each one more tragic than the next. For these storytellers, the end of their story was this: the free world no longer exists.

Were it not for the cruelty of the joke, Huong Nguyen might find her story laughable. A woman who laughed easily despite her circumstances, she said, "I ran out of tears. So now I just laugh when I can." Her sons, who share the same history as their mother, now live in Santa Ana, California. Their mother, on the other hand, has become a "living ghost."

When forced repatriation began in July 1989 it provoked an international uproar. A few years later, it has become international acceptance. Britain, running Hong Kong for a few years yet, even signed a treaty with Vietnam making repatriation of the Hong Kong people possible.

The stateless population, in the meantime, is growing. More and more are born into no-man's-land. Hong Kong refugee camps have one of the highest birth rates in the world.

Consider the children. Refugee children know next to nothing about policies regarding them. Although stateless the moment they opened their eyes, like children anywhere else they played where they could, and in the afternoon at Whitehead their laughter rang out.

Yet, it is hard to imagine a happy childhood in such a desolate place. Theirs is a world of chicken wings in red plastic buckets, wet gooey rice in rusted tin pails, bunk beds that sheltered whole families, tick bites and rashes, unbearable temperatures, and odious stench. Under oppressive corrugated-roof hangars in punishing humid summer heat often reaching 100 degrees, people ate and slept. Fights broke out regularly and every few weeks or so someone would hang him or herself in the latrines. In the camps, hurried and banal and careless sex went on behind flimsy, ragged curtains next to which children played hopscotch or sang.

High overhead jumbo jets soared across the Hong Kong sky, going to who knows where. But for a child born in one of those camps the plane might as well belong to a world of fantasy. His world is grounded to a reality that is defined by smallness, and the borders of his country are made of chicken wire fences, ones he cannot cross. One child who had never lived in a real house, never, for that matter, seen one with his own eyes, referred to the bunk bed he shared with his family of four as "my house."

A scene came back to me recently and I was surprised that I could have forgotten it. One late afternoon in Whitehead a group of children were trying to retrieve a bright red wildflower growing a few feet outside the fence using a thin stick of firewood. Nature was all around the center, the sea sparkled and gleamed, but it was all out of reach. I remember a guard standing outside the fence watching, idly smoking a cigarette while the children tried in vain to retrieve the flower.

I had told myself I would get those kids some flowers the next time I came back into the camp but then, so busy taking notes and listening to people with life and death stories, I simply forgot.

"Is it true, Uncle," a child about seven asked me one early morning, "that at the red light you stop and at the green light you go?" Other boys were listening intently. They had been betting—with what I didn't know—as to who was right. Born inside the camps, they had never seen traffic lights before, except on the TV in the communal cafeteria.

"You go when it's green," I told them. "You stop when it's red."

For the West the lesson about itself is sobering. Our compassion for those who fled from our enemies' territories—President Reagan, who saw himself as someone who had defeated communism, in his farewell speech recalled a Vietnamese boat person calling out to an American sailor, "Hey, Freedom Man" before being rescued—turned into what everyone now begins to call fatigue.

We suffer from compassion fatigue, the pundits tell me. There are too many refugees. Haitians. Cubans. Afghans. Tibetans. Chinese. You name it. Don't you know the borders have melted? The West frets. Lady Liberty turns her back. Too many love the USA. Too many love freedom. It is not necessarily, in the final analysis, a good thing in the post–cold war era.

A refugee from a communist country once had a role in the story Americans told themselves. He who risked his life jumping over the barbed wire fence in Berlin or sailed across the treacherous sea from Vietnam to search for freedom reassured those at the end of the exodus trail that the American way of life represented something worth having, that they lived on the right side of the cold war divide.

Once, the West readily opened its arms to these poor souls to validate the myth, and to score political points in their constant vigilance against communism. *Give us your tired, your poor, your huddled masses . . .*

Overnight, so now it seems, refugees and illegal immigrants and migrant workers and even the domestic homelessness have melted into an indistinguishable blur. Recoiling from our earlier idealism, we Americans tell ourselves homelessness is now an inherent part of the New Disorderly World and something out of our control.

As it is, "the outside of Vietnam," Diep Tran told me, sighing, "has become the same as the inside of Vietnam. You have no rights if you are homeless and countryless. You don't even have the rights to your own story, your own words."

"Hong Kong simply has had enough with refugees," said Duyen Nguyen, a Vietnamese American in his late thirties who is a deputy director for the US Joint Volunteer Program in Hong Kong. A consummate fighter for refugee rights, Duyen always looked tired. As he talked to me he took off his thick glasses and looked out the window of his office to the crowded, mildew-stained buildings in Kowloon, where Hong Kong Chinese lived in tiny spaces. Descendants from refugees of another war, their colorful laundry hung on wires of every tiny balcony like a thousand Mark Rothko paintings. "Besides, there is pressure to get rid of the problem by the time China takes over in 1997," he added.

The United Nations High Commission for Refugees, according to several disaffected former staff members, has capitulated to the process because it believes the only way to solve the problem is to make life so difficult for the Vietnamese refugees that they would rather volunteer to go home. "In fact, forced repatriation is working—the number of asylum seekers has dropped dramatically," said a former UNHCR staff member. "Forget human rights and compassion—the bottom line is to find a quick fix for the refugee crisis."

In the *South China Morning Post*, letters to the editors are mostly anti-refugee to the point of being rabid. After almost two decades, Hong Kong is fed up. One resident urged that "Vietnamese people should be sent to labor camps to work as slaves." Other letters suggested Hong Kong should force everyone back to Vietnam regardless of screening. These are presumably the same people who are themselves searching frantically for visas out of Hong Kong before China takes power in 1997.

These days no one will speak up for the Vietnamese refugees in Hong Kong or, for that matter, the refugees scattered in various camps in Southeast Asia, but perhaps that is beside the point. The boat people, kicking and screaming as they are carted off to airplanes for the journey home, warn us that maybe it is also our misfortune that we can no longer hear them. Our own idealism wanes; we too, like them, sit in the dark, our hands on our ears, poor, huddled masses.

On the bunk bed where he stored all that he owned, where he wrote and slept and ate with his wife and two kids, Lieu Tran, 31, offered me lunch. One afternoon we sat cross-legged with the curtain drawn and had fried chicken wings—a staple here in the camp—along with porridge.

"I just got my second chicken wing last week," he said matter-of-factly. This expression is something of an in-house joke. You get your first "chicken wing" when you receive your letter from the Hong Kong immigration authorities informing you that you have failed your interview with immigration officials—that you have been deemed an "economic refugee." You are allowed to appeal to the court under UNHCR's observation. When you get your second chicken wing it means your appeal has come back and, if the answer is still no, you're out of luck. With two chicken wings, Lieu said, laughing, "you can fly home to communist paradise."

Below Lieu's pillow were stacks of notebooks and letters. Life in the camp had given him plenty of time to reflect. His whole life, he said, had bled into these notebooks and letters—"an autobiography of a stateless man," he called it. He took one out and said, "If you could publish this in America I would really appreciate it."

I was tempted to write something about Lieu's life, but having read the following letter, I thought it best if he told it himself, translated here in full:

"This letter I write to you in the free world begging for help. You can lend your voice and scream for us, we who scream constantly but are never heard. You who live on stable ground can reach out to a people who live on the edge of an abyss.

"I grew up in the city of Hue, Vietnam. My father served in the South Vietnamese Army during the war as a sergeant. He was shot and killed by the Viet Cong in September 1973 while on his way home on leave.

"After 1975, South Vietnam fell into the hands of the communists. The communist regime began to confiscate our property and put many of us on trial. Because my father was in the army, my family was tried for having committed 'crimes against the Party and the People.'

"We owed them, our accusers said, for our 'crimes of blood.' In January 1978 we were forced to leave Hue for the high mountain wilderness in Dac Lac, an area the communists call the New Economic Zone.

"How we suffered! Those years in the NEZ we were slaves. Each day we went into the forest to clear brush. We planted vegetables, which got taxed by the state so we had little left. We had to survive on tree roots and yams.

"We suffered diseases and many accidents. There was no medicine. Many who were sent there with me died slowly from malaria. There were no schools, no churches, no temples. We had nowhere to turn.

"My siblings and I couldn't take it anymore and we fled. In the city we begged on the streets and worked as coolies and tried to avoid government officers who would send us back to the NEZ if they found us.

"We thought that if life in Vietnam continued this way, we would die slowly. In 1988, my sister, my wife, my little daughter, and I escaped from Vietnam. Our boat was made of bamboo, and with thirty others we sailed out to sea. Some of us died of thirst, some of starvation, but at least the dead found peace at the bottom of the sea. It was better this way—to risk becoming fish bait for a chance of freedom.

"Those who survived among us arrived in Hong Kong after twenty-five days. Immediately we were placed in a detention center called Thai-A-Chau. We lived on cement floor like animals. Each of us got two bowls of rice daily. In winter we went without blankets. Our daily lives consisted of waiting in food lines and trying to protect ourselves from beatings by the Hong Kong police.

"A year after I arrived in Hong Kong I was screened for my refugee status. The interpreter, who was Chinese, did not speak Vietnamese very well. The screening officer did not allow me to explain but only to answer questions. When I said something he didn't like, he shouted at me. 'You're a liar,' he screamed.

"The worst thing was that he would not write down important events about my past so that the court could see that I was truly a political refugee. All was lost when a letter came back to my barracks informing me that I was an 'economic migrant'—ineligible for asylum. My family and

I live in constant fear of repatriation, afraid of having to return to the prison of communist Vietnam.

"Our home these last months has been a place called Whitehead Detention Center. Life has gotten worse for people who live here. Some have gone crazy because of the crowded conditions; others have gotten sick because there is so little medicine. A few I know have committed suicide. I fear most for the children. What future is there for children who live without a place to play, who live behind an iron fence?

"Vietnam and the United Kingdom have agreed to return all boat people from Hong Kong to Vietnam. Facing that impending action, we live in anguish and pain. But my family and I have agreed to this: we are determined to commit mass suicide here in Hong Kong, if necessary, rather than return to Vietnam where one has no right to be human.

"Perhaps you Americans can recognize in us a kindred people who treasure freedom more than life."

The screening process Hong Kong uses to determine which Vietnamese fit political refugee status is controversial and has been condemned by Amnesty International and the Lawyers' Committee for Human Rights. Many interpreters are Chinese immigrants from Vietnam who can't speak Vietnamese very well. The people aren't allowed to tell their stories. The process has declared that fewer than eight percent of the boat people are eligible for political asylum, a number that has stayed consistent for months, suggestive of a quota. The rest are to be shipped home.

I asked Lieu if he knew the difference between involuntary repatriation and voluntary repatriation. "Those too weak to fight when the police raid this place for potential repatriates will be termed voluntary," he answered. "Those of us who fight to the death will be called involuntary."

Then he showed me his knife. He had taken a metal bar that once supported his bunk bed and rubbed it onto the cement floor until it had become a kind of sharp swing blade. "I will never go home," he said and gripped it until his knuckles turned white.

In Section 6 a woman named Xuan Le, who had the look of someone malnourished for years, told me how she and her family nearly drowned while escaping from Hai Phong Province. In her mid-forties, she looked ten years older, her face darkened by the sun, the wrinkles deep, her shoulder blades protruding. She stood about five feet tall, weighing no more than ninety pounds. Her hair had turned almost all gray.

"One night my family and I decided to escape. There were three of us in the family. My husband was still in a reeducation camp. My sister lives in Canada. She sent money home and I kept saving until I had enough to buy seats on the boat. I took my two little boys and left from Hai Phong in the middle of the night.

"A few days out and our boat hit a coral reef. God, it was so terrifying. Water started to rise. Children were crying. It was winter. The sea was ice cold. It began to sink.

"I stood there for maybe eight to ten hours. The water went slowly up to my knees, then my waist. My two children, I would not let the water touch them. One hung onto my neck and the smaller one sat on my shoulders . . .

"I don't know how I got my strength. I thought we were going to die. Everyone on the boat thought so too. People started praying. But I just stood. I didn't move at all. I would die first before my children, I decided. I turned into stone."

Then a miracle happened to Xuan Le. A Hong Kong patrol boat came by and rescued the despondent refugees. As the patrolmen pulled her and her children out of the freezing water, Xuan Le said she couldn't feel her own body at all. "I was no longer human. I was something else. It took a week or so before I had feeling in my fingers again. It was . . . it was as if I had turned into Hon Vong Phu," recalled the gray-haired woman, laughing hysterically.

Up in the coastal province of Quang Ninh there was a rock in the shape of a woman holding a child. It was called Hon Vong Phu— the Rock Waiting for Her Husband. According to legend, the stone figure had once been a real woman. A thousand years ago, as she awaited the return of her war-faring husband who was most likely never to return, a thunderstorm turned her and the baby in her arms into stone. Over time she became a local goddess, and villagers and fishermen prayed to her for good weather.

I told Mrs. Xuan that she was very brave. But she shook her head adamantly. "Look around you," she said and gestured toward the squatting women washing their children by the washing area out in the bright cement courtyard. "Tell me which Vietnamese mother would react differently?"

Save me! Save us!

You're our savior.

You are our only hope.

There is a famous photo of two Vietnamese women screaming for help from behind white metal bars. It was taken on December 12, 1989, in Hong Kong. One woman has her hands outstretched; the other, on her knees, wearing a white headband, prays.

A couple of hours after this picture was taken, the two women, their families, and other inmates from the Phoenix House Detention Center—fifty-one people in all—were sent back to Vietnam against their will, flown by Cathay Pacific Airlines.

The main reason I was sent to Hong Kong was because forced repatriation not only affected the thirty-five thousand Vietnamese boat people living in refugee camps across Southeast Asia but all of the thirty million internationally displaced persons now scattered across the globe. It was becoming a universally accepted practice.

But I also went because of that picture. For days I couldn't get it out of my head after I first saw it, especially the image of the praying woman, her white headband, and the way she looked into the camera. The white headband is the Vietnamese funeral garment. Vietnam's national forehead, one might even say, is bound with this white strip of cloth. Over the years it has become this woman's unofficial flag—her symbol of suffering, of struggle, of death.

When I first saw the photo I immediately thought of my mother: it could have been her. It could have been us.

The photo brought back painful memories. One afternoon in the refugee camp in Guam, my mother came back to our tent with her clothes all wet and her eyes full of tears. The American GIs had built the shower stalls without roofs, and while the women took their showers the GIs parked their army truck next to the stalls and stood atop the hoods and watched. Water was rationed; there was no second chance. Mother bit her lips and took the shower with her clothes on.

Another time, a GI tossed a quarter at me. I bent to pick it up from the muddy ground, despite my better judgment, trying not to look at his face. I had come from an upper-class family in Vietnam. I had seen urchins begging on the streets of Saigon. When I came back to our tent and gave the coin to my mother she looked at me astonished. But she did not say anything and took the coin. I don't remember saying anything either. Just the same, we recognized the look in each other's face: shame and humiliation.

I went to Hong Kong not knowing what I would find, but I knew what I felt: rage against the treatment of boat people, rage against the West. I had wanted to do something. I had wanted to help. But I went not purely out of my own piousness. There was no denying it: a cub reporter, I jumped at the rare opportunity. I had connections and I knew I was going to be the only American journalist who spoke Vietnamese there and, therefore, could get into the notorious Whitehead Detention Center as an interpreter. The fact was, despite everything else, thrilling throughout my time in Hong Kong: me, going undercover, alone, watching an important post–cold war story unfold.

What I hadn't prepared for, however, was that I was too close to the story. Go back a few years and it could easily be me mired in this camp. Worse, throughout my presence in that detention center, I was bewildered. I had no clear sense of where my true alliance lay, where exactly I stood. Was I an activist, an interpreter, or a journalist? So many people with so many stories and I was the only receptacle for their tragedies. I was dizzy, and each time I entered that camp I felt like I was drowning in their sorrow and sadness.

What was the true nature of my relationship with the boat people?

I was both connected and disconnected from the refugee's narrative. My experience belonged to the cold war story, one where I fled the oncoming communist army and was taken in by a generous America. I lived the American Dream, grew up as an American in an American suburb, and graduated from a good university. I went on further. I fancied myself a writer. I saw myself living a cosmopolitan life, a premise of ever expanding opportunity and choices.

The boat people who fled after the cold war ended, on the other hand, left Vietnam too late. And all over the world the business of protecting refugees has turned into the business of protecting the West from asylum seekers themselves. Movement toward resettlement countries, UN officials will now tell you, is movement in "the wrong direction."

Perhaps nowhere else but among Vietnamese refugees lost in no-man's-land and facing deportation would a Vietnamese from America, however deep his sympathy, however fierce his rage, cease to simply be a Vietnamese. He confronts a crucial self-realization: he is no longer a refugee, no longer an inheritor of one set of history.

In America I had nurtured a hidden psychic wound, a stigma to which I had uncritically attached myself and, over the years, I wore it like a scar or a badge of honor. I had seen myself as a refugee living in America. I was obsessed with my own story, my expulsion from my homeland. Among those whose future was as dark as that of a condemned prisoner facing a firing squad, I was made keenly aware that I had been self-indulgent. They may love the USA but the USA can no longer afford to love them. I, who left Vietnam earlier as a child, on the other hand, have been generously embraced by the West and have, in turn, embraced it.

The refugee sobriquet no longer fits. I was a free man, someone who grew up in California, took vacations to Europe and Mexico, someone who attended a prestigious university, someone with an American passport, a press pass, and various credit cards that, in an age where borders are becoming increasingly porous, seem to open every door and customs gate.

Indeed, after a few weeks in Hong Kong, confronted with the boat people's profound grief, I began to miss my friends in America, my life in America. I felt that I began to tense up each time I walked through the barbed wire gate while the armed Chinese guards gave me dirty looks. Looking back I realized that I had unconsciously made the point of looking different from the boat people. I dressed impeccably. I ironed my shirt. I could not have possibly been mistaken as a boat person were a riot to break out and the Hong Kong police had to come in with their batons and tear gas.

I was no savior, no hero. I wasn't even sure how much, as a writer, I could help. If anything, I was, in stealth, trying to save myself from them.

Among almost all the people I met and deeply admired—Hung Tran, Pam Baker, Duyen Nguyen, Quyen Vuong, Phu Bui, and many more— lawyers, social workers, NGO (non-governmental organization) officials, scholars, and so on—people who dedicated months if not years of their lives to helping the boat people in Hong Kong, there was almost a pallid pall that hung over their lives. They lived and breathed refugee policies. Boat people's cases piled up high on their desks. They took tragedies home with them.

But even if compassion fatigue hadn't defeated them, it was at least wearing them down. Duyen Nguyen, for instance, rarely cracked a smile and I never once heard him laugh. Quyen, a Fulbright scholar, was informed by her own journey as a boat person, but her smile was infinitely sad. Others—volunteers, workers for NGOs who returned to help—bickered among themselves, disagreed as to which was the best tactic to help those facing deportation. One night at a hush-hush secret meeting between social workers and lawyers and NGO workers who had wanted to go beyond their professional capacities to help boat people's causes, one man just plain lost it, stood up and screamed, then promptly stomped out.

If they agreed on anything at all, it was that I was a lightweight, a fly-by-night sort who came in for a story and no more, whereas they . . . they were entrenched. They had chosen their battle. I, though sympathetic, hadn't chosen mine. I was merely a visitor to the front line. By gathering and disseminating news from inside, I might be able to be of some help, but by all estimates, considering how global generosity has dwindled in the face of millions upon millions of stateless people, not by much.

I had initially wanted to dissuade them of that notion, but soon I came to accept that it was true. I didn't want to be consumed like a Duyen Nguyen or like that unrivaled champion of refugees Pam Baker, attorney at law, who worked tirelessly and who didn't seem to need sleep or food, just cigarettes. I was, less than a month into the fight—and I hated to admit it at the time—already tired and worn out. I brightened up one morning when the phone rang and my office told me that my assignment to Europe in the spring had been approved. I couldn't wait to leave. Lightweight indeed.

There's more. I slept badly at night in my hotel room throughout my time in Hong Kong and had horrid, vivid dreams. The summer heat was getting to me. In the center, I was getting tick bites, rashes. I never got used to the fetid smell of the entire place.

The division between Northerners and Southerners who did not trust each other made the situation worst, and many fights that broke out were due to this century-old demarcation. Gangs referred to as "bear heads" by the internees were also a problem, as Vietnam released its worst elements and let them escape and Hong Kong authorities allowed them to mix with various sections as a way to create unrest and disorganization. Though I could not confirm it, rape was reportedly occurring in the camp with impunity, and though no one would talk about it, young women without men were free for all.

There was a kind of pettiness among some of the people in the center that greatly irked me. A few times, when I had listened to someone for too long, another would come along and say, "His story is not as good as mine. He lies. I don't lie. Let me tell you mine." It was as if I was the UNHCR official myself and could decide their fates.

One windless afternoon I nearly passed out. It was right before Dai Nguyen had wanted me to touch his scars, as if to validate what I saw with my other senses. "Touch them," he said and I smiled and shook my head no. "That's okay. I believe you, Brother." I suddenly realized that until that moment I had been holding my breath.

And so, if I left for Hong Kong with rage against the West for closing its doors on the boat people, I was coming back with more or less the same rage but with one caveat, a self-knowledge I didn't expect: I was having compassion fatigue of my own.

On my last day in Whitehead a young woman named Tuyet wanted to talk with me. I had talked to her before and she had asked if I could send letters she'd written to friends in America on her behalf, a request to which I said yes.

Within earshot of several young women friends of hers, Tuyet asked for another favor. "Do you think I'm pretty?" she began.

"Yes," I answered politely. She hadn't really stood out among her friends; average was my assessment. It occurred to me as I said this, however, that she was wearing makeup, which was unusual in the center.

"Would you marry me?" she asked softly. Her voice had perceptibly changed. She was trembling. "Save me, Brother, please," she whispered. "If you marry me, I won't be sent back. Save me. I'll be your servant for the rest of my life."

The night before, the women in Section 6 were tearing white cloths for headbands and some were sharpening knives fashioned out of metal bars pulled from their bunk beds. There were rumors of an impending raid to take more people back. As far as many were concerned they were being ushered back to their own funeral, and they were not going without a fight.

I looked at Tuyet. She couldn't have been more than twenty. If I can't save them all, why not just one? Others have done it. New brides have walked out of this barbed wired prison on the arms of the NGO worker-heroes while the rest looked on with envy and awe.

For a few seconds, under the burning sun, I hesitated. I didn't say anything. I kept looking at her. It felt as if the culmination of my own confusion and conflict seemed to have come to rest at this juncture.

In my mind's eye I saw a fading ghost of myself saying yes. I saw another narrative taking place other than the one I was after. Tuyet and I would be married. We would stay and fight the good fight. Then, when it was all over, I would take my new bride home to America, to glorious California, the Golden State, the ultimate destination for all refugees, to see my family, and beyond that the events were invisible and innumerable, beyond my imagination.

Then, just like that, I started to break out in a cold sweat. I saw my own future as dead-ended as her own. Instead of doing the story I was sent to Hong Kong to do, I would end up married to it. It was not a narrative that I had imagined for myself. And it was not what I had given up going to medical school and picked up the pen for. I had yearned to be free from the past. This was why I had become a writer, wasn't it? Or, was this—the past, the war, and its aftermath—the story I was ready to tell and, by saying yes to Tuyet, willing to live with for the rest of my life?

In the end, I was both a coward and, typical of myself in the face of someone else's great distress, indecisive. I became helpless. In retrospect, I dearly wish I had been deliberate instead of circumspect and just said no. Instead, I told a lie. "I am so tired, Tuyet. Listen, I'll come in tomorrow and we'll talk then, all right?"

Tuyet smiled and thanked me profusely as I walked out of the center for the last time. I felt her stare on my back from behind the chicken wire fence. I was sure she was beaming. I dared not look back. In my hesitation, I had given her false hope.

And no, I am not unaware that I had become a bit like the West itself; the West, that is, writ very, very small.

––––––

Mid-flight back to San Francisco, I woke from a dream in which many indistinguishable dark faces from behind barbed wire fences stared out at me. I saw those laughing children playing hide-and-seek among the barracks, their bare, dirty little feet slapping against the cement surface of the courtyard. It was an early dawn and out the plane's window, far down below, the Pacific Ocean glowed like an iridescent mirror while above it my plane softly hummed and soared. Why is it some can travel back and forth over its vast expanse with ease and others die trying to traverse its treacherous waters? And what are the moral obligations of a free man to his countrymen who are not?

I had no easy answers. I still live with the questions.

On the plane, the backpack on which I rested my feet was bulging with unpublished biographies and poems and letters that people had entrusted to me. They could not very well take them back to Vietnam or these stories and testimonies would, ironically, be counted as evidence against the state, reasons enough for imprisonment, or worse. Vietnam was the only country willing to use the boat people's biographies verbatim against them.

But having read many of their stories I realized they offered me no answers, only added to my sense of guilt for having survived, for being what one religious gray-haired woman in the center called me, "the blessed one." The stewardess who tapped me on the shoulder to offer me various choices of drinks was as startled as I when I turned from the window: my face was full of tears.

The boat people once raced toward the promised land when the iron curtain still divided the world, and it was understood that risking one's life to be free was a good thing. But the myth ended midway in their flight. Their misfortune was not that they were liars but that history, having taken a sharp turn around a bend, made liars of them.

Hon Vong Phu, so I read recently, had crumbled and fallen into the ocean. The stone woman and her child, broken into many fragments, are scattered now on the ocean floor. Their curse, released at last, clings to the fleeing people of Vietnam.

LÊ THỊ DIỄM THÚY was born in Phan Thiet, Southern Vietnam. She and her father left Vietnam in 1978, by boat, eventually settling in Southern California. Lê is a writer and solo performance artist and her works "Red Fiery Summer" (Mua He Do Lua), "the bodies between us," and "Carte Postale" have been presented at, among other venues, the Whitney Museum of American Art at Philip Morris, USA; the International Women Playwright's Festival in Galway, Ireland; and the Vineyard Theater in New York City. She is the recipient of fellowships from the Guggenheim Foundation and the Radcliffe Institute for Advanced Study. A 2008 United States Artists Ford Fellow in Literature, she is currently at work on her second novel.

THE GANGSTER WE ARE ALL LOOKING FOR

Vietnam is a black-and-white photograph of my grandparents sitting in bamboo chairs in their front courtyard. They are sitting tall and proud, surrounded by chickens and a rooster. Between their feet and the dirt of the courtyard are thin sandals. My grandfather's broad forehead is shining. So too are my grandmother's famous sad eyes. The animals are oblivious, pecking at the ground. This looks like a wedding portrait though it is actually a photograph my grandparents had taken late in life, for their children, especially for my mother. When I think of this portrait of my grandparents in their last years, I always envision a beginning. To or toward what, I don't know, but always a beginning.

———

When my grandmother, a Catholic schoolgirl from the South, decided to marry my grandfather, a Buddhist gangster from the North, her parents disowned her. This is in the photograph, though it is not visible to the eye. If it were, it would be a deep impression across the soft dirt of my grandparents' courtyard. Her father chased her out of the house, beating her with the same broom she had used every day of her life, from the time she could stand up and sweep to that very morning that she was chased away.

The year my mother met my father, there were several young men working at her parents' house, running errands for her father, pickling vegetables with her mother. It was understood by everyone that these men were courting my mother. My mother claims she had no such understanding.

She treated these men as brothers, sometimes as uncles even, later exclaiming in self-defense: I didn't even know about love then!

Ma says love came to her in a dark movie theater. She doesn't remember what movie it was or why she'd gone to see it, only that she'd gone alone and found herself sitting beside him. In the dark, she couldn't make out his face but noticed that his profile was handsome. She wondered if he knew she was watching him out of the corner of her eye. Watching him without embarrassment or shame. Watching him with a strange curiosity, a feeling that made her want to trace and retrace his silhouette with her fingertips until she memorized every feature and could call his face to mind in any dark place she passed through. Later, in the shadow of the beached fishing boats on the blackest nights of the year, she would call him to mind, his face a warm companion for her body on the edge of the sea.

I n the early days of my parents' courtship, my mother told stories. She confessed elaborate dreams about the end of war: food she'd eat (a banquet table, mangoes piled to the ceiling); songs she'd make up and sing, clapping her hands over her head and throwing her hair like a horse's mane; dances she'd dance, hopping from one foot to the other. Unlike the responsible favorite daughter or sister she was to her family, with my father, in the forest, my mother became reckless, drunk on her youth and the possibilities of love. Ignoring the chores to be done at home, she rolled her pants up to her knees, stuck her bare feet in puddles, and learned to smoke a cigarette.

S he tied a vermillion ribbon in her hair. She became moody. She did her chores as though they were favors to her family, forgetting that she ate the same rice, was dependent on the same supply of food. It seemed to her the face that now stared back at her from deep inside the family well was the face of a woman she had never seen before. At night she lay in bed and thought of his hands, the way his thumb flicked down on the lighter and brought fire to her cigarette. She began to wonder what the forests were like before the American planes had come, flying low, raining something onto the trees that left them bare and dying. She remembered her father had once described to her the smiling broadness of leaves, jungles thick in the tangle of rich soil.

O ne evening, she followed my father in circles through the forest, supposedly in search of the clearing that would take them to his aunt's house. They wandered in darkness, never finding the clearing much less the aunt she knew he never had.

"You're not from here," she said.

"I know."

"So tell me, what's your aunt's name?"

"Xuan."

"Spring?"

"Yes."

She laughed. I can't be here, she thought.

"My father will be looking for me—."

"It's not too late, I'll walk you home."

In the dark, she could feel his hand extending toward her, filling the space between them. They had not touched once the entire evening and now he stood offering his hand to her. She stared at him for a long time. There was a small scar on his chin, curved like a fingernail. It was too dark to see this. She realized she had memorized his face.

My first memory of my father's face is framed by the coiling barbed wire of a military camp in South Vietnam. My mother's voice crosses through the wire. She is whispering his name and with this utterance, caressing him. Over and over, she calls him to her, "Anh Minh, Anh Minh." His name becomes a tree she presses her body against. The calling blows around them like a warm breeze and when she utters her own name, it is the second half of a verse that begins with his. She drops her name like a pebble into a well. She wants to be engulfed by him, "Anh Minh, em My. Anh Minh, em My."

The barbed wire gates open and she crosses through to him. She arrives warm, the slightest film of sweat on her bare arms. To his disbelieving eyes she says, "It's me, it's me." Shy and formal and breathless, my parents are always meeting for the first time, savoring the sound of a name, marveling at the bones of the face cupped by the bones of the hand.

I trail behind them, the tip of their dragon's tail. I am drawn along, like a silken banner on the body of a kite.

For a handful of pebbles and my father's sharp profile, my mother left home and never truly returned. Picture a handful of pebbles. Imagine the casual way he tossed them at her as she was walking home from school with her girlfriends. He did this because he liked her. Boys are dumb that way, my mother told me. A handful of pebbles, to be thrown in anger, in desperation, in joy. My father threw them in love. Ma says they touched her like warm kisses, these pebbles he had been holding in the sun. Warm kisses on the curve of her back, sliding down the crook of her arm, grazing her ankles and landing around her feet on the hot sand.

What my father told her could have been a story. There was no one in the South to confirm the details of his life. He said he came from a semi-aristocratic northern family. Unlacing his boots, he pulled out his foot and directed her close attention to how his second toe was significantly longer than the others. "A sure sign of aristocracy," he claimed. His nose was high, he said, because his mother was French, one of the many mistresses his father had kept. He found this out when he was sixteen. That year, he ran away from home and came south.

"There are thieves, gamblers, drunks I've met who remind me of people in my family. It's the way they're dreamers. My family's a garden lying on their backs, staring at the sky, drunk and choking on their dreams." He said this while leaning against a tree, his arms folded across his bare chest, his eyes staring at the ground, his shoulders golden.

She asked her mother, "What does it mean if your second toe is longer than your other toes?"

"It means . . . your mother will die before your father," her mother said.

"I heard somewhere it's a sign of aristocracy."

"Huh!"

When my mother looked at my father's bare feet she saw ten fishing boats, two groups of five. Within each group, the second boat ventured ahead, leading the others. She would climb a tree, stand gripping the branch with her own toes and stare down at his. She directed him to stand in the mud. There, she imagined what she saw to be ten small boats surrounded by black water, a fleet of junks journeying in the dark.

She would lean back and enjoy this vision, never explaining to him what she saw. She left him to wonder about her senses as he stood, cigarette in hand, staring at her trembling ankles, and not moving until she told him to.

I was born in the alley behind my grandparents' house. At three in the morning, my mother dragged herself out of the bed in the smaller house where she and my father lived after they married. My father was away, fighting in the war. Ma's youngest sister had come to live with her, helping with my older brother, who was just a baby then. Ma left the two of them sleeping in the hammock, my brother lying in the crook of my aunt's arm, and set out alone.

She cut a crooked line on the beach. Moving in jerky steps, like a ball tossed on the waves, she seemed to be bounced along without direction. She walked to the schoolhouse and sat on the ground before it, leaning against the first step. She felt grains of sand pressing against her back. Each grain was a minute pinprick, and the pain grew and grew. Soon she felt as though her back would erupt, awash in blood. She thought, I am going to bleed to death. She put her hands on her belly. We are going to die.

In front of the schoolhouse lay a long metal tube. No one knew where it came from. It seemed to have been there always. Children hid inside it, crawled through it, spoke to each other from either ends of it, marched across it, sat upon it and confided secrets beside it. There had been so little to play with during the school recess. This long metal tube became everything. A tarp was suspended over it, to shield it from the sun. The tube looked like a blackened log in a room without walls. When the children sat in a line on the tube, their heads bobbing this way and that in conversation, it seemed they were sitting on a canopied raft.

The night I was born, my mother, looking at the tube, imagined it to be the badly burnt arm of a dying giant buried in the sand. She could not decide whether he had been buried and was trying to get out or whether he had tried to bury himself in the sand but had failed to cover his arm in time. In time for what? She had heard a story about a girl in a neighboring town who was killed during a napalm bombing. The bombing happened on an especially hot night, when this girl had walked to the beach to cool her feet in the water. They found her floating on the sea. The phosphorous from the napalm made her body glow, like a lantern. In her mind, my mother built a canopy for this girl. She started to cry, thinking of the buried giant, the floating girl, these bodies stopped in mid-stride, on their way somewhere.

S he began to walk toward the tube. She had a sudden urge to be inside it. The world felt dangerous to her and she was alone. At the mouth of the tube, she bent down, her belly blocking the mouth. She tried the other side, the other mouth. Again, her belly stopped her. "But I remember," she muttered out loud, "as a girl I sometimes slept in here." This was what she wanted now, to sleep inside the tube.

"Tall noses come from somewhere—"

"Not from here."

"Not tall noses."

———

Eyes insinuate, moving from her nose to mine then back again. Mouths suck in air, color it into the darkest shade of contempt, then spit it at her feet as she walks by. I am riding on her hip. I am the new branch that makes the tree bend but she walks with her head held high. She knows where she pulled me from. No blue eye.

M a says war is a bird with a broken wing flying over the countryside, trailing blood and burying crops in sorrow. If something grows in spite of this, it is both a curse and a miracle. When I was born, she cried to know that it was war I was breathing in, and she could never shake it out of me. Ma says war makes it dangerous to breathe, though she knows you die if you don't. She says she could have thrown me against a wall, until I broke or coughed up this war that is killing us all. She could have stomped on it in the dark, and danced on it like a madwoman dancing on gravestones. She could have ground it down to powder and spat on it, but didn't I know? War has no beginning and no end. It crosses oceans like a splintered boat filled with people singing a sad song.

E very morning Anh wakes up in the house next to mine, a yellow duplex she and I call a town since we found out from a real estate ad that a town house is a house with an upstairs and a downstairs. My father calls Anh "the chicken egg girl." Early each morning Anh's mother loads a small pushcart with stacks of eggs and Anh walks all over Linda Vista selling eggs before school. Her backyard is full of chickens and one rooster. Sometimes you can see the rooster fly up and balance himself on the back gate. From his perch, he'll crow and crow, on and off, all day long, until dark comes.

W e live in the country of California, the province of San Diego, the village of Linda Vista. We live in old Navy Housing bungalows built in the 1940s. Since the 1980s, these bungalows house Vietnamese, Cambodian, and Laotian refugees from the Vietnam War. When we moved in, we had to sign a form promising not to put fish bones in the garbage disposal.

We live in a yellow house on Westinghouse Street. Our house is one story, made of wood and plaster. Between our house and another one-story house are six two-story houses. Facing our row of houses, across a field of brown dirt, sits another row of yellow houses, same as ours, watching us like a sad twin. Linda Vista is full of houses like ours, painted in peeling shades of olive green, baby blue, and sun-baked yellow.

There's new Navy Housing on Linda Vista Road, the long street that takes you out of here. We see the Navy People watering their lawns, their children riding pink tricycles up and down the cul-de-sac. We see them in Victory Supermarket, buying groceries with cash. In Kelley Park they have picnics and shoot each other with water guns. At school their kids are Most Popular, Most Beautiful, Most Likely to Succeed.

Though there are more Vietnamese, Cambodian, and Loatian kids at the school, in the yearbook we are not the most of anything. They call us Yang because one year a bunch of Loatian kids with the last name Yang came to our school. The Navy Housing kids started calling all the refugee kids "Yang."

Yang. Yang. Yang.

Ma says living next to Anh's family reminds her of Vietnam because the blue tarp suspended above Anh's backyard is the bright blue of the South China Sea. Ma says, isn't it funny how sky and sea follow you from place to place as if they too were traveling.

Thinking of my older brother, who was still in Vietnam, I asked Ma, "If the sky and the sea can follow us here, why can't people?"

Ma ignores my question and says even Anh reminds her of Vietnam, the way she sets out for market each morning.

Ba becomes a gardener. Overnight. He buys a truck full of equipment and a box of business cards from Uncle Twelve, who is moving to Texas to become a fisherman. The business cards read "Tom's Professional Gardening Service" and have a small green picture embossed on them, a man pushing a lawn mower. The man has his back to you, so no one holding the card can tell it's not Ba, no one who doesn't already know. He says I can be his secretary because I speak the best English. If you call us on the business phone, you will hear me say: "Hello, you have reached Tom's Professional Gardening Service. We are not here right now, but if you leave a message, we will get back to you as soon as possible. Thank you."

It is hot and dusty where we live. Some people think it's dirty but they don't know much about us. They haven't seen our gardens full of lemongrass, mint, cilantro, and basil. Driving by with their windows rolled up, they've only seen the pigeons pecking at day-old rice and the skinny cats and dogs sitting in the skinny shade of skinny trees. Have they seen the berries that we pick, that turn our lips and fingertips red? How about the small staircase that Ba built from our bedroom window to the backyard so I would have a shortcut to the clothesline? How about the Great Wall of China that snakes like a river from the top of the steep hill off Crandall Drive to the slightly curving bottom? Who has seen this?

It was so different at the Green Apartment. We had to close the gate behind us every time we came in. It clanged heavily, and I imagined a host of eyes, upstairs and down, staring at me from behind slightly parted curtains. There were four palm trees planted at the four corners of the courtyard and a central staircase that was narrow at the top and broad at the bottom. The steps were covered in fake grass, like the set of an old Hollywood movie, the kinds that stars an aging beauty who wakes up to find something terribly wrong.

We moved out of the Green Apartment after we turned on the TV one night and heard that our manager and his brother had hacked a woman to pieces and dumped the parts of her body into the Pacific Ocean in ten-gallon garbage bags that washed up onshore. Ma says she didn't want to live in a place haunted by a murdered lady. So we moved to Linda Vista, where she said there were a lot of Vietnamese people like us, people whose only sin was a little bit of gambling and sucking on fish bones and laughing hard and arguing loudly.

Ma shaved her head in Linda Vista because she got mad at Ba for gambling away her money and getting drunk every week during *Monday Night Football*. Ba gave her a blue baseball cap to wear until her hair grew back and she wore it backward, like a real badass.

After that, some people in Linda Vista said that Ma was crazy and Ba was crazy for staying with her. But what do some people know?

When the photograph came, Ma and Ba got into a fight. Ba threw the fish tank out the front door and Ma broke all the dishes. They said they never should've got together.

Ma's sister sent her the photograph from Vietnam. It came in a stiff envelope. There was nothing else inside, as if anything more would be pointless. Ma held the photograph in her hands. She started to cry. "Child," she sobbed, over and over again. She wasn't talking about me. She was talking about herself.

Ba said, "Don't cry. Your parents have forgiven you."

Ma kept crying anyway and told him not to touch her with his gangster hands. Ba clenched his hands into tight fists and punched the walls.

"What hands?! What hands?!" he yelled. "Let me see the gangster! Let me see his hands!" I see his hands punch hands punch hands punch blood.

Ma is in the kitchen. She has torn the screen off the window. She is punctuating the pavement with dishes, plates, cups, rice bowls. She sends them out like birds gliding through the sky with nowhere in particular to go. Until they crash. Then she exhales "Huh!" in satisfaction.

I am in the hallway gulping air. I breathe in the breaking and the bleeding. When Ba plunges his hands into the fish tank, I detect the subtle tint of blood in water. When he throws the fish tank out the front door, yelling, "Let me see the gangster!" I am drinking up the spilt water and swallowing whole the beautiful tropical fish, their brilliant colors gliding across my tongue, before they can hit the ground, to cover themselves in dirt until only the whites of their eyes remain, blinking at the sun.

All the hands are in my throat, cutting themselves on broken dishes, and the fish swim in circles; they can't see for all the blood.

Ba jumps in his truck and drives away.

When I grow up I am going to be the gangster we are all looking for.

The neighborhood kids are standing outside our house, staring in through the windows and the open door. Even Anh, the chicken egg girl. I'm sure their gossiping mothers have sent them to spy on us. I run out front and dance like a crazy lady, dance like a fish, wiggle my head and whip my body around. At first they laugh but then they stop, not knowing what to think. Then I stop to stare them down, each one of them.

"What're you looking at?" I ask.

"Lookin' at you," one boy says, half giggling.

"Well," I say, with my hand on my hip, my head cocked to one side, "I'm looking at you too," and I give him my evil one-eyed look, focusing all my energy into my left eye. I stare at him hard as if my eye is a bullet and he can be dead.

I turn my back on them and walk into the house.

Ma is sitting in the window frame. The curve of her back is inside the bedroom while the rest of her body hangs outside, on the first of the steps Ba built from the bedroom to the garden. Without turning to look at me, she says, "Let me lift you into the attic."

"Why?"

"We have to move your grandparents in."

I don't really know what she is talking about, but I say O.K. anyway.

We have never needed the attic for anything. In fact, we have never gone up there. When we moved my grandparents in, Ma simply lifted me up and I pushed open the attic door with one hand while, with the other, I slipped the stiff envelope with the photograph of my grandparents into the crawlspace above. I pushed the envelope the length of my arm and down to my fingertips. I pushed it so far it was beyond reach. Ma said that was all right; they had come to live with us, and sometimes you don't need to see or touch people to know they're there.

Ba came home drunk that night and asked to borrow my blanket. I heard him climbing the tree in the backyard. It took him a long time. He kept missing the wooden blocks that ran up the tree like a ladder. Ba had put them in himself when he built the steps going from the bedroom window into the garden. If you stood on the very top block, your whole body would be hidden by tree branches. Ba put those blocks in for me, so I could win at hide-and-go-seek.

When Ba had finally made it onto the roof, he lay down over my room and I could hear him rolling across my ceiling. Rolling and crying. I was scared he would roll off the edge and kill himself, so I went to wake Ma.

She was already awake. She said it would be a good thing if he rolled off. But later I heard someone climb the tree, and all night two bodies rolled across my ceiling. Slowly and firmly they pressed against my sleep, the Catholic schoolgirl and the Buddhist gangster, two dogs chasing each other's tails. They have been running like this for so long, they have become one dog, one tail.

Without any hair and looking like a man, my mother is still my mother, though sometimes I can't see her even when I look and look and look so long all the colors of the world begin to swim and bob around me. Her hands always bring me up, her big peasant hands with the flat, wide nails, wide like her nose and just as expressive. I will know her by her hands and by her walk, at once slow and urgent, the walk of a woman going to the market with her goods bound securely to her side. Even walking empty-handed, my mother's gait suggests invisible bundles whose contents no one but she can reveal. And if I never see her again, I will know my mother by the smell of the sea salt and the prints of my own bare feet crossing sand, running to and away from, to and away from, family.

When the eviction notice came, we didn't believe it so we threw it away. It said we had a month to get out. The houses on our block had a new owner who wanted to tear everything down and build better housing for the community. It said we were priority tenants for the new complex, but we couldn't afford to pay the new rent so it didn't matter. The notice also said that if we didn't get out in time, all our possessions would be confiscated in accordance with some section of a law book or manual we were supposed to have known about but had never seen. We couldn't believe the eviction notice so we threw it away.

The fence is tall, silver, and see-through. Chain-link, it rattles when you shake it and wobbles when you lean against it. It circles our block like a bad dream. It is not funny like the clothesline whose flying shirts and empty pants suggest human birds and vanishing acts. This fence presses sharply against your brain. We three stand still as posts. Looking at it, then at one another—this side and that—out of the corners of our eyes. What are we thinking?

At night we come back with three uncles. Ba cuts a hole in the fence and we step through. Quiet, we break into our own house through the back window. Quiet we steal everything that is ours. We fill ten-gallon garbage bags with clothes, pots and pans, flip-flops, the porcelain figure of Mary, the wooden Buddha and the Chinese fisherman lamp. In the arc of our flashlights we find our favorite hairbrushes behind bedposts. When we are done, we clamber, breathless. Though it's quiet, we can hear police cars coming to get us.

We tumble out the window like people tumbling across continents. We are time traveling, weighed down by heavy furniture and bags of precious junk. We find ourselves leaning against Ba's yellow truck. Ma calls his name, her voice reaching like a hand feeling for a tree trunk in darkness.

In the car, Ma starts to cry. "What about the sea?" she asks. "What about the garden?" Ba says we can come back in the morning and dig up the stalks of lemongrass and fold the sea into a blue square. Ma is sobbing. She is beating the dashboard with her fists. "I want to know," she says, "I want to know, I want to know . . . who is doing this to us?" Hiccupping she says, "I want to know, why—why there's always a fence. Why there's always someone on the outside wanting someone . . . something on the inside and between them . . . this . . . sharp fence. Why are we always leaving like this?"

Everyone is quiet when Ma screams.

"Take me back!" she says. "I can't go with you. I've forgotten my mother and father. I can't believe . . . Anh Minh, we've left them to die. Take me back."

Ma wants Ba to stop the car, but Ba doesn't know why. The three uncles, sitting in a row in the bed of the truck, think Ma is crazy. They yell in through the rear window, "My, are you going to walk back to Vietnam?"

"Yeah, are you going to walk home to your parents' house?"

In the silence another shakes his head and reaches into his shirt pocket for his cigarettes.

Ba puts his foot on the gas pedal. Our car jerks forward, and then plunges down the Crandall Drive hill. Ma says, "I need air, water . . . " I roll the window down. She puts her head in her hands. She keeps crying, "Child." Outside, I see the Great Wall of China. In the glare of the streetlamps, it is just a long strip of cardboard.

I n the morning, the world is flat. Westinghouse Street is lying down like a jagged brushstroke of sun-burnt yellow. There is a big sign within the fence that reads

Coming Soon
Condominiums
Town Homes
Family Homes

Below these words is a copy of a watercolor drawing of a large pink complex.

———

We stand on the edge of a chain-link fence, sniffing the air for the scent of lemongrass, scanning this flat world for our blue sea. A wrecking ball dances madly through our house. Everything has burst wide open and sun down low. Then I hear her calling them. She is whispering, "Ma/Ba, Ma/Ba." The whole world is two butterfly wings rubbing against my ear.

Listen . . . they are sitting in the attic, sitting like royalty. Shining in the dark, buried by a wrecking ball. Paper fragments floating across the surface of the sea.

There is not a trace of blood anywhere except here, in my throat, where I am telling you all this.

NAM LE was born in Vietnam in 1978 and migrated to Australia in 1979. His first book, *The Boat*, was translated into fourteen languages and received more than a dozen major awards in America, Europe, and Australia, including the PEN/ Malamud Award, the Anisfield-Wolf Book Award, the Dylan Thomas Prize, and the Australian Prime Minister's Literary Award. *The Boat* was selected as the best debut of 2008 by *New York* magazine and the *Australian Book Review*, and a book of the year by over thirty venues around the world including the *New York Times*, the *Los Angeles Times*, *The Guardian*, and *The Independent*. Its stories have been widely anthologized, adapted, and taught. Le spends his time in Australia and abroad.

LOVE AND HONOR AND PITY AND PRIDE AND COMPASSION AND SACRIFICE

My father arrived on a rainy morning. I was dreaming about a poem, the dull *thluck thluck* of a typewriter's keys punching out the letters. It was a good poem—perhaps the best I'd ever written. When I woke up, he was standing outside my bedroom door, smiling ambiguously. He wore black trousers and a wet, wrinkled parachute jacket that looked like it had just been pulled out of a washing machine. Framed by the bedroom doorway, he appeared even smaller, gaunter, than I remembered. Still groggy with dream, I lifted my face toward the alarm clock.

"What time is it?"

"Hello, Son," he said in Vietnamese. "I knocked for a long time. Then the door just opened."

The fields are glass, I thought. Then tum-ti-ti, a dactyl, end line, then the words *excuse* and *alloy* in the line after. *Come on,* I thought.

"It's raining heavily," he said.

I frowned. The clock read 11:44. "I thought you weren't coming until this afternoon." It felt strange, after all this time, to be speaking Vietnamese again.

"They changed my flight in Los Angeles."

"Why didn't you ring?"

"I tried," he said equably. "No answer."

I twisted over the side of the bed and cracked open the window. The sound of rain filled the room—rain fell on the streets, on the roofs, on the tin shed across the parking lot like the distant detonation of firecrackers. Everything smelled of wet leaves.

"I turn the ringer off when I sleep," I said. "Sorry."

He continued smiling at me, significantly, as if waiting for an announcement.

"I was dreaming."

He used to wake me, when I was young, by standing over me and smacking my cheeks lightly. I hated it—the wetness, the sourness of his hands.

"Come on," he said, picking up a large Adidas duffel and a rolled bundle that looked like a sleeping bag. "A day lived, a sea of knowledge earned." He had a habit of speaking in Vietnamese proverbs. I had long since learned to ignore it.

I threw on a T-shirt and stretched my neck in front of the lone window. Through the rain, the sky was as gray and striated as graphite. *The fields are glass* . . . Like a shape in smoke, the poem blurred, then dissolved into this new, cold, strange reality: a wind-blown, rain-strafed parking lot; a dark room almost entirely taken up by my bed; the small body of my father dripping water onto hardwood floors.

I went to him, my legs goose-pimpled underneath my pajamas. He watched with pleasant indifference as my hand reached for his, shook it, then relieved his other hand of the bags. "You must be exhausted," I said.

He had flown from Sydney, Australia. Thirty-three hours all up—transiting in Auckland, Los Angeles, and Denver—before touching down in Iowa. I hadn't seen him in three years.

"You'll sleep in my room."

"Very fancy," he said, as he led me through my own apartment. "You even have a piano." He gave me an almost rueful smile. "I knew you'd never really quit." Something moved behind his face and I found myself back on a heightened stool with my fingers chasing the metronome, ahead and behind, trying to shut out the tutor's repeated sighing, his heavy brass ruler. I realized I was massaging my knuckles. My father patted the futon in my living room. "I'll sleep here."

"You'll sleep in my room, Ba." I watched him warily as he surveyed our surroundings, messy with books, papers, dirty plates, teacups, clothes—I'd intended to tidy up before going to the airport. "I work in this room anyway, and I work at night." As he moved into the kitchen, I grabbed the three-quarters-full bottle of Johnnie Walker from the second shelf of my bookcase and stashed it under the desk. I looked around. The desktop was gritty with cigarette ash. I threw some magazines over the roughest spots, then flipped one of them over because its cover bore a picture of Chairman Mao. I quickly gathered up the cigarette packs and sleeping pills and incense burners and dumped them all on a high shelf, behind my Kafka Vintage Classics.

At the kitchen swing door I remembered the photo of Linda beside the printer. Her glamour shot, I called it: hair windswept and eyes squinty, smiling at something out of frame. One of her ex-boyfriends had taken it at Lake MacBride. She looked happy. I snatched it and turned it facedown, covering it with scrap paper.

As I walked into the kitchen I thought, for a moment, that I'd left the fire escape open. I could hear rainwater gushing along gutters, down through the pipes. Then I saw my father at the sink, sleeves rolled up, sponge in hand, washing the month-old crusted mound of dishes. The smell was awful. "Ba," I frowned, "you don't need to do that."

His hands, hard and leathery, moved deftly in the sink.

"Ba," I said, halfheartedly.

"I'm almost finished." He looked up and smiled. "Have you eaten? Do you want me to make some lunch?"

"*Thoi*," I said, suddenly irritated. "You're exhausted. I'll go out and get us something."

I went back through the living room into my bedroom, picking up clothes and rubbish along the way.

"You don't have to worry about me," he called out. "You just do what you always do."

The truth was, he'd come at the worst possible time. I was in my last year at the Iowa Writers' Workshop; it was late November, and my final story for the semester was due in three days. I had a backlog of papers to grade and a heap of fellowship and job applications to draft and submit. It was no wonder I was drinking so much.

I'd told Linda only the previous night that he was coming. We were at her place. Her body was slippery with sweat and hard to hold. Her body smelled of her clothes. She turned me over, my face kissing the bedsheets, and then she was chopping my back with the edges of her hands. *Higher. Out a bit more.* She had trouble keeping a steady rhythm. "Softer," I told her. Moments later, I started laughing.

"What?"

The sheets were damp beneath my pressed face.

"What?"

"*Softer*," I said, "not *slower*."

She slapped my back with the meat of her palms, hard—once, twice. I couldn't stop laughing. I squirmed over and caught her by the wrists. Hunched forward, she was blushing and beautiful. Her hair fell over her face; beneath its ash-blond hem all I could see were her open lips. She pressed down, into me, her shoulders kinking the long, lean curve from her back of her neck to the small of her back. "Stop it!" her lips said. She wrested her hands free. Her fingers beneath my waistband, violent, the scratch of her nails down my thighs, knees, ankles. I pointed my foot like a ballet dancer.

Afterward, I told her my father didn't know about her. She said nothing. "We just don't talk about that kind of stuff," I explained. She looked like an actress who looked like my girlfriend. Staring at her face made me tired. I'd begun to feel this way more often around her. "He's only here for three days." Somewhere out of sight, a group of college boys hooted and yelled.

"I thought you didn't talk to him at all."

"He's my father."

"What's he want?"

I rolled toward her, onto my elbow. I tried to remember how much I'd told her about him. We'd been lying on the bed, the wind loud in our room—I remember that—and we were both tipsy. Ours could have been any two voices in the darkness. "It's only three days," I said.

The look on her face was strange, shut down. She considered me a long time. Then she got up and pulled on her clothes. "Just make sure you get your story done," she said.

I drank before I came here too. I drank when I was a student at university, and then when I was a lawyer—in my previous life, as they say. There was a subterranean bar in a hotel next to my work, and every night I would wander down and slump on a barstool and pretend I didn't want the bartender to make small talk. He was only a bit older than me, and I came to envy his ease, his confidence that any given situation was merely temporary. I left exorbitant tips. After a while I was treated to battered shrimps and shepherd's pies on the house. My parents had already split by then, my father moving to Sydney, my mother into a government flat.

That's all I've ever done, traffic in words. Sometimes I still think about word counts the way a general must think about casualties. I'd been in Iowa more than a year—days passed in weeks, then months, more than a year of days—and I'd written only three and a half stories. About seventeen thousand words. When I was working at the law firm, I would have written that many words in a couple of weeks. And they would have been useful to someone.

Deadlines came, exhausting, and I forced myself up to meet them.

Then, in the great spans of time between, I fell back to my vacant screen and my slowly sludging mind. I tried everything—writing in longhand, writing in my bed, in my bathtub. As this last deadline approached, I remembered a friend claiming he'd broken his writer's block by switching to a typewriter. You're free to write, he told me, once you know you can't delete what you've written. I bought an electric Smith Corona at an antique shop. It buzzed like a tropical aquarium when I plugged it in. It looked good on my desk. For inspiration, I read absurdly formal Victorian poetry and drank Scotch neat. How hard could it be? Things happened in this world all the time. All I had to do was record them. In the sky, two swarms of swallows converged, pulled apart, interwove again like veils drifting at crosscurrents. In line at the supermarket, a black woman leaned forward and kissed the handle of her shopping cart, her skin dark and glossy like the polished wood of a piano.

The week prior to my father's arrival, a friend chastised me for my persistent defeatism.

"Writer's block?" Under the streetlights, vapors of bourbon puffed out of his mouth. "How can you have writer's block? Just write a story about Vietnam."

We had just come from a party following a reading by the workshop's most recent success, a Chinese woman trying to immigrate to America who had written a book of short stories about Chinese characters in stages of immigration to America. The stories were subtle and good. The gossip was that she'd been offered a substantial six-figure contract for a two-book deal. It was meant to be an unspoken rule that such things were left unspoken. Of course, it was all anyone talked about.

"It's hot," a writing instructor told me at a bar. "Ethnic literature's hot. And important too."

A couple visiting literary agents took a similar view: "There's a lot of polished writing around," one of them said. "You have to ask yourself, what makes me stand out?" She tag-teamed to her colleague, who answered slowly as though intoning a mantra, "Your *background* and *life experience*."

Other friends were more forthright: "I'm sick of ethnic lit," one said. "It's full of description of exotic food." Or: "You can't tell if the language is spare because the author intended it that way, or because he didn't have the vocab."

I was told about a friend of a friend, a Harvard graduate from Washington, D.C., who had posed in traditional Nigerian garb for his book-jacket photo. I pictured myself standing in a rice paddy, wearing a straw conical hat. Then I pictured my father in the same field, wearing his threadbare fatigues, young and hard-eyed.

"It's a license to bore," my friend said. We were drunk and walking our bikes because both of us, separately, had punctured our tires on the way to the party.

"The characters are always flat, generic. As long as a Chinese writer writes about *Chinese* people, or a Peruvian writer about *Peruvians*, or a Russian writer about *Russians* . . ." he said, as though reciting children's doggerel, then stopped, losing his train of thought. His mouth turned up into a doubtful grin. I could tell he was angry about something.

"Look," I said, pointing at a floodlit porch ahead of us. "Those guys have guns."

"As long as there's an interesting image or metaphor once in every *this* much text"—he held out his thumb and forefinger to indicate half a page, his bike wobbling all over the sidewalk. I nodded to him, and then I nodded to one of the guys on the porch, who nodded back. The other guy waved us through with his faux-wood air rifle. A car with its headlights on was idling in the driveway, and girls' voices emerged from inside, squealing, "Don't shoot! Don't shoot!"

"Faulkner, you know," my friend said over the squeals, "he said we should write about the old verities. Love and honor and pity and pride and compassion and sacrifice." A sudden sharp crack behind us, like the striking of a giant typewriter hammer, followed by some muffled shrieks. "I know I'm a bad person for saying this," my friend said, "but that's why I don't mind your work, Nam. Because you could just write about Vietnamese boat people all the time. Like in your third story."

He must have thought my head was bowed in modesty, but in fact I was figuring out whether I'd just been shot in the back of the thigh. I'd felt a distinct sting. The pellet might have ricocheted off something.

"You could *totally* exploit the Vietnamese thing. But *instead*, you

choose to write about lesbian vampires and Colombian assassins, and
Hiroshima orphans—and New York painters with hemorrhoids."

For a dreamlike moment I was taken aback. Cataloged like that,
under the bourbon stink of his breath, my stories sank into unflattering
relief. My leg was still stinging. I imagined sticking my hand down the
back of my jeans, bringing it to my face under a streetlight, and finding it
gory, blood-spattered. I imagined turning around, advancing wordlessly
up the porch steps, and drop-kicking the two kids. I would tell my story
into a microphone from a hospital bed. I would compose my story in a
county cell. I would kill one of them, maybe accidentally, and never talk
about it, ever, to anyone. There was no hole in my jeans.

"I'm probably a bad person," my friend said, stumbling beside his bike
a few steps in front of me.

I f you ask me why I came to Iowa, I would say that Iowa is beautiful
in the way that any place is beautiful: if you treat it as the answer to a
question you're asking yourself every day, just by being there.

That afternoon, as I was leaving the apartment for Linda's, my father
called out my name from the bedroom.

I stopped outside the closed door. He was meant to be napping.

"Where are you going?" his voice said.

"For a walk," I replied.

"I'll walk with you."

It always struck me how everything seemed larger in scale on Summit
Street: the double-storied houses, their smooth lawns sloping down to
the sidewalks like golf greens; elm trees with high, thick branches—the
sort of branches from which I imagined fathers suspending long-roped
swings for daughters in white dresses. The leaves, once golden and red,
were turning brown, dark orange. The rain had stopped. I don't know
why, but we walked in the middle of the road, dark asphalt gleaming
beneath the slick, pasted leaves like the back of a whale.

I asked him, "What do you want to do while you're here?"

His face was pale and fixed in a smile. "Don't worry about me," he
said. "I can just meditate. Or read."

"There's a coffee shop downtown," I said. "And a Japanese restaurant." It sounded pathetic. It occurred to me that I know nothing about what my father did all day.

He kept smiling, looking at the ground moving in front of his feet.

"I have to write," I said.

"You write."

And I could no longer read his smile. He had perfected it during our separation. It was a setting of the lips, sly, almost imperceptible, which I would probably have taken for a sign of senility but for the keenness of his eyes.

"There's an art museum across the river," I said.

"Ah, take me there."

"The museum?"

"No," he said, looking sideways at me. "The river."

We turned back to Burlington Street and walked down the hill to the river. He stopped halfway across the bridge. The water below looking cold and black, slowing in sections as it succumbed to the temperature. Behind us six lanes of cars skidded back and forth across the wet grit of the road, the sound like the shredding of wind.

"Have you heard from your mother?" He stood upright before the railing, his head strangely small about the puffy down jacket I had lent him.

"Every now and then."

He lapsed into formal Vietnamese: "How is the mother of Nam?"

"She is good," I said—too loudly—trying to make myself heard over the groans and clanks of a passing truck.

He was nodding. Behind him, the east bank of the river glowed wanly in the afternoon light. "Come on," I said. We crossed the bridge and walked to a nearby Dairy Queen. When I came out, two coffees in my hands, my father had gone down to the river's edge. Next to him, a bundled-up, bearded figure stopped over a burning gasoline drum. Never had I seen anything like it in Iowa City.

"This is my son," my father said, once I had scrambled down the wet bank. "The writer." I glanced quickly at him but his face gave nothing away. He lifted a hot paper cup out of my hand. "Would you like some coffee?"

"Thank you, no." The man stood still, watching his knotted hands, palms glowing orange above the rim of the drum. His voice was soft, his clothes heavy with his life. I smelled animals in him, and fuel, and rain.

"I read his story," my father went on in his lilting English, "about Vietnamese boat people." He gazed at the man, straight into his blank, rheumy eyes, then said, as though delivering a punch line, "*We* are Vietnamese boat people."

We stood there for a long time, the three of us, watching the flames. When I lifted my eyes, it was dark.

"Do you have any money on you?" my father asked me in Vietnamese.

"Welcome to America," the man said through his beard. He didn't look up as I closed his fist around the damp bills.

My father was drawn to weakness, even as he tolerated none in me. He was a soldier, he said once, as if that explained everything. With me, he was all proverbs and regulations. No personal phone calls. No female friends. No extracurricular reading. When I was in primary school, he made me draw up a daily ten-hour study timetable for the summer holidays, and punished me when I deviated from it. He knew how to cane me twenty times and leave only one black-red welt, like a brand mark across my buttocks. Afterward, as he rubbed Tiger Balm on the wound, I would cry in anger at myself for crying. Once, when my mother let slip that durian fruit made me vomit, he forced me to eat it in front of guests. *Doi an muoi cung ngon.* Hunger finds no fault with food. I learned to hate him with a straight face.

When I was fourteen, I discovered that he had been involved in a massacre. Later, I would come across photos and transcripts and books; but that night, at a family friend's party in suburban Melbourne, it was just another story in a circle of drunken men. They sat cross-legged on newspapers around a large blue tarpaulin, getting smashed on cheap beer. It was that time of night when things started to break up against other things. Red faces, raised voices, spilled drinks. We arrived late and the men shuffled around, making room for my father.

"Thanh! Fuck your mother! What took you so long—scared, no? Sit down, sit down—"

"Give him five bottles." The speaker swung around ferociously. "We're letting you off easy, everyone here's had eight, nine already."

For the first time, my father let me stay. I sat on the perimeter of the circle, watching in fascination. A thicket of Vietnamese voices, cursing, toasting, braying about their children, making fun of one man who kept stuttering, "It has the power of f-f-five hundred horses!" Through it all my father laughed good-naturedly, his face so red with drink he looked sunburned. Bowl and chopsticks in his hands, he appeared somewhat childish squashed between two men trading war stories. I watched him as he picked sparingly at the enormous spread of dishes in the middle of the circle. The food was known as *do nhau*: alcohol food. Massive fatty oysters dipped in salt-pepper-lemon paste. Boiled sea snails the size of pool balls. Southern-style shredded chicken salad, soaked in vinegar and eaten with spotty brown rice crackers. Someone called out my father's name; he had set his chopsticks down and was speaking in a low voice.

"Heavens, the gunships came first, rockets and M60s. You remember that sound, no? Like you were deaf. We were hiding in the bunker underneath the temple, my mother and four sisters and Mrs. Tran, the baker, and some other people. You couldn't hear anything. Then the gunfire stopped and Mrs. Tran told my mother we had to go up to the street. If we stayed there, the Americans would think we were Viet Cong. 'I'm not going anywhere,' my mother said. 'They have grenades,' Mrs. Tran said. I was scared and excited. I had never seen an American before."

It took me a while to reconcile my father with the story he was telling. He caught my eye and held it a moment, as though he were sharing a secret with me. He was drunk.

"So we went up. Everywhere there was dust and smoke, and all you could hear was the sound of helicopters and M16s. Houses on fire. Then through the smoke I saw an American. I almost laughed. He wore his uniform so untidily—it was too big for him—and he had a beaded necklace and a baseball cap. He held an M16 over his shoulder like a spade. Heavens, he looked nothing like the Viet Cong, with their shirts buttoned up to their chins—and tucked in—even after crawling through mud tunnels all day."

He picked up his chopsticks and reached for the *tiet canh*—a specialty—mincemeat soaked in fresh congealed duck blood. Some of the other men were listening now, smiling knowingly. I saw his teeth, stained red, as he chewed through the rest of his words.

"They made us walk to the east side of the village. There were about ten of them, about fifty of us. Mrs. Tran was saying, 'No VC no VC.' They didn't hear her, not over the sound of machine guns and the M79 grenade launchers. Remember those? Only I heard her. I saw pieces of animals all over the paddy fields, a water buffalo with its side missing—like it was scooped out by a spoon. Then, through the smoke, I saw Grandpa Long bowing to a GI in the traditional greeting. I wanted to call out to him. His wife and daughter and granddaughters, My and Kim, stood shyly behind him. The GI stepped forward, tapped the top of his head with the rifle butt and then twirled the gun around and slid the bayonet into his throat. No one said anything. My mother tried to cover my eyes, but I saw him switch the fire selector on his gun was automatic to single-shot before he shot Grandma Long. Then he and a friend pulled the daughter into a shack, the two little girls dragged along, clinging to her legs.

"They stopped us at the drainage ditch, near the bridge. There were bodies on the road, a baby with only the bottom half of its head, a monk, his robe turning pink. I saw two bodies with the ace of spades carved into the chests. I didn't understand it. My sisters didn't even cry. People were now shouting, 'No VC no VC,' but the Americans just frowned and spat and laughed. One of them said something, then some of them started pushing us into the ditch. It was half full of muddy water. My mother jumped in and lifted my sisters down, one by one. I remember looking up and seeing helicopters everywhere, some bigger than others, some higher up. They made us kneel in the water. They set up their guns on tripods. They made us stand up again. One of the Americans, a boy with a fat face, was crying and moaning softly as he reloaded his magazine. 'No VC no VC.' They didn't look at us. They made us turn back around. They made us kneel back down in the water. When they started shooting, I felt my mother's body jumping on top of mine; it kept jumping for a long time, and then everywhere was the sound of helicopters, louder and louder like they were all coming down to land, and everything was dark and wet and warm and sweet."

The circle had gone quiet. My mother came out from the kitchen, squatted behind my father, and looped her arms around his neck. This was a minor breach of the rules. "Heavens," she said, "don't you men have anything better to talk about?"

After a short silence, someone snorted, saying loudly "You win, Thanh. You really *did* have it bad!" and then everyone, including my father, burst out laughing. I joined in unsurely. They clinked glasses and made toasts using words I didn't understand.

Maybe he didn't tell it exactly that way. Maybe I'm filling in the gaps. But you're not under oath when writing a eulogy, and this is close enough. My father grew up in the province of Quang Ngai, in the village of Son My, in the hamlet of Tu Cung, later known to the Americans as My Lai. He was fourteen years old.

L ate that night, I plugged in the Smith Corona. It hummed with promise. I grabbed the bottle of Scotch from under the desk and poured myself a double. *Fuck it*, I thought. I had two and a half days left. I would write the ethnic story of my Vietnamese father. It was a good story. It was a fucking *great* story.

I fed in a sheet of blank paper. At the top of the page, I typed "ETHNIC STORY" in capital letters. I pushed the carriage return and scrolled to the next line. The sound of helicopters in a dark sky. The keys hammered the page.

I woke up late the next day. At the coffee shop, I sat with my typed pages and watched people come and go. They laughed and sat and sipped and talked and, listening to them, I was reminded again that I was in a small town in a foreign country.

I thought of my father in my dusky bedroom. He had kept the door closed as I left. I thought of how he had looked when I checked on him before going to bed: his body engulfed by blankets and his head so small among my pillows. He'd aged in those last three years. His skin glassy in the blue glow of dawn. He was here now, with me, and already making the rest of my life seem unreal. I read over what I had typed: thinking of him at that age, still a boy, and who he would become. At a nearby table, a guy held out one of his iPod earbuds and beckoned his date to come around and sit beside him. The door opened and a cold wind blew in. I tried to concentrate.

"Hey." It was Linda, wearing a large orange hiking jacket and bringing with her the crisp, bracing scent of all the places she had been. Her face was unmaking a smile. "What are you doing here?"

"Working on my story."

"Is your dad here?"

"No."

Her friends were waiting by the counter. She nodded to them, holding up one finger, then came behind me, resting her hands on my shoulders. "Is this it?" She leaned over me, her hair grazing my face, cold and silken against my cheek. She picked up a couple of pages and read them soundlessly. "I don't get it," she said, returning them to the table. "What are you doing?"

"What do you mean?"

"You never told me any of this."

I shrugged.

"Did he tell you this? Now he's talking to you?"

"Not really," I said.

"Not really?"

I turned around to face her. Her eyes reflected no light.

"You know what I think?" She looked back down at the pages. "I think you're making excuses for him."

"Excuses?"

"You're romanticizing his past," she went on quietly, "to make sense of the things he did to you."

"It's a story," I said. "What things did I say?"

"You said he abused you."

It was too much, these words, and what connected to them. I looked at her serious, beautifully lined face, her light-trapping eyes, and already I felt them taxing me. "I never said that."

She took half a step back. "Just tell me this," she said, her voice flattening. "You've never introduced him to any of your exes, right?" The question was tight on her face.

I didn't say anything and after a while she nodded, biting one corner of her upper lip. I knew that gesture. I knew, even then, that I was supposed to stand up, pull her orange-jacketed body toward mine, speak words into her ear, but all I could do was think about my father and his excuses. Those tattered bodies on top of him. The ten hours he'd waited, mud filling his lungs, until nightfall. I felt myself falling back into old habits.

She stepped forward and kissed the top of my head. It was one of her rules: not to walk away from an argument without some sign of affection. I didn't look at her. My mother liked to tell the story of how, when our family first arrived in Australia, we lived in a hostel on an outer-suburb street where the locals—whenever they met or parted—hugged and kissed each other warmly. How my father—baffled, charmed—had named it "the street of lovers."

I turned to the window: it was dark now, the evening settling thick and deep. A man and woman sat across from each other at a high table. The woman leaned in, smiling, her breasts squat on the wood, elbows forward, her hands mere inches away from the man's shirtfront. Throughout their conversation her teeth glinted. Behind them, a mother sat with her son. "I'm not playing," she murmured, flipped through her magazine.

"L," said the boy.

"I said I'm not playing."

H ere is what I believe: We forgive any sacrifice by our parents, so long as it is not made in our name. To my father there was no other name—only mine, and he had named me after the homeland he had given up. His sacrifice was complete and compelled him to everything that happened. To all that, I was inadequate.

At sixteen I left home. There was a girl, and crystal meth, and the possibility of greater loss than I had imagined possible. She embodied everything prohibited by my father and plainly worthwhile. Of course he was right about her: she taught me hurt—but promise too. We were two animals in the dark, hacking at one another, and never since have I felt that way—that sense of consecration. When my father found out my mother was supporting me, he gave her an ultimatum. She moved into a family friend's textile factory and learned to use an overlock machine and continued sending me money.

"Of course I want to live with him," she told me when I visited her, months later. "But I want you to come home too."

"Ba doesn't want that."

"You're his son," she said simply. "He wants you with him."

I laundered my school uniform and asked a friend to cut my hair and waited for school hours to finish before catching the train home. My father excused himself upon seeing me. When he returned to the living room he had changed his shirt and there was water in his hair. I felt sick and fully awake—as if all the previous months had been a single sleep and now my face was wet again, burning cold. The room smelled of peppermint. He asked me if I was well, and I told him I was, and then he asked me if my female friend was well, and at that moment I realized he was speaking to me not as a father—not as he would to his only son—but as he would speak to a friend, to anyone, and it undid me. I had learned what it was to attenuate my blood but that was nothing compared to this. I forced myself to look at him and I asked him to bring Ma back home.

"And Child?"

"Child will not take any more money from Ma."

"Come home," he said finally. His voice was strangled, half swallowed.

Even then, my emotions operated like a system of levers and pulleys; just seeing him had set them irreversibly into motion. "No," I said. The word just shot out of me.

"Come home, and Ma will come home, and Ba promises Child to never speak of any of this again." He looked away, smiling heavily, and took out a handkerchief. His forehead was moist with sweat. He had been buried alive in the warm, wet clinch of his family, crushed by their lives. I wanted to know how he climbed out of that pit. I wanted to know how there could ever be any correspondence between us. I wanted to know all this but an internal momentum moved me, further and further from him as time went on.

"The world is hard," he said. For a moment I was uncertain whether he was speaking in proverbs. He looked at me, his face a gleaming mask. "Just say yes, and we can forget everything. That's all. Just say it: Yes."

But I didn't say it. Not that day, not the next, not any day for almost a year. When I did, though, rehabilitated and fixed in new privacies, he was true to his word and never spoke of the matter. In fact, after I came back home he never spoke of anything much at all, and it was under this learned silence that the three of us—my father, my mother, and I, living again under a single roof—were conducted irreparably into our separate lives.

The apartment smelled of fried garlic and sesame oil when I returned. My father was sitting on the living room floor, on the special mattress he had brought over with him. It was made of white foam. He told me it was for his back. "There's some stir-fry in the kitchen."

"Thanks."

"I read your story this morning," he said, "while you were still sleeping." Something in my stomach folded over. I hadn't thought to hide the pages. "There are mistakes in it."

"You read it?"

"There were mistakes in your last story too."

My last story. I remembered my mother's phone call at the time: my father, unemployed and living alone in Sydney, had started sending long emails to friends from his past—friends from thirty, forty years ago. I should talk to him more often, she'd said. I'd sent him my refugee story. He hadn't responded. Now, as I came out of the kitchen with a heaped plate of stir-fry, I tried to recall those selections where I'd been sloppy with research. Maybe the scene in Rach Gia—before they reached the boat. I scooped up a forkful of marinated tofu, cashews, and chickpeas. He'd gone shopping. "They're *stories*," I said, chewing casually. "Fiction."

He paused for a moment, then said, "Okay, Son."

For so long my diet had consisted of chips and noodles and pizzas I'd forgotten how much I missed home cooking. As I ate, he stretched on his white mat.

"How's your back?"

"I had a CAT scan," he said. "There's nerve fluid leaking between my vertebrae." He smiled his long-suffering smile, right leg twisted across his left hip. "I brought the scans to show you."

"Does it hurt, Ba?"

"It hurts." He chuckled briefly, as though the whole matter were a joke. "But what can I do? I can only accept it."

"Can't they operate?"

I felt myself losing interest. I was a bad son. He'd separated from my mother when I started law school and ever since then he'd brought up his back pains so often—always couched in Buddhist tenets of suffering and acceptance—that the cold, hard part of me suspected he was exaggerating, to solicit and then gently rebuke my concern. He did this. He'd forced me to take karate lessons until I was sixteen; then, during one of our final arguments, he came at me and I found myself in fighting stance. He had smiled at my horror. "That's right," he'd said. We were locked in all the intricate ways of guilt. It took all the time we had to realize that everything we face, we faced for the other as well.

"I want to talk with you," I said.

"You grow old, your body breaks down," he said.

"No, I mean for the story."

"Talk?"

"Yes."

"About what?" He seemed amused.

"About my mistakes," I said.

I f you ask me why I came to Iowa, I would say that I was a lawyer and I was no lawyer. Every twenty-four hours I woke up at the smoggiest time of morning and commuted—bus, tram, elevator, without saying a single word, wearing clothes that chafed and holding a flat white in a white cup—to my windowless office in the tallest, most glass-covered building in Melbourne. Time was broken down into six-minute units, friends allotted eight-minute lunch breaks. I hated what I was doing and

I hated that I was good at it. Mostly, I hated knowing it was my job that made my father proud of me. When I told him I was quitting and going to Iowa to be a writer, he said, "*Trau buoc ghet trau an.*" The captive buffalo hates the free buffalo. But by that time he had no more control over my life. I was twenty-five years old.

The thing is not to write what no one else could have written, but to write what only you could have written. I recently found this fragment in one of my old notebooks. The person who wrote that couldn't have known what would happen: how time can hold itself against you, how a voice hollows, how words you once loved can wither on the page.

"Why do you want to write this story?" my father asked me.

"It's a good story."

"But there are so many things you could write about."

"This is important, Ba. It's important that people know."

"You want their pity."

I didn't know whether it was a question. I was offended. "I want them to remember," I said.

He was silent for a long time. Then he said, "Only you'll remember. I'll remember. They will read and clap their hands and forget." For once, he was not smiling. "Sometimes it's better to forget, no?"

"I'll write it anyway," I said. It came back to me—how I'd felt at the typewriter the previous night. A thought leapt into my mind: "If I write a true story," I told my father, "I'll have a better chance of selling it."

He looked at me a while, searchingly, seeing something in my face as though for the first time. Finally he said, in a measured voice, "I'll tell you." For a moment he receded into thought. "But believe me, it's not something you'll be able to write."

"I'll write it anyway," I repeated.

Then he did something unexpected. His face opened up and he began to laugh, without self-pity or slyness, laughing in full-bodied breaths. I was shocked. I hadn't heard him laugh like this for as long as I could remember. Without fully knowing why, I started laughing too. His throat was humming in Vietnamese, "Yes . . . yes . . . yes," his eyes shining, smiling. "All right. All right. But tomorrow."

"But—"

"I need to think," he said. He shook his head, then said under his breath, "My son a writer. *Co thuc moi vuc duoc dao.*" How far does an empty stomach drag you?

"*Mot nguoi lam quan, ca ho duoc nho,*" I retorted. A scholar is a blessing for all his relatives. He looked at me in surprise before laughing again and nodding vigorously. I'd been saving that one up for years.

A fternoon. We sat across from one another at the dining room table: I asked questions and took notes on a yellow legal pad; he talked. He talked about his childhood, his family. He talked about My Lai. At this point, he stopped.

"You won't offer your father some of that?"

"What?"

"Heavens, you think you can hide liquor of that quality?"

The afternoon light came through the window and held his body in a silver square, slowly sinking toward his feet, dimming, as he talked. I refilled our glasses. He talked above the peak-hour traffic on the streets, its rinse of noise; he talked deep into evening. When the phone rang the second time I unplugged it from the jack. He told me how he'd been conscripted into the South Vietnamese army.

"After what the Americans did? How could you fight on their side?"

"I had nothing but hate in me," he said, "but I had enough for everyone." He paused on the word *hate* like a father saying it before his infant child for the first time, trying the child's knowledge, testing what was inherent in the word and what learned.

He told me about the war. He told me about meeting my mother. The wedding. Then the fall of Saigon. 1975. He told me about his imprisonment in reeducation camp, the forced confessions, the introductions, the starvations. The daily labor that ruined his back. The casual killings. He told me about the tiger-cage cells and connex boxes, the different names for different forms of torture: the honda, the airplane, the auto. "They tie you by your thumbs, one arm over the shoulder, the other pulled around the front of the body. Or they stretch out your legs and tie your middle fingers to your big toes—"

He showed me. A skinny old man in Tantric poses, he looked faintly preposterous. During the auto he flinched, then, a smile springing to his face, asked me to help him to his foam mattress. I waited impatiently for him to stretch it out. He asked me again to help. *Here, push here. A little harder.* Then he went on talking, sometimes in a low voice, sometimes grinning. Other times he would blink—furiously; perplexedly. In spite of his Buddhist protestations, I imagined him locked in rage, turned around and forced every day to rewitness these atrocities of his past, helpless to act. But that was only my imagination. I had nothing to prove that he was not empty of all that now.

He told me how, upon his release after three years' incarceration, he organized our family's escape from Vietnam. This was 1979. He was twenty-five years old then, and my father.

When finally he fell asleep, his face warm from the Scotch, I watched him. I felt like I had drifted into dream too. For a moment I became my father, watching his sleeping son, reminded of what—for his son's sake—he had tried, unceasingly, to forget. A past larger than complaint, more perilous than memory. I shook myself conscious and went to my desk. I read my notes through once, carefully, all forty-five pages. I reread the draft of my story from two nights earlier. Then I put them both aside and started typing, never looking at them again.

Dawn came so gradually I didn't notice—until the beeping of a garbage truck—that outside the air was metallic blue and the ground was white. The top of the tin shed was white. The first snow had fallen.

He wasn't in the apartment when I woke up. There was a note on the coffee table: *I am going for a walk. I have taken your story to read.* I sat outside, on the fire escape, with a tumbler of Scotch, waiting for him. Against the cold, I drank my whiskey, letting it flow like a filament of warmth through my body. I had slept for only three hours and was too tired to feel anything but peace. The red geraniums on the landing of the opposite building were frosted over. I spied through my neighbors' windows and saw exactly nothing.

He would read it, with his book-learned English, and he would recognize himself in a new way. He would recognize me. He would see how powerful was his experience, how valuable his suffering—how I had made it speak for more than itself. He would be pleased with me.

I finished the Scotch. It was eleven-thirty and the sky was dark and gray-smeared. My story was due at midday. I put my gloves on, treaded carefully down the fire escape, and untangled my bike from the rack. He would be pleased with me. I rode around the block, up and down Summit Street, looking for a sign of my puffy jacket. The streets were empty. Most of the snow had melted, but an icy film covered the roads and I rode slowly. Eyes stinging and breath fogging in front of my mouth, I coasted toward downtown, across the College Green, the grass frozen so stiff it snapped beneath my bicycle wheels. Lights glowed dimly from behind the curtained windows of houses. On Washington Street, a sudden gust of wind ravaged the elm branches and unfastened their leaves, floating down them thick and slow and soundless.

I was halfway across the bridge when I saw him. I stopped. He was on the riverbank. I couldn't make out the face but it was he, short and small-headed in my bloated jacket. He stood with the tramp. Both of them staring into the blazing gasoline drum. The smoke was thick, particulate. For a second I stopped breathing. I knew with sick certainty what he had done. The ashes, given body by the wind, floated away from me down the river. He patted the man on the shoulder, reached into his back pocket and slipped some money into those large, newly mittened hands. He started up the bank then, and saw me. I was so full of wanting I thought it would flood my heart. His hands were empty.

If I had known then what I knew later, I wouldn't have said the things I did. I wouldn't have told him what he had done was unforgivable. That I wished he had never come, and that he was no father to me. But I hadn't known, and, as I waited, feeling the wind change, all I saw was a man coming toward me in a ridiculously oversized jacket, rubbing his black-sooted hands, stepping through the smoke with its flecks and flame-tinged eddies, who had destroyed himself, yet again, in my name. The river was behind him. The wind was full of acid. In the slow float of light I looked away, down at the river. On the brink of freezing, it gleamed in large, bulging blisters. The water, where it still moved, was black and braided. And it occurred to me then how it took hours, sometimes days, for the surface of a river to freeze over—to hold in its skin the perfect and crystalline world—and how that world could be shattered by a small stone dropped like a single syllable.

T.K. LÊ grew up in Westminster, California, and currently resides in Los Angeles. She obtained her MA in Asian American Studies at UCLA, exploring how two war monuments, a cemetery near her parents' place, and An-My Lê's photography provide alternatives to US nationalist memory of the Vietnam War. After that she birthed a chapbook called *The Labor of Longing*, a series of meditations about her mother. The chapbook is a companion to *A Roof and Some Refuge*, a collection of poems and stories about her father. She is currently exploring new forms of writing to bridge war memory and the ongoing violence and erasures produced by US empire building. She turns to crafting, cats, and *Steven Universe* for therapy.

PART OF MEMORY IS FORGETTING

I'm not a social butterfly. I like the warmth of my cocoon. It was only after a year of dodging invitations and one particularly difficult teaching day that I agreed to attend a happy hour with my co-workers. We arrived at the bar, assembled tables together, shuffled chairs, and before I knew it, I was locked somewhere in the middle, unable to make a getaway without getting my chair's legs tangled with those of someone else's. We exchanged the usual pleasantries. Work, weather, drinks of choice. And like clockwork, exactly what I was expecting to happen did.

"So," she said, shifting her gaze from her cocktail to my face, "What . . . is your ANCESTRY?" My coworker's eyes got wide and the sleeves of her dress shirt swept up and around, reflecting a loose timeline of how far back she wanted me to go.

My initial reaction was to challenge her, but I reeled myself in because she was someone who worked above me and anyway, she seemed to be choosing her words carefully. Most of all, she seemed nervous, and I kinda like making white people nervous. So I was about to answer politely, but before I could utter a single word, another coworker interrupted me.

"*She* is a Viet Cong," she said, taking a long gulp of her beer. And she laughed. I stated as firmly as I could that I didn't consider it funny, which made her laugh even more.

I listened to her laugh echo in the bar. It was as if something about my face was a riddle, a joke, and Viet Cong was the punchline.

———

Surely you have seen the photograph. On February 1, 1968, south Vietnamese troops captured a suspected officer from the north by the name of Nguyen Van Lem. The police chief from the South, Nguyen Ngoc Loan, held a gun to the head of the soldier from the North, and in that moment there was the sound of two clicks: first the gun, and then of Eddie Adams' camera. Nguyen Van Lem's face was twisted in utter fear while the police officer's face remained stoic. The shock value of violence held still long enough for examination made this photo infamous. It was used as a message against the war in Vietnam. Eddie Adams won a Pulitzer for it.

When I was a teenager, I saw Dave Navarro give a tour of his crib on MTV. In the entrance of his home, not far from wherever the magic happens, he had a wall-sized image of this execution. He said something along the lines of being reminded that he's living, or some shit like that. Humanity and whatnot.

My dad worked as a photographer during this American war and told me that he got more money if he fit soldiers from the North and South into the frame. 100 USD.

———

Early last year, I saw an item go up for sale on Etsy. It was the identification card of a young Vietnamese girl, a black and white portrait of her stared at me from the left-hand side of the card. Her hair, parted down the middle, framed her expressionless face. Her fingerprints had been pressed on the other side of the card. The description said:

MAKE ME AN OFFER I CAN'T REFUSE!

Female's date of birth: October 1, 1958

The card was issued in Tan-Binh, Vietnam on December 18, 1973. These cards were issued to civilians in South Vietnam during the Vietnam War. After the fall of Saigon in September [*sic*]1975 they were no longer issued and are now invalid. This is one of the many ID cards that my husband had in his collection. He served in Vietnam with 3rd Marine Division in 1965.

Due to the age of the card the corner on the lower back has started to slightly curl. Identities for sale. I wondered if that woman were still alive. She would have been around my mother's age. My lip curled, slightly.

———

I could talk to my coworkers about how my parents were both refugees and about the life or death decisions they had to make at ages younger than ours. I could talk about the My Lai massacre, about the systematic rape of entire villages that meant even less than "just making a point." Agent Orange, burning skin, landmine amputees, and all the dead children. But I won't satisfy her with the gratuitous imagery of a war I never knew.

The violence, after all, is written in her everyday lexicon: I killed the job interview. I raped that test. I'll shoot you an email.

I speak that same language, fluently. And even though I wasn't alive during the war, I've been living through it since I was born.

Part of memory is forgetting. In Vietnamese, there is no verb conjugation; we understand a sentence is in the past by the context of the words around it. I have kept my ear close to the floor of our house for years now, listening for anecdotes of my family's history. It wasn't until recently that I realized that silence is the history.

U.S. history books triumph the 60s and 70s for the peace movement and advancement in journalism—literature and film critics hail this as an artistic renaissance, changing the ways in which stories are told, stories that reflect the ambiguities the Americans felt in fighting the war.

Make the other poor bastard die. Good morning, Vietnam. Five dolla. The horror, the horror.

And now I suppose my coworker's calling me a Viet Cong could be a punchline, but about bombing and maiming a country already broken, and then calling it art.

———

At the bar, I let the flow of the conversation wash over me. They had already begun on a new topic, sports or travel or work minutiae. As more people arrived, it turned into a shouting match of life experiences.

I participated at a minimum and gave short responses to their inquiries. I found it useless to give answers to people who had them already.

I took the bus home, enveloped myself in the memory of the night, and searched for a language I would use to write it down.

ADA LIMÓN is the author of four books of poetry, including *Bright Dead Things*, which was named a finalist for the 2015 National Book Award in Poetry, a finalist for the 2015 National Book Critics Circle Award, and one of the Top Ten Poetry Books of the Year by *The New York Times*. Her other books include *Lucky Wreck*, *This Big Fake World*, and *Sharks in the Rivers*. Her stepfather is a Vietnam veteran and she grew up keenly aware of the trauma of war that reverberates for years after the war's end.

LISTEN

"I have always been disturbed by the romanticizing, the glorification of war. There's nothing good about it, it's kill or be killed. Nothing glorious."

Sometime around 2 AM in the canyon dark, no moon, the house wailed open with a guttural yell that shook me awake on the couch. In an instant I knew what it was, that painful loud bellow that echoes around the quiet night like a siren long after the fire's gone out. For years, this is how my stepfather, B, awakes from a bad dream. A violent yell that makes my heart beat so fast that I can't sleep for hours afterwards. When I was a kid, I remember him coming into my room to make sure I knew he was okay. "It was just a dream," he would tell me, "go back to sleep." He never talked about the nightmares, but we knew what they were about.

Just last weekend, we all traveled together to Southern California for my grandparents' 67th wedding anniversary. It was on the second night, in a friend's condominium where we were staying, that he woke with one of his shouts. It made sense. That night after dinner, B and Grandpa were discussing the wars, their different and individual stories of serving in the United States Army. My grandfather, raised a rural farmer and woodworker, fought in the battle at Monte Cassino at 18. He had never had a meal in a restaurant. My stepfather was 19 when he went to Vietnam with the 4th Division. He couldn't legally drink or vote at the time. When family members have been to war, it becomes an impossible subject to avoid. My grandfather is asked why he married so young: "Well, we knew I'd be drafted and time was running out." Which turns into the story of how B ended up in Vietnam.

Despite their darkness, their heaviness, the stories are achingly wonderful. They are not heroic or served with false bravado. They could be stories about growing up poor, or having a heart broken for the first time. They are their life experiences. Simple and painful and human. Both men are inherent storytellers, deft at the nuances of balancing pain with a humor that can only come from the most honest of places. Everyone is rapt, empty glasses in front of them, dirty dishes. They stop for a second. We're quiet. The refrigerator roars louder. Then another question. Vietnam and World War II are diametrically opposed wars in so many ways, the country behind them, the global community, the different eras of consciousness. But they are also the same. These men, kind, funny, tender, the men you want every man to be, have done unimaginable things. Have seen their good friends die in the most horrific circumstances. Gruesome images that cannot be erased, but must be lived with. These are their coming of age stories.

―――

When you live with a veteran, the language of war becomes a natural thing. When I went away to college, B walked all around the neighborhood of my first apartment. We watched him from the window. "He's checking the perimeter," Mom said. In the car on the way to my grand-parents' house, my mom talks about some purse she saw online and I make a joke about how she's obsessed with purses. I tell her I'm going to write a book called, *The Things She Carried*. The only thing B has ever expressed great hatred for is rats. I don't know too much about the origin of this hatred, but I do know that there are rats referred to as "corpse rats" in almost every war. On a hike in Kauai, the landscape reminds him of the Vietnam jungle sparking a two-hour fascinating conversation about the conditions during the war. This is family conversation. The unfolding of our histories passed on. What we don't ever discuss, and for this I am grateful, are the contents of his nightmares.

According to the Department of Veterans Affairs, nightmares are 1 of 17 symptoms associated with Posttraumatic Stress Disorder. Also, "If you have been suffering from nightmares for more than 3 months, you are encouraged to contact a mental health professional . . ." More than 3 months? How about more than 42 years? According to the Interna-tional Association of the Study of Dreams, somewhere between 5–10% of adults suffer from nightmares on a monthly basis. In their descriptions of what causes nightmares, veterans are specifically mentioned. "Many people experience nightmares after they have suffered a traumatic event, such as surgery, the loss of a loved one, an assault or a severe accident. The nightmares of combat veterans fall into this category. The content of these nightmares is typically directly related to the traumatic event and the nightmares often occur over and over." My mother says that B should come with a sign that reads, "This man should not sleep alone."

My grandmother believes that you have to eat something before you tell someone your dreams, or else they'll come true. For my entire upbring-ing, my family members have rushed to the kitchen to shove something in their mouths before recounting a disturbing dream. Carl Jung said, "The dream is a little hidden door in the innermost and most secret recesses of the soul . . ."

The night before B shouted himself, and us, awake he was telling us about how, just two days after he left Vietnam, his Infantry Company was essentially wiped out. The man who replaced B as the RTO (Radio Telephone Operator, who carries a 25 pound radio on his back in addition to the 50 pound rucksack) was taken as a POW for six years. He was eventually released and he and B still talk.

When I ask if B remembers what the dream was about he just looks at me, a stark look that means he won't repeat it. "I guess you do," I answer. We eat toast and watch the sun come up over the desert skyline.

Two days later, in the Ontario airport, we are surrounded by service men and women in their fatigues. Most of them seem older than the age both Grandpa and B went to war. I like to think that that fact alone will better their chance for survival and mental health. Going through security, we both notice that their shoulder patches are 4th Division. And B points out the Second Lieutenant. She is a woman, a few years younger than me. She has the face of my best friend growing up. Her eyes are steeled and focused. I feel like I would trust her. I smile; she nods sternly. The group closest to me is headed to Fort Bragg and then to Iraq. Many of them are returning for their second tours.

My mother, B, and I sit near the window and wait for the plane. We talk about my life in New York, laugh about the roadside chapel we saw off Highway 10 called Mystical Memories, and how good the grandparents seem after 67 years of marriage. The sun is bright off the tarmac. I watch my parents board and walk over to my gate near the majority of the soldiers. I listen to their stories, one is talking about his kids, another on the phone with the base. They seem strong and capable. It seems like there are millions of them when they board my plane.

According to the U.S. Census Bureau there are 23.2 million veterans in the United States and growing. At the U.S. Department of Veterans Affairs they offer this advice under, How Can I Help?: "Tell your loved one you want to listen and that you also understand if he or she doesn't feel like talking." Although B and I talk about everything, he will never tell me about the contents of his nightmares. And yes, I understand.

When I get home, after a few days, I ask B if it's okay if I write about him. I ask if he'd like to add anything. He does:

The VN war was more worthless than most wars and I have, to say the least, mixed feelings about having fought in it. Once you're in it, as an individual, you have an allegiance and responsibility to your fellow soldiers and I tried to live up to that responsibility. I was nineteen when I went to war, a lot older when I came back. Paul Fussell, historian/writer, says something to the effect of, "Those of us who have fought in combat know something about ourselves—and it's not very nice." I'd have to agree. My ability to go quickly to that cold place where it's me or you still gives me pause. Aging hasn't softened that, it's just made me less able to deliver on it. I have always been disturbed by the romanticizing, the glorification of war. There's nothing good about it, it's kill or be killed. Nothing glorious. I don't mean to suggest you think that there is. I suppose I just wish the seminal experience of my life, and I guess Grandpa's too, had been something of beauty rather than destruction and grief.

BRIAN MA was born in North Carolina to Vietnamese parents of Chinese descent. On both sides, family members have been executed or jailed by all warring parties. He is a graduate of the Creative Writing Program at New York University, and he currently lives and works in Seoul, Korea.

JULY IN VIETNAM

Only two generations before they spoke French
and then Russian,
and now the Soviet guns are still around.
Dawns skinny soldier-boys march the square
in this country where

there is no snow, never snow,
and no potatoes. I came for a reason
but his prison is a school now,
my family's house a pharmacy.

It is cramped, in the alleyways
laundry hangs on strings.
After eating I sweep the fish-heads
from the table and cats take what they can.

I have registered my name and address
at the police station,
changed my money at the jewelry store.
Meeting the ex-prisoners was raucous,

I ate snake and frog because I was drunk.
We were all drunk
and they were telling the waitress I was from America.

My observations are rarely confident.
Every now and then
I get sick because of this air,

heavy with particulates.
They play music too loud in the clubs
so that whenever I leave,
I can't even hear the motor-traffic.

In this country the landscape loves
apologizing to me and I love this generosity.
Every day I eat the vegetables and fruit here,
I eat the ice.

AERIAL

This military plane from an old war
gutted then fit with seats
carries me

over jungles and swamps.
The morning burns what fog it can.
Did I look out the windows at first, I can't remember.
I thought I felt the hull-plates rattle
against loose bolts.

Flying homeward as though to a dying parent
the propellers are so loud I feel them on my skin.

Distances and blood.
In coming here all threads snap,
there's no easy way back.

The jungle breathes its dark mists,
its incoherent stillness puts me on guard.

As I descend the sun at my level
makes me squint,
my eyes drooped as though in arrogance.
But as usual the boundaries are hard to discern.
The guilt is like a fog; in the fog there are people.

SJOHNNA McCRAY studied at Ohio University and earned an MFA from the
University of Virginia where he was a Hoyns Fellow. McCray also received an
MA in English Education from Teachers College, Columbia University. His poetry
collection, *Rapture*, was selected by Tracy K. Smith as the winner of the 2015
Walt Whitman Award from the Academy of American Poets and was published
by Graywolf Press in 2016. His honors include the AWP Intro Journal Award, Ohio
University's Emerson Poetry Prize, and a Pushcart Prize nomination.

HOW TO MOVE

I cannot look at anything
    so black as my father's leg
        or used-to-be-leg below the knee

now a stump. If a child's doll lost
    its flexible hand, the surface
        underneath would be as round

as father's stump. I've touched it once.
    And my brother, who is five,
        is not afraid to touch the stump.

Men on the corner used to holler
    that dad was a high yellow nigger
        or if the sun had darkened him

and pulled the red to the surface of his skin,
    a red nigger. I am thinking of colors
        because the prosthesis comes in colors.

His first leg was the color of oatmeal,
    maybe the color of peaches. Khaki,
        yellow and pink: a simulated sunset.

I am thinking of technicians
    with photographs creating
        perfect shades of negroness

for limbless negroes, every negro
    matched to a swatch or chart with names
        like fingernail polish. When my brother

touches the stump, the stump
    that has shrunk and hardened to look
        like an oversized, uncircumcised penis,

when my brother takes the brown
    almost black debris of father's life
        into small hands that marvel

at catching spiders in jars, he is not afraid.
    When we discover death, shaking
        in the gravel driveway, he knows it

immediately, the dark gray body
    of the robin, the red and slightly pink
        shaggy belly. The fuzz of the robin's round belly

like a fuzz of new tennis balls.
    The robin is on its side with the right wing
        moving slowly, back and forth.

At the same time, the beak is opening
    And closing. There's hardly any sound, no song
        except the sound of short, jagged gasps. All

elements working in unison: wing
    moving back and forth, beak
        opening and closing, the rhythm inherent

in knowing and not knowing when anything
    is coming, but wanting to finish it, gracefully.
        Even while dying. But maybe grace

has nothing to do with it; maybe
    it's desire that pulls our limbs, the robin's
        wing on concrete, to fly even in shadow

of a man and a boy, the boy with his eyes
    out of his mind, celestial. Maybe
        the desire is to show us how to move.

When we are at home,
    my brother takes the stump in his arms
        holds on to it like a prize or an unexpected gift

        that father has given us.

BEDTIME STORY #1
—*Seoul, Korea, 1971*

Father gave her a little extra. How could she not
    fall for him? He was handsome
but still a boy. In the depot where soldiers
    took such women, his skinny body clung
too close to hers and his narrow ass still
    belonged to his mother. The other men
knew the routine and how much to pay.
    She loathed their accent and American swagger.
The sweat would barely cool and dry
    before another shook the cot and bucked his hips
out of rhythm—in some other time zone.

    However, he began to offer other things
besides money. He brought sweets from the base
    and the minute he touched his pocket
the face she reserved for his English crumbled
    like sweet toffee. Because he didn't know how
to say what he wanted to say, no time
    was spent on uneasiness. Chocolate
caramel and peanuts spoke best, secured
    his place. He hooked his arms through hers as if
they could stroll the lane like an ordinary couple:
    the unassuming black and the Korean whore
in the middle of the Vietnam War.

GARDNER MCFALL lost her Navy pilot father in the Vietnam War when she was 14 years old; his A4-Skyhawk was never recovered from the Pacific, where he was training for a second tour of duty in Vietnam. Her first book of poems, *The Pilot's Daughter,* was an elegy for him that subsequently became the basis for her libretto for the 2010 opera *Amelia*, commissioned by Seattle Opera. *Russian Tortoise*, her second poetry collection, contains a section of poems derived from her travel to Vietnam in 2006. McFall has received a "Discovery"/*The Nation* award, *The Missouri Review*'s Thomas McAfee Prize, and residencies to Yaddo, the Mac-Dowell Colony, and Virginia Center for the Creative Arts.

MISSING

For years I lived with the thought
of his return. I imagined he had ditched
the plane and was living on a distant
island, plotting his way back
with a faithful guide; or, if
he didn't have a guide, he was sending
up a flare in sight of an approaching ship.

Perhaps, having reached an Asian capital,
he was buying gifts for a reunion
that would dwarf the ones before.
He would have exotic stories to tell,
though after a while, the stories
didn't matter or the gifts.

One day I told myself, he is not coming
home, though I had no evidence,
no grave, nothing to say a prayer over.
I knew he was flying among the starry
plankton, detained forever.
But telling myself this was as futile
as when I found a picture of him

sleeping in the ready room,
hands folded across his chest,
exhausted from the sortie he'd flown.
His flight suit was still on,
a jacket collapsed at his feet.
I half thought I could reach out

and wake him, as the unconscious
touches the object of its desire
and makes it live. I have kept
all the doors open in my life
so that he could walk in, unsure
as I've been how to relinquish
what is not there.

ON THE LINE

The line where you were,
like the equator, divided the world
in two. Whatever the latitude,
the planes roared off the carrier.
Their bombs fell vertically
on target. In a letter, you wrote:

"Each day we bomb the Ho Chi Minh Trail,
they reconstruct it by night.
We can't win, but don't quote me."
You were a kind man.
You loved your family.
For years I've tried to figure

what you loved more—
not the military life with tours of duty
or the jungle war. You loved
Duty itself, a word, an abstraction.

Now our lines of communication
are cut, except for your blood in me.

These words, strange as your death,
fall as on foreign villages,
unpronounceable names,
all lost on American ears.
I am traveling fast, propelled
by you, doing what I must,
ready to answer for it.

BLUE RAFT
for my daughter

The first month you floated in me
at the beach of my childhood,
the sun burned my shoulders.
Black crows appeared
among the sandpipers and gulls.
The crows were the only darkness,
out of place with their splayed crow feet,
unable to run or dive like sea-birds.
I watched them on the shore,
donax in their sharp beaks.
I couldn't say whether theirs
was a taste born of necessity or desire.
One looked at me with its hard, berry eyes,
and I looked back,
each of us suspecting the other.
Then, I took the blue raft
from summers before and went out
beyond the waves to flutter-kick and drift.
The ocean was smooth as a platter,
strewn with stars.
I wanted to drift for hours

in forgetful peace,
right into oblivion,
with only the ocean to buoy me
and no one in the houses to call me.
The houses seemed very small
and far away.
When I drifted close to the shrimpers,
a shrill whistle woke me.
I was out too far.
I started to paddle and kick.
All the while I thought of you
floating inside me.
Out too far, out too far.
At last I reached the point
where waves swell,
and a wave lifted the raft
high, then down.
The foam enveloped me
the way it would when I'd ride
on my father's back,
a knapsack, a small burden
among salty pleasure.
I skidded over the broken shells
to ankle-deep water, and as I rose,
taking the blue raft lightly under my arm,
salt and sand clinging to me,
I thought of how my father would say,
lying on a raft in the Atlantic,
"This is the life." He was dead,
but you were floating in me,
and the crows, like some new part
of myself, stood on the beach,
exquisitely black, shining.

PHILIP METRES was born on the Fourth of July. His father served as a naval officer during the Vietnam War, and in the mid-1970s, the family sponsored and hosted a Vietnamese refugee family in their home. Metres is the author of *Pictures at an Exhibition* (2016), *Sand Opera* (2015), *I Burned at the Feast: Selected Poems of Arseny Tarkovsky* (2015), *To See the Earth* (2008), and others. His work has garnered a Lannan fellowship, two NEAs, six Ohio Arts Council Grants, the Hunt Prize for Excellence in Journalism, Arts & Letters, the Beatrice Hawley Award, two Arab American Book Awards, a Watson Fellowship, a Creative Workforce Fellowship, the Cleveland Arts Prize, and a PEN/Heim Translation grant. He is professor of English at John Carroll University in Cleveland.

THE THINGS THEY CARRIED THAT WE CARRY

When I was five, the Vietnam War officially ended. In some sense, though, wars never really end—not for those cauterized by their fire. Forty years later, my father, who served as a U.S. naval advisor on a South Vietnamese patrol gunboat and survived the Tet Offensive holed up in the Saigon hotel, would visit Vietnam with fellow veterans, and was stunned to see that his Vietnam no longer existed. The Saigon of 1968 was gone, except for the one he carried in his head, suffusing his body, flaring out into our family room at moments of helplessness and despair.

A few years back, talking to my students in "Literature of War and Peace," my father surprised me when he said the best thing he did in Vietnam was volunteer at a Catholic orphanage, teaching English. When he asked the head of the orphanage, Sister Regina—who'd been airlifted out before the fall of Saigon—what he could do, she suggested sponsoring a refugee family. Despite having two small children, he and my mother agreed.

I have a blurry memory of an endless expanse of tents, stretching into the distance. Camp Pendleton, California. What was promised to be a family of five had now bloomed into fourteen. The Nguyen family stood outside a dusty tent, awaiting a life they could not imagine. They'd lost everything but the clothes on their bodies, and Hoa, the matriarch, had her four children and old mother hold onto a string as they walked in the camps in Guam and Philippines, so they wouldn't get separated.

I would share my room with Lam and Dủng—boys a few years older than me—while my parents would battle landlords reluctant to rent to foreigners. I remember, more than anything, the Nguyens' kindness and generosity, the appealing scents of their houses.

Thirty years later, when we visit the Nguyen family, Ba tells the story of how we became one family. He does not hold back his tears—tears of gratitude, tears of sorrow—as memories of that war flood back. Hoa played with our three-year-old daughter as if she were her own. They have lived out classic immigrant narrative—all their children success-ful professionals—yet they carry with them where they came from. *Big heart*, Ba said, *your parents have big heart*. When he said *heart*, it sounded like *hurt*. His eyes shined. *We tell you this*, Hoa said, *so that you can help someone also.*

War always comes home. In Great-uncle Charlie, who spent his entire adult life in an asylum when he returned from the Great War, though his siblings were told that he was dead. In the anger and grief of my vet-eran father. In the men who wept behind dark sunglasses as my father pinned medals onto their worn fatigues during the 1986 Vietnam Vet-eran parade in Chicago—the first parade for Vietnam Veterans, over ten years after the war was over. In the scars in the skull of my Palestin-ian ex-brother-in-law. In the paranoid gaze that a woman gave me on an international flight after 9/11, as I, a somewhat swarthy Arab American, slowly removed my shoes.

Writing, for me, has been a practice pitched against the forces of war—the dislocation, trauma, and pain that trail in their wake. As Herodotus once wrote, I write to "prevent these deeds from drifting into oblivion," striving not only to chronicle what has happened, but also to carve out the contours of a better world. Naomi Shihab Nye articulated this paradoxical vision of hope in "Jerusalem": "it's late but everything comes next."

In the past decade, I have been inexorably drawn to writing about the depredations in the Middle East. "Hung Lyres" is a sequence of poems from *Sand Opera* (2015), a book-length meditation on the post

9/11 years. What began as outrage, as testimony, as grief, morphed into
a keen-song of survival, watching my children surprise me back into joy.
Witness without love is like death without life. I write to work our way
back toward what Rumi called "the field"—that place of the imagination,
beyond the realm of good and evil.

FROM *HUNG LYRES*

@

When the bombs fell, she could barely raise
her pendulous head, wept shrapnel

until her mother capped the fire
with her breast. She teetered

on the highwire of herself. She
lay down & the armies retreated, never

showing their backs. When she unlatched
from the breast, the planes took off again.

Stubborn stars refused to fall . . .

@

Downstairs, the baby monitor opened its one-way channel
to the fitful breathing. My brother-in-law uncorked a bottle,

doled out the steak and silver. On TV: a portrait of a marine,
dress blues. His eyes still open. At the Vietnam Veteran

parade, Chicago '86, I saw sideburned men bivouacked
behind shades, awkward as my father pinned stacks

of ribbons to unbuttoned fatigues, still returning from the war
ten years later. *What I remember*, Rob said, *was John. Every dinner*

his father rehearsed the arguments: containment, the Reds. He stewed
in silence. Until, once, he grabbed his father, pulled him to the backyard.

We'd reached the bottom of the bottle. *He took a kitchen knife*
and gouged the dirt. Rob looked at the well of glass, its last smutch

of red. I'm underwater, looking up at a milky light.
Inside the box was a necklace of ears. The son said: this is your war.

Did it happen that way, the circle of ears—a symbol so readymade
it's already fiction? The scholar teaching "The Dream of the Rood"

declares: *any time a poet repeats himself, he really means it.*
I have my doubts. Still: *inside the box was a necklace of ears.*

Above us, someone stirred, the monitor chirring.
We held our breath. No one was crying.

@

What does it mean, I say. She says, it means
to be quiet, just by yourself. She says, there's

a treasure chest. Inside. You get to dig it out.
Somehow, it's spring. Says, will it always

rain? In some countries, I say, they are
praying for rain. She asks, why do birds sing?

In the dream, my notebook dipped in water,
all the writing lost. Says, read the story again.

But which one? That which diverts the mind
is poetry. Says, you know those planes

that hit those buildings? Asks, why do birds sing?
When the storm ends, she stops, holds her hands

together, closes her eyes. What are you doing?
I'm praying for the dead worms. Says, listen:

MỘNG-LAN, writer, former Stegner Fellow at Stanford University, Fulbright Scholar, has published six books of poetry and artwork and two chapbooks, and has won prizes such as the Juniper Prize, the Pushcart Prize, and the Great Lakes Colleges Association's New Writers Awards, among others. Frequently anthologized, including in *Best American Poetry Anthology*, she has finished a novel, with an excerpt in the *North American Review*. A former college professor with an MFA in creative writing from the University of Arizona, she left her native Vietnam on the last day of the evacuation of Saigon. Also a musician, composer, visual artist, and dancer, she has released nine albums of jazz piano and tangos, which showcase her poetry. Her new show is "Ocean of Senses: Dream Songs & Tangos: one woman's journey from Sài Gòn to Buenos Aires via America."

FIELD

Crows land like horses' neighs
rush of rocks

how many buffaloes
does it take to plow a disaster?
how many women to clean
up the mess?

shoots of incense
hotly in her hands

she bows towards the tombstones
face of her son
how many revolutions for us to realize?

her windless grey hair
becomes her   she knows this
there is no reason
to dye what she's earned

rain quiet as wings
on her back

A NEW VIỆT NAM

I

sweat of bolts & nails
muscle like steel & metal

architects' work at a ripping pitch
pounding out a new capitol

around the lakes
morning to evening   the ground explodes
liquid concrete
mercury ambling down streets

you think you are the noise

men pick at French-laid concrete like crows

shovels and picks at shoulders
they stand   knees in earth

                              pain trots down the street

how life would've been　　more than noise

                    how events should've happened

2

　Huế—what do you make of chance
                    life's but a dollar a day

                    what should you say when a person
dies each day in the Demilitarized Zone　　scrounging for scrap metal
shrapnel　unexploded
                    bullets & bombs on trays like shrimp
        before tourists?

the hills　　now there　　now disappearing
        white claws stream down　　from dumped chemicals
                              a fun house of horror

still after decades the Khe Sanh Combat Base
            is nearly flat; the Hồ Chí Minh trail winds
thirty minutes to Laos, & National Highway 1 threading
            the country in one

is it chance that the Huế dialect is a giddy
                              fish never to be hooked?

the language is imagined by the land's vapors
                fluctuating hills
                    the mirage of white sand

by dreams of the brood
                of cows walking through white mountains

     a woman fries her smoky meal
                       next to a moon crater

3

      honey-moon light swoops over the valleys
                           upon the Dà Lạt mountains
                   like squadrons

a man buys two bunches of bananas in half a second
      I linger   & face the remark
                    of the vendor   *"chúi nào cũng như vậy hết*
                  cỏ hiền quá   *đi vào buôn bán đi"*
("the bananas are all the same   you're too naive   go into business")

I pass the Nuclear Research Center
                        prop from an old movie
          on a deserted mountain

    toward the Domaine de Marie Convent   a pink
church   "once house to 300 nuns"   someone waves

   then past the cemetery   a mountain of crosses
                       which doesn't stop rising

JUAN J. MORALES is the author of *The Siren World* and *Friday and the Year That Followed*. He is a CantoMundo Fellow, the Editor of *Pilgrimage Magazine*, and an Associate Professor of English at Colorado State University—Pueblo. He is the son of an Ecuadorian mother and Puerto Rican father, who spent 31 years in the US Military. His father is a two-time Purple Heart recipient who served in the Korean Conflict and completed two tours during the Vietnam Conflict. Morales writes to preserve the conflicted perspective on the soldier's experience and its mixture of sacrifice, opportunity, and the lasting impact of PTSD on his father and family.

THE CLOVERLEAF

The day Pop gets shot, he follows every order and procedure. He repeats prayers, reads letters from home twice, cleans his gun. His lieutenant tells him to use the Cloverleaf with five men to sweep the next mile, to move the unit up. They stem up, make three-circled sweeps. Pop counts steps, ending one leaf at the start of the next. Then, on their last loop, automatic fire traps them, echoes in their helmets, a sound hot as splintered tree bark. They take cover near the hole the V.C. stops digging when he hears Pop's patrol.

Bullets rip through air and leaves. Pop doesn't see his wound until the radioman points to where bullet cleaves past ligaments, bone, and slides through his shoulder. The tiny slit drips until his sleeve soaks dark green. *Bullshit*, he yells, shooting on an emptied clip. They regroup after Kennedy flanks the V.C. Even Pop shakes his head and looks away when Kennedy cusses at the corpse. When they withdraw, Pop leans on McDaniels.

At base camp, pain scrapes into Pop's thoughts. Violet smoke swirls then fizzles upward with the voices lost in the propellers. A medic lays him on the gurney, bandages him up. When the helicopter takes off, McDaniels and the big black man, whose name Pop forgets, waves. Before

he loses them behind the tree line, Pop watches both relax, light ciga-
rettes, and study the grass folded under their boots. He wonders if they'll
be alive when he comes back. The helicopter is cold. He ignores the land-
scape, the lucky gash beginning to scar his shoulder.

PHOBIAS

You rub your hands together and shiver when you tell me the story.
In Panama, every soldier in your unit builds rafts out of branches,
weaves of grass, and ponchos. One at a time,

everyone moves across the Chagres. Your raft, near the center
of the murky current, unravels. Under your breath and river's grinding,
you feel something like leeches seep into your clothing

and fill your boots. The young soldier, you call him strong swimmer,
tucks the damp rope in his mouth to drag you
and the remaining bits of raft. Seeing through waves

lapping in my eyes, I imagine myself hearing the silence
then rush of the Chagres, and the kicking ache of my legs struggling
to float. My arms extend, then spear us forward. I know you cannot
    swim,

but the way you tell the story, of how you nearly drowned
without getting your hair wet, makes me taste river froth
spitting down my chin, and see the bank becoming bigger and bigger.

After the river devours your hat, the rope braids
into itself and jerks in your hands. You close your eyes
to feel him kick his legs through the current.

JOHN MURILLO is the author of the poetry collection *Up Jump the Boogie*, finalist for both the Kate Tufts Discovery Award and the Pen Open Book Award. His honors include the J. Howard and Barbara M. J. Wood Prize from the Poetry Foundation, a Pushcart Prize, and fellowships from the National Endowment for the Arts, the *New York Times*, Bread Loaf Writers Conference, Fine Arts Work Center in Provincetown, Cave Canem Foundation, and the Wisconsin Institute for Creative Writing. He has taught in the creative writing programs at Cornell University, the University of Miami, Columbia College Chicago, and currently teaches at Hampshire College and New York University.

TROUBLE MAN

It's the bone of a question
      Caught in your throat,
Pre-dawn sighs of the day's
      First traffic, shoulders like
Fists under your skin. Say
      it's raining this morning,
You've just left a woman's
      Blue musk and duvet,
To find devil knows what
      In the world, your wet collar,
Too thin jacket, no match
      For pissed off sky gods,
And say this car pulls near,
      Plastic bag for passenger
Side window, trading rain
      For music. Marvin Gaye.
And maybe you know
      This song. How long
Since a man you called father
      Troubled the hi-fi, smoldering
Newport in hand, and ran
      This record under a needle.
How long since a man's

Broken falsetto colored
Every hour indigo. Years
        Since he drifted, dreaming
Into rice fields, stammered
        Cracked Vietcong, gunboats
And helicopters swirling
        In his head. Years since
His own long walks, silent
        Returns, and Marvin's
Many voices his only salve.
        He came up harder than
You know, your father.
        Didn't make it by the rules.
You father came up hard,
        Didn't get to make no rules.
Graying beard, callused hands,
        Fingernails thick as nickels,
You were the boy who became
        That man, without meaning
To, and know: A man's
        Life is never measured
In beats, but beat-downs,
        Not line breaks, just breaks.
You hear Marvin fade down
        The avenue and it caresses you
Like a brick: You father,
        Marvin, and men like them,
Have already moaned every
        Book you will ever write.
This you know, baby. This
        You know.

NGÔ TỰ LẬP, son of a People's Army colonel, was born in 1962 in Hanoi and spent his childhood in the countryside during the Vietnam War. He has published three collections of poetry, five books of fiction, six books of essays, and many translations from Russian, French, and English. He has won seven prizes for his writing, which has been translated into English, French, German, Swedish, Czech, and Thai. He is currently director of the International Francophone Institute (Hanoi). His book *Black Stars* (translated by Martha Collins and the author) was nominated for the PEN International Award in 2014.

MARTHA COLLINS (Translator) is the author of eight books of poetry, most recently *Admit One: An American Scrapbook* (2016), *Day Unto Day* (2014), *White Papers* (2012), and the book-length poem *Blue Front* (2006), which won an Anisfield-Wolf Award. A protestor during the Vietnam War, Collins has also co-translated four collections of poems from the Vietnamese, including *The Women Carry River Water* by Nguyen Quang Thieu (1997, with the author), *Green Rice* by Lam Thi My Da (2005, with Thuy Dinh), and *Black Stars* by Ngo Tu Lap (2013, with the author).

WOMEN FROM THE 1960s (I)

The first women I ever saw
Were huge and dark, with warm breasts
And tired eyes like sad stars

While I played with a snail
In a bomb shelter flooded with rain
The women disappeared without a sound

Thirty years later I still see them
Millions of breasts cut from suffering bodies
Fallen to earth like young coconuts
Full with milk even in the grave

Thirty years later they still come back
To prepare the alluvial fields for corn
Their tears falling like crystals

A woman crouches behind the fence
Old, dried like a dead acacia
A woman from the 1960s
Who knows things half of us never will know
        —Translated from the Vietnamese by Martha Collins
          and the author

A BULLET FIRED INTO THE NIGHT

Like a falling leaf in a dream
Or an arm in a dream, dangling
A night flight, with eyes wide open

A June night, an astonished look
No one sees the vanished smile
The soldier's dark face above the barrel
No one fears the barrel now—
An eel sniffing the mud

In a garden, banana leaves still catch dew
A nest of storks sleeps soundly on tall bamboo
Only an ancient bat startles

In a closed house, a mother turns up her lamp
Not knowing she will be lonelier now
And a girl will sorrow in secret

No one knows: the soldier was once a man
All summer long, crows will convene
In a row of bright green trees
        —Translated from the Vietnamese by Martha Collins
          and the author

BICH MINH NGUYEN was born in Saigon in 1974. When she was eight months old her family fled the fall of Saigon, eventually settling in Grand Rapids, Michigan. She received an MFA in creative writing from the University of Michigan and currently teaches creative nonfiction and fiction at the University of San Francisco, where she directs the MFA in Writing Program. She is the author of three books: *Stealing Buddha's Dinner* (2007), which received the PEN/Jerard Fund Award from the PEN American Center; *Short Girls*, which received an American Book Award; and *Pioneer Girl* (2014). She and her family live in the Bay Area.

THE GOOD IMMIGRANT STUDENT

My stepmother, Rosa, who began dating my father when I was three years old, says that my sister and I used to watch *Police Woman* and rapturously repeat everything Angie Dickinson said. But when the show was over Anh and I would resume our Vietnamese, whispering together, giggling in accents. Rosa worried about this. She had the idea that she could teach us English and we could teach her Vietnamese. She would make us lunch or give us baths, speaking slowly and asking us how to say *water*, or *rice*, or *house*.

After she and my father married, Rosa swept us out of our falling-down house and into the middle-class suburban Grand Rapids, Michigan. Our neighborhood surrounded Ken-O-Sha Elementary School and Plaster Creek, and was only a short drive away from the original Meijer's Thrifty Acres. In the early 1980s, this neighborhood of mismatching street names—Poinsettia, Van Auken, Senora, Ravanna—was home to families of Dutch heritage, and everyone was Christian Reformed, and conservative Republican. Except us. Even if my father hadn't left his rusted-through silver Mustang, the first car he ever owned, to languish in the driveway for months we would have stuck out simply because we weren't white. There was my Latina stepmother and her daughter, Cristina, my father, sister, grandmother, and I, refugees from Saigon; and my half-brother born a year after we moved to the house on Ravanna Street.

Although my family lived two blocks from Ken-O-Sha, my step-mother enrolled me and Anh at Sherwood Elementary, a bus ride away, because Sherwood had a bilingual education program. Rosa, who had a master's in education and taught ESL and community ed in the public school system, was a big supporter of bilingual education. School mornings, Anh and I would be at the bus stop at the corner of our street quite early, hustled out of the house by our grandmother who constantly feared we would miss our chance. I went off to first grade, Anh to second. At ten o'clock, we crept out of our classes, drawing glances and whispers from the other students, and convened with a group of Vietnamese kids from other grades to learn English. The teachers were Mr. Ho, who wore a lot of short-sleeved button-down shirts in neutral hues, and Miss Huong, who favored a maroon blouse with puffy shoulders and slight ruffles at the high neck and wrists, paired with a tweed skirt that hung heavily to her ankles. They passed out photocopied booklets of Vietnamese phrases and their English translations, with themes such as "In the Grocery Store." They asked us to repeat slowly after them and took turns coming around to each of us, bending close to hear our pronunciations.

Anh and I exchanged a lot of worried glances, for we had a secret that we were quite embarrassed about: we already knew English. It was the Vietnamese part that gave us trouble. When Mr. Ho and Miss Huong gave instructions, or passed out homework assignments, they did so in Vietnamese. Anh and I received praise for our English, but were reprimanded for failing to complete our assignments and failing to pay attention. After a couple of weeks of this Anh announced to Rosa that we didn't need bilingual education. Nonsense, she said. Our father just shrugged his shoulders. After that, Anh began skipping bilingual classes, urging me to do the same, and then we never went back. What was amazing was that no one, not Mrs. Eunice, my first grade teacher, or Mrs. Hankins, Anh's teacher, or even Mr. Ho or Miss Huong said anything directly to us about it. Or if they did, I have forgotten it entirely. Then one day my parents got a call from Miss Huong. When Rosa came to talk to me and Anh about it we were watching television the way kids do, sitting alarmingly close to the screen. Rosa confronted us with "Do you girls know English?" Then she suddenly said, "Do you know Vietnamese?" I can't remember what we replied to either question.

For many years, a towering old billboard over the expressway downtown proudly declared Grand Rapids "An All-American City." For me, that all-American designation meant all-white. I couldn't believe (and still don't) that they meant to include the growing Mexican-American population, or the sudden influx of Vietnamese refugees in 1975. I often thought it a rather mean-spirited prank of some administrator at the INS, deciding with a flourish of a signature to send a thousand refugees to Grand Rapids, a city that boasted having more churches per square mile than any other city in the United States. Did that administrator know what Grand Rapids was like? That in school, everywhere I turned, and often when I closed my eyes, I saw blond blond blond? The point of bilingual education was assimilation. To my stepmother, the point was preservation: she didn't want English to take over wholly, pushing the Vietnamese out of our heads. She was too ambitious. Anh and I were Americanized as soon as we turned on the television. Today, bilingual education is supposed to have become both a method of assimilation and a method of preservation, an effort to prove that kids can have it both ways. They can supposedly keep English for school and their friends and keep another language for home and family.

In Grand Rapids, Michigan, in the 1980s, I found that an impossible task.

I transferred to Ken-O-Sha Elementary in time for third grade, after Rosa finally admitted that taking the bus all the way to Sherwood was pointless. I was glad to transfer, eager to be part of a class that wasn't in my mind, tainted with knowledge of my bilingual stigma. Third grade was led by Mrs. Alexander, an imperious, middle-aged woman of many plaid skirts held safe by giant gold safety pins. She had a habit of turning her wedding ring around and around her finger while she stood at the chalkboard. Mrs. Alexander had an intricate system of rewards for good grades and good behavior, denoted by colored star stickers on a piece of poster board that loomed over us all. One glance and you could see who was behind, who was striding ahead.

I was an insufferably good student, with perfect Palmer cursive and the highest possible scores in every subject. I had learned this trick at Sherwood. That the quieter you are, the shyer and sweeter and better-at-school you are, the more the teacher will let you alone. Mrs. Alexander should have left me alone. For, in addition to my excellent marks, I was nearly silent, deadly shy, and wholly obedient. My greatest fear was being called on, or in any way standing out more than I already did in the class that was, except for me and one black student, dough-white. I got good grades because I feared the authority of the teacher; I felt that getting in good with Mrs. Alexander would protect me, that she would protect me from the frightful rest of the world. But Mrs. Alexander was not agreeable to this notion. If it was my turn to read aloud during reading circle, she'd interrupt me to snap, "You're reading too fast" or demand, "What does that word mean?" Things she did not do to the other students. Anh, when I told her about this, suggested that perhaps Mrs. Alexander liked me and wanted to help me get smarter. But neither of us believed it. You know when a teacher likes you and when she doesn't.

Secretly I admired and envied the rebellious kids, like Robbie Andrews who came to school looking bleary-eyed and pinched, like a hungover adult; Robbie and his ilk snapped back at teachers, were routinely sent to the principal's office, were even spanked a few times with the principal's infamous red paddle (apparently no one in Grand Rapids objected to corporal punishment). Those kids made noise, possessed something I thought was confidence, self-knowledge, allowing them to marvelously question everything ordered of them. They had the ability to challenge the given world.

Toward the middle of the third grade Mrs. Alexander introduced a stuffed lion to the pool of rewards: the best student of the week would earn the privilege of having the lion sit on his or her desk for the entire week. My quantity of gold stars was neck and neck with that of my two competitors, Brenda and Jennifer, both sweet-eyed blond girls with pastel-colored monogrammed sweaters and neatly tied Dock-Sides. My family did not have a lot of money and my stepmother had terrible taste. Thus I attended school in such ensembles as dark red parachute pants and a nubby pink sweater stitched with a picture of a unicorn rearing up. This only propelled me to try harder to be good, to make up for everything I felt was against me: my odd family, my race, my very face. And I craved that stuffed lion. Week after week, the lion perched on Brenda's desk or Jennifer's desk. Meanwhile, the class spelling bee approached. I didn't know I was such a good speller until I won it, earning a scalloped-edged certificate and a candy bar. That afternoon I started toward home, then remembered I'd forgotten my rain boots in my locker. I doubled back to school and overheard Mrs. Alexander in the classroom talking to another teacher. "Can you believe it?" Mrs. Alexander was saying. "A foreigner winning our spelling bee!"

I waited for the stuffed lion the rest of that year, with a kind of patience I have no patience for today. To no avail. In June, on the last day of school, Mrs. Alexander gave the stuffed lion to Brenda to keep forever.

The first time I had to read aloud something I had written—perhaps it was in fourth grade—I felt such terror, such a need not to have any attention upon me, that I convinced myself that I had become invisible, that the teacher could never call on me because she couldn't see me.

More than once, I was given the assignment of writing a report about my family history. I loathed this task, for I was dreadfully aware that my history could not be faked; it already showed on my face. When my turn came to read out loud the teacher had to ask me several times to speak louder. Some kids, a few of them older, in different classes, took to pressing back the corners of their eyes with the heels of their palms while they chanted, "Ching-chong, ching-chong!" during recess. (This continued until Anh, who was far tougher than me, threatened to beat them up.)

I have no way of telling what tortured me more: the actual snickers and remarks and watchfulness of my classmates, or my own imagination, conjuring disdain. My own sense of shame. At times I felt sickened by my obedience, my accumulation of gold stickers, my every effort to be invisible.

Yet Robbie Andrews must have felt the same kind of claustrophobia, trapped in his own reputation, in his ability to be otherwise. I learned in school that changing oneself is not easy, that the world makes up its mind quickly.

I've heard that Robbie dropped out of high school, got a girl pregnant, found himself in and out of first juvenile detention, then jail.

What comes out of difference? What constitutes difference? Such questions, academic and unanswered, popped up in every other course description in college. But the idea of difference is easy to come by, especially in school; it is shame, the permutations and inversions of difference and self-loathing, that we should be worrying about.

Imagined torment, imagined scorn. When what is imagined and what is desired turn on each other.

Some kids want to rebel; other kids want to disappear. I wanted to disappear. I was not brave enough to shrug my shoulders and flaunt my difference; because I could not disappear into the crowd, I wished to disappear entirely. Anyone might have mistaken this for passivity.

Once, at the end of my career at Sherwood Elementary, I disappeared on the bus home. Mine was usually the third stop, but that day the bus driver thought I wasn't there, and she sailed right by the corner of Ravanna and Senora. I said nothing. The bus wove its way downtown, and for the first time I got to see where other children lived, some of them in clean orderly neighborhoods, some near houses with sagging porches and boarded-up windows. All the while, the kid sitting across the aisle from me played the same cheerful song over and over on his portable boom box. *Pass the doochee from the left hand side, pass the doochee from the left hand side.* He and his brother turned out to be the last kids off the bus. Then the bus driver saw me through the rearview mirror. She walked back to where I was sitting and said, "How come you didn't get off at your stop?" I shook my head, I don't know. She sighed and drove me home.

I was often doing that, shaking my head silently or staring up wordlessly. I realize that while I remember so much of what other people said when I was a child, I remember little of what I said. Probably because I didn't say much at all.

I recently came across in the stacks of the University of Michigan library *A Manual for Indochinese Refugee Education 1976–1977.* Some of it is silly, but much of it is a painstaking, fairly thoughtful effort to let school administrators and teachers know how to go about sensitively handling the influx of Vietnamese children in the public schools. Here is one of the most wonderful items of advice: "The Vietnamese child, even the older child, is also reported to be afraid of the dark, and more often than not, believes in ghosts. A teacher may have to be a little more solicitous of the child on gloomy, wintery days." Perhaps if Mrs. Alexander had read this, she would not have upbraided me so often for tracking mud into the classroom on rainy days. In third grade I was horrified and ashamed of my muddy shoes. I hung back, trying to duck behind this or that dark-haired boy. In spite of this, in spite of bilingual education, and shyness, and all that wordless shaking of my head, I was sent off every Monday to the Spectrum School for the Gifted and Talented. I still have no idea who selected me, who singled me out. Spectrum was (and still is) a public school program that invited students from every public elementary school to meet once a week and take specialized classes on topics such as Middle Ages, Ellis Island, and fairy tales. Each student chose two classes, a major and minor, and for the rest of the semester worked toward final projects in both. I loved going to Spectrum. Not only did the range of students from other schools prove to be diverse, I found myself feeling more comfortable, mainly because Spectrum encouraged individual work. And the teachers seemed happy to be there. The best teacher at Spectrum was Mrs. King, whom every student adored. I still remember the soft gray sweaters she wore, her big wavy hair, her art-class handwriting, the way she'd often tell us to close our eyes when she read us a particular story or passage.

I believe that I figured out how to stop disappearing, how to talk and answer, even speak up, after several years in Spectrum. I was still deeply self-conscious, but I became able, sometimes, to maneuver around it.

S pectrum may have spoiled me a little, because it made me think about college and freedom, and thus made all the years in between disappointing and annoying.

In seventh grade I joined Anh and Cristina at the City School, a seventh through twelfth grade public school in the Grand Rapids system that served as an early charter school; admission was by interview, and each grade had about fifty students. The City School had the advantage of being downtown, perched over old cobblestone roads, and close to the main public library. Art and music history were required. There were no sports teams. And volunteering was mandatory. But kids didn't tend to stay at City School; as they got older they transferred to one of the big high schools nearby, perhaps wishing to play sports, perhaps wishing to get away from City's rather brutal academic system. Each half-semester, after grades were doled out, giant dot-matrix printouts of everyone's GPAs were posted in the hallways.

I didn't stay at City, either. When my family moved to a different suburb, my stepmother promptly transferred me to Forest Hills Northern High School. Most of the students there came from upper-middle-class or very well-to-do families; the ones who didn't stood out sharply. The rich kids were the same as they were anywhere in America: they wore a lot of Esprit and Guess, drove nice cars, and ran student council, prom, and sports. These kids strutted down the hallways; the boys sat in a row on the long windowsill near a group of lockers, whistling or calling out to girls who walked by. Girls gathered in bathrooms with their Clinique lipsticks.

High school was the least interesting part of my education, but I did accomplish something: I learned to forget myself a little. I learned the sweetness of apathy. And through apathy, how to forget my skin and body for a minute or two, almost not caring what would happen if I walked into a room late and all heads swiveled toward me. I learned the pleasure that reveals itself in the loss, no matter how slight, of self-consciousness. These things occurred because I remained the good immigrant student, without raising my hand often or showing off what I knew. Doing work was rote, and I went along to get along. I've never gotten over the terror of being called on in class, or the dread in knowing that I'm expected to contribute to class discussion. But there is a slippage between being good and being unnoticed, and in that sliver of freedom I learned what it could feel like to walk in the world in plain, unself-conscious view.

I would like to make a broad, accurate statement about immigrant children in schools. I would like to speak for them (us). I hesitate; I cannot. My own sister, for instance, was never as shy as I was. Anh disliked school from the start, choosing rebellion rather than silence. It was a good arrangement: I wrote papers for her and she paid me in money or candy; she gave me rides to school if I promised not to tell anyone about her cigarettes. Still, I think of an Indian friend of mine who told of an elementary school experience in which a blond schoolchild told the teacher, "I can't sit by her. My mom said I can't sit by anyone who's brown." And another friend, whose family immigrated around the same time mine did, whose second grade teacher used her as a vocabulary example: "Children, this is what a *foreigner* is." And sometimes I fall into thinking that kids today have the advantage of so much more wisdom, that they are so much more socially and politically aware than anyone was when I was in school. But I am wrong, of course. I know not every kid is fortunate enough to have a teacher like Mrs. King, or a program like Spectrum, or even the benefit of a manual written by a group of concerned educators; I know that some kids want to disappear and disappear until they actually do. Sometimes I think I see them, in the blurry background of a magazine photo, or in a gaggle of kids following a teacher's aide across the street. The kids with heads bent down, holding themselves in such a way that they seem to be self-conscious even of how they breathe. Small, shy, quiet kids, such good, good kids, *immigrant, foreigner,* their eyes watchful and waiting for whatever judgment will occur. I reassure myself that they will grow up fine, they will be okay. Maybe I cross the same street, then another, glancing back once in a while to see where they are going.

HOA NGUYEN was born in the Mekong Delta and raised in the Washington, DC, area. She studied Poetics at New College of California in San Francisco. Author of four full-length books of poetry, her titles include *As Long As Trees Last* and *Red Juice, Poems 1998–2008*. In the fall of 2016, Publishers Weekly selected her book *Violet Energy Ingots* as one of the top 10 poetry books published in the fall of 2016. Nguyen teaches at Ryerson University, for Miami University's low residency MFA program, for Bard College the Milton Avery School for Fine Arts, and in a long-running, private poetics workshop.

AGENT ORANGE POEM
after Emily Dickinson

What justice foreigns for a sovereign
We doom in nation rooms

Recommend & lend   resembling fragrant
Chinaberry spring

Here we have high flowers⠀⠀a lilac in the nose
"The Zeroes—taught us—Phosphorus"

and so stripped⠀⠀the leaves⠀⠀to none

INDEPENDENCE DAY 2010

Can be cracked or am that⠀⠀⠀⠀you didn't
consider me or I thought so
recovering in a nap⠀⠀⠀⠀You took the 4th
of July beers

⠀⠀In the movie
she was Asian and playing an Asian
part⠀⠀singing white on white in the white
room

⠀⠀⠀⠀I want to strum
or mask this day

⠀⠀Ask a question
of the large "picture" window
like why and why and also why
to think of the napalmed girl
in the picture

HIEU MINH NGUYEN is the author of *This Way to the Sugar* (Write Bloody Press, 2014). Hieu has received grants and fellowships from Kundiman, the Vermont Studio Center, and the Loft Literary Center. He is a poetry editor for *Muzzle Magazine* and an MFA candidate at Warren Wilson College. His work has appeared or is forthcoming in *Poetry Magazine*, *BuzzFeed*, *Guernica*, *Gulf Coast*, *Ninth Letter*, and elsewhere. His second collection of poetry, *Not Here*, is forthcoming from Coffee House Press in 2018. His work explores the intersectional identities that come with being a queer child of Vietnamese refugees.

BUFFET ETIQUETTE

My mother and I don't have dinner table conversations
out of courtesy. We don't want to remind each other
of our accents. Her voice, a Vietnamese lullaby
sung to an empty bed. The taste of her hometown
kicking on the back of her teeth.

My voice is bleach. My voice has no history.
My voice is the ringing of an empty picture frame.

       :::
I am forgetting how to say the simple things
to my mother. The words that linger in my periphery.
The words, a rear view mirror dangling from the wires.
I am only fluent in apologies.

       :::
Sometimes when I watch home movies,
I don't even understand myself. My childhood
is a foreign film. All of my memories
have been dubbed in English.

       :::
My mother's favorite television shows are all '90s sitcoms.
The ones with laugh tracks. The prerecorded emotion
that cues her when to smile.

::::

In the first grade I mastered my own tongue. I cleaned
my speech, and during parent teacher conferences
Mrs. Turner was surprised my mother was Asian.
She just assumed I was adopted. She assumed
that this voice was the same one I started with.

::::

As she holds a pair of chopsticks, a friend asks me
why I am using a fork. I tell her *it's much easier.*
Her voice, the same octave as my grandmother's,
she says *but this is so much cooler.*

::::

I am just the clip-art. The poster boy of whitewash. My skin
has been burning easier these days. My voice box is shrinking.
I have rinsed it out too many times.

::::

My house is a silent film.
My house is infested with subtitles.

::::

That's all. That's all.
I have nothing else to say.

COCKFIGHT

I met my brother once
in a small village in Vietnam
who, upon meeting me
grabbed my small arm
& dragged me into the woods
behind his house
where a group of men
all wearing our father's face

stood in a circle, cheering
while the two roosters
whose beaks had barbed hooks
taped to them, pecked
& clawed each other open
until the mess of bloodied feathers
were replaced by two clean birds
one, my brother's. The other
a man's, who I am told is deaf
but vicious. He told me
our father calls him long distance
from America, every week.
I can't help but wonder how
they tell the roosters apart
since the blood has turned their feathers
the same shade of burgundy.
I told him how our father, who lives
only three miles away from me
avoids making eye-contact at supermarkets.
I can tell this made him happy.
Though, he didn't cheer
when the crowd cheered, when one rooster
fell to the dirt with a gash in its neck.
I knew he was the winner
when he lowered his head to hide
his smile, how he looked at me
then snatched his earnings
from the vicious man's hands.
I learned what it was like to be a brother
by watching the roosters
& how, at first, the air was calm
until they were introduced
& then they knew:
there could only be one.

TATER TOT HOT-DISH

The year my family discovered finger food
recipes, they replaced the roast duck with a turkey,
the rice became a platter of cheese and crackers,
none of us complained. We all hated the way the fish
sauce made our breath smell. When the women
started lightening their hair, we blamed it on the sun.
When Emily showed up with blonde highlights
and an ivory boyfriend, we all started talking
about mixed babies. Overjoyed with the possibility
of blue eyes in the family photo. That year
I started misspelling my last name, started reshaping
myself to have a more phonetic face. Vietnam
became a place our family pitied, a thirsty rat
with hair too dark and a scowl too thick.
We stopped going to temple and found ourselves
a church. That year my mother closed her eyes
and bowed her head to prayers she couldn't understand.

PHONG NGUYEN is the author of the novel *The Adventures of Joe Harper* and two short fiction collections. He is also the son of Hien Nguyen, whose mother and brother were killed in a French air raid during occupation, and whose father was interrogated by the communists during the war. He grew up in a household that appreciated how Vietnam is so much more than its history of conflict, but a household that was also deeply affected by that history.

THE WHEEL OF HISTORY

The wheel of history will run you over.

—Khmer Rouge slogan

MAP

History begins at 2:10 p.m. The chairs are attached to their desks, arranged in jagged rows from a full day's use. The walls are blocks of peach stucco, and a lone poster in the corner half-heartedly asks its viewers to "Make a Difference."

It is the third month of eighth grade, and I want to step outside of my metal-cage seat and crouch on the floor. When you sit on one of these bone-hard chairs of indeterminate material, it presses back with such force that it leaves marks on the flesh. I am used to wearing down my knees picking beans and the dull ache of a stooping back. But eight hours of sitting leaves my elbows and ass cheeks red and sore. Eventually, I will become used to it, and sitting will be as natural as walking.

When my friend Jason stands up to use the bathroom, the legs of his desk-chair jerk back, making a scraping sound against the tile floor. Jason and I hold spitting contests, and he challenges me to a race nearly every day. Even his loud standing is like throwing a stone. He seems to be saying, *Now it's your turn.*

Hanging out at his place after school, we have been known to wrestle until the first nosebleed, to out-lie each other with stories of our imagined sexual exploits, and to enter into spontaneous chip-eating contests. We've grown fat on each other's company.

During the revolution, I was just a chubby kid on the side of the road as the army passed. I was strangely unfrightened by their blood-red headbands. Their loose black clothes. Their bayoneted rifles.

"Do you speak French?" they said, their eyes like spear-points.

"No," I said. At five, I barely even spoke Khmer.

"That's good, that's good. Everything we've ever had was stolen from us by the French, then sold back to us. The colonials are responsible for all our troubles, Comrade. Don't you agree?"

I agreed. I must have agreed, because I lived.

They gave me a wet cigarette, and promised to be back someday to make me a soldier.

After they passed, looking back at the place they were leaving, I saw what appeared to be a bonfire. The wooden stakes our neighbors used to hold up the sheets when they bathed were now skewers for the dead.

In History class, when we finish watching a documentary on the Vietnam War, Mrs. Lee starts directing her questions at me. I know hardly anything about the American Presidents, and nothing at all about the anti-war movement. "Why do you think Johnson escalated the war, even though there was no clear path to success? . . . Map?"

"I think, maybe, Johnson was a hard-working man. He was like a coffin-maker," I say.

"A coffin-maker?" says Mrs. Lee, skeptically.

When put under a spotlight, I tend to ramble. "He cannot think too hard about what he's making, or else he will stop. But if he stops, it does not keep the armies from making more dead."

"OK . . ." Mrs. Lee says. "Anyone else?"

I used to say "I don't understand," if I didn't want to speak up in class. But Jason knows my English is good, and he would call me out on it. That's the way we are: best friends who tell on each other.

"Yeah, my dad fought in 'Nam and he says we could have won if we just kept on fighting," Jason says. "It was the Americans at home who wussed out."

"OK . . ." Mrs. Lee says. "And what would winning mean, in that case?"

"Defeating the enemy," Jason says, with enviable simplicity. "Beating them."

———

The old man said, "Go away!" It was just something the old man said. He had said it to kids around the neighborhood a hundred thousand times. If they buzzed around him like flies, he tolerated them like flies. If they skimmed too close to his ear, he waved his arms and shouted again in impotent rage: "Go away!"

But when they heard the old man shout, "go away," these Khmer Rouge kids in their war-costumes stung like wasps. They seized him by the arms and dragged him into the market, where among the bitter melon and durian, he was clubbed with rifle butts and kicked by twelve little feet, shod in sandals cut from old tire.

So the children beat the man. I cannot express what a strange feeling it provoked in me. I had seen a man beating a child before. But never had I seen a child beating a man. With every strike, the earth seemed to wobble on its axis until the tilt of the earth was changed. The horizon was horribly askew; the vegetable carts seemed to roll themselves.

While the thrashing continued, one tall boy with a cracked voice stood facing the gathering crowd with his hands held behind his back, his shoulders straight and his chin raised at attention. "This man is an enemy of Khmer and has been involved with numerous Western plots against Angkar. Do not feel sympathy for him. Do not defend him. He is a prisoner." The word he used, *neok theos*, meant both "prisoner" and "guilty person."

"What is his name?" asked one woman, full with child, sweating in the heat, a basket on her hip.

For a moment, the soldier looked almost friendly, then quickly resumed the mask-like expression of his office. "Don't concern yourself with who he is. Go home and take care of your children. They are the future of Khmer, and they are Angkar's children too."

And the crowd immediately fell to crumbs like stale bread, going their separate ways as though scattered by the wind. I kept on staring at the old man on the floor; I could not help it. One soldier pointed his automatic rifle at the prisoner.

"No! Foolish!" the tall boy said. "Use the bayonet. Ammunition is precious."

———

During break, Mrs. Lee says, "Is there anything you miss about Cambodia?"

The only thing I can think of is the early-morning-time, when we all sat under the window and talked about our dreams. But that ritual had ended with the revolution.

"Why did you and your family stop talking about your dreams?" she asks.

How to explain? "The *chhlop* would listen outside the window, and with dreams, you cannot control them. Talking about them, you could say the wrong things."

"What are the wrong things?" she says, genuinely curious.

Teacher, how can I explain? Saying "What are the wrong things?" could mean the end of you.

But I am not the only one who has stopped talking about dreams. Dreams in America are like secrets that are kept; it is as though they never happened at all. The only time I even hear the word is when, in history class, they play a video of Dr. Martin Luther King standing on the steps of the Lincoln Memorial.

Other times, the word "dream" means something that will never come to pass. "You think that Lindsay Bradner even knows who you are? You're dreaming," Jason says after break, while Mrs. Lee writes a series of dates on the board.

"I *know* she knows who I am," I say. "She's my tutor."

Jason's eyes light up like flares. "You lucky fuck." He looks genuinely impressed, as though I had done something of my own merit. "If I forget how to speak English, do you think I could get a hot girl to tutor me?"

"It's not . . . we're not going out. I'm just saying, she has a good spirit. I am happy when I am with her. That's all," I say, warmed by the thought of her.

Jason smiles with half of his face. "Sure, I get you," he says, nodding.

"You want to make babies with her." He pauses, struck by inspiration. "Lindsay. Bradner. . . . You want to bet to see who gets there first?"

———

Dream #1: My American mother has given birth to a giant baby. It grows, every moment it grows, but I cannot tell her how horrible it is, I cannot tell anyone. It is forbidden to say anything about his inhuman proportions. It eats not with its mouth, but with its navel. The baby's mouth is for crying only.

It never leaves the house, so food must be brought to it. When I bring meat, it tears the flesh and bone out of my hands and shoves it directly into the stomach. If I bring carrots, it chews them into little orange pieces, then throws them up on the floor. I stare at it, and it stares back at me, not with anger, but with stone-faced judgment.

If I fail to bring it food, what will happen then?

If it grows any bigger, how will the house remain standing?

———

I don't know if I remember this part correctly. We were all in bed. The man showed up alone, and he shouted before knocking on the door, "Comrade Heng!" Even though he announced himself with such authority, we were still surprised to see he was actually an officer. If it had been the *chhlop*, another group of Khmer Rouge kids, at least we would know what to be afraid of. But the crisp green uniform threw us all off our guard.

"Angkar needs the people's help; our soldiers fight so that your land is not overrun by the enemy. Now you must help Angkar feed the soldiers. Your share is four crates."

My father spoke in whispers, as though someone were sleeping. "Officer Heng, I thank you for this visit, and I will help you in any way I can. But our overseer is called Odom Oum, and we bring our crates to his outpost after every harvest. If you ask him—"

"—I am not here on behalf of the *chhlop*, or Comrade Odom; I am here for Angkar. Four crates, please, for the fighting men of Khmer."

Father looked our way, with shadows all over his face, out of which shone the most hopeless eyes. "We will have to harvest them," he said.

"I will wait," said the officer. He sat in the swinging chair that mother had used to soothe us as babies. He unbuttoned his shirt and lit a cigarette in the dark.

The cicadas ululated over everything, moving the night with the slightest tremble. As I stepped over the grassy dunes into the fields, I secretly prayed that this was the sensation of being shaken awake. Father pointed a flashlight down where our hands scooped and plucked the immature mung beans, then emptied them through our fingers into a canvas sack. "Four crates!" My father said. "Let us please have enough for four crates!"

As I picked, I could not help but glance repeatedly toward the horizon, hoping that with the sunrise would come some kind of salvation. Instead, I saw only the dark silhouette of the thousand-fingered sleng tree, the poison-fruit tree, whose branches stabbed upward and outward and, where it ran up against the concrete wall of a prison, the branches bent back upon themselves and stabbed inward, cutting into its own bark.

When we returned to our own front porch like beggars, dirty-kneed and tired-eyed, the officer stood up from the hammock and frowned down deliberately, performing his displeasure. He was joined now by two *chhlop* who must have been there all along, hiding under the house, among the stilts that kept our home raised for monsoon season.

"Where have you been hiding that flashlight?" he said, gesturing lazily at my father's full hands.

"I haven't been hiding it. I keep it in a special place for emergencies only," my father said.

"No," the officer said, speaking softly, but with one hand resting threateningly on his rifle, "you wanted to have private property, just for yourself."

"I was thinking no such thing," my father said.

The officer continued, as though my father hadn't spoken at all. "So you are stealing from Angkar. It is as Comrade Odom reported."

Rather than speak, Father turned to look at the crates of beans, the faintly lightening sky, and the dirty, hungry children who were his own brood.

"Let Angka Leu decide," the officer said.

Then Father was bound in either rope or cord, he either cried or pled for mercy, and they either marched or dragged him away.

Was I standing there, surrounded by drooping beanstalks, staring down at my frayed and muddy sandals? Did we huddle together in the house, taking turns at the window, praying that we would not be next? I try to remember. I try not to remember. I want to remember. I want to not remember.

———

My brothers claim that poor memory is a blessing. I am the youngest in my American family. Although he is only a year older than I am, Chann is in the eleventh grade, the same as Roth. My brother Sen, who is actually my uncle, is supposed to be writing college-application essays in the guidance counselor's office right now.

Before letting us go, Mrs. Lee asks me to explain the significance of Watergate. I did the reading, but my memory fails me. I know that it led to the disgrace of an American President.

"The President . . . " I begin, "was ashamed of his crimes, and tried to hide them?"

"Yes, and . . . ?" Mrs. Lee prompts me, "what was the effect of it all?"

"When so many people say that a man is a criminal, then he hardens his heart; he becomes a criminal because it is easier than convincing the world that he is not a criminal."

"Did you do the reading, Map?" Mrs. Lee asks.

"Yes," I say, honestly. "But I have trouble with it, and I am distracted."

"OK, Map. I'm not interested in excuses. Do better tomorrow," she says.

I walked to school this morning, as I sometimes do when I become restless waiting for the bus. Passing through the parking lot of a 7-11, I felt something hard in my shoe, and picked it out. It was a quarter. *Oh no, I thought, I've used my good luck on something so small.*

———

Dream #2: I'm walking to school in the early morning—too early, though I do not realize it at first—and everything is strangely quiet. There are birds out, but no other living things, and even the birds are sitting still upon the telephone wire, like the crows' own scarecrows. Then a bus rumbles in the distance until, panicking suddenly, I start to run. A high fence stands to my right, and to my left, home after identical home. And the rumble of the bus goes on.

I run so fast and so far that soon I reach a neighborhood where I've never been. I arrive at a playground, and I seem to be running in place, then floating through space as though upon a moving walkway, inclining gradually upward, a few feet off of the ground.

Here are gathered all the missing people. So *this* is where they hide the dead. Bodies mounted at the bottom of a slide; bodies piled upon a twirl-a-whirl; bodies stacked beneath the monkey bars. The larger the pile of the dead, the bigger are the flies. And the flies, confusing me for the dead, swarm around my own fragile body.

———

"Comrade Odom, please," my mother said, speaking with a tearful whine that I would have thought exaggerated, if I did not know, from my own agitated thoughts, that it was impossible to exaggerate her desperation. "My husband is an innocent man. He cannot be sent to face the Angka Leu."

Odom Oum sat with his hands folded on his desk. The papers laid out in front of him were meticulously arranged. I could not take my eyes away from one particular hand-written document, two inches high, upon which was written, "Activities of Enemies." His handwriting was so neat, so exact. He could have been a monk in ancient times.

"It is better that ten innocent men be thrown in prison than one guilty conspirator goes free," said Odom Oum, reciting yet another party slogan.

"Comrade Odom," my mother persisted. "I knew your father, and I knew you when you were just a naked child, and someday I hope to meet *your* children. When your children learn in school about these times, they will call him a hero who saves the lives of his neighbors."

Odom Oum shook his head with a smile. "In the new state there are no heroes. There are only those who are loyal to Angkar, and counter-revolutionaries like Sangam Chey who conspire against Angkar."

"But he *is* loyal, and *we* are loyal. I am concerned for you, because I know you are a good man, and you do not want to do something you will regret. History is unkind to those who betray their own people." My mother must have known that these were perilous words; but desperation, like any human feeling, could be dangerous in the new state.

"History?" said Odom Oum, showing his teeth like a tiger. Then he took out his pencil and, looking down at the document in front of him, he began writing. "The wheel of history *will run you over*," said Odom Oum.

———

History is over, thank God.

"Why don't you sign up for baseball?" Jason says. "You run good." We are headed to study hall, the last hurdle before the end of the school day, after which Jason will be driven to baseball practice, and I will board the bus home.

"I'm too busy," I say. "I'm behind at school."

"Do you want to arm wrestle?" he says. I do not want to arm wrestle.

We play stick-figure wars instead, taking turns drawing hordes of stick-figure soldiers, cowboys, and flying ninjas, in an ongoing and ever-escalating battle for dominance over one wide-ruled sheet of paper.

After we are done with our war, Jason quickly becomes bored. "Let's play pencil-break," he says, looking at our tragically unused pencils.

But the teacher is watching, daring us to do wrong, until he grows tired of watching, and returns his attention to the document laid out in front of him.

In the *He-Man* cartoon, the villain is a skeleton man who sits on a skeleton throne in a skeleton castle. In *Inspector Gadget*, a claw-handed enemy has a face that you can never see, because you are staring at the back of his chair. The Evil Emperor sits. The hero always stands.

Jason gets up again to run to the bathroom.

———

Dream #3: I am running on a hamster wheel. Then, as I become aware of how unlikely a thing this is, other features start to emerge within the scene, and gradually I find that I am in our family room, watching morning TV, though still running around on my hamster wheel, a see-through plastic sphere that dilutes all light and sound.

And then, without warning, the walls too start to project images from the TV, and suddenly the whole room is bathed in the pale glow of a playfully violent cartoon.

Soon I notice that I am being watched like a TV myself. A *chhlop* is listening outside the window of my American home. And he keeps a journal of all my activities:

8:15am—Family Room—the prisoner runs with the television on. He wastes electricity indulging his appetite for diversion.

8:28am—Family Room—the prisoner keeps running. He will not stop until he, or the wheel, is broken.

The dream is so convincing that, even after I wake, I am sure that the *chhlop* are there, seeing all, recording all, adding up the proof of my guilt.

12:06pm—Bedroom C—the prisoner whimpers in his sleep. There is no dream so pure as revolution. A counterrevolutionary, the prisoner is having impure dreams, in which his life belongs to no one but him.

———

"What will happen next?" I ask Mother. On the way home from the prison, she is suddenly marble-faced like Officer Heng, or like Odom Oum.

This woman, my mother, she looks up at the useless, unhusbanded world, the skin under her eyes as loose as bags of tea. When the wind blows over us, it is as though she made the wind blow. "The *chhlop* will come to our home tomorrow, and they will ask if we have any shovels. Since we have no shovels, they will make us borrow shovels from our neighbors. They will put us on a truck and send us to Tuol Sleng with the others. At nighttime, we will be marched out to a fallow field.

"Then we will use our shovels to dig. Of course we know what will happen when we finish digging, but we will not refuse, because though our bodies ache, we do not ever want the digging to end. Because when the holes are finally big enough, they will flatten our heads with oxcart handles, and push us in." My older brothers are crying. I am still too young to understand. I think she is telling a story, and I think that she is finished. But she is not finished.

"Then the neighbors will be punished," she says.

"Punished for what, Mae Ma?"

"For owning shovels."

———

"So I guess you saw dead people before, right?" Jason says, waiting for the eighth period bell to ring.

He isn't wrong, but the past tense sounds wrong to my ears. "Not since I come to America," I say.

"Was it gross? Were there like, maggots on them and stuff?"

"I don't remember," I reply, honestly.

My eyes follow a path that leads from the alien-drawing scrawled on the desk to the rattling radiator beneath the sill, to the wall of blue construction-paper cut and stapled into letters that spell, "Timeline of WWII."

"Did you ever fire a gun?" he asks.

"Yes, after Sen helped me escape," I say.

"*After* you escaped?"

"Mm-hmm."

Jason blinks a few times, waiting for a story. Outside the window, school busses queue in the semicircle driveway like patient caterpillars.

———

Derrick—an Australian missionary—took Sen and me out to the dam, away from the refugee tents.

He wore a backpack, a ponytail, and a Mauser handgun. When he spoke he used a pidgin of English, Cambodian, and Thai. "Now the Mauser Parabellum ain't the best arm to learn to fire on, but it's good practice for a steady hand. Sen, you've used a firearm before, yeah?"

Sen nodded.

"Great, then you go first," he said, handing Sen the gun. Derrick had set up soup cans and other repurposed food containers on a tree trunk, felled by a recent monsoon.

Sen supported his shooting arm with his other arm, squinting one eye and looking down the sight at the target. Here was my uncle, who saved me and helped me reunite with my brothers. He didn't look at all like an imitation, as I thought he might. He looked like the real thing—a man who was imitated by the movies, rather than the other way around. When he fired, it sounded less like a bomb and more like a cracking rock, less thunderous by far than the automatic rifles used by the army. He hit three targets, and left two standing—a can of Campbell's and a sardine tin.

Holding the gun in my own hands was a different thing. Watching was easy. But the pistol seemed to shake in my grip like an eel in a net. I thought of the old man who always warned, "Go away!" I thought of the young boy who bayoneted him, and the sound of the blade, clicking against the bone.

"Don't be nervous. There's no one in your line of fire. You're aiming perfectly. Now shoot," Derrick said.

It seemed as though the bullet might fly in any random direction. There was no way I could trust the physical world.

I shot, and hit nothing. I shot again, and hit nothing. I shot, and I shot, until I was completely sure that all the rounds were empty.

NGUYEN PHAN QUE MAI was born in 1973 in a village in northern Vietnam and grew up in the Mekong Delta, southern Vietnam. She is the author of eight books of poetry, fiction, and nonfiction published in Vietnamese. Her first international publication, *The Secret of Hoa Sen* (poems, BOA Editions, 2014), was published as part of the Lannan Translations Selection Series. Que Mai's first novel in English is forthcoming with Algonquin Books. She has received the Poetry of the Year 2010 Award from the Hanoi Writers Association, First Prize—the Poetry Competition About 1,000 Years Hanoi, as well as grants and fellowships from the Lannan Foundation, the University of Lancaster, and the Prince Claus Fund for Culture and Development.

BRUCE WEIGL (translator) is the author of more than a dozen books of poetry, several translations, and the best-selling memoir *The Circle of Hanh* (Grove Press). His collection *Song of Napalm* is among the most captivating collections by a poet writing on the Vietnam War. His honors include the Paterson Poetry Prize, fellowships from the National Endowment for the Arts and the Yaddo Foundation, the Robert Creeley Award, and the Poet's Prize from the Academy of American Poets. His work and collaborations have been performed internationally. His most recent collection, *The Abundance of Nothing* (TriQuarterly Press), was a finalist for the 2013 Pulitzer Prize. He lives in Oberlin, Ohio.

THE BOAT GIRL

Hương, like the perfume of the guavas she picked
in the ripe summer of 1986,
before a boat carried her away
into a thick night of the dark ocean.

Under a dome
woven by blurry stars,
I stood watching her go,
her shoulders a trembling thin leaf
among the forest of leaves clinging together in a hurricane.

With the perfume of her guavas
bursting onto my palms, I ran after her

but a neighbor reached out to pull me into the dark.
"Don't cry, my child," she said, "don't reveal the secret of their escape."

I was too young to understand then
about the pain of separation
and the reasons for my country to be slashed in two—
North and South—
the blood of its division bitter in our mouths.

I didn't know that Hương, the perfume of ripe
guavas that summer,
would lose her lovely name
to the towering waves of a surging storm,
one in hundreds of thousands
of Vietnamese refugees adrift at sea.

I didn't know
until her mother reappeared
after twenty-five years of living as Elizabeth
far away, in America.

I brought her a handful of guavas
saved from the dome of stars
that watched Hương leave.
Their perfume still burned my fingers
after all those years,
I had wanted to tell her.
But I couldn't because amidst the pain in her eyes,
I saw Hương dangling on a branch broken in half,
her pure laughter rising up
into raindrops ripe with guava perfume.

> —*Translated from the Vietnamese by*
> *Bruce Weigl and the author*

MY MOTHER

I cross the Lam River to return to my homeland
where my mother embraces my grandmother's tomb in the rain,
the soil of Nghệ An so dry the rice plants cling to rocks.
My mother chews dry corn; hungry, she tries to forget.

I cross the sedge fields to return to Ninh Bình.
Just after my birth, the war dropped bombs there.
To protect me from those storms, my mother spread her wings,
her faded shirt fragrant with the red gạo blossoms.

I cross the Mekong River to return to Bạc Liêu,
the skinny shadow of my mother
imprinted against the afternoon light,
each drop of sweat in exchange for a seed of rice;
yet in spite of this hardship, she always smiles.

I cross time to return to the past.
My mother sends me away among raindrops.
She lights the stove fire, sits there, waiting for me.
I begin to walk, each step the distance of a vast sea.

I cross the distance to return to Sài Gòn.
Oh my mother, her hair is turning white.
She is forever as she was before: gentle, loving, and kind.
Now that I can finally see her love, time has passed away.

I am always far away, and guilty not to be there.
I don't know if I can repay you, my dear mother.
So young, you worked your life hard and were strong,
the way you met so many storms alone.

I overcome my shyness, to hug my mother for the first time
I would love to stay by her side.
Hesitantly, my feet walk the dusty road of life.
I hear my heart cry. A sea of a thousand strings holds me back.
> —*Translated from the Vietnamese by*
> *Bruce Weigl and the author*

QUẢNG TRỊ

The mother runs toward us,
the names of her children fill her eye sockets.
She's screaming "Where are my children?"

The mother runs toward us,
her husband's name carves a hole in her chest.
She is screaming "Return my husband to me."

Time fades her shoulders.

Her ragged hair withers.
Sky spreads sunlight, dragging me along the roads
carpeted with bomb craters like the eyes of the dead,
wide open, staring.
The dry, cracked fields struggle to find their breath.

Flamboyant flowers shed their blood along the road.
Still so deep the wounds, Quảng Trị.
> —*Translated from the Vietnamese by*
> *Bruce Weigl and the author*

NGUYỄN QUANG THIỀU (1957) is a poet, working as editor, fiction writer, play-wright, translator, and children's author, living in Vietnam and holding high office in the Writers' Unions there. Born in Hà Tây Province, Nguyễn Quang Thiều entered Ha Noi University in 1975 and began to write poetry in 1982. He studied Spanish and English in Cuba from 1984 to 1989. He currently lives in Hà Đông. He has published many collections of poetry in Vietnamese as well as the bilingual collection *The Women Carry River Water* (UMass Press, 1997). His forthcoming collection is titled *The Pulse of a New Delta*.

KEVIN BOWEN (Translator) served in Viet Nam in 1968 and 1969. His poetry collections include *Playing Basketball with the Vietcong*, *Forms of Prayer at the Hotel Edison*, *Eight True Maps of the West*, and *Thai Binh/Great Peace*. He has worked as editor and translator with Nguyen Ba Chung and Bruce Weigl on collections such as *Six Vietnamese Poets, Distant Road: Selected Poems of Nguyen Duy,* and *Zen Poems from Early Vietnam*. From 1985 to 2011 he was director of the William Joiner Center for the Study of War and Social Consequences at University of Massachusetts—Boston. In 2011 was awarded the Phan Chu Trinh Award for contributions to Vietnamese Culture. He is co-editor with Nora Paley of *A Grace Paley Reader*, published by Farrar, Strauss and Giroux (2017).

MARTHA COLLINS (Translator) is the author of eight books of poetry, most recently *Admit One: An American Scrapbook* (2016), *Day Unto Day* (2014), *White Papers* (2012), and the book-length poem *Blue Front* (2006), which won an Anisfield-Wolf Award. A protestor during the Vietnam War, Collins has also co-translated four collections of poems from the Vietnamese, including *The Women Carry River Water* by Nguyen Quang Thieu (1997, with the author), *Green Rice* by Lam Thi My Da (2005, with Thuy Dinh), and *Black Stars* by Ngo Tu Lap (2013, with the author).

THE EXAMPLES

For the war widows of my village

Time flows into a huge ancient vase. Like brown locusts, the widows of my village disappear, one by one, behind the grass. Red-flecked winds rush back from the distant horizon, their fingers scratching madly at the thorn grass. I stand on the village road, crying like a boy who's lost his mother. I can't look for widows behind every blade of grass in this vast place.

With poles on their shoulders, the widows walk on roads worn like the curved spines of a thousand hard-working lives. Sleeping, they walk through wild winds that rise when the sun rolls into darkness. Sleeping, they walk into prehistoric rains that fall when dawn gets up from a feverish night. Like a lunatic, I stand and count them; example after example, I count them.

My widows, my examples, don't wear shoes or sandals; they avoid roads that lead to moonlit nights. Their breasts are tired and hard of hearing; they cannot hear the calls of men, who smell of tobacco and muddy rice fields on nights when winds roll in the panting garden. Only the mice eating rice in wooden coffins can wake them up; they lie in fear of the sound of termites feasting on those coffins.

Time rushes silently, silently into the ancient vase. Like locusts, the widows disappear, one by one, they disappear behind the grass. I am a lunatic standing here crying, crying for the examples, who've gone forever.

And when I have no one left to count, the widows come back from behind the grass, walking on moonlit roads strewn with October straw. Their hair, smelling of grapefruit leaves, spills into the moonlight; their breasts lean toward just-kindled fires. First their footsteps, then the sound of opening doors, and then a song rises up through the heads of sleepless lunatics who look at the moon.

The lunatics open their doors and leave their houses. They walk with the song, on and on, until they find a place with no examples.
>   —*Translated from the Vietnamese by Martha Collins*
>   *and the author*

MY FATHER'S LAUGHTER

Not at all like a drunk
My father leaves home at midnight.
Fireflies surround him
Like red-hot wires
Winding around him and snapping.

The noise of barking dogs runs
From our neighborhood to the end of our village
And stops at a wharf with a lonely boat
My father boarded with twenty years
In his hands. He didn't look back.
My mother covered her feet in the sand;
Her tears flowed into the river basin.

Years later my father came back,
His hair no longer black.
Now at night he sits and smokes,
His pipe hissing as if it were trying
To bore a hole through his sadness.

My father's children are not his final goal;
They are only four milestones along his sadness.
He carries his seventy years
To the old wharf and steps on the boat.
Does it rock because his feet are unsteady,
Or because it trembles with fear?

The noise of barking dogs runs
From the end of our village back to our gate
While the white hair of my father looks up and laughs.

    —*Translated from the Vietnamese by*
     Martha Collins and the author

JULY

In the dream, our bodies lie laid out across the bed.
We look like two trees felled in a storm.
Above us, woodsmen wearing masks
Run a plumb line down our torsos.

They rip us up into bloody red pieces.
Their blades cut through us. Flashes of light,
Bright as fireworks, send our lifeblood
Flying like dust through the sparks.

Our bed has turned into a workshop, our lives cut up,
Turned into tables, wardrobes, coffins.
We are everywhere, but the trees don't know us.
We are only a mute memory to them now.

The woodsmen think we'll never come back.
Not from a few bits of sawdust and shavings.
They toss the last few scraps of us into the fire;
Watch our lives burn out through the blaze.

But today the woodsmen are being led from the workshop.
They march out under the trees.
The trees are kind and grant them their last request.
Their faces hooded in masks.

> —*Translated from the Vietnamese by*
> *Kevin Bowen and the author*

AUGUST

In August the persimmon fruit is yellow.
It has the look of a person who's been sick a long time,
Who has little hope of recovering.

I stared up at the persimmon at dusk.
I had courage neither to leave nor to step closer.

Bats were shrieking, climbing up into the trees.
They caught the scent of the persimmon on their cries.

They glided and circled and huddled in dark bunches.
A sickness seemed to settle over the garden.

Only an old image, a persimmon's five pointed star
Splashed against a stucco wall, called me back.

Who knows what illness stepped past me that night in the garden,
As I stood trapped under the persimmon's yellow glow?
            —*Translated from the Vietnamese by*
            Kevin Bowen and the author

VAAN NGUYEN was born in Israel to Vietnamese refugees and raised in Jaffa, near Tel Aviv. Duki Dror's 2005 documentary *The Journey of Vaan Nguyen* documents her family's efforts to reclaim ancestral land in Vietnam. The film also introduced Nguyen's poetry to the Israeli public. *The Truffle Eye (Ein ha-kemehin),* a chapbook of poems, appeared in 2008. An expanded edition, published by Ma'ayan Press, appeared in 2013 in both print and digital editions. Nguyen is affiliated with Gerila Tarbut (Cultural Guerrilla), a collective of Israeli and Palestinian poets, artists and cultural activists, and is at work on her second book.

ADRIANA X. JACOBS (Translator) is Associate Professor of Modern Hebrew Literature at the University of Oxford and author of *Strange Cocktail: Translation and the Making of Modern Hebrew Poetry* (forthcoming). Her translations of modern Hebrew and contemporary Israeli poetry have appeared in various print and online publications, including *Gulf Coast, Poetry International, Zeek, The Ilanot Review, Metamorphoses,* and the *Michigan Quarterly Review.* She is the recipient of a 2015 PEN/Heim Translation Grant for her translation of *The Truffle Eye* by Vaan Nguyen.

MEKONG RIVER

Tonight I moved between three beds
like I was sailing on the Mekong
and whispered the beauty of the Tigris and Euphrates.
Under an endless moment
looking
below the left tit
I have a hole
and you fill it
with other men.
Notes of Tiger beer
on your body.

Alone,
crickets drone south of Laos.
Showers of cold air from Hanoi
the back gasps

the tight ass, an ink stain on the belly.
Draw me a monochrome
flow chart
on fresh
potted flowers.
I'll release roots at your feet,
I want to come to puke specks
of dust
in my crotch. Rest your hand
in my pants. Make it personal
Who abandons an illness in open sea?
> —*Translated from the Hebrew by*
> *Adriana X. Jacobs*

PACKING POEM

In the rice bowl green bananas,
and peels, dry castor beans in a jar,
feathers and mulch outside the window
this is how they still gather evidence.

The chopsticks rest diagonally
matching the movement of birds along a waterfall.
How do they stall the transmission and keep eating rice
before the night migration?
Under the cover of delusions,
all I wanted was to warn everyone "there's Armageddon"
and ask whether foreigners have
inflatable boats.

And those paranoid, paranoid women, have nothing
but these gallows
for overloading muscles
for stretching the body
in the gym
a woman lying naked in the sauna gossips under her breath

and the thoughts escape her
all at once
either the meds work or the mind is numb
but sometimes, if you concentrate, you can hear an airplane landing.
            —Translated from the Hebrew by Adriana X. Jacobs

VIET THANH NGUYEN is the Aerol Arnold Chair of English and professor of English and American Studies and Ethnicity at the University of Southern California. He is the author of *Race and Resistance: Literature and Politics in Asian America* (Oxford University Press, 2002) and the novel *The Sympathizer,* from Grove/Atlantic (2015). *The Sympathizer* won the Pulitzer Prize, Edgar Award for Best First Novel from the Mystery Writers of America, the First Novel Prize from the Center for Fiction, the Carnegie Medal for Excellence in Fiction from the American Library Association, and the Asian/Pacific American Award for Literature in Fiction from the Asian/Pacific American Librarians Association. His book *Nothing Ever Dies: Vietnam and the Memory of War* (Harvard University Press, 2016) was short-listed for the National Book Award and the National Book Critics Circle Award for nonfiction. His next book is *The Refugees*, a short story collection (Grove Press, 2017).

APRIL 30

Today is what many Vietnamese in the diaspora call "Black April." For them it is the anniversary of the Fall of Saigon. I understand their feelings. I grew up in a Vietnamese community in San Jose, and I absorbed their memories and their unspoken trauma. My own family was marked by separation and division, by people and property left behind. And yet, I could never wholeheartedly endorse this sense of loss and grievance, could never bring myself to say "Black April" (not least of all because if we were to speak of mourning, we should say "White April," but that would not go over so well in a white America). Like my narrator in *The Sympathizer,* I see every issue from both sides, and so I see that for some Vietnamese people this is not a day of mourning but one of celebration. The Fall is for some the Liberation.

And yet, it is important to mark this day because it is the symbolic moment when so many Vietnamese people became refugees. Many people have described me as an immigrant, and my novel as an immigrant story. No. I am a refugee, and my novel is a war story. I came to the United States because of a war that the United States fought in Vietnam, a war that the Vietnamese fought with each other, a war that China and the Soviet Union were involved in, a war that the Vietnamese brought to Laos and Cambodia, a war that did not end in 1975, a war that is not over for so many people of so many nationalities and cultures. For Americans to call me an immigrant and my novel an immigrant novel is to deny a basic fact of American history: that many immigrants to this country came because of American wars fought in the Philippines, Korea, Laos, Cambodia, Vietnam. Immigrants are the story of the American Dream, of American exceptionalism. Refugees are the reminder of the American nightmare, which is how so many who are caught under American bombardment experience the United States.

As much as Americans fear refugees and seek to transform refugees into immigrants who fulfill the American Dream, the Vietnamese who stayed in Vietnam have a hard time understanding their refugee brethren. I had breakfast with a former Vietnamese ambassador in Hanoi and she said that the "boat people" were economic refugees, not political refugees. Probably every single Vietnamese refugee would disagree with her, and the ethnic Chinese who were persecuted, robbed, and blackmailed would say that the line between being an economic refugee and a political refugee is a very thin one.

One of my Vietnamese language teachers said that the re-education camps were necessary to prevent postwar rebellion. Perhaps rebellion was in the making, but reaching out a hand in peace and reconciliation would have done so much more to heal the country. The Vietnamese people overseas remember the re-education camps as the ultimate hypocrisy of the Vietnamese revolution, the failure of Vietnamese brotherhood and sisterhood. This, too, is one reason why so many Vietnamese people became refugees and why so many find it hard to reconcile with a Vietnam that will not acknowledge its crimes against its own people, even as it is so ready to talk about the crimes of the South Vietnamese, the Americans, the French, and the Chinese. Nothing is more difficult than to look in the mirror and hold oneself to account. The victorious Vietnamese are guilty of that. So are the defeated Vietnamese.

I've heard more than once from Vietnamese foreign students in the United States that the past is over, that the Vietnamese at home understand the pain of the Vietnamese overseas, and that we should reconcile and move on. These students do not understand what the overseas Vietnamese feel—that they lost a country. It is easier to be magnanimous when one has won. But at least these Vietnamese students want to be magnanimous. At least they reach out a hand in friendship, unlike many of an older generation.

The younger Vietnamese Americans need to reach out that hand, too, even as they feel the deep need of filial piety. They wish to acknowledge the suffering and the pain of their parents and grandparents. If they do not, who will? They live in a country where most Americans know nothing about the Vietnamese people, or about Vietnamese Americans, where Americans care little to remember the Southern Vietnamese who they supposedly fought the war for. So the younger Vietnamese Americans feel that burden to carry on their parents' memories. One day, perhaps, they can let that burden go, but it will be much easier to do so when Vietnam helps to carry that burden by officially acknowledging that every side in that war had its reasons, that every side had its patriots, that we cannot divide the past into heroes and traitors.

As for me, I remain a refugee. My memory begins when I arrived in the United States at age four and was taken away from my parents to live with a white family. That was the condition for being able to leave the refugee camp in Fort Indiantown Gap, Pennsylvania. That experience remains an invisible brand stamped between my shoulder blades. I have spent my life trying to see that brand, to make sense of it, to rework it into words that I can speak to myself, that I can share with others. As painful as that experience was, what I learned from it was not to dwell only on my own pain. I needed to acknowledge that pain, to understand it, but in order to live beyond it, I also needed to acknowledge the pain of others, the worldview of others. This is why I cannot say "Black April," because it is one story of one side, and I am interested in all stories of all sides.

DEBORAH PAREDEZ is the daughter of a Vietnam veteran. Her work explores the workings of memory and the voices of women bearing witness to war and violence. She is the author of the poetry volume *This Side of Skin* and the critical study *Selenidad: Selena, Latinos, and the Performance of Memory*. Her poetry and essays have appeared in the *New York Times*, *Los Angeles Review of Books*, *Poetry*, *Feminist Studies*, *RHINO Poetry Journal*, *Callaloo*, and elsewhere. She teaches poetry and ethnic studies at Columbia University and is co-founder and co-director of *CantoMundo*, a national organization for Latina/o poets.

LAVINIA WRITING IN THE SAND
After Vietnam

Second-hand newlywed bed rocked
by his arched back, gasps for more
air, quickened buckling, then

collapse. This is the first time
his body ricochets
with the crooked electricity,

the first time she sees him
this way, spasm-gripped
as the seizure intercepts his sleep.

Lucky for him, she's fresh
from nursing school, knows
enough to take him into her

arms, still his jaw to keep him
from biting his tongue, turn
his face against the choking.

This is the bed they made
for me. Evenings as a girl
I'd watch him drift off

in the recliner, her voice
from the kitchen, *Make sure
your father doesn't swallow*

his tongue. These days
they say it's not possible
to do such a thing, but

I've seen the body flailing
dusk after dusk after dusk
and the whole house gone

silent.

A HISTORY OF BAMBOO

The bamboo out back
is taking over—infantry

charging—steady invasion
from the neighboring city lot.

Each week another advance
nearer to the bedroom window

the view now only green
reed and yearning

stalk. There is no stopping
the deep-running roots

the garden guide instructs
unless a trench is dug

to uproot the system.
In Laos, a farmer digs

for bamboo shoots
and his spade strikes

a cluster bomb
startled from its mud-cradle.

At night the hollow poles rise
and answer to the wind.

Who knows how many
more will surface by morning.

*Note: Between 1964 and 1973, the US military dropped 2 million tons of explosive ord-
nance on Laos; 10–24 million cluster bombs or unexploded ordnances (UXOs) remain
scattered across the country, killing hundreds each year.*

SUZAN-LORI PARKS is one of the most acclaimed playwrights in American drama today. She is the first African-American woman to receive the Pulitzer Prize in Drama, is a MacArthur "Genius" Award recipient, and in 2015 was awarded the prestigious Gish Prize for Excellence in the Arts. Suzan-Lori teaches at New York University and serves at the Public Theater as its Master Writer Chair. Other grants and awards include those from the National Endowment for the Arts, Rockefeller Foundation, Ford Foundation, New York State Council on the Arts, and New York Foundation for the Arts. She is also a recipient of a Lila-Wallace Reader's Digest Award, a CalArts/Alpert Award in the Arts, and a Guggenheim Foundation Grant. Her father is a Vietnam Veteran and US army officer who reached the rank of colonel.

FATHER COMES HOME FROM THE WARS (PART 1)

FATHER: Hi honey, Im home.
MOTHER: Yr home.
FATHER: Yes.
MOTHER: I wasnt expecting you. Ever.
FATHER: Should I go back out and come back in again?
MOTHER: Please.

> *He goes back out and comes back in again.*

MOTHER: Once more.
FATHER: Yr kidding.
MOTHER: Please.

> *He goes back out and comes back in again.*

MOTHER: Yr home.
FATHER: Yes.
MOTHER: Let me get a good look at you.
FATHER: I'll just turn around.
MOTHER: Please.

> *He turns around once Counterclockwise.*

MOTHER: They should of sent a letter. A letter saying you were coming home. Or at least a telephone call. That is the least they could do. Give a woman and her family and her friends and neighbors a chance to get ready. A chance to spruce things up. Put new ribbons in the hair of the dog. Get the oil changed. Have everything running. Smoothly. And bake a cake of course. Hang streamers. Tell the yard man to—tidy up his act. Oh God. Long story. Oh God. Long story. I woulda invited the neighbors over. Had everyone on the block jump out from their hiding places from behind the brand new furniture with the plastic still on it and say—WHAT? Say: "Welcome Home" of course. And then after a few slices of cake and a few drinks theyd all get the nerve to say what theyre really thinking. For now itll stay unthought and unsaid. Well. You came home. All in one piece looks like. We're lucky. I guess. We're lucky, right? Hhhhh.

FATHER: They sent a letter saying I was coming home or at least they telephoned. Maybe you didnt open the letter. I dont blame you. It could have been bad news. I see yr unopened envelopes piled up. I dont blame you. I dont blame you at all. They called several times. Maybe you were out. Maybe you were screwing the yard man. If you had known I was coming you woulda put new ribbons in the hair of the dog, got the oil changed, baked a cake and invited all the neighbors over so they could jump out of their various hiding places behind the brand-new furniture purchased with the blood of some people I used to know—and some blood of some people I used to kill. Oh God. Long story. Oh God. Long story. And theyd shout at me— WHAT? "Welcome Home" of course. And then after a few slices of cake and a few drinks theyd get the nerve to say what they really think: "Murderer, baby killer, rascist, government pawn, ultimate patsy, stooge, fall guy, camp follower, dumbass, dope fiend, loser." Hhhhh.

MOTHER

FATHER

(Rest)

MOTHER: I can't understand a word yr saying.

FATHER: I dont speak English anymore.

MOTHER: I dont blame you. SIT DOWN, I'LL FIX YOU SOMETHING.

> *He sits. She takes a heavy frying pan and holds it over his head. Almost murder. She lowers the pan.*

MOTHER

FATHER

(Rest)

> *He sits. Again she raises the frying pan and holds it over his head. Almost murder. She lowers the pan.*

FATHER: Where are the children?

MOTHER: What children?

> *Sound of the wind and the rain.*

FATHER COMES HOME FROM THE WARS (PART 3)

> *Father, surrounded by his Soldiers, stands at the door. The Family is at dinner.*

FATHER: Hi, honey, Im home.

> *The family stares.*

1ST SOLDIER: When you hear the word "war" what comes to mind?

FATHER: Dont start that talk here. Im home.

2ND SOLDIER: You dont mind if we wait here do you?

FATHER: Do what you gotta do. Im home.

> *Father sits in his easy chair. His soldiers wait.*

FATHER: Come on, Junior. Lets watch some game shows.

MOTHER: Yr not hungry?

SISTER: Mother and me made a welcome home pie for you. See the writing: "Welcome home from the wars, Father!"

(Rest)

Yr not even looking.

FATHER: All I wanna do is watch some goddamn game shows.

JUNIOR: All thats on is war movies.

FATHER: Fine.

MOTHER: Who are yr friends, honey?

FATHER: Turn up the volume, Junior.

JUNIOR: Im gonna be a soldier just like yr a soldier, right, Pop?

FATHER

FATHER

FATHER: You betcha.

> *Junior turns up the volume and the Soldiers in the doorway make loud war sounds. Father leans back and relaxes.*

PLAYING CHOPSTICKS (FATHER COMES HOME FROM THE WARS, PART 7)

> *A Soldier Dad in army uniform, like he's just come in from jungle combat. He's still got a camouflage suit on, and dark paint covers his face. Maybe even jungle twigs and branches stick out from his helmet and clothing.*
> *He sits on a campstool, a Kid sits with him.*
> *The Soldier Dad is teaching the Kid to use chopsticks. They are moving a mountain of rice into another pile, far across the other side of the stage, making another, hopefully identical mountain.*
> *The Soldier Dad is great with chopsticks. The Kid is hopeless.*
> *Somewhere offstage someone plays the piano.*
> *Theyre playing "Chopsticks" over and over.*

SOLDIER DAD: You wanted yr dad to bring you back something from over there. I brought you something, right?
KID: Right.

(Rest)

Whats "gonorrhea"?

(Rest)

SOLDIER DAD: Thats something for adults, Kid. Lets stick to our chopsticks.
KID: I heard Mom telling Grandmom that you brought her some "gonorrhea" home from the war.

SOLDIER DAD
SOLDIER DAD

SOLDIER DAD: I brought you something nice and yr acting like you dont like it, Kid. Here. Watch Dad do it.

> *Soldier Dad effortlessly picks up a piece of rice and walks over to the other side of the stage where he arranges it carefully on the pile.*

SOLDIER DAD: The idea is to pick up the rice with the chopsticks, carry it over here and put the rice down. And put it down in such a way as we remake the rice mountain over here.
KID: Right.
SOLDIER DAD: Its good practice.
KID: For what?

SOLDIER DAD
KID

> *Soldier Dad smacks Kid upside the head.*
> *The move comes so fast and seemingly out of nowhere.*
> *Like a flash flood.*
> *The Kid's head snaps horribly back, but then, just as quickly, the Soldier Dad's anger is spent.*
> *The Kid doesnt cry or anything.*

SOLDIER DAD: Try it again. Go on. You gotta learn it.

The Kid tries moving the rice with the chopsticks again.

SOLDIER DAD: Not much better. Ok, a little better, but, watch.

Soldier Dad moves several pieces of rice, all one at a time, very quickly and with great fanfare, talking as he moves them.

SOLDIER DAD: Soldier Dad can move them quick. Soldier Dad can hold the chopsticks in his right hand and move rice, and he can hold them in his left hand too. Makes no difference. Soldier Dad can hold the sticks behind his back, doesnt have to look, its just that easy. And every piece of rice gets put in place!

The Kid watches with mounting awe and mounting anger. Offstage the piano gets louder.

SOLDIER DAD (*Yelling to the offstage piano*): CUT THAT OUT, HUH? HOW AM I SUPPOSED TO FUCKING THINK WITH YOU FUCKING, FUCKING THAT MUSIC UP??!!

The music stops.

KID
SOLDIER DAD

KID: You want me to try it again?
SOLDIER DAD: Yr mother used to be a concert pianist.
KID: You want me to try it again?
SOLDIER DAD: Yeah. Go ahead.

The Kid tries moving the rice again. He's much better this time—like a miracle happened—and now he's actually pretty good.

SOLDIER DAD: Wow! Great job, Kid!
KID: Thanks.
SOLDIER DAD: Chip off the old block after all. I was worried. I'd been away for so long and you—you couldnt do the rice thing.

(*Rest*)

It was the only thing I brought you back and you couldnt do it and I was worried. But you can do it. My Kid's my Kid. Good. So let's get to work, huh?

> *The music starts up again and the Kid and Soldier Dad get back to work.*
> *Each is amazing at moving the rice. And they are enjoying themselves. It is*
> *horrible to see them enjoying themselves doing such a pointless task. But they*
> *are building a monument together—and this monument will be a fortress*
> *against the future pain. And the music, playing all the while, seeps into the*
> *walls of the fortress, seeps in and holds it like stone.*

FATHER COMES HOME FROM THE WARS (PART II: HIS ETERNAL RETURN—A PLAY FOR MY FATHER)

> *During this play we hear a war news-in-brief soundtrack, laced with mili-*
> *tary band music thats played at a slower than normal speed. The action is*
> *as follows: A never-ending loop of action—5 Servicemen walk downstage*
> *together. All wear military uniforms from the same side of the same war, but*
> *not necessarily the same branch of Service. They stand upstage and walk very*
> *vibrantly and heroically downstage. Theyre returning home as heroes. As*
> *they reach centerstage, 5 women, their Servicewives, stand up from the audi-*
> *ence, and run toward the men. Just as the Servicemen reach the downstage*
> *edge, the Servicewives meet them. The Servicemen pick up their Service-*
> *wives, twirling them around very joyfully.*
> *Before each wife returns to the ground a Child comes onstage and, racing*
> *towards its respective Mother and Father, jumps for joy.*
> *This action repeats. New Servicemen walk downstage, new wives leap up*
> *from the audience and rush into their arms, new Children run in to cheer.*
> *The action repeats eternally. Long after the audience has emptied of*
> *Women; long after the Men have grown out of the desire to be hugged and*
> *kissed and welcomed; long after the Children have become less cheerful and*
> *more sensible and have taken up trades, like accounting or teaching or real*
> *estate or politics; long after the Children's Children have outgrown joy and*
> *have all grown-up and moved away. Forever.*

ANDREW X. PHAM is the author of *Catfish and Mandala: A Two-Wheeled Voyage Through the Landscape and Memory of Vietnam* (1999) and *The Eaves of Heaven: A Life in Three Wars* (2009). He is also the translator of *Last Night I Dreamed of Peace* (2008). *Catfish and Mandala*, his travel memoir, won the Kiriyama Prize, the QPB Prize, and the Whiting Writers' Award. It was also named a Guardian Prize Shortlist finalist and a *New York Times* Notable Book of the Year. *The Eaves of Heaven*, his biography of his father, was a National Book Critics Circle finalist, an Asian Pacific American Librarian Association Honorary Book of the Year, and one of the *Washington Post*'s Top Ten Books of the Year.

THE FALL OF SAIGON

Sixteen years of fighting had reduced the war to a troublesome liability. We accepted it like an offshore storm that never left. The battles, the bombs, the highway ambushes, the countryside insurgency, the draft cycles, and the ever-mounting casualties had become the ebbs and flows of a long, long war. We never expected victory—our leaders were too corrupt for that—and yet defeat never entered our minds. We convinced ourselves that the ever-present, powerful Americans would never desert us. We had become too dependent, lazy, blind, and selfish to save ourselves.

The end came swiftly. The cities didn't fall; they tumbled, one after another in quick, horrific succession. On March 13, 1975, the first to go was Ban Me Thuot, a key hold in the Central Highlands. Five days later, Pleiku was lost. In three more days, the enemy overran Quang Tri. Hue, the capital of central Vietnam, was abandoned two days after that. President Thieu and his staff of incompetent generals accelerated the downfall with their order to abandon the 1st and 2nd Corps. The stalemate was over. The tide had turned permanently. Within three weeks, eight provinces were forfeited; 40,000 troops were massacred during the retreats. It was devastating, but no one could predict that the Viet Cong would sack Saigon's presidential palace in another twenty-six days.

My brother Hong was working at the Forestry Service of Phu Bon, a province in the Central Highlands. When the VC took the province seat, he escaped to Bao Loc on an L-19, a two-seater propeller plane; it was sheer luck that he had caught his army pilot friend in time. Had he tried to escape by road, he would have been among the tens of thousands of civilians who perished in the forest on their exodus to the coast. From Bao Loc, he caught a bus into Saigon. Hong walked through the door of my father's house empty-handed. He had lost his home and everything he owned. Days later, my brother Hung, a high school principal, fled Ham Tan, a mere sixty-five miles from Saigon. The news Hong and Hung brought home was terrifying.

Madness had descended on the city. People were in a selling and buying frenzy. Refugees sold whatever they had. Others liquidated assets at a fraction of their cost to raise money for passage out of the country. Former northerners like my family, who had lived under Communist rule, were the most anxious to leave. The majority of southerners, however, did not think that a Communist takeover would be disastrous. They snapped up cars, motorbikes, houses, and staples at bargain prices. I sold my car and was in negotiation to sell our four-story house. The prospective buyer backed out of the sale when the Viet Cong approached Phan Thiet.

A day later, as the Viet Cong began encircling Phan Thiet, my wife's mother, brother, and sister fled on their neighbor's fishing boat and arrived in Saigon the next morning. When they came to stay at our house and gave us the news, I immediately rode out to Vung Tau on my Honda motorbike to see if I could find a fishing boat to take us out to sea. The highway was busy in both directions with refugees from the outer provinces heading to safety and Saigonians fleeing to the coast in search of passage out of the country.

Army trucks rumbled into Vung Tau along with hordes of expensive civilian cars. The wealthy and the powerful were flocking to the coast. Vung Tau's population had tripled in the past month. I scoured the docks, but it was hopeless. Every single vessel, including motorized dinghies, was already booked or bought outright. The hotels and vacation houses were filled with people waiting to board their boats; some were already living on them. Vung Tau officials declared the city closed to new refugees.

The cost of buying passports, tourist visas, and plane tickets out of the country had skyrocketed out of our reach by the time we saw that a collapse was inevitable. It had become the choice of the superrich with weighty government connections. Many folks lost their savings in passport cons. Saigon was full of scam artists and opportunists offering gamut of escape options, from airplanes to ferries to overland border crossings via trucks. Every day, my brothers Hung, Hong, Hoang, and I crisscrossed Saigon looking for contacts and deals. The pall of desperation had fallen over us.

My best friend Tat, the handsome buddy from my high school days, came to me with a proposal. His brother Han, who worked at the Ministry of Transportation, had a deal with the captain of a small coastal merchant ship belonging to a Chinese company. The captain, a Vietnamese of Chinese origin, agreed to take twenty passengers at the price of ten gold leaves each. Tat didn't have the money for his family and suggested that if I loaned him the gold, I could take seven members of my own immediate family. We had been close friends for more than twenty years, so I agreed to his terms. I wanted to meet the captain. Han said the captain refused to meet anyone until it was time to go and that the full fee would be due upon embarkation.

Bach Dang pier was near downtown Saigon, and there were many boats and ferries bringing refugees in from other parts of the country. Tat and I found our ship not on the pier but moored offshore on the other side of the Saigon River. It was a pathetic seagoing junk. Packed to the gunwales, it might carry thirty passengers. Without any other viable alternatives, I swallowed my misgivings and hoped for the best.

A week before the city's collapse, I went over to Tat's house. Neither of us had a telephone, but we lived only three blocks apart so it was easy stopping by to see each other several times a day to check on the status of the boat. I thought it was very safe and fortunate that Tat lived only two minutes by motorbike from me. It was going to be very close because southerners like our ship captain were complacent and had no idea of the dangers of waiting to the final hours.

Tat said, "The captain announced that he'll go as soon as the Americans start to leave."

"That's very risky. We don't even know for certain if he would take us. We haven't even met him."

"I told Han the same thing. He said the government hasn't allowed people to take ships to take people to sea yet. The chaos must begin before the captain can leave without permission. By then, no one will care."

"Why can't he bribe the officials? Your brother can help him find the right contact in the Ministry."

"I doubt the captain will want to part with any of his gold. Besides, he probably can get more money at the last moment when people will pay anything to leave."

"So we wait for the end."

"Yes, we wait for the Americans."

President Thieu and his cabinet fled well before the Americans. On April 21, 1975, Thieu abandoned his office and country. He flew to Taiwan with his family, taking along fifteen tons of personal luggage, rumored to be the wealth of the country. His disgraceful exit delivered a detrimental blow to the troops' morale, and on the following day, Xuan Loc, a critical defensive point merely thirty-five miles from Saigon, crumbled into the enemy's hand. It would be remembered as an epic battle, a display of heartbreaking courage against overwhelming odds. Our trusted American allies never came, but the embattled and impoverished ARVN had gallantly fought alone, outnumbered and outgunned.

Refugees poured into the capital, running from the shelling and fighting in the adjacent towns that formed a defense line around the city. The number of refugees swelled dramatically as the Viet Minh pushed the ARVN back toward Saigon. Reality was fast disintegrating into nightmare.

State-controlled television and radio broadcasts lied to keep citizens calm. Even the Voice of America was no longer trustworthy. Only the BBC remained factual, and none of their reports bore good news. Like everyone else, I spent my days dashing back and forth all over the city, gathering information and rumors wherever I could. The latest and most credible news was the firsthand accounts from the tens of thousands of refugees seeking shelter at pagodas throughout the city.

X a Loi temple near my house had more refugees than it had celebrants during the New Years prayers. Hundreds of people huddled and slept wherever they found space. Plastic tarps were strung up in the courtyard and along the sides of the temple to shelter newcomers. They were all in very bad shape. Some were injured. Many were missing family members. Women sobbed, their children crying inconsolably. These people had run for their lives.

At one corner of the yard, a middle-aged man sat alone, calmly smoking a hand-rolled cigarette, oblivious to the chaos around him. His shirt was torn; dried blood stained the sleeves; his pants were caked with mud. I asked him if I could sit next to him. He glanced sideways at me and kept smoking. I sat down and waited for him to talk. Usually, people were anxious to talk about their ordeals, but the man just rolled another smoke. I finally asked him where he came from.

"Nha Trang," he replied without turning.

"Is your family here with you?"

"They didn't make it."

"The VC captured them?"

He closed his eyes and sighed. "They killed them."

Not knowing what to say, I blurted, "Do you think we'll be safe here?"

He ground the cigarette beneath his sandal, stood up, and walked away.

B y April 27, 1975, it looked as if the end of the world had arrived. The Communists had surrounded the capital—the final foothold of the South's forces. Artillery shells, rockets, and bombs tore up the outskirts of the city. ARVN jet fighters screamed across the overcast sky and swooped along the edges of the city, trying to turn back the advancing Communist forces. North, south, and west of Saigon, columns of black smoke curled upward, the blazes spreading. Torrents of refugees poured into the city on every road. Terrified, traumatized, and exhausted, they rolled toward the last sanctuary. They came like an undulating human carpet, filling, choking the new Bien Hoa superhighway as far as the eyes could see.

On April 28, Duon Van Minh took over the role of Chief of State. Fully armed South Vietnam troops appeared on Tran Quo Toan Boulevard, where the Military Assistance Command, Vietnam headquarters was located right around the corner from my father's house. These were the "Red Beret Angels," the South Vietnam elite airborne force. They were our very best men, known for their courage and seen in every parade. They were our heroes, symbolic of South Vietnam's pride and power. Their dedication, ferocity, and sacrifices were legendary. They were the ones who had shown us that we could fight the VC and win. It shook me profoundly to see them sitting on the curb with their heads hung low, their rifles on the sidewalk. Without their confident swagger, they seemed so young, more boys than men. Had it been fifteen years since I was drafted? I walked up and down the street, trying to catch their eyes. I recognized that look of battle fatigue. Their morale was broken. Hopelessness pulled on their limbs. It was plain on their faces; the war was over.

I got on my motorbike and rushed over to Tat's house, determined to convince the captain that we must not wait any longer. I was prepared to pay a premium to make the captain see reason. The moment I saw Tat sitting outside his house, I knew our hopes were dashed.

Tat wouldn't look at me. He mumbled, "They confiscated the boat."

"Who?"

"The police."

"Why?"

He shrugged. "They have family and need to escape too."

"When did you find out?"

"Yesterday evening."

I was speechless. We were dead. It was as simple as that. I sat with him fifteen, twenty minutes, dumbstruck. I could feel the seconds ticking away. I was angry that he hadn't told me earlier, even though I knew I couldn't change a thing.

I said, "We must not give up. We must keep looking. Let me know immediately if something comes up."

He promised he would, and I left on my motorbike.

I didn't know where I was going, but I needed to go somewhere, anywhere. My stomach was souring. Where to start looking all over again? I revved the engine, and sliced and weaved through the bustling streets. I joined the throngs of tens of thousands looking for an escape route. All of Saigon, including the hundreds of thousands of refugees, was on the road, coursing manically in a dozen different directions. Cars, trucks, motorbikes, bicycles, and cyclos jammed the avenues. Accidents clogged the intersections. No one cared, no one stopped. We were like animals trapped in a burning cage. But there was nowhere to go. Fighting blocked the highway to Tan Son Nhat Airport. Streets leading to government and military sites were barricaded. I found one dead end after another.

On Mac Dinh Chi Boulevard, a sprawling mob of Vietnamese and foreigners swarmed the American embassy. They surged at the gate, begging to get into the sanctuary. White foreigners pushed through the crowd and were allowed in first. The Vietnamese clamored and shoved each other to get to the guards, waving documents and shouting their qualifications: employees of American companies, contractors, relatives of Americans, wives and children of American soldiers. I watched from a distance, knowing that a decommissioned officer had no priority, regardless of my service. My office had provided a cover for CIA operatives. If the Viet Cong caught me, I expected to be tortured and executed. My wife and children would be sent to live in the jungle.

I had never felt so much envy toward foreigners as I did at that moment. Since I was a teenager, I could never escape the feeling that they glided on some other plane above us; their dignity, living standards, and privileges thriving in another stratum beyond our reach. I had never bothered looking upward until now. Even other Asians—the Filipinos, the Taiwanese, the Koreans, the Japanese—were passing right over us. My people were at the bottom of the hierarchy, and we were about to sink even lower once the Communists took control.

I went home, put my arms around Anh, and told her the bad news. Rather than breaking down as I'd feared, she insisted that we see our physician, who was a good friend. We had known Dr. Nguyen Duy Tam for the fourteen years since he opened his first modest clinic. He had become one of the most successful doctors in Saigon and had powerful connections. His clientele consisted of generals, politicians, and business moguls. He was also a prominent congressman.

When we arrived at his modern clinic in an upscale neighborhood, it was nearly deserted. Three patients were attended by two distracted young nurses who seemed on the verge of bolting out of the office. Dr. Tam took us into his office and confided that he had plans to go to France. He offered to take my family if we had one hundred bars of gold for the fare. The agent would need twenty bars as a deposit. We rushed home and brought back the gold. The flight would leave the next morning. Dr. Tam said he would send a car for us.

In the evening, I went over to my father's house. My brothers were out roaming the city, looking for an escape. Father was sipping tea with his opium cohorts. Father's cousin and confidant, Mr. Tri, droned on about his theory that the Americans would strike a deal with the Viet Cong once the fighting was over. According to Mr. Tri, there was no need to leave the country. Father's two neighbors, both southerners, insisted that at least with the Communists there would be less corruption in the government. They couldn't see why the Communists would want to take revenge on former northerners like us for migrating south twenty-one years ago.

I sat with them as long as I could because I wanted to spend some time with my father. I considered telling him about Dr. Tam's offer, but in the end, I couldn't bring myself to do it. He had become extremely cynical, and he believed solely in Mr. Tri's counsel. My stepmother and sisters could do nothing. Their fates lay squarely with him. Father wanted Hung, Hong, Hoang, and me to escape, because life for us would be very dangerous under the Communist regime. As for himself, Father had decided that he was old enough to die. He had the resigned calm of someone stricken by a terminal illness. He had decided to face the Communists together with his neighbors and Mr. Tri, his most trusted friend.

That night of April 28, Anh and I stayed up and watched over our three-year-old son, who was very ill with a high fever. We didn't talk. There was too much to say and nowhere to begin. Our entire life was here in this house, all the years of hard work, the memories, our families to be left behind. What to bring, what to leave? Too many difficult choices, so we packed nothing, save some warm clothes for the children and one envelope filled with photos. Anh brewed a strong pot of tea and we sat together looking out our second-floor window at the dark street.

It was 7:00 A.M., just after dawn, when the first convoy of military vehicles thundered down Ly Thai To Boulevard in front of our house. Private cars sped after them toward the center of the city. Something was afoot. I had a strong urge to jump on my motorbike and follow them, but I was afraid we might miss Dr. Tam's car. It was nerve-racking to see hordes of people heading toward downtown while we sat still. By 8:00 A.M., I couldn't wait any longer and I took Anh to see the doctor.

A smell of rot permeated Saigon. Trash, clothes, baggage, housewares, blankets, baskets of food, and just about everything else littered the streets. A horse-drawn cart full of luggage and trunks was ditched on the side of the road, the horse gone. A beautiful hardwood chair and sofa were left on the sidewalk. Cars parked crookedly, their doors hanging open. Overnight, the ARVN soldiers had vanished into the alleys and byways, their uniforms and weapons discarded in the gutters. Unlike other surrendering cities, there were no robberies or looting by renegade soldiers or gangsters.

In Dr. Tam's clinic, the head nurse sat alone at the front desk reading a novel. She greeted us with a sad smile and said that Dr. Tam had left with his family around 3:00 A.M. They had gone to Ton Son Nhat Airport by helicopter and flew out of the country on a civilian plane. I felt the earth drop away from my feet. Anh clutched my arm.

"He promised us," Anh insisted. "He promised to take us with him. There was supposed to be a car. This morning, he said."

"I'm so sorry, Sister Anh. The doctor told me to tell you that he tried, but couldn't negotiate to take anyone else besides his own family. He's very sorry he couldn't help you."

Anh turned to me. "He promised us."

I put my arm around her shoulder and led her out. The nurse stopped us at the door and handed us a small box sealed with tape—our gold deposit.

After taking Anh home, I was going over to my father's house when I saw a helicopter lifting off the MACV headquarters. The once-busy compound was empty, the main doors closed. The steel gates were shut, the familiar U.S. MPs gone. Anyone who was going to be saved was already inside the main building. On the rooftop, helicopters were evacuating American personnel and some lucky Vietnamese who worked for them. Watching them rising away effortlessly, I thought I could smell the stink of death seeping into the city. It was truly over. The Americans weren't just leaving, they were running, flying, bolting out as fast as possible.

Father was in the living room drinking tea with a neighbor. He said Hung had gone over to my home to tell me that there were ferries taking evacuees out to sea at Ben Bach Dang. Hong was already there, and Hoang had just left. Hien was still at the police academy in Thu Duc. Father had decided that my stepmother, three sisters, and youngest brother would stay in Vietnam with him. Escape was too dangerous for them. I rushed back home, missing Hung by minutes.

"We have to go to the ferries now!" I said to Anh.

"We don't have a car," she said.

"Get the kids ready. Tell your brother, sister, and mother that if they want to come with us, they must be ready in ten minutes."

"You go first and find us a place on the ferry. I'll get a car and follow you. We'll meet you there."

"I'll wait for you by the pier, at the lamppost next to the banana vendor."

The eight-mile drive to Ben Bach Dang took twice as long as usual. Traffic was crazy. I saw half a dozen crashes. Throngs of people were fleeing to the pier. The military vehicles and cars that I had seen early this morning were now parked haphazardly by the riverside. The dock was littered with abandoned cars, bicycles, motorbikes, and luggage. No one even bothered to pick them up. I arrived just in time to see the last ferry cast off its moorings. The ship was dangerously overloaded, every inch of its deck packed. People hung onto the railing, calling to friends and relatives who didn't make it aboard. Some jumped into the churning water and swam after the ship. I pushed my way to the edge of the dock. Hoang was on the ferry. I yelled and waved at him, but he didn't see me. I didn't see Hung anywhere. If Hoang was on this last ferry, there was little chance Hung was on it as well. After telling Hoang about the ferries, Hung had wasted more time crossing the city to look for me. My heart pounded violently in my chest. What if Hung had gotten into an accident on the way back here? I screamed out his name, my voice lost in the cacophony. Hung had taken an immense risk trying to help his brothers escape. In this desperate panic when everyone was solely focused on his own survival, my dear brother Hung did not think of himself, but instead jeopardized his last chance of escape to save me. I felt nauseous. My single wish then was to see Hung standing on that ferry. But it was getting farther and farther from me. I kept looking at it until distance fused the passengers into a single mass, between us, a stretch of brackish water as dark and forbidding as abyss.

I was drowning on the dock. Another chance to escape had slipped through my fingers. If only I hadn't counted on Dr. Tam's help. If only he had sent word to us when he knew he couldn't keep his promise. If only I had trusted my instincts this morning and followed those cars. If, if, if . . .

I came to see Tat. His house was locked. No one was home. His neighbor told me that Tat and his brother Han, our Ministry of Transportation insider, had known about the evacuation and left early this morning with his huge family and relatives—more than forty people. They had boarded one of the first ferries. Tat's house was three blocks from mine. We had seen each other several times a day for the past month. My best friend had left without taking a moment to share the information that would have made a world of difference for me. I would have had plenty of time to save not only my own family, but also my brothers and in-laws. This was someone whom I had tutored and guided throughout high school and college. I had seen Tat through the death of his father, performing many of the duties as though I was a member of his family. When he had been summoned to the draft center, I held his full-time teaching position to keep the school from replacing him. After bribing himself another exemption, Tat returned, and I gave him back his job and the entire month's salary that I had earned teaching his classes. He was like a brother.

It broke my heart. I couldn't bring myself to tell my wife the news.

All through the darkest night, the most quiet and peaceful night Saigon ever had, I wrestled with fate. Dawn revealed a ghost town. I looked out from my second-story window at a vacant street. I couldn't eat and hadn't slept in two days. I felt detached, drunk with fatigue.

Mid-morning, a convoy of camouflaged trucks roared through the street, heading to the city center. The North Vietnam Army was entering Saigon without resistance or a single gunshot. It was chilling. The air had somehow gone bad.

The victors entered Saigon in the late morning on a medley of vehicles: American Jeeps, army trucks, civilian pickups, and sedans. They were the South Vietnam Communist troops, the PAFL, the paramilitary units, and Saigon's own underground Communists. They brandished weapons and wore mismatched uniforms, black pajamas, T-shirts, and even jeans. Pickup trucks with loudspeakers declared the surrender of the South Vietnam government, announcing that we were now "liberated" from tyranny and capitalism. Cheering packs of Saigon youths followed the convoy with their mopeds and bicycles. People stepped outside timidly. They stood drowsily in front of their homes as if they were just waking from a long sleep.

Late in the afternoon, my father came riding his creaky bicycle, dressed in a pair of gray slacks and a white shirt. Bent over the handlebars, he looked ghastly thin—as vulnerable as a pauper. I hadn't seen him pedaling his bike for years. I was afraid he was going to fall over.

He came to make sure I didn't do something crazy like commit suicide or hike to the Cambodian border. Father knew that sooner or later, the Communist's ax would fall on my neck and he wanted to be there with me when bad things began. He had always said that our family had been extremely blessed compared to all those around us, the countless others who had suffered heartbreaking losses. He believed it was karma. He came to remind me that we had lived with good intentions. He wanted to give me hope.

We climbed to the fourth-story rooftop together. He said he believed Hung had escaped on the ferries along with my cousin Tan and my brothers Hong and Hoang. Father sighed and admitted that his trusted friend and confidant, Mr. Tri, who had advised everyone to stay, had fled without a word of good-bye or warning. I could tell the betrayal wounded him deeply. I felt very sorry for Father. I wanted to comfort him, but it wasn't our way to show weakness or emotion. I was forty years old. Father was an old man entering the last stage of his life. This was the most serene silence we shared, standing shoulder to should in the fading light.

The sun simmered on the skyline. The day was closing, and with it an era. I could feel the city, my city, kneeling down. The vast orange heaven, pillars of smoke, the ragged cityscape. It was a beautiful sight. It was like standing at the helm of a ship. The whole city was sinking.

Father turned and stared at me. The unforgiving years had carved themselves into his gaunt face, deep scars of a life I had known but never dared study. I saw it then, the immense sorrow brimming in his eyes. It was staggering. I could tell he wanted to say it, but didn't know how. All at once, our barriers fell, and I saw through the blurred seasons of our history, our pains, his disappointments, my childhood fear of this distant man. For the first time in my life, I felt the fullness of my father's love. It was crushing, the lateness of the hour.

AIMEE PHAN is the author of the story collection *We Should Never Meet* and the novel *The Reeducation of Cherry Truong*. She has received fellowships from the NEA, the Rockefeller Foundation's Bellagio Center, MacDowell Colony, and Hedgebrook. She is a core member of the Diasporic Vietnamese Artists Network, an alliance of writers and artists of Southeast Asian descent, and co-directs the Diasporic Vietnamese Literary Festival. Her writing has appeared in the *New York Times*, *USA Today*, *Salon*, and *The Rumpus*, among others. She currently teaches at California College of the Arts in San Francisco.

MOTHERLAND

The first impression: gazing, gawking, analysis of the site and its surroundings, discussion on whether it lives up to photographs from history books and brochures. Nods, murmurs, and smiles of recognition. It seems bigger. No, smaller. Opinions vary.

Then the historical context: tour guide Leah in her red visor and matching "Vietnam Specialist" T-shirt, motioning for them to keep up with her.

The Reunification Palace has gone through many transformations during the different political regimes in Vietnam, Leah says, her hand sweeping over her head for effect.

Once the home of the French governor, it is best known as the former central headquarters of the South Vietnamese government. The palace has survived several attacks and renovations through the years and now stands as a museum for us.

Members of the tour consider her their cultural ambassador, eagerly absorbing every word, since Leah has been leading tours in Southeast Asia for almost five years. She says without irony that she considers herself an honorary Vietnamese, to which her travelers, most of whom are white, nod approvingly.

While the palace, with its modern architecture and beautifully manicured gardens and fountains, is impressive, Huan is distracted by the activity surrounding it. On the main boulevard leading to the palace, mopeds and cars noisily tangle in five-lane rush hour. In the gardens around the palace, other tour groups snap pictures of the landmark, while pushcart vendors in conical hats and slippers creep around them, hoping to lure customers with their hot pastries and roasting meats.

Visual recordings come next and usually last the longest. Cameras and camcorders, of various sizes and qualities, emerge frantically once Leah steps out of the way. Postcardlike shots of the site, zoom in and out, then individual photos, and, finally, the group picture, which never takes less than ten minutes to organize.

All right, everyone, Leah yells, squinting behind the company camera. There is an option after the trip to purchase her professional-quality photos. Get real close. We're one big family, right?

Huan must resist the urge every time to flee the mass photo op, wary of squeezing into another photograph with all those red shirts. But his mother insists. Gwen's eyes plead with him when he tries to edge away, and the dutiful son must acquiesce. He stands next to his old friend Mai, who rests her head against his shoulder. She, too, is tired of the group atmosphere, but they know it is ending soon, at least for today.

They've been sightseeing all morning: the former U.S. embassy, the Notre Dame Cathedral, the Old Post Office, and the Remnants of War Museum. Individually interesting, but packaged in one day, exhausting. The next stop is the Binh Tay market, where Leah promises brief commentary and ample leisure time to wander.

Fifteen minutes are allotted for souvenirs while Leah flags down their motor coach. She instructs them to remain inside the palace garden, so that no one is left behind. She is always worried about losing people.

Do you want something? Gwen asks. The group is dispersing to various gift stands along the plaza, Mai already waiting in line at a dessert vendor. Although Huan's mother already has a large tote bag full of embroideries, a conical hat, and a miniature bronze Buddha statue, she is ready to hunt for more.

No, Huan says. I'm fine. His only purchases so far are postcards to send back to a few coworkers and friends.

Don't you want to come browse with me?

I'm tired, Mom. You go ahead. I'll wait for you here.

Okay. I'll look, and if I find something you might like—

Go, Mom. The bus will be here soon.

She leaves her tote bag with Huan and hustles to the nearest souvenir vendor. Ho Chi Minh City is a land of bargains, anything and everything on sale, an ideal match for Huan's mother, an avid shopper. Yesterday, Gwen was throwing up in the hotel bathroom all afternoon from a dubious rice pudding purchased from a sidewalk peddler. Today, fully recovered, she happily haggles with a vendor over a plastic replica of the palace.

Huan feels a tug on his pant leg. He peers over his sunglasses to the impediment.

A small boy grins a toothless smile, holding a stained cardboard box full of crumpled cigarette boxes, candy, and soda cans. He wears only shorts and rubber sandals. He bumps his merchandise against Huan's thigh. You buy now, suh.

Huan shakes his head.

C'mon. You rich American. Lots of dollahs.

He doesn't smile like he had this morning, when these child peddlers were still new and endearing. Their relentless pursuit and broken, cackling English have gnawed through his patience. Leah's advice is to avoid eye contact with tenacious vendors and beggars, and they will eventually move on. But Huan tries a different tactic, looking directly at the boy, hoping to intimidate him away permanently.

The stare-off lasts several minutes, the boy beaming and Huan scowling. The child thinks it's some kind of game with a prize at the end. Huan grows suspicious that the boy's patience can be greater than his own.

Have you made a friend? Gwen asks, quickly snapping a picture of the two.

Mom, don't, Huan says, as his mother slips the boy a Vietnamese coin piece, but it is too late. The child squeals victoriously and scampers off.

Oh, it's all right.

You've made yourself a target. Now they'll be chasing us down all afternoon.

You're exaggerating.

I'm not. He's going to tell all his friends to look for the American red-haired lady in the red T-shirt. She's giving away money.

Does somebody need a nap?

Mom.

Sweetie, his mother says, squeezing his shoulder. Relax. We're here to enjoy ourselves.

She is determined to do this. Traveling, especially in groups, is much more her thing than Huan's. On their first day, she quickly learns the names, occupations, and home states of all their fellow travelers. In exchange, they know all about Gwen and her Amerasian son's trip to Vietnam, a belated quest to discover his roots, visit the Saigon orphanage he once lived in. She divulges this story to anyone who asks, so proud of Huan's decision to learn more about his native country, something she has encouraged his whole life.

Huan realizes this must come out sooner or later. It is obvious that he and his mother are not biologically related: she, a chubby Caucasian redhead, and he, a lanky half-black, half-Vietnamese with fuzzy black hair. Gwen's enduring strategy to combat raised eyebrows and sneers is to explain their situation frankly: she and her husband adopted Huan once he arrived in America with the Operation Babylift evacuation. The way she gushes over her miraculous family and beautiful son, even the most cynical keep their opinions to themselves.

To her credit, Gwen doesn't mention, not even once to their tour companions, that she isn't supposed to be on this trip. That she is taking the place of Emily, who originally suggested this vacation to Huan for their three-year anniversary. She thought it would be fun to explore his past. Huan didn't even want to go after their breakup, but since they didn't think to buy travel insurance, his mother convinced him not to waste such a lovely trip. She even called his friend Mai, who was teaching in Japan for the year, and persuaded her to meet up with them in Vietnam. Gwen said she was doing this for Huan. It will be good for him to get away and appreciate what he does have, which is so much. His mother tries to see the best in everything and, especially now, is determined to pass this trait down to her son.

———

The Binh Tay market is in the Cholon district, a half hour's drive away, so the travelers use the downtime to rest in their tinted, air-conditioned motor coach. There are enough seats for everyone to take two and lie down, but Huan's mother likes for them to sit together. They are on vacation.

The bus is quiet. They are normally a noisy, awkward band of travelers: a mix created solely by coincidental vacation times. They are mostly families, some with small children. One family is Vietnamese, the Vus, who immigrated to America shortly after the Fall and are returning for their first visit. There's a senior couple, the Lewises, who are spending their retirement savings to see the world. There are three U.S. war veteran buddies who never seem embarrassed by their prolific dropping of words like *gooks* and *'Nam*. The old men stare at Huan when they think he's not looking, almost tempting Huan to ask if they left behind their own bastard child in Vietnam.

Mai sits across from them, napping. Her long black hair fans across the cushioned seat, reminding him briefly of Emily. He hasn't seen Mai in a few years and not regularly since high school. She seems comfortable in Vietnam, not complaining like the other tourists of the heat and humidity, probably because she's lived in Asia for the past year.

After college, Mai left for graduate school in England. Then a consulting job in Beijing. Now teaching English in Japan. She is living with a fellow teacher, a Canadian named Gordon, whom Huan has never met.

Too bad, Gwen later says, privately to Huan. She's become so pretty since high school. Good teeth.

Mom. Don't start.

I'm not saying anything. Leah is rather charming, don't you think? I know you don't usually date Caucasian girls, but she seems worldly. Fluent in three languages.

Gwen claims she wants him to date regardless of color, but he knows she is worried that he has never brought home a white girl. His last few girlfriends, including Emily, were Asian. She wants to know why her race is being unilaterally rejected.

Out the window, pink dust filters through the air, illuminating the abandoned colonial French mansions along the wide boulevards. The mopeds, cyclos, and pedestrians around their bus hustle past these ghosts, obsolete remnants of a forgotten foreign invader. The focus is on the bright gold pagoda, the center of the market, leading into hundreds of wooden vendor stalls. Twinkle lights, stuffed animals, and dangling clumps of neon rubber sandals decorate the market's tarp ceilings.

Under the pagoda, Huan's mother eyes him warily. I suppose you want to go off on your own now.

Mom, I love you.

Forget him, Mai says, leaning into Gwen. He'll just get in the way of shopping. Huan's mother smiles. She has always liked Mai.

Fine, Gwen says. Do you want to meet us for dinner then?

Sure.

Should we set up a meeting place?

I'll just find you.

As he wanders through the stands, Huan realizes there is no farmers' market like this in America. People bump against him, the locals, who are there to do business. Different languages barter and negotiate. Vietnamese, Chinese, Russian. In the livestock section, customers bend over wire cages, poking the live ducks, chickens, and pigs inside. Behind wooden tables soaked dark with blood, butchers prepare fresh meat for customers.

He walks through the aisles, stopping occasionally to watch and listen to exchanges between peddlers and patrons. Sometimes Huan believes if he listens carefully, he will understand the language. At a chicken stall where a woman is plucking a fresh kill, a policeman stares pointedly at Huan. He is wearing a tattered olive green uniform and muddy black boots. A black nightstick and a clunky archaic pistol are prominently displayed on his plastic belt. The cop has to be at least a foot shorter than Huan.

Huan smiles, unsure what else to do. When the policeman only glares, Huan casually turns around, shoving his hands deep in his pockets, and walks away. A few minutes later, he notices the same policeman peering at him from behind a pile of bananas. Huan doesn't stop at any of the stands anymore, the cop only a few paces behind him. Huan pretends not to see him and continues walking, until reaching the edge of the market, then turns around, and walks again.

Twenty minutes of this and the policeman finally approaches him. One hand clenching his nightstick, jaw locked, he barks something at Huan.

Huan shakes his head. I don't understand.

This seems to infuriate the cop even more. He stalks in a circle around Huan, muttering. Huan looks around for the nearest merchant to intercede, but they all avoid eye contact, refusing to get involved. He broadens his circle for help, spotting Mai at a vegetable stall in another aisle. His mother isn't with her.

Mai! Huan yells. The policeman jumps back at this outburst. Embarrassed, the cop begins shouting and jabbing his finger at Huan's chest. His other hand nervously fumbles for the whistle around his neck. Huan realizes if other cops are called in, he will be in more trouble.

Mai walks up to them, carrying a small sack of mangoes. She interrupts the cop's railing, says something in Vietnamese, and the policeman quickly turns his anger on her. They stand eye to eye. She doesn't raise her voice, but she doesn't back down. She listens to what he says and responds calmly. Then she looks over to Huan.

Take your hands out.

What? The cop returns his attention to him.

He thinks you're hiding something in your pockets, Mai says. Show him you're not.

Huan obeys, making a big show of waving his hands in the air.

The policeman huffs another order.

Mai bites her lip and looks at Huan. He wants to pat you down.

Are you kidding?

He thinks you stole something. Just let him do it.

By then, a curious crowd has gathered. Teenage girls, old men, tourists with cameras. Trouble happening to other people is always interesting. Huan hopes his mother is far away in another section of the market. Once Huan nods, granting permission, the cop nearly jumps him, quickly slapping into Huan's arms, legs, and midsection. Huan stares at the ground, trying to control his breathing, attempting to expel his growing rage.

The cop looks triumphant afterward, the humiliation complete. After releasing Huan, he nods, wags his finger at them, and walks off. The audience disperses.

Mai walks up to him. You okay?

Huan looks at her. I want to leave.

They go to the deli section, where faded plastic tables and chairs lie strewn around for weary customers. Mai buys them a plate of pâté chauds, golden flaky pastry shells with spicy meatball middles. They eat them in silence.

It's not fair, Huan finally says.

Yeah, Mai says.

It's bullshit. Did you get that guy's name?

What for?

I'm going to complain.

Mai looks around the market and back at him. To whom?

The police chief, the American embassy, Leah. Someone.

What were you expecting? For everyone to be nice to you?

I didn't expect to be harassed.

This is Vietnam. If they can tell you're at least part-Vietnamese, they're going to have issues with you. I've been dealing with it, too. If you want courtesy for the rest of the trip, go stand next to Leah.

It's different for me.

It's not just you, Mai says. The authorities hate overseas Vietnamese. They think we're rude and arrogant to come back home, throw money around, and expect to be treated like royalty.

I'm not acting like that.

No. They don't know you. So don't take it personally.

He doesn't know why he is. He has experienced discrimination before, plenty of it, in America, though his parents did their best to shield him from it. But it bothers him that the Vietnamese are looking down at him, angry at him. They want to show him how un-Vietnamese he is. Well, he knows that. He always has.

As he tries to relax, Huan focuses on his calm, patient companion. Hey, he says, patting her hand. Thanks. He realizes it's a little strange to have Mai, little Mai, rescuing him. Two years older, Huan remembers how nervous and awkward Mai was in high school, how she always sought him out for advice. She has matured during their years apart. She's grown up.

She pats him back. You're welcome.

Where's my mom?

She's standing in line to see a fortune-teller.

A scam.

No, just fun. It's cheap anyway.

Did she talk to you?

Mai hesitates, then smiles her answer.

I'm sorry, Huan says, staring at his food. She doesn't know when to shut up.

She's worried about you.

This isn't the first time I've been dumped.

I know it's not about Emily.

I don't know what I'm doing here, Huan says. This trip was never my idea. First, it was Emily's, and now my mom's.

Mai looks down at the table. But it's a good idea. So what if it isn't yours?

I'm glad you're here.

Me too.

It's been years, Mai. Are you ever planning on coming back to America?

Sure I am. She takes a bite of her pastry and fastidiously wipes her mouth with a napkin. Huan decides not to press her on when.

She tells him more about her classes in Japan and her boyfriend Gordon. He tells her about the new responsibilities at his job and how much work he'll have on his desk once he returns. They reminisce about old high school and college friends. She laughs for the first time on their vacation, a reminder of the old Mai.

What are you doing tomorrow morning? Huan asks.

Why?

We're not going to the tunnels until the afternoon. My mom and I are visiting the nursery center that handled my adoption.

Her face doesn't change at all, and Huan suddenly remembers. Mai is an orphan, too.

If you're busy, it's okay. He feels terrible. How can he forget? Mai grew up in foster homes her whole life. Sometimes she spent college breaks at his family's house.

I'm not, Mai finally says. I'll come.

Okay, Huan says. Thanks. Embarrassed, he looks away, into the crowded market, everywhere heads full of smooth, black hair.

The Children of Mary's Adoption Center is located in an old government building on the western side of District One. The morning traffic on the main boulevard in front of the center is heavy and noisy, and the children are instructed to stay within the building's gates at all times.

In the courtyard, young orphans bustle around Huan's mother. They coo at Gwen with outstretched hands, softly chanting the English word *please* over and over. She smiles at them, struggling with a plastic trash bag in her arms, and dramatically hands each child a stuffed animal, rubber ball, or plastic toy.

When one of the little girls gives his mother a kiss, Huan turns around and heads back inside. He remembers the argument he had with his mother before leaving for Vietnam, when he discovered half her luggage space devoted to these toys. She couldn't understand why he was so angry about the gifts.

These children don't have anything, Huan. What's wrong with giving if we can?

He couldn't bring himself to tell her. The toys would be played with for a few days, but they'd eventually get dirty, break, get thrown away, and the orphans would still be destitute. They didn't need this kind of charity.

He finds Mai in the hallway, looking at photographs of children on the wall. Huan walks up behind her.

Are you looking for her? he asks. Mai's childhood friend Kim was also on the Babylift. Huan never knew her very well, except that she always seemed angry, blaming the bad things that happened in her life on everyone else, often Mai.

Mai nods sheepishly. I don't even know which adoption agency she left from.

Too bad she couldn't come.

She's too busy with her kids and work. Besides, I don't think she would've anyway.

Why not?

Mai pauses for a moment. I think she might hate Vietnam more than she hates America.

Huan can understand that. He wonders if it is one of the few things he and Kim would ever agree on.

Do you ever talk to the Reynoldses anymore? Huan asks.

We write. Christmas cards, birthdays.

No plans to visit?

Mai shakes her head. Not right now. I'm busy, they're busy. They have a new foster child. He's only seven.

They walk along the halls, scrutinizing each picture. Mai slowly wanders ahead of him. Huan hangs back, remembering that Mai doesn't like people watching over her shoulder. She couldn't stand other people looking at the same picture as she at museums. She prefers observing alone.

Huan is grateful that Mai decided to come today. Their cyclo driver got lost twice, raising suspicions that he was trying to pad his fare. Mai sharply threatened him in Vietnamese. A few minutes and two turns later, they arrived at the center.

Eight years ago, the Vietnamese government granted permission for the adoption center to reopen in Ho Chi Minh City. The facilities look spare, but well maintained, with a fresh coat of paint on the building's exterior and vibrant potted plants in each room. The staff and children seem happy. The orphans stare unabashedly at Huan, recognizing his mixed heritage and that he was once like them. But he isn't. These children are pure Vietnamese.

There are no more Amerasian children, the despised products of American military men and Vietnamese women finally aborting with the war's end. No, those bastards are grown. Some gone, but not all. Huan realizes he should be more worried about other Amerasians in Vietnam than anyone else. The Amerasians who were left behind have good reason to hate Huan. They had to bear the brunt of a country's devastation and poverty. Huan searches for them in the streets of Ho Chi Minh City, but he hasn't spotted any yet. Perhaps they have learned to fade into the scenery, granting the country's wish just to disappear. The children of the dust mercifully dissipated, the last bitter reminders of a hated war.

Huan feels a tickle on his elbow. Sophie, the center's founder and president, smiles at him. A bone-thin white haired American in her seventies, she looks at him like Gwen does, with naïve, hopeless affection. He is getting this a lot today, his status of Babylift orphan suddenly elevating him to Christ child. Sophie was on the same evacuation flight as Huan. She is the one who placed him in Gwen's arms twenty-six years ago.

Thanks again for taking the time to meet with us, Huan says.

Oh, it's my pleasure, hon. I always enjoy seeing my babies all grown-up and successful.

Well, I don't know about that.

Oh, hush. She shakes her head at him. So many people loved you, Huan, so many wanted you for their own. I remember.

Huan smiles wanly. She probably says this to every orphan.

Brunch is ready, Sophie says, looking around. Where's your mother?

She's still giving away her toys.

She is such a generous soul, Sophie says, shaking her head. You are so lucky to have her.

Brunch is set up on the patio, tame American cuisine of sandwiches and salads, which Gwen is grateful for.

Not that I don't love all the new, exotic things we're trying here, but I do miss plain, good American food. Am I right?

Sophie and the other staff at the table smile at her. Huan looks over at Mai, whose face appears carefully blank.

They have mementos to share. Sophie passes around photo albums taken during the Babylift, and in those washed out black-and-white pictures, they try to distinguish Huan from crowds of little faces. There is only one individual photograph of Huan, which Gwen already has a copy of back home. His identification picture, full name Huan Anh Cung, scrawled on a sheet of paper and held in front of his gaunt, confused face.

The admittance and medical records are next. In a thick, faded green book on pages that record many other orphans' lives, they locate Huan's information. He stayed in Sophie's adoption center for nine months before the Babylift evacuation. His biological parents are listed as unknown. He was named by the nuns at the orphanage where he was abandoned. His medical records indicate he suffered from bronchitis, ear infections, and boils.

None of this is new. Huan's mother requested his background information from the adoption center long ago. But he nods and smiles when he is supposed to, because he knows they are all watching him, expecting gratitude and humility.

This information would have been more interesting for Emily. She was always curious about his vague heritage and couldn't understand why he wasn't, too. Emily was not adopted. Born to Korean immigrant parents, she was close to them and her extended family and cousins, aunts, uncles, and grandparents. Huan agreed to go to Vietnam with her, for her, because he liked that she was so interested in his past. He never realized until afterward that her motivation to learn about Vietnam was to prove to her family that he really was Asian, not just black. Her work went unfinished. She broke up with him after realizing her mother would never ultimately approve. Maybe if he were half-white it would be different, all Asian even better. She offered to buy out her half of the trip. She even suggested he still go with someone else.

You know, we arranged reunion tours for the adoptees last year, Sophie says, looking at Huan. I thought we sent the information packet to you.

He feels the others' eyes on him, expecting an explanation for the rejection. I couldn't take off work, Huan says.

That's too bad. Sophie grins. You would have enjoyed it. We organized the adoptees to visit the orphanages or maternity hospitals where they were first found. If I remember your file correctly, you came to us from Blessed Haven. That's just south of here in the Delta.

We're going to the Delta, his mother says. Tomorrow as part of our tour.

How lovely, Sophie says. Well, if you'd like to visit I can make a call.

That would be wonderful, Gwen says, eagerly leaning forward.

Huan doesn't bring it up until after they leave the center. He wants to wait until they get back to their hotel room, but he can't. They are in a taxicab, Mai is sitting in front, and Huan tries his best to keep his voice down.

I never said I wanted to visit the orphanage.

Gwen looks at him, surprised. Why wouldn't you?

Maybe I don't feel like it. Maybe today has been enough.

I don't understand, she says. Why would we come all this way without talking to the people who once knew you and took care of you? Sophie says there is a nun who believes she remembers you.

You don't get to make that decision for me.

Why are you getting so angry?

If I wanted to do this, I would have asked. The reason you asked is because you wanted to.

Fine. If you don't want to go, we don't have to go.

They're already expecting us.

I'll call Sophie tomorrow. I'll fix it, don't worry.

Gwen is crying. From the front seat, Mai reaches over and hands her a tissue. For the remainder of the ride they listen to street noise from the driver's rolled-down window. In the sun's noon position, Huan can see the city's smog hovering over its inhabitants. They breathe the pollution in easily, accepting the foul sight and smell as natural.

I n a dense forest forty-five miles outside of Ho Chi Minh City, a guide in faded green army attire leads the tour group to an open-sided hut. They sit in dusty plastic chairs while a woman in black pajamas turns on the big-screen television.

Beautiful shade trees and smiling, simple Vietnamese peasants, nature, serenity, safety in the town of Cu Chi. And then the looming American B-52s unleash their bombs. Bursts of gunfire crackle from the television speakers. Clouds of smoke overwhelm the screen, making the peasants on screen cry and suffer. Out of dust, the valiant Communist liberators emerge. Young, beautiful, courageous faces. They will rescue their country.

The female guide must notice the audience fidgeting uncomfortably. She appears to expect this, laughs as she turns the video off, explaining that it is old, times have changed, and everyone, American and Vietnamese, are all friends now.

For their paying friends, Cu Chi Tunnels, the 250-kilometer underground headquarters of the Viet Cong during the war, is now a popular tourist attraction. The maze of tunnels especially widened to accommodate larger Western sightseers, a recreational firing range where visitors can shoot AK-47 rifles, souvenir booths selling Zippo lighters, pens made from bullets, rubber sandals, keepsake T-shirts.

Leah and the Vietnamese tunnel guide assure their group that the tunnels are safe and well maintained for the public. They are both much shorter than Huan. The tunnel guide climbs down the ladder first, and one by one, each traveler follows. Some of the older, heavier people struggle to fit down the snug hole, with Leah's help. The ceiling in the underground areas barely reaches six feet and the tunnels themselves only three. They get on their hands and knees and crawl farther into the tunnels, the guide in front loudly reciting the tunnel's history.

Huan can't help admiring this vast underworld. These Vietnamese rat people whom the Americans so underestimated hand-dug and created a three-level network that once stretched to the Cambodian border. Protected by tiger pits, punji stake traps, and firing posts, the tunnels successfully endured American bombs, allowing their intricate subterranean maze to flourish with kitchens, hospitals, sleeping chambers, and even a small theater. The American veterans are especially impressed, their eyes memorizing these once mythical caverns, finally permitted to see Charlie's side.

The damp earthy walls and moist air are making Huan dizzy. He is tired of bumping into people's sweaty bodies, aware they can't help it, but desperately needing space. There is no space here. Everyone is on top of each other. These Cu Chi guerrillas must have had incredible endurance. Huan feels he is not selfish about many things, but air, he decides, he cannot share.

As they crawl into another narrow tunnel, Huan stops, falling back on his heels. Although the guide has advised them to take small, short breaths, he inhales a lungful of stale air and immediately begins coughing.

Hey, Mai says. He feels her hand on his shoulder. You okay?

The exit is only twenty yards ahead. Huan creeps faster. When he sees sunlight poking along the walls, an adrenaline boost propels him forward, fingers digging through the clay earth until he reaches the surface. Then he remembers Mai is behind him and helps pull her out.

At the next tunnel-crawling station, which the guide warns is even smaller and longer than the first, Huan decides to sit out. Mai offers to keep him company and he doesn't argue.

They sit at a rusted picnic table, next to a B-52 crater pit the size of a small fishing pond.

I'm not claustrophobic, Huan says.

Yeah, Mai says. Neither am I.

No really, Huan says. It was very unreasonable down there.

I agree.

Huan takes a long drink of the bottled water he bought at a vendor's cart. The water tastes cloying, metallic, and Huan suspects it is a used bottle refilled with tap water. A skinny boy carrying a pail of soft drinks sneaks up to them, tapping Huan on the shoulder. Coca? he asks, grinning and nodding vigorously.

Huan shakes his head and looks away. But the child is persistent. He runs to Huan's other side and asks again.

No buy, Huan says firmly.

It doesn't work. He won't leave, even when Mai sternly scolds him in Vietnamese. The boy pants loudly and steadily through his mouth. Whenever he feels Huan glancing his way, his posture straightens, his arms struggling to raise his scratched pail higher.

Help me, the boy says. Buy fresh Coca. Help me.

When the child nudges him again with the pail, Huan slams his water bottle down on the table, startling the boy and Mai.

I don't want your stupid drink, Huan says fiercely. Get the hell away from us.

The child jolts in shock, his mouth dropping open. Huan realizes the boy probably doesn't understand what he said, it is just the yelling that scares him. The boy's eyes turn red, his jaw begins to shake. But instead of tears, the child lets out a terrible howl.

You look down? the boy screams, dropping his pail. No better! You no better! The child is shaking violently, like he is suffering a seizure.

Mai stands up, trying to put a hand on the child's arm, but he ignores her, angry with her, too, continuing to scream. Tourists wander out of the gift booths, staring. The boy is crying in such terror. Finally, one of the tunnel guides rushes from the gate and grabs the boy by the arm, dragging him away, howling.

The boy's pail has fallen over in the rage, his soft drink cans scattered over the dusty ground. Mai begins picking them up.

I can't leave my hotel room, Huan says.

You didn't have to yell at him, Mai says, setting the pail on the table.

I know, Huan says. It was stupid.

Then why are you doing it?

I don't know. I don't know why I'm here.

You didn't want to come?

No. I was talked into it. I knew better, too, that's what pisses me off. Finding the past doesn't make anyone feel better when it's just bad.

What's bad?

Are you kidding? They hate me.

Who?

You've seen it. Cops, little boys, everybody.

Mai shakes her head. They don't even know you.

They don't have to. They hate Amerasians. They wish I didn't exist.

You can't blame them for not wanting to be here. They didn't do this.

I did?

Yes. Whoever said learning about your past is supposed to feel good? This is you, Huan, about how you feel. You're the one who hates them.

Huan sees two Vietnamese guides taking a cigarette break. They never wanted me, Huan says.

You don't know why your parents gave you up.

I'm supposed to accept that? It's different for you. You know your mother died and didn't abandon you on purpose. I have nothing to go on.

Do you really want answers? Then go to the orphanage tomorrow. I'll go with you.

It didn't help going to the adoption center.

That was your fault. Do you know how many orphans would love to know their histories? Remember Kim? She has no idea. And look what happened to her—married to a man she doesn't respect, with kids she doesn't want. You're taking it for granted.

Right, I should be more grateful.

Mai stands up suddenly. Forget it.

I'm sorry, Huan says. Really, I'm being a jerk. I don't mean to snap.

I know, Mai says, looking up. There's our group. We should go.

Across the woods, Huan can see the guide beginning to pull their travel companions from the hole in the ground. They poke their heads out and emerge into the sunlight, disoriented, panting for air. His mother is one of the last to surface. Her hair is disheveled, face pink with perspiration. She looks around frantically, until she sees Huan. Her relieved smile is genuine. Huan finishes his water and rejoins the group.

———

In the morning, they take a ferry and bus ride to the Delta, which, Leah says, is often referred to as the rice bowl of Vietnam. Out of the city, the air is fresh, the landscape clean and unspoiled. The tour charters a banana boat ride through local estuaries, where villages of wooden huts balance precariously on tall stilts and half-naked children splash in the yellow water. They visit a floating market and gaze at sampans overloaded with colorful vegetables, fruit, and fish.

Huan sits between Mai and his mother on the boat. While Gwen and the other tour members exclaim wonder over the various sights, Mai remains silent. Huan observes his friend, who seems absolutely unaffected by the scenery around her. In retrospect, Huan realizes that Mai hasn't really expressed any great pleasure or disappointment in their last few days of sightseeing. She has declared no favorite landmark. Except for food, she has purchased no souvenirs.

During the bus ride through the rice paddies, Huan's mother spots a peasant family plowing a field with a water buffalo. Though Huan pleads with her not to, his mother convinces Leah to stop the bus to take pictures. Some of the other tourists think it is a good idea, too, pulling out their own cameras. The peasants appear irritated, confused by all the attention. His mother squints behind her camera, fiddling with the zoom function, trying to capture the perfect photographs. When she reboards the bus, smiling with satisfaction, Huan can't even look at her.

For lunch, they feast on a home-cooked meal at a family's sugarcane plantation. The food is diverse and sumptuous, probably not what this albeit wealthy family has for lunch every day. Everything, the housemistress joyously boasts, is fresh from the Delta: catfish, mangoes, rice, cabbage, pork, poultry, and, of course, sugar.

The tour group is encouraged to spend time exploring the grounds of the plantation estate. Huan stands at the balcony, looking down at the winding rows of sugarcane. Huan's mother approaches him, tapping him on the shoulder hesitantly.

I talked to Sophie this morning, Gwen says. She said that they won't expect you, but if you change your mind, you are welcome.

Okay, Huan says.

So I think you should. I think you want to, and if my being there will be distracting, then I'll stay with the tour.

Huan considers this. You sure?

His mother blinks in surprise, and Huan realizes she really does want to come. Yes, she says. Of course.

I'll see you tonight, Huan says.

Huan finds Mai outside, silently watching the laborers shuck sugar-cane. Do you want to go? he asks.

Mai looks at him in confusion, then remembers. Oh.

You don't have to, Huan says. The afternoon activities they would miss include visiting a snake farm, a silkworm factory, and a Buddhst pagoda. Maybe she'd rather do that.

No, Mai says. I'll go.

They make plans to meet up with the group that evening for the ferry ride back to Ho Chi Minh City. Huan's mother insists he take her camera, in case he might want to take pictures. Leah arranges for a motorbike taxi to take them to the orphanage, which is near the Vinh Long province.

They drive past Delta villages, where the poverty is even worse than the homeless they see in the city. Young girls slap wet clothes against large rocks in the river. Small children run after their taxi, fading in the clouds of dust the motorbike kicks up.

After following a long dirt road for nearly twenty minutes, the taxi driver slows. Unlike the adoption center, the orphanage doesn't appear to have been renovated since Huan left. Only half a gate remains as the entrance to a run-down building connected to a chapel. Vegetation stretches over the chipped concrete walls.

Inside, Mai talks with a younger nun, Sister Trieu, who takes them inside to the prayer room to wait for Sister Phuong. She is one of the few remaining nuns who worked at the orphanage when Huan was still there.

Mai sits in a wooden chair, waiting, while Huan paces around the room.

Where are the kids? Huan asks. It is too quiet. He can hear his own footsteps and breathing.

Maybe it's not an orphanage anymore, Mai says.

An older nun comes in with Sister Trieu. They converge in the middle of the room. The three women talk, and Huan listens. Occasionally, the older woman looks at him, but then returns to speaking to Mai.

Mai turns to Huan. Sister Phuong says she remembers you.

Huan nods and smiles obediently.

Sister Phuong points at Huan's face and laughs.

Mai smiles. She says you've grown into your big ears.

They confirm it is the orphanage, but it is on the second floor. Sister Phuong invites them to come upstairs with her to look around.

In a small office stuffed with neglected bookshelves and filing cabinets, Sister Phuong peers over a large record book fingering each name down the list, turning each page slowly.

Mai and Huan sit across from her and wait. The office door is open, and Huan can hear the children moving around on the floor. They are remarkably quieter than the orphans at the adoption center, not much laughter or yelling, children's usual markers. Maybe it's naptime. One young girl passes their door. Her shoulders hunch over, her feet shuffle across the floor. She isn't curious enough to look in at the new visitors.

Ah, Sister Phuong says, looking up triumphantly. She gestures for Huan and Mai to come to her side and look.

The print is faded and nearly legible. Huan looks at Mai.

It's your name, Mai says, her eyes lifting from the book. You weighed six pounds when you arrived. They estimated you were only a few days old.

Huan stares at where the nun's finger is still pointing, the first evidence of his existence. Though he realizes the information is sketchy and unreliable at best, he believes it.

They walk through the nursery, where Sister Phuong says Huan lived. It is a large room with rows and rows of wooden cribs. Several nuns tend to the crying children. Some of the babies are strong enough to stand, their small hands gripping the rails. Most, however, are not.

Sister Phuong asks if they'd like to hold a baby. It occurs to Huan that the older nun may think he and Mai are a couple, perhaps wanting to adopt. But Mai wants to. She holds a baby girl close to her chest, caressing the child's face and cooing into her ear.

What do you think the chances are of this baby getting adopted? Mai asks, looking at Huan.

I don't know.

Mai presses her lips against the child's forehead. The baby struggles in Mai's near-suffocating embrace. Yes, you do, she says. The Babylift is over.

The taxicab is supposed to pick them up at four o'clock, but it is late. Since Mai and Huan have already said their good-byes, they stand at the orphanage gate by the side of the road, waiting.

You know she really can't remember me, Huan says.

What do you mean?

You saw the book. There were a dozen more on the shelves. There were hundreds of babies. Do you really think she remembers one baby from over twenty-five years ago?

Mai glares at him. I think she was very nice.

I'm not saying she wasn't nice.

Why would she lie to you? What good does it do? You were here, you know they took care of you and found you a good home, and you still want more?

Why are you so upset?

You have so much to be grateful for. And all you've done since coming here is complain.

Okay, enough. Stop acting like you're so fine with everything here.

Excuse me?

I don't love it here. And neither do you. If you did, you wouldn't be living in China or Japan. We both have a right to be pissed. This country orphaned you, too.

Just because I'm not disowning this country every other minute doesn't mean I don't have a problem with it.

I know, Huan says. He takes a breath. Then why don't you ever talk about them? Why can't you just tell me?

Mai shrugs, looking away. I don't know.

They sit on the dusty ground, leaning against the concrete wall, shoulder to shoulder.

I haven't said anything, Mai says, because I'm not sure.

Huan waits for several breaths until he speaks again. Why haven't you come to Vietnam until now? You must have had chances.

I meant to. I think I got scared. I didn't want to go alone, or even when Gordon offered to come with me. When Gwen called, I knew this was my chance. She looks at Huan. I knew I could come here with you and your mom. Even if I wasn't completely ready.

Is it hard for you to be here? Huan asks hesitantly. For all the years he's known Mai, she has never talked about this, beyond admitting a few facts. But now that she has seen so much of his past, he feels more comfortable asking about hers. He thinks she might want him to.

No, Mai says. She pauses for a long time.

My mother was from the North. No one knew who her family was when she died. So our neighbor used the money my mother left behind and some of her own to put me on a boat escaping from Saigon. She attached a note on me that I should be adopted by an American family. I still have it. The social worker gave it to me a few years ago.

Huan knows very little of the boat refugee experience except what he has read in textbooks. The escapes were difficult, horrifying even, especially if they were caught by the Communists, or worse, Thai pirates.

Do you remember the boat ride?

I remember sleeping a lot. They kept telling us kids to sleep so we wouldn't think about how hungry we were. We got sick. I don't even remember how we got to the refugee camp.

Do you remember your mother?

A little. I was very young. We used to sleep in the same bed. When she was still alive, she used to comb my hair, which she let grow long because she thought it was pretty. When she died, our neighbor cut it off. It wasn't practical. I cried so much. I thought I looked like a boy.

You're lucky that you knew her.

Mai glances sideways at him, annoyed. Huan, you have a mother.

Huan pulls away from her. I know that.

Then why does it matter if your biological mother willingly gave you up or not? Why do you only care about the people who've rejected you?

I don't.

Your mother tries so hard. Mai shakes her head. It might feel suffocating sometimes, but all that effort—it's for you.

The taxi has still not arrived. Huan looks back at the dilapidated convent and orphanage, his first home. Can I ask you another favor? he says.

What? Huan hands her his mother's camera. He jogs over to stand in front of the orphanage and waits for her to take the picture.

————

Huan can never really complain about his parents. They always showed him love, even during his angry years when he threw their devotion into their faces, sneering that they treated him like a charity case, their trendy Vietnamese baby whose life they rescued. How could they really love him? They didn't even know him.

They forgave him for all of this. They continued to love him, even when he couldn't believe or accept it. Though the workers at the orphanage and adoption center looked after hundreds of babies, Huan realizes they aren't to blame either.

It is Sunday night in Ho Chi Minh City, and the youths of the town are out to celebrate. They don their best clothes, buff their motorpeds to a shine, and prepare to coast the streets. There is no speed or weaving through the streets tonight, no near accidents trying to rush from one place to another. No destination. The pleasure is in the journey, in the twenty-kilometer-per-hour ride.

It is Huan's idea to go out. It isn't on the itinerary. His mother is tired from their day in the Delta, but it is their last night in Ho Chi Minh City. Tomorrow they leave for central Vietnam. Huan hears from the hotel concierge that downtown on Sunday night is not to be missed. They are on vacation. Surprised but pleased, Gwen agrees to go out with him and Mai.

They sit at a sidewalk café on a busy boulevard, with an unobstructed view of the cruisers loitering on the streets. Children effortlessly balance on the back of motorbikes without holding on, smiling and waving at passing friends and family. High school girls with bobbed black hair sail through traffic on bicycles, their brilliant white *ao dai* fluttering behind them. Street musicians strum mandolins and whistle into flutes for spare change. Teenage boys ignite firecrackers in the alleys, splashing smoky colors into the ink night.

I'm sorry you didn't come, Huan says to his mother. Mai has left to browse at the gift shop next door. That I didn't let you. It would have been nice.

I'm just glad you went. Gwen smiles at him. He thinks this isn't enough of an apology, but she is his mother. She knows who he is.

Mai returns with a gift bag. She shows them a deep red jade bracelet she has purchased. It is smooth, unblemished, with flecks of gold in it.

It's beautiful, Gwen says. It will look lovely against your skin.

It's for a friend, Mai says. But thank you.

Though it is getting late, the streets still grow crowded. They share the roads generously, so different from during the day when people viciously maneuver for room. For cruising, the more, the better. Huan's mother cannot resist any longer. She must come closer and take pictures.

I was afraid of hating everyone here, Mai says.

Huan looks at her.

They sent us to America because of you. Mai shrugs her shoulders. Our parents saw pictures of you full of food and in rich people's arms. They thought we'd get that, too. But we came too late. We weren't babies anymore, so nobody wanted us. It was no different from Vietnam.

Nearby, a little girl claps two blocks of wood together, enticing customers to come to her family's pho stall for fresh noodle soup. Eager patrons squat on plastic footstools, slurping warm broth, simmering beef strips, and vermicelli noodles.

How do you feel now? Huan asks.

I know better. It's not our parents' fault. Or anyone else's here. How could I be angry with them, expect them to do right when there was no such thing? When everything here was wrong?

Huan nods, understanding. It was a war.

It was.

They look out onto the street again. The cruisers, so proud and happy. They are young, born after the war. They only know Ho Chi Minh City, while Saigon is a memory that their parents and grandparents speak of. Their futures are pure.

A young man and woman slowly ride past the café. He is wearing a leather jacket, his hair slick with styling gel. She wears a bright yellow dress, her hair in a braid down her back. The woman's arms are wrapped around the man's waist, not because she needs to, but because they are obviously in love. When the couple passes their table, they wave. After a moment, Huan and Mai wave back.

BAO PHI is a two-time Minnesota Grand Slam champion and a National Poetry Slam finalist. He has appeared on HBO Presents *Russell Simmons Def Poetry*, featured in the live performances and taping of the blockbuster diasporic Vietnamese variety show *Paris By Night 114: Tôi Là Người Việt Nam*, and a poem of his appeared in the 2006 *Best American Poetry* anthology. The *New York Times* wrote of his first collection of poetry, *Sông I Sing* (Coffee House Press), "In this song of his very American self, every poem Mr. Phi writes rhymes with the truth." In 2012, the *Star Tribune*'s inaugural Best of Minnesota issue named Bao Phi as Best Spoken Word Artist.

WAR BEFORE MEMORY: A VIETNAMESE AMERICAN PROTEST ORGANIZER'S HISTORY AGAINST *MISS SAIGON*

I'm born in Saigon, just inside the Year of the Tiger. My dad is half Vietnamese, half Chinese. My mom is mostly Vietnamese, she's pretty sure. Both lovers of poetry, they name me Thien-bao: treasure from heaven.

Three months later, bombs are falling from the sky as they shell the airport, trying to kill us. My mom and dad take turns holding me in the bomb shelter, as the world around us shakes and explodes all night. I don't learn this until years later, and it's an odd thing to hear from your own family: we were almost killed before you had the ability to form memory.

———

1975, my parents raise six kids and take care of my paternal grandfather in Phillips, South Minneapolis. Our house is two blocks from Little Earth housing projects. The neighborhood is densely populated with American Indians, a people who know about a great many things, including broken American promises. Many years later, as a teenager, I'll march with American Indian activists in solidarity as they protest a visiting football team that, like *Miss Saigon*, claims to honor the people that they exploit. I'll also read somewhere that Phillips is the largest, poorest, and most racially diverse neighborhood in the Twin Cities.

But when I was a little kid, I just knew it was rough. My earliest experience with multiculturalism is on the school bus: kids of all hues, from all over the world, call me chink.

———

When I was a baby, I didn't have to do much to escape death. Growing up in Phillips, I soon realized that a lot of people in the world wanted to hurt me. Because I was Vietnamese, because I was Asian, because I was not like them, because I was not a part of their crew, because I was around and they were bored, because I was not white and therefore suspicious, because they had been hurt and wanted to hurt someone else, because I could never be American. I learned to be fast on my feet. Rumor has it, one of my distant relatives was an activist who fled from China and took up an assumed surname: Phi, meaning swift, fast running or flying. In Phillips I live up to my namesake.

———

I'm not more than ten when my dad brings me to an Oriental—excuse me, Asian—grocery store in Saint Paul. While he shops, I go to the front of the store to watch a young white boy play a video game. Other small Asian boys flock there too, quietly watching him play. His older sister glares at us, and says to her brother, "these gooks are surrounding us." As if we were the ones who torched her people's hamlets.

———

Around the same time, my mom takes me to Frank's Nursery and Crafts. She loves to garden, and they're having a sale. When the sales clerk finishes ringing us up, my mom looks at the final price and says, I think it's too much. The clerk checks and says, no, this is what you owe. My mom asks her to check it again, so she goes over the receipt. There is a long line of customers behind us; they start to shuffle uncomfortably. The cashier says she checked—there's nothing wrong, pay up. My mom hesitates, then says, "no, you are wrong, it's too much." The people behind us groan, and the look they give my mom is unmistakable. They don't have to say it. The way my mom's shoulders get stiff shows all of us she can feel their glares. The manager comes over. He checks the receipt and finds that the cashier hit 22 instead of 2, and tried to overcharge my mom by $40 dollars. The people in line behind us murmur, embarrassed at their assumption, and chuckle uncomfortably. But my mom doesn't wait for an apology from any of them—she sets her lips, holds my hand, and we leave without looking back.

———

I'm a teenager, shopping with my mom for groceries at Cub Foods. In the parking lot, a Vietnam Vet starts shouting at a Hmong family, two parents and two kids. "I fought for your people, you owe me!" he screams at them. They don't look at him, they keep walking, their shoulders turn in towards each other as if they're trying to make themselves as small a target as possible. I see this and I want to say something, but I don't. I feel like an unlit match.

———

The first Persian Gulf War, and I have two brothers in the military overseas. I fancy myself a teenage activist. I go to all the rallies and say my family has already been torn apart by war once, I don't want to see it happen again, don't want to see it happen to another country and culture and people. Even though I am still living in Phillips, I am only attracted to white women, and I don't think there's anything wrong with that. In my high school, the Vietnamese students in the Asian club ask me why I get involved in all of these political causes but never participate in Asian club. I have no answer for them.

———

> *Tonight I bet that you and I will get along*
> *Forget about the threat, forget the Viet Cong.*
> —"The Heat Is On In Saigon," Miss Saigon

Miss Saigon is a play about a Vietnamese prostitute in desperate need of rescue from evil Vietnamese men and the war-torn Third World. It may be a nice place to visit but it sure doesn't seem like a good place to raise kids. Shut your mouth—there's a helicopter in it! On stage! The production values! Well there were helicopters in Vietnam, and prostitutes, and white soldiers, and bad Vietnamese men, and mixed race orphans, so the play must be historically accurate and shit. The Vietnamese woman shoots herself in the stomach so she can sing one last song while dying in the arms of the white man. I am much, much younger when I ask my mom if she wants to go see this play, because it's about Vietnam. She shakes her head and says, in Vietnamese, "that is not about us." She says it like she's explaining to me that Santa Claus doesn't really exist.

———

I have no problem with stories about prostitutes, if they are written by prostitutes wanting to tell their story.

———

A couple of years later, and it's the first *Miss Saigon* protest. It's freezing, we stamp our feet on the streets of downtown Minneapolis. Many white people walk by us in fur coats, but many of them smile apologetically. Some of them even turn away in solidarity, and decide not to go see *Miss Saigon*. An elderly woman, Esther Torii Suzuki, is protesting with us. Over the years I grow to admire her and see her as my mentor, treasuring her plucky stories about internment camp and wearing pantsuits. David Mura is there, with his young daughter. The Ordway creates Community Cultural Committees, including an Asian American one. When they bring the play back in 1999, they don't even mention it to the Asian American Cultural Committee.

———

My mom and I go to Vietnam. It's the first time she's been back since the war, it's the second time I've been back. I finally get to meet my uncles, crazy Northerners, hardcore nationalists who stayed North after Dien Bien Phu while my parents, seeking an education, went South. Vietnamese people, you know what this means. My mom had not seen her brothers in over 40 years due to war. They miss their little sister, they joke with her and they lecture each other, they are kind to me, her youngest son. But something is underneath. Whether or not they feel my dad fought for the wrong side. The inter-village beef, the resentment that their little sister can afford to lend them American dollars—we're poor in America, but what few dollars we have are gigantic in Vietnam. We can even save those big dollars, and if we get enough, we have the privilege to buy tickets to Broadway musicals that insist that they're historically accurate depictions of what happened to our family, our people.

———

The play *Miss Saigon* is here in Minnesota for the second time. The actress who plays Kim, the female lead, is in a nearby park for a meet and greet. I stand patiently in line as men and women walk up to her, shake her hand, and tell her what an inspiration she is. Her smile is bright but she looks tired. When it's my turn, I smile, and I tell her I'm one of the principal organizers of the protests of *Miss Saigon* here in Minnesota, but that I want to make sure she knows we're not protesting her or any of the other Asian American actors in the play. I've never seen a smile disappear so quickly. She tells me I shouldn't be protesting the play because her character is a strong Asian woman. She also says the play "tells the truth" about Vietnam.

I tell her I was born in that country during the war. My mom and dad survived, made sure I and my siblings survived. My mom held me when the bombs fell. My parents raised six kids in an economically poor neighborhood in a country that didn't want them. My parents' story tells a truth about Vietnam too. Why isn't anyone interested in their truth? I ask her.

The woman who plays Kim says nothing—she turns away from me, reaches for the next hand to shake, and smiles.

———

SPOILER ALERT: the brown person dies, and the white people, though saddened, live to learn a valuable lesson.

———

I am standing on the sidewalk at the Ordway, handing out informational leaflets with information about the stereotypes, the racism and the sexism, of *Miss Saigon*. I have been instructed to be polite, not to argue with anyone no matter how rude they are to me, to always take the high ground in all encounters. An Asian woman drives her car slowly by me, and her daughter, a mixed race girl no more than ten, glares at me from the passenger side window. "You're stupid!" she yells while looking directly at me. "How can you protest love?" You really should be wearing a seat belt, I think to myself. The Asian woman turns her car around in a slow loop, so that her daughter can yell insults at me again. "You're stupid," she yells at me, again and again. Her mother loops the car around about three times, glares at me wordlessly as she drives by at a crawl each time, a cruel smile on her face, as her young daughter harangues me from the passenger seat. It's like groundhog's day for their venom. "How can you protest love?" the little girl yells at me. You don't even understand your own hate, I want to tell her, how can you understand what love is?

___

In a strong G.I.'s embrace
flee this life
flee this place!
—"*The Movie in My Mind,*" Miss Saigon

My dad was a soldier who fought on the battlefields of his own country for 10 years for South Vietnam, he lost his brother and sister-in-law to a bomb. Nobody ever asks about his truth.

___

In 2003, Vietnamese American undercover police officer Duy Ngo is shot by a fellow police officer. Even though the officer who shot him opened fire with an MP5, a non-regulation sub machine gun he was not authorized to use while on duty, nearly killing Ngo, the Minneapolis police department attempted to blame Ngo for the incident. Duy Ngo committed suicide in 2010.

Vietnamese men, they can't tell when we're friend or foe, and pretty soon we can't either.

___

Is the white man's truth always bigger than ours?

___

Many years later, I'm reading a book by Anthony Bourdain, a white man whom I admire. He compares Vietnam to meeting a woman and immediately falling in love. "You sense that given the opportunity, this is the woman you want to spend the rest of your life—" Stop it.

———

It's now. The United States is on the brink of bombing Syria. The Ordway is bringing *Miss Saigon* back to Minnesota for the third time. This play, that romanticizes war, marches back to us on musical heels. My parents are still in Phillips, me and my family are not too far away— literally and figuratively. At daycare, our daughter's surroundings are much like mine were when I was her age—her cohorts are Native American, Black, Chicano/a, white. No one has made fun of her race or gender. Please, I beg the world, let that last as long as possible.

I hire a babysitter so that I can go to a community debate with the Ordway at MPR. I don't even want to go—why waste money and time when we know the discussion will do no good. They'll claim that they're using art to provoke discussion. They will find Asians who agree with them, then reward them. They will magnify the voices of the Asians who take their side. They will find people who say it's not so bad, or that there are more important things to protest.

But I go. I am encouraged to see quite a few Asian American community members there, and also some allies of color, indigenous allies, female allies, white allies, queer allies, and of course, some whose identities are intersections of all of these. Some of us in attendance—Rose, Janet, Ed, myself, and a few others—have been a part of some or all of the three protests against the Ordway over the last twenty years. I've spent the two weeks beforehand reading and re-reading materials about *Miss Saigon*, reading the text of the shitty songs, staging debates in my head. I'm like a boxer ready to get in the ring. I want to be ready to debate anyone, handle any argument they throw my way. I tell myself, over and over again: don't lose it. Be rational, no matter how stupid they are, no matter how dismissive.

The President and CEO of the Ordway, a white woman, suggests that we all see the show so that it can provoke feelings in us. Though several of us have in fact seen the play, I can't help it. "My entire family was almost wiped out in that war," I blurt out. "You think I need to go see your play in order to have my emotions provoked?" There goes my resolve to avoid losing my cool.

I feel raw. Can barely sit still. I want to vent, to rage, to add my perspective as a Vietnamese person, but I also don't want to dominate the conversation. I listen to several Asian American women talk about how men assume they or their mothers are prostitutes, or see them as submissive sex objects who will do anything for a white man—a behavior that *Miss Saigon* reinforces. David Mura is there. His daughter has graduated college. My daughter, not yet four years old, is at home. Her middle name is the Japanese name of Esther Suzuki, who died shortly after the second protest of *Miss Saigon* at the Ordway.

Our daughter has a greater chance of someone assuming she is a submissive sex object without agency or a voice, than the Ordway promising that they won't bring this colonialist, racist, sexist play back. People will look at her and assume she has it better in America than whatever country she is from, though she was born in Saint Paul. The co-producers of the play can't even manage a simple apology. "We're sorry you're hurt," the CEO says. That's like punching us in the face three times and instead of apologizing for causing us violence, they say: sorry that you happened to get hurt by our fist.

Miss Saigon, which has been called "the greatest love story of our time," is an expensive production. It has raked in a ton of money, and it will continue to do so. Human beings seem to have an endless appetite for racism, sexism, and colonialism. Most of the people paying hundreds of dollars to see *Miss Saigon* would hate to be called racists, I'm sure, or would deny that they are supporting something that reinforces Orientalism, sexism, and human trafficking. But they'll open up their wallets all the same.

At home, our daughter asks me to cut out heart shapes from paper. She tapes them onto a large round circle from another piece of paper. "What is this?" I ask her. "It's a Valentine's Day card for everyone in the whole wide world!" she exclaims, and she means it. Her gesture of love is inexpensive, but not cheap.

BEN QUICK is an author, teacher, veterans' advocate, and father who splits his time between Da Nang, Vietnam, and Tucson, Arizona. He holds an MFA in non-fiction writing from the University of Arizona where he also served as the Beverly Rogers Nonfiction Fellow. He has taught writing for the past fifteen years, most recently at the University of Arizona and the University of Foreign Language Studies in Da Nang, Vietnam. His literary interrogations of fatherhood and the war have won many awards including the Pushcart Prize.

THE BONEYARD

The first thing I see are the tails of the planes. They jut like hundreds of dorsal fins rising from prehistoric fish that have been lined up by a butcher on a massive table of thin brown grass. It is a surreal sight, and I allow my eyes to settle into the rhythm of motion—not quite focused, not quite gone—watching the rows of sharp metal ridges whir past at fifty miles per hour.

As I crest a small rise, the bodies of the craft come into full view: rows and rows of warplanes, all shapes and sizes, stretching on forever, it seems. I force myself back to the task at hand, navigating the approach to the Aerospace Maintenance and Regeneration Center (AMARC) on the southeast side of Tucson, Arizona. I turn right at the traffic light on Kolb Road into a small parking lot and find a space.

Ten minutes later, I'm riding shotgun in a black van with government plates. My driver, head of public relations at AMARC, is Terry. Middle-aged, handsome, and soft in her talk and manners, Terry asks me what I want to see. I hesitate—not because I don't know, but because I'm not sure how to tell her that I've come to bear witness to American folly, to rest my eyes on the flying machines that flattened the forests of Southeast Asia, poisoned its people, and changed my life.

"The C-123s," I say.

She looks at me quizzically, pushes her index finger to her lower lip. I'm nervous to begin with, having never been on an air base, having very little in the way of credentials, and having tried, however awkwardly, to obscure the true reason for my visit. I'd told her I was doing a piece on Vietnam-era warplanes for graduate school when we talked on the phone.

I mutter these words—*My father is a veteran*—and I'm suddenly taken by the irrational fear that I may have given the impression of an apologist looking to take some photos for a nostalgic slide show. My fear is compounded by the fact that today is September 11, the anniversary of the day some folks, especially those in the military, have come to view as off-limits for dissent. That I find myself moderately attracted to Terry only complicates matters. I'd expected a formal woman in military garb, spit-shined boots, and the works, but AMARC employees are civilian contractors. And the loose-fitting sundress, designer shades, and casual tone of the woman beside me have caught me off guard. I'm entirely unsure of myself and my purpose.

"The C-123s? I'm not sure if we have any of them. They might have one in the museum."

"Well I saw one in this book." I reach down between my legs, flip open my bag, and produce the picture book I'd found at the public library. Glossy and oversized, *The Desert Boneyard* by Philip Chinnery is filled with aerial photos of AMARC, snatches of aviation history, and nostalgic recollections of past commanders and famous aircraft. An honest appraisal of the Air Force arsenal and its capacity for destruction it is not, but like many seemingly frivolous research tools, it has served a vital purpose. It has shown me that AMARC—known affectionately as The Boneyard—had, at one point in time, housed the airplanes I came here to find.

"Oh, you got you a book. Let's see . . . " Resting the book on the cup holders in the space between the seats, I turn to page seventy-five. I can feel beads of sweat on my forehead.

"Oh. Those. Oh sure, we have two of them on the west side, but the rest are fenced off. You can't get to 'em. Nobody goes in there."

"Why?"

"Well, the toxin."

January 20, 1961: Eight inches of snow fall on Washington, DC, initiating one of the worst traffic jams ever in the nation's capital as John F. Kennedy takes his inaugural vows. Up to this point, American involvement in the turmoil of Southeast Asia has been secondary, mainly involving the grudging flow of money and arms to the fragile Diem regime in South Vietnam. But conservatives in the capital are calling for more than a half-hearted attempt to fill the vacuum left by France's withdrawal from the region. And the new American president is young and Irish-Catholic, a suspect combination in midcentury American politics. He is worried that Republicans will paint him pink if he doesn't hold the South from Communist guerrillas. So he sets out to do so, and to do it with gusto, expanding U.S. military operations in a manner later described by Noam Chomsky as a move "from terror to aggression."

The word *counterinsurgency* begins to appear more and more frequently in the speeches of American politicians. A long and awkward utterance, it is a word that depends on the existence of the root word *insurgency*, defined by *Webster's* as "a condition of revolt against a government that is less than an organized revolution and that is not recognized as belligerency." In the case of Vietnam, the people charged with perpetuating the state of revolt—the insurgents—are a loose but growing number of Communist soldiers recently given the tacit approval of the Hanoi government in North Vietnam. They have begun conducting night raids on military posts and villages in the South under the name National Liberation Front and have become known condescendingly to Diem supporters as the Viet Cong.

In Vietnam, countering these insurgents means denying the Viet Cong and their allies in the countryside and hills the apparatus of survival: food and forest. Before long, the primary method of denial becomes the aerial application of a variety of defoliants. In 1961, accepting a joint recommendation from the State and Defense departments, President Kennedy signs a resolution accelerating the program. Spraying will intensify in three distinct plant communities: the dense broadleaf vegetation that blankets the Vietnam outback and turns roads and supply routes into ambush zones, the mangroves that line swamps and provide habitat for the catfish and shrimp that are staples of the Vietnamese diet, and the fields of foodstuffs—rice, manioc, and sweet potatoes.

Before 1961 is up, Kennedy sends scientist James Brown to the newly established United States/Vietnamese Combat Development and Test Center (CDTC) in Saigon to explore the effectiveness of a variety of herbicides for use as counterinsurgency tools. The results of Brown's work are a cluster of compounds that come to be known as the "rainbow agents" for the colors of the identification bands that encircle barrels of the herbicides. Agents White, Purple, and Blue will all see use in the jungles of Southeast Asia, but the most intensively employed by far will be Agent Orange, a fifty-fifty mix of the n-butyl esters 2,4-dichlorophenoxyacetic acid (2,4-D) and 2,4,5-trichlorophenoxyacetic acid (2,4,5-T).

The origins of Agent Orange lie in an obscure laboratory at the University of Chicago where, during World War II, the chairman of the school's biology department, E. J. Kraus, discovered that direct doses of 2,4-D can kill certain broadleaf vegetation by causing the plants to experience sudden, uncontrolled growth not unlike that of cancer cells in the human body. Kraus, thinking his findings might be of use to the Army, informed the War Department, which initiated testing of its own but found no use for the stew of hormones prior to the end of the war. But experiments with 2,4-D and 2,4,5-T continued through the 1950s.

Late in 1961, Brown and the technicians at the CDTC decide the time is right, the testing complete, the dispersal methods sound. On January 13, 1962, three Air Force C-123s—twin-propellered short-range assault transport planes—lift off from Tan Son Nhut airfield in South Vietnam, each loaded down with more than a thousand gallons of Agent Orange. The planes fly low over the canals and deltas of the Ca Mau Peninsula—the claw-shaped tip of the nation—occasionally taking fire from the swaths of jungle below. When they finally reach the prescribed site, the chemical cargo is sprayed continuously from three groups of high-pressure nozzles jutting from internal dispensers, the entire load dropped in minutes. A mist can be seen settling over mangroves as the planes turn back toward Saigon. Operation Ranch Hand is underway.

Fifteen thousand gallons of herbicide will be sprayed over the forests and fields of Vietnam that first year. By 1966, the annual application will have increased to 2.28 million gallons. In retrospect, the ecological and human consequences of the spraying program will seem catastrophic. But in 1962, in the thick of an increasingly desperate conflict with a silent enemy hiding in the bush, the extermination of mangroves and rice crops, the destruction of hundreds of thousands of acres of forest canopy, and the desertification of land adjacent to supply routes are embraced as steps toward creating the conditions for winning the war, conditions that nevertheless seem to be slipping farther and farther away from American military strategists in Washington and Saigon.

The kerosene stench of chemical rain that falls on American troops as they slink through the hinterlands in search of Viet Cong is seen as a bearable nuisance. The lethality of the fog that settles on the farms of South Vietnamese peasants and the convoys of American soldiers, like so many war costs, will remain hidden.

My father returned to the Midwest after his tour in the jungles of Vietnam accompanied by a dehumanizing terror. But along with the images and the guilt was something more tangible, a rash that covered his back, raised hivelike splotches that didn't go away for five years—until I was nearly three. The name for this rash is chloracne; its cause, prolonged exposure to herbicides.

I entered this world on a muggy July evening in 1974, the sun beginning to sink down into the hardwoods that separate the town of Morrison, Illinois, from miles upon miles of cornfields—fields that would have been at least six feet tall by then, ripening with line upon line of fat yellow ears sheathed in green. The delivery went without complication. There was my mother's low moaning, the usual frenzy of female nurses, and the old doctor reaching his latexed hands to cradle my small wet head as it emerged from the birth canal. There was much crying and celebration, the ceremonial cutting of the cord by the father, the grandparents waiting anxiously in the hallway, aunts and uncles, friends. But there was something else as well, something curious: although in every other way I fit the normal profile of a baby boy, my left hand was almost round, and at first glance, fingerless. Looking closer, one could see that there were indeed fingers in the flat bell of flesh and bone, but no space between them, and the bones were either misshapen or missing altogether. Instead of clutching at nipples and beards, it flew from side to side like the club on the tail of a prehistoric beast. My grandmother was horrified.

Despite my evident uniqueness, I ran through the first half of my childhood like any other midwestern boy, playing soccer and baseball, fishing, running around the neighborhood with other children in packs. I played war games in the local woods, snuck off to the candy store with my younger brother, dug up earthworms in the big garden between rows of tomatoes and hot peppers, watching with delight as aphids and sow bugs crawled over my hands. Although I endured a number of surgeries in a prolonged attempt to separate fingers, and although I was forced to wear a series of uncomfortable bracelike contraptions to bed—sterile plaster meant to force the bones to bend into a more functional formation— these were happy times for me. Too young to feel self-conscious, stubborn and creative enough to circumnavigate any limitations, I didn't really stop to think that I was different from other children. I climbed trees, played catcher in Little League, kept goal for my soccer team, won sprints in swim meets.

Still, I have to believe an awareness was growing. There must have been innocuous comments from neighborhood boys, partially hidden conversations, questions. And parents, even kind and well-meaning parents, can fumble with answers.

I must have been close to ten years old the day my mother and I ambled through the automatic door of Eagle's Supermarket and across the chipped green and white checkers of tile. We came for just a few items, the only memorable one being the ice cream. We were gliding across that tile, headed straight for the open freezers of the dairy section, me in my shorts and t-shirt, my mother in her gardening clothes. We were moving fast, were so close to the freezers that I could almost feel the chill, could almost see the dense coating of hoarfrost on the inner chambers, when she ran her eyes from my face to my shorts and asked with impatience: "Why do you keep your hand in your pocket? Don't you think people know?" Hiding my flaw was beginning to become second nature, an act of instinct rather than will.

Terry's been at the boneyard for eighteen years. She shoots down the gravel road like a person who's done it a thousand times before, pointing out an array of aircraft, telling me stories as we bounce through the past. Here sit the Grumman Tomcats. There, in the tall grass, the

Rockwell B-1Bs. And over there, on the near side of the wash, the Lockheed Hercules, the Huey transporters, the Cobra gunships. This F-14 bombed one of Saddam's bunkers in the second Gulf War. That 119 was Westmoreland's ride. Airplanes, helicopters, and missile casings, all in different shapes, sizes, ages, and states of dismemberment, are lined up like trinkets in a jewelry booth at a country fair—the earrings in this quadrant, the bracelets in that, the bolos over here, the brass buckles over there. Three thousand acres' worth.

Some are stripped for parts. As evidence I see the glint of naked metal on exposed engines and radiators and, in big black drums beside hoodless frames, the jumbled masses of fuel pumps and belts. Some will be called back to service with the Air Force or Navy, maintenanced and flown away to bases in Utah and Nevada. Others, especially the historic planes, are destined for museums. And still others will end up in the hands of foreign armies, sold to the highest—and often most unsavory—bidder or shipped off, at discount rates, to allies in Tel Aviv or Seoul.

Through this broad yard of history we roll, the faded marks of the military all around us. Terry gradually slows down and comes to a stop. On one side is a row of unarmed nuclear warheads; on the other, the noses of two green and tan cargo planes.

"Here we are."

Stepping down from the van, I tear my disposable camera from its foil package, unpack my tape recorder, and walk toward the aircraft.

"So these were not part of Ranch Hand?"

"No. I think these guys were just transporters."

"Just transporters."

They look like smiling whales, these two transporters. Smiling whales with propellered wings. Like all the planes in The Boneyard, the windows, air ducts, and doors of the 123s are covered in thick white latex. Spraylat, it is called, and it keeps the interiors of the planes cool. Without the Spraylat, temperatures in the cargo holds and cockpits can rise to two hundred degrees Fahrenheit, baking everything inside. The white coating makes the planes look like ghost ships, mummies in an aviation graveyard. But I came to see the other planes, the ones that devastated a vast and peopled landscape, the ones that maimed me before I was born.

O peration Ranch Hand dissolved in 1970 under intense pressure fueled by increasing awareness of the dangers of Agent Orange. By then, one-seventh of Vietnam's total land area had been sprayed with herbicides, one-fifth of its forest flattened. Studies would eventually show that the spray missions flown by the men of Ranch Hand had little or no effect on the path of the war, that the millions of gallons of herbicide dropped on nipa palm and mangrove, on tropical rainforest, on trails and swamps and roads, on military barracks and rice paddies, saved few American lives. Studies would also show that the substance held in the striped barrels was more dangerous than its handlers had realized, and that American military leaders had known this for a long time.

Peter Schuck, author of *Agent Orange on Trial*, notes, "as early as 1952, Army officials had been informed by Monsanto Chemical Company, later a major manufacturer of Agent Orange, that 2,4,5-T was contaminated by a toxic substance." The substance he refers to is dioxin, a chemical that the Environmental Protection Agency has described as "one of the most perplexing and potentially dangerous chemicals ever to pollute the environment." Lab tests in the 1940s had shown that even the tiniest amounts of dioxin, concentrations as small as 4 parts per trillion— an amount equivalent to one drop in 4 million gallons of water—induced cancer in rats. In slightly larger doses, the substance brought on virulent symptoms leading to quick death. When barrels of Agent Orange were shown to contain dioxin concentrations as high as 140 parts per million, questions about the effects of human exposure began to swell.

By the 1970s, for Vietnamese living and working in spray zones, the answers to these questions had already started to become clear and painful: babies born with massive birth defects, some with skeletons that bended and twisted as they grew, some with organs on the wrong side of skulls and ribs, some with conditions so bad they survived only days. Even though American servicemen came into contact with the toxin over the course of months rather than years, soldiers—particularly those serving at the apex of Ranch Hand, men dropping on knees to fill canteens with odd-looking water pooled in bomb craters, men walking with handheld weed sprayers around the flanks of base camps, men sleeping on naked ground—still ran the risk of lethal exposure. The risk was so real, in fact, that as Yale biologist Arthur Galston put it, all soldiers "who worked with Agent Orange or saw duty in the heavily defoliated zones of Vietnam have a legitimate basis for asking the government to look into the state of their health."

Concern about long-term effects on the people and ecology of Vietnam and the health of American G.I.s prompted groups of critical American scientists to publicly denounce the use of Agent Orange and other herbicides as early as the mid-1960s. In 1966 and 1967, a coalition led by the well-respected American Association for the Advancement of Science sent petitions to the Johnson White House calling for an end to all chemical and biological warfare. At the same time, international anxiety was growing. In 1969, after three years of failed attempts, the United Nations succeeded in passing—despite sustained and often menacing opposition from the U.S.—a resolution declaring Operation Ranch Hand a violation of the 1925 Geneva Convention Protocol limiting the use of chemical weapons. Still, the spraying continued.

Finally, evidence showed up that was too damning to be stonewalled or intimidated away. In late 1969, Matthew Meselson, a broad-shouldered Harvard scientist fond of bow ties and no friend of war boosters, obtained a copy of a National Cancer Institute report confirming the teratogenicity—the ability of a compound to cause embryonic or fetal malformation—of 2,4,5-T in rats and mice. Meselson convinced Lee DuBridge, his former colleague at the California Institute of Technology and science advisor to the then newly elected Richard Nixon, to convene meetings to discuss the implications of the findings. In spite of the continued reluctance of many in the Pentagon to acknowledge the seriousness of the data, administration officials could read the changing tea leaves of public tolerance, and on April 15, 1970, application of Agent Orange and most other defoliants was suspended indefinitely.

Years later, a sad and fitting epitaph for the Agent Orange saga would come from James Clary, an Air Force scientist and author of the official history of Operation Ranch Hand, in a statement to Senator Tom Daschle: "When we initiated the herbicide program in the 1960s we were well aware of the potential for damage due to dioxin contamination in the herbicide. We were even aware that the military formulation had a higher dioxin concentration than the civilian version, due to the lower cost and the speed of manufacture. However, because the material was to be used on the enemy, none of us were overly concerned."

B y the time I reached adolescence, there was no longer any doubt as to whether I was like other young men. I was different, less than, not quite whole. Instead of attempting to come to terms with what I have now come to realize is a minor glitch in DNA, instead of facing up to my own uniqueness, the shape of my particular handprint, I tried hard to deny it, to prove to myself that I was in no way distinct from the two hundred boys and girls I entered Dixon High School with in 1988. On the surface, I succeeded. I joined sports teams and—I'm sure this was a conscious act of rebellion—put myself in positions that required the use of both hands in order to succeed. I wrestled and won matches as a freshman, earned four varsity letters as a soccer goalkeeper, brought home trophies and plaques. What's more, I had awkward sex with teenage girls, drank beer and smoked pot, grew my hair long, hung out with the right crowd, took a cheerleader to the prom.

Inside, I was a wreck. I recall the summer between my junior and senior year and a girl named Krista, younger than I, brown hair, green eyes, slender, carrying always the smell of Elizabeth Taylor Passion. Krista was the first girl I spent more than one or two nights with, and I fell for her hard. Along with my friend Josh and his girlfriend Billy, we spent the better part of the summer together. It was a hot summer, hot in the manner that all midwestern summers are, so thick with vapor that even the loosest clothing sticks to skin, and sunglasses slide down noses. That whole summer, when I was in the company of Krista—which was most of the time—I wore long sleeves. I would rush into my bedroom to change clothes each time she came to my house. There was a particular red cotton shirt a friend had loaned to me that I must have worn three times a week. I wore it in the water when we swam in the moonlight at the abandoned rock quarry; I wore it during sex on the gravelly shore; I wore it when to do so must have been agonizing. I thought the sleeves would hide my hand.

And the long-sleeved t-shirt was not the only mechanism employed for hiding the truth of who I was. I took to wearing thick goalkeeper's gloves that kept the shape of their fingers against gravity when I shook hands with players from opposing teams after soccer games (in retrospect, I wonder if the gloves weren't part of the appeal of the position). I would bury both hands deep in the pockets of my letterman's jacket as I flirted with girls from other schools at track meets or wrestling matches. I became skilled at striking a variety of postures to keep my dreaded deformity out of sight, turning this way or that, sitting down just so. I learned to live in a state of contortion.

It would be comforting to look back and to sense some kind of turning point, some theatrical beginning of a healing process, a link between the discord of those years and the relative stillness of the present. The truth is this: like most authentic change, most real letting go, mine has happened gradually, and beneath the surface of things. A decade and a half of life—of marriage and divorce, of fatherhood and graduate school, of love affairs and rafting swift rivers, of university teaching and Buddhist meditation—have swept away much of the hidden shyness and dread. But still, at the age of thirty-three, I'm finding that old habits die hard. If I've lost myself momentarily while driving, reading a book, or engaging in some other task that requires a chunk of my brain, I sometimes find that, without intending to, I have tucked my left hand gently behind my right elbow. Lying in bed at night before sleep takes hold, I'll notice my left hand resting underneath the ruffles of the blanket while my right hand sits bare and comfortable on top. Or I'll think about a class I've taught on a particular morning, coming to a sudden realization that all the gesturing and hand-waving was done with one arm. I will pause for a moment and make a mental note. Sometimes, I will curse.

Terry pumps the brakes to keep from skidding, drags the gearshift into park, and points out the driver's-side window. From behind a chain-link fence, I stare at a fleet of seventeen C-123s beached on the desert playa. A two-foot square of aluminum, white with red block letters, clasped to the fence at shoulder height, reads AUTHORIZED PERSONNEL ONLY, meaning Air Force specialists wearing hazmat suits. I must make do with the view from the fence line, which is fine with me, since the nearest contaminated aircraft are less than fifty feet away.

I climb out of the van and gawk. Forty years before, these olive planes, arranged before me now like neglected toys on the top shelf in a child's bedroom, unloaded over 10 million gallons of dioxin-laden herbicide on a countryside halfway across the world, the same countryside my father tromped through with a gun at his side for one full year at the peak of the spraying. And now, on the edge of the desert metropolis, beneath wisps of cloud shifting and breaking in the morning sky, in the checkered shadow of the chain-link fence, as much as I would like to deny it, I find myself looking for catharsis—a burst of emotion that will finally and emphatically wash it all away.

I know how lucky I am—that things could be much worse. I've seen the pictures of the Vietnamese tending the earth after the fire. The parents who cut and burned the trunks of leafless trees to keep their children warm in winter. The beautiful young girls with jet black hair and loose blouses trimming grass for baskets. The peasants planting saplings in barren ground.

And I've seen the photos of jars filled with the stillborn at the Tu Du hospital in Ho Chi Minh City. Babies born with two faces and three ears. Dead babies with limbs like ropes, long, slender, twisted like pale pretzels in formaldehyde. Siamese twins with melting heads, gathered in a lovers' tangle, the lips of one pressed to the neck of the other in the softest kiss. Shelves full of pickle jars holding the rawest fruit.

And the living, the children of the damned. Children with eyes like marbles, huge and rolling and blank. Children with skin like birch bark, skin that peels and flakes in small squares, covering their bodies in checkerboards of dying flesh, pushing up from scalps like duff on a forest floor. Children with alien heads, their skulls ten times the size of their jaws. I've seen the feet turned in on themselves, the blackened arms, the hands like clamps.

I look down at my hand in its present state, nearly three decades after the last surgery, after I finally said no more—no more casts, no more stitches, no more IV needles, no more Darth Vader masks spewing anesthesia into my lungs. I look down at the rumpled flesh, the grafts sewn between the spaces opened up to give me fingers, grafts of crotch skin, grafts that grow hair, and the lines of scars from the stitching, and the two tiny inner digits, and the middle knuckle that bears no crop, and the pinky that juts straight out, and the short, thick thumb, and I am glad that at six years of age I finally said no. They wanted to do more surgeries, wanted to cut a little more here, tweak the bone structure a little more there. And I said no.

A gust of wind rakes an old Pepsi can along the base of the fence. It rattles to a stop on the crown of an anthill, teeters for a moment, and rolls to my feet like an empty shell. Out here on the scabland of memory where scorpions scurry under B-52s, jackrabbits bound over chopper blades in tufts of never-green grass, and the sun burns through everything, there are no epiphanies. There are only dirt and space, dreams and loneliness, and—I realize with a start—confrontations with the past that will never quite fill the gaps. Taken with an incredible urge to urinate, I snap one last photo and hop in the van, trying hard not to look back.

ASHLEY ROMANO holds a Master of Fine Arts in Creative Writing from New York University and works at Adobe. Her dad served in the Vietnam War as a US Marine, and his account of the time spent in Vietnam has been a major influence on the narrative of Ashley's writing. Her work has appeared in *Narrative Magazine*. She currently lives in Astoria, Queens, under the Hell Gate Bridge.

JERSEY CITY
for Robert

I.

To the place you grew up
      in a railroad
           apartment with your brother,
      mother and father.
Where you worked on a chicken farm
      and stayed in a bungalow

on the shore every summer.
      To the place you played
high school football and broke
      your nose. Where you decided
            to walk into a Marine's recruiting office
      during Vietnam and then into a tattoo
parlor where you got a sailor skunk
      on your bicep with the 18
            dollars you had. Where you would send
      letters and maps to your parents,
people I would never meet,
      telling them where you were sleeping,
            wrapped in a trench
      and Qui Nhơn. A snippet of stories.
I am this.

II.

Barry Mann and Frankie Lymon couldn't even answer
the questions they asked. Who put the bomp in the bomp
bah bomp bah bomp and why do fools fall in love?
Your advice: *try to find better music to fall in love to.*
You found Mom, your Linda Sue, in between those doo-wop
beats. She found you after dating the Four Seasons drummer.
Teenagers in love even when singing *Duke of Earl*
in between watch shifts during the Helicopter War.
It wasn't about the answers but the way to shake hips,
to pin a carnation boutonniere at homecoming,
to find someone to share a malted and *ssh boom* with.

I haven't found something better.

III.

My dad only gave me one photo of him in the war: his rifle aimed
at the cameraman, standing on top of a truck, cigarette between his lips.
Only after he died did I get the photos of him in his Marine uniform

with his parents. In them I saw I inherited a dimple on the left cheek.
The stories my father told me of him being in the war were dropping
acid and smoking dope. There were no stories of how his best friend

got blown up by a land mine, because every Vietnam vet has one,
only tales of seeing little red monkeys from his watch station
and jumping out of helicopters to *What a Wonderful World.*

The scars my father had were little white nicks on both of his calves,
multiple souvenirs he carried with his to tell only he knew. I'll never
    know
if he took his malaria pill each week, or if he incorrectly discarded a
    wooden

ammo box which could be turned into an electrical mine, or practiced
    his religion
just as A Marine's Guide told him. I only have his words and dimples
    like the
Vietcong instructions *Is the enemy strong? Avoid him. Is the enemy weak?*
    Attack.

IV.

I was born a child of rock 'n' roll and war and this crazy thing
we call love. Out through Mother and passed to the calloused
hands of Father. So when Dad died, out went the Doobie Brothers,
Boz Scaggs, and ZZ Top. Out went the stories of getting fined
for shooting a water buffalo in a rice paddy and taking opium
during a watch shift. Out went the Christmases where the ham
would be carved to a soundtrack of Johnny Mathis. Out went
the birthday cards signed love, Mom & Dad, the television
playing Gladiator with commercials even when owned on DVD,
the singing of Runaround Sue while vacuuming. In came dinners
quiet as bread rising on the counter, the head of the table never full.

JOSEPHINE ROWE is an Australian writer of fiction, poetry, and essays. She is the author of two story collections and a novel, *A Loving, Faithful Animal* (Catapult, 2017), which follows an Australian family attempting to move beyond the long shadow of the Vietnam War. Rowe's writing has appeared in *McSweeney's Quarterly Concern*, *Best Australian Stories*, *The Iowa Review*, *Harvard Review*, *Narrative Magazine*, and elsewhere. She holds fellowships from Yaddo, Writers Omi, and the University of Iowa's International Writing Program, and was a 2014–2016 Wallace Stegner Fellow in fiction at Stanford University. She currently lives in Tasmania.

VANELLINAE

And I know now, about the birds—their Latin name, their
population and international distribution. I know their

migratory patterns, have watched footage of them in
flight; could write about the slow, irregular beat of wing or

shrillness of call, but still do not know how to write about
you   standing at the window that morning at the

repatriation clinic, grey in the early light alongside the other
old soldiers and all of you just watching the birds in the grass

outside. Seven of you there at the window, not speaking only
smoking as you'd smoked through decades of daily crossword

instant coffee, broken families, anger management, repeat
prescriptions, therapy through wood and leather work and

all those things nobody talks about. You stood smoking and
watched the birds build a nest, and though I know the word

Vanellinae   I still do not know how to write about what
you and those grey men were waiting for.

WHAT I KNOW OF DOORWAYS

I.

Here, I am five years old or eight years old
or ten
between my father
(wild; throwing punches and hard words and spit)
and my mother
(saying nothing, now
the door-handle pressed into the small of her back).
My mother's body is soft and warm as sleep
as my father beats a hole
beside her head.
(Years later my mother slips through this hole.
The door is replaced so that I cannot follow).

2.

Watching sheet-lightning
through a screen door
in Bairnsdale. I sit in the hallway and
lean forward when the sky turns
silver.
In the next room are relatives
I do not know.
Their children
stand back from the windows
eat slowly
are adequate.
They don't pretend
to like me.

3.

My sister and I get up at dawn.
The back door creaks
so we open it slowly, by inches.
Everything is grey—
our faces and breath,
the house and hills.
We climb onto the roof,
staining the palms of our hands
and the soles of our feet
red with dust from the tiles.
We are waiting. I can't remember what for.

LOVE

He is teaching her how to break bottles against the side of the house. A whiskey bottle works best, he tells her. She thinks this is very lucky, because that is what they have the most of—he has spent the last few weeks emptying them. So whiskey bottles are what they are using. Now, he says. Like this. Crack. So that you get something like a shiv, not just a fistful of glass and stitches. Like this, he says. Crack. And she feels a great swell of pride in her sparrowy chest—he gets it perfect, every time. Now you, he says, and he hands her the next bottle. Because a father can't always be there, he says, and she nods and tries to look solemn, to make him believe she understands. The bottle does not break on the first try. She swings harder on the second try and gets it, but it is a bad break. Her father does not say this, but she knows. Too close to the neck. Shards of glass from other afternoons shine dully in the dry earth at their feet. He hands her another bottle and the second break is better, the glass jutting out like the snaggled teeth of some prehistoric fish.

She tries to imagine when she will need this—how things will ever get so bad. Her idea of evil is a slinking, unknowable thing, formless and weightless and impossible to hurt. She takes another bottle and tries to give the evil a shape, eyes and lips and things, all squinty and sneering—

a composite of all the villains and monsters she has seen in films and picture books. And although she finds the result is less terrifying than something incorporeal, she does not know how she will ever be brave enough—will she ever be able to do that to somebody, evil or otherwise?

They both know she will not. Later there will be men and dark rooms and lost hours, a thousand little cruelties and she will never, not once in her life, save herself in the way he shows her now.

But there are so few things he feels he can teach her, so little he can offer before the night calls him back, swallows him whole without leaving any trace but the small change on the bedside table, half a pack of cigarettes and a new bruise on her mother's arm.

That is not important now. That is for later, and for now there is the smooth neck of the Jameson's bottle in her small hand, the cool glass warming with the heat of her palm, another crack against the wall of their coffee-brick house.

On the other side of the wall her mother stands in the center of the lounge room and listens, not understanding, her pale hands making light fists and her head lowered in preemptive defeat.

Outside, the setting sun has turned her father to a featureless silhouette somewhere just to the right of her, watching. When she tries to retrieve this moment from the clutter of early childhood—and she will, over and over again, looking for reasons, warning signs, answers—she will not remember how his face was set. But she will remember the sound of breaking glass, and she will understand this as love.

LEVI RUBECK's poems have appeared in *No, Dear, Wreck Park, Analog Science Fiction*, and elsewhere. He is a former editor at NYU's *Washington Square Review*, co-edits the online journal *Paperbag*, and writes on games for *Kill Screen*. (More info at dangerhazzard.com.) Later in his life, Levi's father finally began to reckon with and share his experience as a Navy sailor during the Vietnam War. Levi explores his father's denial of the legitimacy of his role in that war, and how it affected his marriages, children, and sense of place in the world.

YELLOW FLARE

I feel like Creedence should
be playing. It might be
why you don't watch the news.
You told me you wonder
where's your tumor, Scott
got one the size of a handball
but he died sober. Did I ever
see you otherwise? I remember
a trip to the small hospital
and a bowl of candy, a room
of tore-up board games and
old men playing cards. I'm not
so sure. The officers tested
aggression-enhancing drugs
on monkeys sleeping in your boat,
which was still hot from the nukes
it carried in 1944. You should
be dead or shrieking but in
this photo you're at Sturgis
wrapped in a leather vest,
shaking hands, in this one
showing off your soft-tail.
We answer the phone
with the same color
but who knows where
we got it from.

MALL FLARE

I can count the hair on your face.
Two types of boys come here: those
with fathers and those without.
Our office is in the only mall for
one hundred miles, across
the theater, down the hallway from
the arcade with guns in candy
colors, light swaying in the breeze.
Gateway guns. I can put a helmet
on your head but you best not lose
either. An example of losing your head:
sleepwalking through Turkey,
picking a fight with a cab driver,
barely avoiding manslaughter charges.
You will lose it anyways, it's true.
Why you should join the Navy
rather than the Army: we teach our
boys not to pee on their hands.
A buddy sent me this video he took
on his boat of missiles launching.
He wasn't supposed to take it
but the boys are filming everything,
it's so easy now. Even though
you can't really see anything,
there's the sound of the air boiling
and then some cheers.

KAREN RUSSELL's debut novel, *Swamplandia!*, was a finalist for the 2012 Pulitzer Prize for Fiction and winner of the New York Public Library's 2012 Young Lions Fiction Award. She was named a National Book Foundation "5 Under 35" young writer honoree at a November 2009 ceremony for her first book of short stories, *St. Lucy's Home for Girls Raised by Wolves*, which won the Bard Fiction Prize in 2011. She is the recipient of the Mary Ellen von der Heyden Berlin Prize and Fellow at the American Academy in Berlin. A 2013 MacArthur Fellow, Russell is currently a visiting writer at the Iowa Writers Workshop. Her latest collection is *Vampires in the Lemon Grove.*

UNDERGROUND IN VIETNAM

As tourists in Vietnam, my friend Vince and I ate coconut candy and rode bicycles around the Mekong Delta. We lunched on a fish that looked like Harry Dean Stanton and joked uneasily about Agent Orange. Now, as part of the same package tour, our no-name bus took us to the Cu Chi Tunnels, the infamous Viet Cong network that snakes below the jungle northwest of Ho Chi Minh City. We were going to slot our bodies into a hole in the ground and try not to entomb ourselves.

Before coming to Ho Chi Minh City, I had the sort of familiarity with Vietnam that comes from hearing one abbreviation throughout my childhood: "Nam." To my siblings and me, it meant the place where an unrecognizably youthful naval officer disappeared and came out on the other side as our father. A slice of the country had lodged in my dad's brain, a bloody shard of time, but I knew only the sliver he talked about with us, and I confess that I was shocked when the place had an airport. Shocked that it was possible to land here, walk around, pay a purplish currency for goods I recognized—T-shirts, ice cream. The reality of modern Vietnam seemed too vast and overflowing with life. At the Sheraton hotel, my father's stories felt suddenly fictional, unreal.

I suppose I hoped that the tunnels might be a literal portal, a way to enter the deep grammar of my dad's past; now I felt desperate to get back on the big anonymous bus before I'd know for certain that I was wrong to come to this country and to this "attraction."

During the war, the tunnels stretched 125 miles from the outskirts of

Saigon all the way to the Cambodian border, permitting the V.C. forces to coordinate intelligence over great distances. Many thousands of men, women, and children lived underground. Schools and hospitals operated sunlessly. Babies were born in the tunnels, our tour guide, Hai, told our group, but sick civilians and wounded soldiers died buried. In inverted funerals, their bodies had to be put aboveground.

Today Cu Chi is a theme park. The blood-soaked ground has sprouted a cafe and a gift shop. Shrapnel is sold as a souvenir; you can buy U.S. servicemen's lighters and bullets, bagged like carnival goldfish. Hai showed us an exhibit of many whimsically named booby traps: Tiger Trap, Spinning Trap. Bamboo spikes that looked like old lion's teeth grinned at us. "No Babies Trap," he said, and demonstrated how they would snap shut on a soldier's penis. "Trap makes a lady-man. Understand? Ha ha! No babies." Some of our faces contorted with horror; others' laughed maniacally. Hai's turned red. Nobody seemed to know what to do with this history. Earlier, Hai cornered Vince and me, the only Americans on the trip, to ask if we had seen *his* father; the man left Saigon for Houston when Hai was 3.

As a courtesy, the entrance to the tunnels had been dilated for our large, Western bodies. Still, it was a tight fit. One Dutch girl in a silver jacket slid into it, like a light ray entering a blind eye. Vince went down next, and I followed. There were dim red lamps in the tunnels, and there wasn't a breath of sun. Everybody crawled forward on all fours in a human chain. This chain was incredibly slow-moving. At first there was banter, but then the heat smothered it. I wanted to yell to be let up, but I was at least eight bodies from the entrance, so I stayed silent, shamed into it by those amiable Dutch kids, whose big bodies were practically humming with good nature even as they blocked the exits. In the underground acoustics, my brain became a megaphone for such unhelpful information as: YOU HAVE TO PEE. YOU CAN'T STAND THIS FOR ONE MORE MINUTE. If I had hoped to get a deeper sense of the war, I was currently connected to only my own shallow panic.

Then we stopped moving. Anyone who has been on a roller coaster when it grinds to a halt midflight knows this terror.

"Hey, what's going on?" "How long till we surface?" Somebody thought Hai had said seven minutes. "Seven, right?" a voice cracked. "And not, like, 70?" Sixty seconds, times seven. Somewhere back in the sun, I assented to enter this nightmare. Now I was the middle segment of a long worm. Move, I threatened the worm. If you don't move, I'll scream.

The scariest stories, to me, are always about what we *can* bear, the hells we construct and endure. Soldiers and even children lived in these conditions for years. My father fought aboveground, but he tells a similar story: "I can go no further!" turned out to be a bluff the war would call him on again and again.

Eventually we did start moving. We pushed on, helpless to do otherwise, on the assumption that we'd turn a corner, find an exit. One by one we did make it out of the tunnel, gulping at a blue sky. We'd been down there for less than 20 minutes. We had seen, Hai reminded us, only a tiny fraction of the entire thing.

BRIAN SCHWARTZ's short stories and essays have appeared in *Harvard Review*, *Ascent*, *Blackbird*, and *Painted Bride Quarterly*, among other journals. At University of California Irvine, he was awarded a Regents Fellowship and the Cheng Fellowship in Fiction, and his work has been nominated for a Pushcart Prize. Schwartz is a senior lecturer in the Expository Writing Program at NYU and he has also taught at UC Irvine, San Francisco State, and in Bard College's Language & Thinking program. His father Mayer served in Vietnam as a doctor in the US Army Medical Corps with the rank of captain and received a Bronze Star for meritorious service.

INVASION

We kept the new house closed up but every day a couple lizards found their way inside; this happened early in the morning or at twilight, when it was cooler. From the start, my wife Donna was a lizard sympathizer. She liked to take the little things outside and set them free so they could sunbathe their cold blood and infiltrate our home again in the dark of night. During our first week in Florida, we found one lizard in the bedroom of our new home, one in the TV room, one in the kitchen.

The kitchen one died of a coronary: Donna picked it up, and it fell onto its side in the palm of her hand. These lizards scare easily.

We were living in Pelican Row, a gated community in Cole County, Florida, in a Pelican Row townhouse, with a small kidney-shaped swimming pool. The maintenance fees were very reasonable. As soon as we got to Pelican Row, we installed an alarm system, but we kept having problems with it. Something to do with the electrical wiring. Several times we came home from the deli or the symphony or the beach and the minute we unlocked our front door horns blew and a theatrical Bible voice boomed into the thick air: GO BACK! YOU ARE TRESPASSING! THE AUTHORITIES ARE ON THEIR WAY! GO BACK!

But it was our home now—we owned it.

Shortly after our move to Florida I discovered a bundle of old letters I'd written to my wife from Vietnam. Donna had kept all the letters together faithfully, a thick stack, more than 350 pages, but then over the years we'd forgotten about them. I found the letters as we unpacked, sifting through our boxes of shared belongings, a mound of old creased paper browned at the folds like the tanning, wrinkled hide of a beach-bound retiree. "Look at this, Donna!" I called out through the cool air of our new concrete garage. We read through several of the letters together, standing side by side, scanning through those pages from the distant past.

Dear Donna, I'd written on page after page.

Dear Donna,

Dear Donna,

Dear Donna,

Dear Donna, over and over, day after day, a 26-year-old Army doctor, reaching back home for loving language, some sign of the beautiful familiar. My youthful penmanship was surprisingly legible. My letters were inquisitive and polite. They were full of little incidents I no longer have any memory of, very different from the stories that have stuck with me all these years, the things I can't forget. I've always done my best to contain my memories of Vietnam, put them together in a tight file in my brain, secure and closeable. I saw what doctors saw over there in that far-away place: I saw bullet holes, wet stumps where limbs should be. I saw corpses. But on a lot of days nothing happened, no one was hurt, I was bored out of my mind. I had plenty of time to write home.

Here's one story I never put in a letter: I'm in the Quonset hut playing cards with some docs one night, and we all hear a wailing outside. It's a sad howl, almost like a child's. First I'm careful to put my cards face down on the table and pocket my piastres; then I lead a pair of medics outside to see who's making that sound, and why.

There's a grunt there in the dark with a shovel in his hand. He smells like liquor. I'm looking all over to see—is he bleeding, is he hurt. Is there a hole in his shoulder or his groin. But he's in a t-shirt, his limbs seem fine, body fine, he is a drunk G.I. holding a shovel crying about something.

It was a cobra, he wails.

Now I'm looking at his ankles, his feet, which are in black boots, but there, at his feet, there's a dark snake on the ground. It's cut in half, two thick lines in the dust. It was a cobra.

Were you bitten? I ask him.

No, he says. He holds his shovel at me, shaking it. I sliced it right in half, he cries.

The guy was fine. If he'd missed with his first swing he might have died. That's how death was there; it was like a weather condition. It was in the forecast or it wasn't, depending on the day.

D onna was a speech therapist when we lived in upstate New York; she began studying for her Florida state license in speech pathol-ogy after we moved. I asked Donna one day—we were out on the golf course—"Haven't you considered just not working?"

"Not really," she said. She was wearing a pink sun-visor. She used to work with elementary school children who couldn't say their "R"s; now she wanted to work in hospitals, like I used to do. She wanted to get up in the morning and visit patients. She thought she'd like to work with stroke survivors—her father died after a stroke.

"But look, honey, we've only been in Florida for a month," I said.

"Why don't you take the whole year off? I mean, we're retired. We can do anything we want. We live in a virtual paradise down here." I gestured to the golf course. We could see retirees everywhere we looked, on other distant patches of manicured grass, in light-colored clothes, hauling clubs or scooting along in white carts. There were palm trees and sand traps. Everything was blurred by the sun.

"I have never heard you use words like that before," Donna said. "Paradise? Can't you wait until you're dead for that?"

"I don't believe in life after death," I told my wife.

"Me neither," she said. "I believe in life before death. Oh, there's my ball."

We stopped so she could set up her shot. I was steamed at the things she was saying. Then she got out a five-iron; I told her she wanted a different angle, and she thought about it a moment. "The hell with it," Donna said. She swung the five-iron violently at the nesting ball, and I don't think we ever found it. We probably didn't look too hard: there are copperheads in that part of Florida, blunt-headed, sticky-fanged, masters of the quick strike. They like to hide near trees.

S ome nights I would read a letter or two out loud to Donna; other nights she would read one to me, rendering my younger self in her fine woman's voice. It became an after-dinner ritual. We were working our way through the whole stack, my 1967 epistles. I'd never written so much in my life—and I never will again, either. And some of my letters were boring. But some made us laugh out loud, Donna and me, reclining on our cushy new Florida furniture and trying to remember who exactly we were back then. Kids, when you get down to it. Anyway, one night I called our son Jason in Wisconsin because Donna and I found a letter that made us both laugh out loud. "Jason, you got a minute?" I said. "Have I told you that your mother and I found a stack of old letters I sent home from Vietnam? Have I mentioned that to you?"

"What?" he said. Jason had two young kids; I often found myself repeating things to him because he couldn't hear me over the sounds of his lovely screeching brood.

"The letters I wrote to your mother from Vietnam," I said again. "Can I read one to you?"

"Sure," he said, sounding a little doubtful. But I went ahead anyway. The letter was about what happened during a monsoon. *Dear Donna*, I wrote, *The rains are upon us. It seems like they'll never stop. Other than that everything is okay and I'm fine. A man here named Martin has taken to walking around outside wearing nothing but his boots, because he says everything gets soaked in one second flat and what's the point? So off with his clothes and we have all been seeing much more of Martin than we care to. Predictably enough this has earned Martin a nickname: but nevermind about that, it's a little off-color. Rest assured I am wearing clothes as usual.*

I started laughing but the best my son could manage was a forced chortle.

"What was the guy's nickname?" Jason wanted to know.

"Who knows? Can you believe that happened to me?" I asked my son. "You realize how young I was when I was in Nam?" Then I saw one of those damn lizards scamper out from under our oven. Pinkish little vermin, almost like a wiggly crayon. "Whoop—Hold on, Jason. Donna, hey, we have a visitor in here. Donna?"

"Leave it alone," Donna called from the other room.

"Jason, sorry, I have to go," I said. Despite my wife's protests I was not inclined to leave the lizard be.

Winter of the previous year, our last Christmas in the old house, Jason brought his kids to upstate New York. When we were all there together in the old ancestral home for the holidays, I watched the movie *Peter Pan* with Jason's kids—the oldest was seven—and I was rooting for Captain Hook. He's the only character in that damn story who's subject to age. Hook's ridiculous mustache, his old man's chin and obsolete outfits—he's like a middle-aged guy trapped in a never-ending shopping mall filled with adolescent punks. And there's his missing hand, torn off by a suddenly-lunging crocodile: a glorified lizard. The hook struck me as awful and almost real last time I watched; age does that, it curls and numbs your extremities, turns your body into something you can't entirely trust, something that could betray you in the middle of an innocent nap as you go to scratch your cheek. The kids giggled whenever Hook was in trouble, but I didn't think it was funny.

nother story: I'm sitting at a folding table under a tent with one of the medics. We're at the edge of a small city called Pleiku—it's clinic day. We have a military directive to perform community service for the South Vietnamese, so on Friday mornings we sit out here, as the heat builds in wet layers, and we try to relieve the residents' aches and pains. But they almost never come to us when they're seriously ill. Instead they line up with stomach ailments, nagging sores, odd-shaped bruises. We give out decongestants and plastic bandages, which Uncle Sam packages in olive green tins. They call me *dai-wee-boxee*, which means Captain Doctor, and they use hand motions to indicate where they hurt. One man, a thin short guy, very short black hair, comes up to me at the table, and he points to his head. I point to my head. "Your head?" I say. "You have a headache?" He's pointing to his forehead and grimacing. There are no cuts or discolorations. "Okay, you have a headache," I say. I hand over two aspirin tablets.

The village guy looks down at the two white tablets I've placed in his palm. He looks up at me. He's not sure what to do with the aspirin.

"Swallow them. Eat them," I say. I point to my mouth.

He smiles and nods; he throws the aspirin into his mouth. He chews them; instead of swallowing, though, he spits the aspirin into his hand. Then he rubs the chalky paste he's made into the skin of his forehead. The man thanks me by giving a wave of his hand and walks away with a white smear on his forehead. I see him meet his wife, who is waiting for him near the tent entrance; he points to his forehead. She smiles and touches his face, then brings her hand down to his shoulder and says something to him. They both smile, and as they leave the tent together I think of Donna. At that point I haven't seen Donna for eight months. Jason is a year and a half old, changing every day and I couldn't see any of it. They are living in Chicago. Donna sent me a recording of Jason's sounds and words, his remarkable voice; for days after I received the tape, I listened and rewound and listened again. My body was filled by that music.

One evening, Donna got home from our new local library and found me sitting at my desk, half-soused on three whiskey sours and most of a can of beer. She came into the room to say hello. She bent and kissed me on the cheek, but she didn't mention the smell of whiskey. She looked at the computer screen. I was researching lizards. I said, "I like to know what I'm up against."

"Harold, they're not hurting anything," said Donna. "You should leave them alone."

"Right," I said, "but they're in our house."

"What's that?" she said, pointing to the screen. "Is that the kind we have here?"

The lizards we get are small, pale-skinned except for the reddish pigment along their spines. I started clicking through the different images I'd found. It was beginning to feel like a ridiculous exercise: How was this going to help? Was I going to type the lizards away? Was I going to search them out of existence? It was pathetic—I was sitting there drinking, showing Donna my pastiche of little lizard pictures, as though it were a garden I'd made for her.

"Oh, look," she said. She liked a delicate yellow one with a loose sack of scaly flesh under its chin.

"You smell good," I told Donna. She smelled like salt from the beach, and like herself, a scent that's vaguely floral. Sort of like an orchid, if you've ever smelled one of those.

After I finished on the Web, I went out to the back to fire up the grill. Donna had brought home some fresh snapper, and it was almost dinnertime (I thought it was, anyway: when you stop working, dinnertime can become the focus of your day, and somehow your preparations for dinner stretch on hours longer than they ever did when you worked, when you were a doctor with a small practice in a little town way up north, the thought of it can make you shiver). Our grill was on the little patio by the side of the kidney-shaped pool. As I stumbled through the sliding glass doors, hauling the bag of coals, I began to hear a splashing. Donna was behind me in the kitchen, and we didn't have any guests, but at first I didn't think to worry about what might be swimming around in our pool. My mind was fixed on the grill, and, curiously enough, it remained fixed on the grill for a second after I slid the doors open, stepped out back, and saw the large black turtle paddling in our bright clean poolwater. These damn creatures were every-fucking-where: reptiles, amphibians, what have you. I walked around the edge of the pool, watching the turtle, until I reached the grill and opened its top. But then I set down the charcoal and went back into the house.

"Donna, look at this," I called. She came and stood by me at the sliding glass doors.

"Oh," she said.

"Can you believe that?"

"Harold," she said, "let it find its way out."

But the black shell went around and around. The turtle had a strange snout; it seemed to have a little black funnel instead of a mouth, some little suction device to breathe in its food, its air. I couldn't figure it out—another little alien species in Florida. How do you live a life like that, swimming around in someone's pool without a mouth? And how the hell do you grow into a twenty-five pound turtle if you can't eat solids? (Because this turtle looked to weigh about twenty-five pounds.) So the wide dark shell continued its kidney-shaped circuit around our pool, that liquid emerald bean, giant and sunken, where all my grandchildren will learn to swim. That was a decision I made when Donna and I moved down here: the pool would be for the grandkids. They would be swimmers, and their comfort in water would make them more confident and able on land. I would contribute to their lives with the shape of my home, and with the weather my new home state could provide.

And now here was this turtle in my pool.

"It looks trapped," Donna said.

It was her pool too; couldn't I keep my wife happy and secure in our home?

"But just leave it alone," Donna said.

I went into the garage for the shovel.

The shovel is an heirloom, a relic, an old, banged-up garden shovel, heavy and brown, and we've had it since our first house in upstate New York. Why we brought it down to Florida, I have no idea. There was always something to shovel in New York; the snow or the soil of the zucchini patch or the rocks that stuck up out of the grass. But in Florida, there is no snow, and everything else has been dug for you before you arrive. I went out back holding the shovel tight, my right hand wrapped like an unlucky starfish around the wood handle, my left hand stabilizing the shaft.

"Harold," Donna said, "no. Leave it alone."

"I just want to help it," I told her.

I looked into the pool, and there came the circling turtle, like some monster aquatic version of a toy train, making quiet splashes with its rubbery black feet. The shallow lines in its shell looked as though they were drawn by children. The turtle eyed me, I swear it did, slightly twisting its strange snout to get a better look. In its eye I saw a kind of understanding—it was a martyr for wilderness. It knew it.

"You're going to hurt it!" Donna said. Her voice was raised and the skin of her face was flushed and angry.

"Donna," I said, "this is our pool." When it passed under me, I dug into the water with the shovel and trapped the turtle against the side of the pool. Adrenaline surged through me; I lifted and the thing came out of the water with the shovel. I was trembling, my whole body shaking, lifting just that modest living weight. Donna circled around the pool towards me. She was not calm. She was agitated, making little movements with her head, and reprimanding me loudly: "Let it go! What are you doing, Harold? Drop the turtle!"

I could feel the grip loosening in my right fingers and thumb. "Donna, open the gate that leads out by the garage. Hurry, babe. The gate."

"Is this what our retirement's going to be?" she cried out in anguish and wonder. "Just a bunch of baggage about whether you're still strong enough to keep everything in order? To protect your little piece of the world?"

"Will you help me?" I said back. My arms were shaking; the turtle was still at the end of the shovel. Donna's neck was flushed and her lips were wet. If I was old, she was old. But Donna didn't seem old to me. Donna opened her mouth to speak, but then I let go, and there was a great splash. I heard her say something about love. The shovel dropped in after the turtle. My wife walked into our perfectly new Florida townhouse, still flushed, all that blood up close to the skin of her face. When the animal control worker arrived, I gave him an idea of what had happened—why there was a shovel at the bottom of the pool in addition to a turtle, now barely staying afloat in its slow circle. "It's almost always better to call us," he said. He produced a blue net from the back of his truck, scooped up the exhausted swimmer, and hauled it away. It left a trail of water.

In Nam we had green military-issue shovels, lightweight and collapsible; because I was a doctor, I only used my shovel near the base. We had to set up what were called piss tubes to urinate in, which were very long artillery shell casings placed a few feet into the ground into a bed of stone. I helped dig in one set of piss tubes: they were placed at a 15–20 degree angle so that you weren't urinating straight down at a 90 degree angle to the ground, but rather at an angle compatible with the natural urinary stream of the average man. The height of these tubes was about 3.5 feet and the diameter of the opening was 4–5 inches. The area was enclosed by a brown canvas material to shield you from view during the act of micturation.

Besides the piss tubes, we had to build shitters, wooden sheds with a slab of wood inside under which were 55-gallon drums cut in half, holding a few inches of kerosene. We shared latrine duty on a rotating basis, burning the old drums and replacing them with new ones. There was a lot of gagging and fleeing upwind.

Right after the incident with the turtle, I went shopping for a new bottle of whiskey, to get away from Donna and give myself time to think. I didn't even feel like a drink, really. I bought an expensive bottle so I could worry about the price of it, worry about my retirement funds and investments, instead of worrying about what had passed between me and my wife. I put the bottle on the kitchen counter when I got home and stood looking at it. I didn't want any whiskey, but the bottle caught my attention. When I heard Donna's footsteps behind me I didn't turn around. I kept my eyes on the smooth red wax that had been poured over the top of the whiskey bottle by the manufacturer, over the cap and neck of the bottle, a regal, shining seal. My temptation to break that seal was like a kid's need to jump in a puddle.

"Harold," Donna said.

I turned to face her. Her hair was wet from the shower, and she was wearing a bra and a pair of shorts. "New whiskey," I said, and I tapped the bottle.

Donna was quiet for a second.

"You know, when I was walking on the beach earlier today," she finally said, "it got me thinking. The beaches down here are so pristine, and they're never crowded—they're elitist beaches. They're almost perfect. But I was walking along the water, and then I didn't want to be there anymore. All these leather-skinned, sun-darkened, gold-wearing . . . "

"Don't say 'old,'" I warned her.

"That's not the point," Donna said. "It was their bodies. They were all baking their almost-naked bodies, stretched out on chaise lounges. It wasn't pleasant; I didn't like it."

"What does this have to do with us, Donna?" I dreaded her answer; I'm a bit of a sunbather myself.

"It has to do with the place we live in, Harold," she said. "I don't feel the same down here. I don't feel like myself, and I don't feel similar to other people who live here. Let's be honest: How many of the women down here *don't* have plastic surgery? I want to move."

"You want to move? Where would we move?"

"Away," she said. "Or—just to a different place."

"Move out?" I said. "You're going to leave me," I said. "Are you going to leave me?" I hadn't been away from her, not really, since my year in Vietnam. The worst year of my life.

"I don't want to leave you," she said. "But I want to move."

"But this place," I said. "It's for us, for the grandkids, the family."

"It might be for them," Donna said, "but it's not for us. It's not for me, at least."

"We've been married 39 years," I said. That's all I could say. We'd never disagreed about a home.

Donna told me she was moving back up north, and I could go with her or stay in Florida, it was my decision. "I'm thinking Boston, maybe Chicago," she said. "You're welcome anytime."

"This feels like a divorce," I said.

"Please: I have no interest in divorcing you," she said.

That night, we had excellent lovemaking. Then I had a dream.

I dreamt of another invader in the swimming pool. But this time instead of a turtle in our pool, it was something larger. For a while Donna and I watched it through our sliding glass doors, until, despite a chorus of protests, I went out to the pool with the shovel. Except it wasn't our old garden shovel; somehow I held in my hands my collapsible Army shovel from Vietnam. The intruder in our pool—some primordial reptile—was gliding like a giant scaly squid stained in its own ink. A scaly squatter, a living tree limb, a floating dark exclamation mark in our emerald green pool. With eyes like bubbles that wouldn't pop. I dug into the water; I lifted the beast—gigantic, five times my size, with teeth springing from a sweet muddy mouth, plus a tail like a wrecking ball, or a whip—and I stared right at the maw. The long reptile began to creep to me along the shaft of the shovel, moving on its sharp claws like a cat.

I woke up, and Donna was holding me, at least, curled into me with a knee up near my groin and an arm over me. She was sleeping with her mouth open, breathing loudly, which was just like her. I stared into the darkness of her mouth for a moment, and, assured that she was near me, I got myself to sleep.

MONICA SOK is a Cambodian American poet from Lancaster, Pennsylvania. She is the recipient of the 2016–2018 Stadler Fellowship and is the author of *Year Zero*, winner of a Poetry Society of America Chapbook Fellowship. Sok received honors from Hedgebrook, Kundiman, MacDowell Colony, the Elizabeth George Foundation, and elsewhere. Her parents lived through the Khmer Rouge regime and in 1979, when Vietnamese forces invaded Cambodia, fled to Khao-I-Dang. Sok's poems discuss intergenerational trauma, familial silence, and growing up Cambodian American in Lancaster.

KAMPUCHEAN SKIN

i used to be her daughter
                    skin once caught in war
grew back rugged   as the land she was
        a crushed nose dripping
                    watercolor on pictures
            worth 4000 *riel* each
one dollar for smooth
                    stone faces of Angkor
    i walked to her first
            left my american friends behind
ignored the affordable glamour   sequined
        scarves   checkered *krama*   elephant blankets
                fringed in gold   all that bloomed there
            to be bought   woman with no face

    wandering around with her pictures
            in the marketplace   i dug
                    into my pocket
            waved a Washington   for all the watercolors
                    of Angkor

                        inside each illustration   red blurry figures bicycling
                            tuk tukking in circles   around
        a single stone face observing east
                west after failing   *where are you from*

where do you live   in my mother's tongue
       she nodded to my friend
       whose baby skin sprouted up like daisy
flowerbeds in thick silk   yes she was beautiful
       but when she called her skin   *sah att*
         before she called my skin   *sah att*
         which she didn't
            i can't tell you how much my face hurt
    kmao pockmarked   colonized and mined like hers

LEFT-BEHIND LOOKS FOR THE APSARAS

Left-Behind saw apsara crowns floating in milk,
churning underneath a poached sun.
She watched the red-and-white-checkered Krama Man
smash skulls sometimes. He couldn't see her
—small inside a tree trunk above the courtyard.
Soon, it would turn red over the kingdom.
Nobody liked that color, not since the evacuation,
especially the jungle. Strong smells of smoke prayers
rising above Ta Prohm temple's roof. Left-Behind
scuttled back to her nest, climbed the neck
of the Octopus Tree to find the source of fire.
Where are the apsaras? she asked the trees.
But the trees pretended not to know anything.
Below, stone heads nodded to her, watching over
Angkor Thom. Smoke clouds sealed their mouths, shut
their eyes. Left-Behind squinted through the haze
to make clear the shrieks she heard. To tell you what she saw,
she would have to whisper through this flute she found
in a branch. She couldn't go near the circle of dancing women
or where the soldiers took them—near the palm trees
whose leaves blushed again and again, again and again.

WHEN THE WAR WAS OVER

He was cornered by the men in blue
at the bottom of the stairs outside.

One pointed a gun at him
made his hands flail

upward in alarm. He cowered behind
Pol Pot—ten times his stature, hands

on his hips as if he were the hero
protecting the victim.

Around the building he ran for it,
found me and told me the war was over,

kissed me, thrust me against the table—
I take his hand, climb the stairs

of my school, twist
the doorknob of a locked classroom

and round our way to the EXIT
where we climb the steps

of an ancient world wonder
from a pre-Angkorian time.

In the open air, we admire the valleys below.
We are small against the carvings

exploring something we missed
only to find the natives

excavating our temple.

KIM THÚY was born in Saigon in 1968. At the age of 10, she left Vietnam with her parents and two brothers. After a stay in a refugee camp in Malaysia, the family arrived in Granby, in the Eastern Townships of Quebec. She pursued studies at the Université de Montréal where she completed degrees in linguistics and translation, then in law. Her first novel, *Ru,* fictionalizes her family's long journey from Vietnam to Quebec. The novel has been translated into several languages. Thúy is the recipient of the Grand Prix RTL-Lire and Canada's Governor General's Literary Award.

SHEILA FISCHMAN (translator) is a Canadian translator who specializes in the translation of works of contemporary Quebec literature. She holds an MA from the University of Toronto. She is a founding member of the Literary Translators' Association of Canada and founding co-editor of *Ellipse: Œuvres en traduction/Writers in Translation.* She has been the recipient of the Governor General's Award for Translation, the Canada Council Prize for Translation, and the Félix-Antoine Savard Award offered by the Translation Center, Columbia University, among others. Her translation of *Ru* by Kim Thúy has been selected for Canada Reads: *Next Episode.* She currently lives in Montreal.

FROM *RU*

I came into the world during the Tet Offensive, in the early days of the Year of the Monkey, when the long chains of firecrackers draped in front of houses exploded polyphonically along with the sound of machine guns.

I first saw the light of day in Saigon, where firecrackers, fragmented into a thousand shreds, colored the ground red like the petals of cherry blossoms or like the blood of the two million soldiers deployed and scattered throughout the villages and cities of a Vietnam that had been ripped in two.

I was born in the shadow of skies adorned with fireworks, decorated with garlands of light, shot through with rockets and missiles. The purpose of my birth was to replace lives that had been lost. My life's duty was to prolong that of my mother.

———

Because of our exile, my children have never been extensions of me, of my history. Their names are Pascal and Henri, and they don't look like me. They have hair that's lighter in color than mine, white skin, thick eyelashes. I did not experience the natural feelings of motherhood I'd expected when they were clamped onto my breasts at 3 a.m., in the middle of the night. The maternal instinct came to me much later, over the course of sleepless nights, dirty diapers, unexpected smiles, sudden delights.

Only then did I understand the love of the mother sitting across from me in the hold of our boat, the head of the baby in her arms covered with foul-smelling scabies. That image was before my eyes for days and maybe nights as well. The small bulb hanging from a wire attached to a rusty nail spread a feeble, unchanging light. Deep inside the boat there was no distinction between day and night. The constant illumination protected us from the vastness of the sea and the sky all around us. The people sitting on deck told us there was no boundary between the blue of the sky and the blue of the sea. No one knew if we were heading for the heavens or plunging into the water's depths. Heaven and hell embraced in the belly of our boat. Heaven promised a turning point in our lives, a new future, a new history. Hell, though, displayed our fears: fear of pirates, fear of starvation, fear of poisoning by biscuits soaked in motor oil, fear of running out of water, fear of being unable to stand up, fear of having to urinate in the red pot that was passed from hand to hand, fear that the scabies on the baby's head was contagious, fear of never again setting foot on solid ground, fear of never again seeing the faces of our parents, who were sitting in the dark surrounded by two hundred people.

———

My mother waged her first battles later, without sorrow. She went to work for the first time at the age of thirty-four, first as a cleaning lady, then at jobs in plants, factories, restaurants. Before, in the life that she had lost, she was the eldest daughter of her prefect father. All she did was settle arguments between the French-food chef and the Vietnamese-food chef in the family courtyard. Or she assumed the role of judge in the secret love affairs between maids and menservants. Otherwise, she spent her afternoons doing her hair, applying her makeup, getting dressed to accompany my father to social events. Thanks to the extravagant life she lived, she could dream all the dreams she wanted, especially those she dreamed for us. She was preparing my brothers and me to become musicians, scientists, politicians, athletes, artists and polyglots, all at the same time.

However, far from us, blood still flowed and bombs still fell, so she taught us to get down on our knees like the servants. Every day, she made me wash four tiles on the floor and clean twenty sprouted beans by removing their roots one by one. She was preparing us for the collapse. She was right to do so, because very soon we no longer had a floor beneath our feet.

————

I know the sound of flies by heart. I just have to close my eyes to hear them buzzing around me again, because for months I had to crouch down above a gigantic pit filled to the brim with excrement, in the blazing sun of Malaysia. I had to look at the indescribable brown color without blinking so that I wouldn't slip on the two planks behind the door of one of the sixteen cabins every time I set foot there. I had to keep my balance, avoid fainting when my stools or those from the next cabin splattered. At those moments I escaped by listening to the humming of flies. Once, I lost my slipper between the planks after I'd moved my foot too quickly. It fell into the cesspit without sinking, floating there like a boat cast adrift.

————

I am waiting until Pascal is a few years older before I make the connection between the story of the mother from Hoa Lu and Tom Thumb. In the meantime, I tell him the story of the pig that traveled in a coffin to get through the surveillance posts between the countryside and the towns. He likes to hear me imitate the crying women in the funeral procession who threw themselves body and soul onto the long wooden box, wailing, while the farmers, dressed all in white with bands around their heads, tried to hold them back, to console them in front of the inspectors who were too accustomed to death. Once they got back to town, behind the closed doors of an ever-changing secret address, the farmers turned the pig over to the butcher, who cut it into pieces. The merchants would then tie those around their legs and waists to transport them to the black market, to families, to us.

I tell Pascal these stories to keep alive the memory of a slice of history that will never be taught in any school.

———

I went back to Vietnam to work for three years, but I never visited my father's birthplace some two hundred and fifty kilometers from Saigon. When I was a child, I would vomit the whole way whenever I made that twelve-hour journey, even though my mother put pillows on the floor of the car to keep me still. The roads were riddled with deep fissures. Communist rebels planted mines by night and pro-American soldiers cleared them away by day. Still, sometimes a mine exploded. Then we had to wait hours for the soldiers to fill in the holes and gather up the human remains. One day a woman was torn to pieces, surrounded by yellow squash blossoms scattered, fragmented. She must have been on her way to the market to sell her vegetables. Maybe they also found the body of her baby by the roadside. Or not. Maybe her husband had died in the jungle. Maybe she was the woman who had lost her lover outside the house of my maternal grandfather, the prefect.

———

For many immigrants, the American dream has come true. Some thirty years ago, in Washington, Quebec City, Boston, Rimouski or Toronto, we would pass through whole neighborhoods strewn with rose gardens, hundred-year-old trees, stone houses, but the address we were looking for never appeared on one of those doors. Nowadays, my aunt Six and her husband, Step-uncle Six, live in one of those houses. They travel first class and have to stick a sign on the back of their seat so the hostesses will stop offering them chocolates and champagne. Thirty years ago, in our Malaysian refugee camp, the same Step-uncle Six crawled more slowly than his eight-month-old daughter because he was suffering from malnutrition. And the same Aunt Six used the one needle she had to sew clothes so she could buy milk for her daughter. Thirty years ago, we lived in the dark with them, with no electricity, no running water, no privacy. Today, we complain that their house is too big and our extended family too small to experience the same intensity of the festivities—which lasted until dawn—when we used to get together at my parents' place during our first years in North America.

There were twenty-five of us, sometimes thirty, arriving in Montreal from Fanwood, Montpelier, Springfield, Guelph, coming together in a small, three-bedroom apartment for the entire Christmas holiday. Anyone who wanted to sleep alone had to move into the bathtub. Inevitably, conversations, laughter and quarrels went on all night. Every gift we offered was a genuine gift, because it represented a sacrifice and it answered a need, a desire or a dream. We were well acquainted with the dreams of our nearest and dearest: those with whom we were packed in tightly for nights at a time. Back then, we all had the same dreams. For a long time, we were obliged to have the same one, the American dream.

———

Once it's achieved, though, the American dream never leaves us, like a graft or an excrescence. The first time I carried a briefcase, the first time I went to a restaurant school for young adults in Hanoi, wearing heels and a straight skirt, the waiter for my table didn't understand why I was speaking Vietnamese with him. At first I thought that he couldn't understand my southern accent. At the end of my meal, though, he explained ingenuously that I was too fat to be Vietnamese.

I translated that remark to my employers, who laugh about it to this day. I understood later that he was talking not about my forty-five kilos but about the American dream that had made me more substantial, heavier, weightier. That American dream had given confidence to my voice, determination to my actions, precision to my desires, speed to my gait and strength to my gaze. That American dream made me believe I could have everything, that I could go around in a chauffeur-driven car while estimating the weight of the squash being carried on a rusty bicycle by a woman with eyes blurred by sweat; that I could dance to the same rhythm as the girls who swayed their hips at the bar to dazzle men whose thick billfolds were swollen with American dollars; that I could live in the grand villa of an expatriate and accompany barefoot children to their school that sat right on the sidewalk, where two streets intersected.

But the young waiter reminded me that I couldn't have everything, that I no longer had the right to declare I was Vietnamese because I no longer had their fragility, their uncertainty, their fears. And he was right to remind me.

———

Around that time, my employer, who was based in Quebec, clipped an article from a Montreal paper reiterating that the "Québécois nation" was Caucasian, that my slanting eyes automatically placed me in a separate category, even though Quebec had given me my American dream, even though it had cradled me for thirty years. Whom to like, then? No one or everyone? I chose to like the gentleman from Saint-Félicien who asked me in English to grant him a dance. "Follow the guy," he told me. I also like the rickshaw driver in Da Nang who asked me how much I was paid as an escort for my "white" husband. And I often think about the woman who sold cakes of tofu for five cents each, sitting on the ground in a hidden corner of the market in Hanoi, who told her neighbors that I was from Japan, that I was making good progress with my Vietnamese.

She was right. I had to relearn my mother tongue, which I'd given up too soon. In any case, I hadn't really mastered it completely because the country was divided in two when I was born. I come from the South, so I had never heard people from the North until I went back to Vietnam. Similarly, people in the North had never heard people from the South before reunification. Like Canada, Vietnam had its own two solitudes. The language of North Vietnam had developed in accordance with its political, social and economic situation at the time, with words to describe how to shoot down an airplane with a machine gun set up on a roof, how to use monosodium glutamate to make blood clot more quickly, how to spot the shelters when the sirens go off. Meanwhile, the language of the South had created words to express the sensation of Coca-Cola bubbles on the tongue, terms for naming spies, rebels, Communist sympathizers on the streets of the South, names to designate the children born from wild nights with GIs.

———

Most of those children of GIs became orphans, homeless, ostracized not only because of their mother's profession but also because of their father's. They were the hidden side of the war. Thirty years after the last GI had left, the United States went back to Vietnam in place of their soldiers to rehabilitate those damaged children. The government granted them a whole new identity to erase the one that had been tarnished. A number of those children now had, for the first time, an address, a residence, a full life. Some, though, were unable to adapt to such wealth.

Once, when I was working as an interpreter for the New York police, I met one of those children, now adult. She was illiterate, wandering the streets of the Bronx. She'd come to Manhattan on a bus from a place she couldn't name. She hoped that the bus would take her back to her bed made of cardboard boxes, just outside the post office in Saigon. She declared insistently that she was Vietnamese. Even though she had *café au lait* skin, thick wavy hair, African blood, deep scars, she was Vietnamese, only Vietnamese, she repeated incessantly. She begged me to translate for the policeman her desire to go back to her own jungle. But the policeman could only release her into the jungle of the Bronx. Had I been able to, I would have asked her to curl up against me. Had I been able to, I'd have erased every trace of dirty hands from her body. I was the same age as her. No, I don't have the right to say that I was the same age as her: her age was measured in the number of stars she saw when she was being beaten and not in years, months, days.

———

Just recently in Montreal, I saw a Vietnamese grandmother ask her one-year-old grandson: "*Thương Bà d-ể d-âu?*" I can't translate that phrase, which contains just four words, two of them verbs, *to love* and *to carry*. Literally it means, "Love grandmother carry where?" The child touched his head with his hand. I had completely forgotten that gesture, which I'd performed a thousand times when I was small. I'd forgotten that love comes from the head and not the heart. Of the entire body, only the head matters. Merely touching the head of a Vietnamese person insults not just him but his entire family tree. That is why a shy Vietnamese eight-year-old turned into a raging tiger when his Québécois teammate rubbed the top of his head to congratulate him for catching his first football.

If a mark of affection can sometimes be taken for an insult, perhaps the gesture of love is not universal: it too must be translated from one language to another, must be learned. In the case of Vietnamese, it is possible to classify, to quantify the meaning of love through specific words: to love by taste (*thích*) without being in love (*thường*); to love passionately (*yêu*); to love ecstatically (*mê*); to love blindly (*mù quáng*); to love gratefully (*tính nghĩa*). It's impossible quite simply to love, to love without one's head.

I'm lucky that I've learned to savor the pleasure of resting my head in a hand, and my parents are lucky to be able to capture the love of my children when the little ones drop kisses into their hair, spontaneously, with no formality, during a session of tickling in bed. I myself have touched my father's head only once. He had ordered me to lean on it as I stepped over the handrail of the boat.

—*Translated from the French by Sheila Fischman*

PAUL TRAN is the poetry editor at *The Offing* and Chancellor's Graduate Fellow in the Writing Program at Washington University in St. Louis, Missouri. Their work appears in *The New Yorker*, *Prairie Schooner*, *RHINO*, which gave them a 2015 Editor's Prize, and elsewhere. A recipient of fellowships from Kundiman, VONA, Poets House, Lambda Literary Foundation, Vermont Studio Center, The Conversation, Palm Beach Poetry Festival, Miami Writers Institute, and the Fine Arts Work Center in Provincetown, Tran is the first Asian-American since 1993 to win the Nuyorican Poets Café Grand Slam, placing in the Top 5 at the National Poetry Slam.

SELF-IMMOLATION

In the world before this one,
      all my lovers fell to my feet
like soldiers in a bombed gully.

I placed framed photographs
of them in the Thien Mu Temple,
        arranged fresh oranges on a plate.

August 1963: Thich Quang Duc
        took a baby-blue Austin Westminster
to Phan Dinh Phung Boulevard.

He sat in the lotus position
while another monk poured petrol
        over his darkening robes.

Police in white-and-khaki uniforms
        kept protesters from hurling
into the flames with their batons.

Black smoke exploded like wings
from his body, which did not move
        except to bow before the Buddha.

When he fell back on the street,
        a camera lunged forward to record
his final minutes in this universe.

Everything burned
but his heart, which remained intact
        and wrapped in sunlit cloth.

In dreams, I touch his handsome face
        and blaze in the battlefield
where my past loves wait.

I'm the field. I'm the fire
unwilling to release them in fear
        no one else will want me.

HEIRLOOM

We know how the story goes.
A pirate leads her off the boat, onto the shore.
He rapes the other women first, shoots them in the head,
feeds their bodies to the ocean's aching blue mouth.

A pirate leads my mother from the boat to the shore.
He strips her down to her soiled cotton underwear,
feeds her aching body to the ocean's blue mouth.
She swears he did not rape her.

When he strips me down to my cotton underwear,
my father sets me on his lap like a Barbie doll.
My mother swears he did not rape me.
She tells me to stop making things up.

My father sets me on his lap. Like a Barbie doll,
I obey when he commands me to open, to keep it a secret.
He warns me not to make things up.
His touch leaves a stain I cannot scrub clean.

I obey. Every time he commands me to open, I keep it a secret.
Even now, years later, long after he disappeared like a ghost,
his touch remains a stain I cannot scrub clean.
I am not asking for you to believe me.

Even now, years later, long after he disappeared like a ghost,
my mother still sees the pirate in her dreams, the ocean's infinite
    hunger.
She is not asking, but I believe her.
Truth finds a way to exact its obscene measures.

My mother still sees the pirate in her dreams. The ocean's infinite
   hunger
swallows her in its waves. She wakes and pretends it never happened.
But truth finds a way to exact its obscene measures,
even when denial appears to be our only choice to survive.

Rising from the waves, I refuse to pretend it never happened.
My father rapes me while my mother is asleep in the other room.
Even when denial appears to be our only choice, to survive
we know how the story goes.

JULIE THI UNDERHILL is a poet, essayist, fiction writer, artist, photographer, filmmaker, performer, and historian. In 1976 she was born in the United States to a mother from Viet Nam, a Cham-French war widow who had evacuated during the Fall of Saigon. During the war in Viet Nam, her American father was a civilian contractor, and her American stepfather flew combat helicopters. She has published in *Veterans of War, Veterans of Peace* (2006), *Embodying Asian/American Sexualities* (2009), *Troubling Borders* (2014), and elsewhere. She received a Rockefeller Fellowship from the William Joiner Institute for the Study of War and Social Consequences (UMass-Boston). Underhill obtained her MA from University of California Berkeley. She is currently a lecturer at California College of the Arts.

THE SILENT OPENING

Despite the rust of ocean winds burnishing
that bright metallic nip of blood
of the same waters we swallow at birth
we came north by boat two thousand years ago
and flourished in kingdom, built master Indic temples
two by two, alone in pairs, or simply alone
is that right?

How were we supposed to learn our culture
when we had to struggle in war to survive
you think it's so easy to know?!
my mother chokes upon the lullabies
losing history, legend, literature, and song
in plenitudes of nightmares.

Yet I live an unsettling night, mother, just like you
my good blood commingled with the enemy, just like you
I've lost my family, displaced by war, just like you
I return with hesitation and tangled words
to speak vocabularies imposed during 600 years
of conquest, containment, and conversion of our people
collapsing our borders and eroding our knowledge
by the frictions of extermination and fear.

And neither my nor your name will inscribe a map of losses
masquerading in paper calm, eulogizing our possible pasts
while lighting candles and offering fruit to our ancestors
who may still recognize us, after all. Perhaps.

I've searched dream rooms for our dead, regardless,
sometimes finding the gate to my dream locked, a hush
held back, the silent opening of locks illuminated
by a small search light revealing hidden vocabularies
translating loss as home, departure for arrival,
now and again.

WAR DREAMS

i am crossing water on a boat
with refugees when it capsizes
close to shore. i dive beneath
the water to save two children,
both under the age of six. one at a time.

yet even after bringing them to a pier
& expelling water from their lungs
they each died. almost everyone
sank to ocean's bottom.
then fast forward
to years later, when i get
a letter from someone
whom i'd thought had drowned
that day.
i read it
uncomprehending.

*

i am working in a country
in central Africa that suffers
famine, ethnic cleansing, disease
& civil war, when i am assigned
by my supervisors to dig
a mass grave on the outskirts
of town. i go to the town's edge
to assess the area.
yet when i begin to dig,
i hit skulls, only to realize
that i am digging
into a preexisting mass grave.
i move & discover more of the same.
nearly every scrap of dirt
was stretched thin over piles of bodies;
i never find a place to begin
again.

MAI DER VANG is the author of *Afterland* (Graywolf Press, 2017), which received the Walt Whitman Award from the Academy of American Poets. She will serve as a 2017–18 Visiting Writer in the MFA Writing Program at the School of the Art Institute of Chicago. Her writing has appeared in *Poetry*, *Virginia Quarterly Review*, the *New York Times*, the *Washington Post*, and elsewhere. As an editorial member of the Hmong American Writers' Circle, she is co-editor of *How Do I Begin: A Hmong American Literary Anthology*.

LIGHT FROM A BURNING CITADEL

Once this highland was our birthplace. Once
we were children of kings.

Now I am a Siamese rosewood on fire.
I am a skin of sagging curtain.
I am a bone of bullet hole.
I am locked in the ash oven of a forest.

      Peb yog and we will be.

The sky sleeps quilted in a militia of stars.

Someone has folded
gold and silver spirit
money into a thousand tiny boats.

      Peb yog
      hmoob and we will be.

I am hungry as the beggar who cracked
open a coconut to find
the heart of a wild gaur.

      Hmoob and we
      will be.

The tree is more ancient
than its homeland,
shedding its annual citrine
as hourglass dripping honey.

> *Peb yeej ib txwm yog*
> *hmoob.*

I dig and dig for no more roots to dig.
I soldier with my severed
legs, my fallen ear.

I've become the shrill
air in a bamboo pipe—the breath
of an army of bells.

**

> *Peb yog:* "We are."
> *Peb yog hmoob:* "We are Hmong."
> *Peb yeej ib txwm yog hmoob:* "We have always been Hmong."

I THE BODY OF LAOS AND ALL MY UXOS

It's been forty years of debris
turning stale, and submunitions

still hunt inside the patina of my mud.
I'm stumbling with ankles steeped

in my little wrecked chimneys.
A foot wedged inside a sandal.

The bandage wraps my chest and I
sense the new branches of a cypress

within me, waiting to tear open
the gauze. Where are the high verandas

that once guarded elephants.
What ends the deepening numbers,

resounding into night, a planeload
releases every eight minutes forever.

Left only with cistern walls dismantled
in this era of widows, this is no way

to be lived, clawed and de-veined by
steel splinters concealed. The ground

knows more than a child will ever.
No way to seal the gaps, when a smuggled

climate spills over my body, taints me
with cobwebs spun from overseas.

WHEN THE MOUNTAINS ROSE BENEATH US, WE BECAME THE VALLEY

I won't ask why the saola came
To you, father, or of the poacher who

Followed, but I ask of the country
You lost, the one I never had, unlike

The midwife who sketched birth
Maps on a girl's body and found

A rainforest in her belly. I ask why
A body is born to save money

But can't pay to cross hell's ferry,
Or why snow tells us heaven

Is cold. A sunken missile maddens
Radiant as firework to the eyes

Of a tribesman, witnessing for
The first time. How did an ancient

Boy drown in a homeless river. I ask
Why the warsick warrior who hunts

With claws is hiding a poem. A piece
Of paper hides a garden. What

Harrowed you most arriving at the last
Minute to catch your brother's

Final breath on the hospital bed.
Can a unicorn kindle the night,

Haloed by its flame, torches jutting
From its head. Live on. Ask me how I've

Saved us. Ask me to build our temples
So rooted, so stone, we won't ever die out.

CHI VU was born in Vietnam and came to Australia in 1979. After studying at the University of Melbourne, she worked as a theater maker, dramaturg, writer, and artistic director. Chi Vu's plays, which include the critically acclaimed and widely studied *A Story of Soil, The Dead Twin,* and *Vietnam: A Psychic Guide,* have been performed in Melbourne and Sydney, and her short stories have appeared in various publications, including the Macquarie PEN *Anthology of Australian Literature.* Her novella, *Anguli Ma: A Gothic Tale,* is published by Giramondo.

THE UNCANNY

I

One of the tasks of a migrant is to move from a sense of alienation in the new country to a sense of being comfortable with that alienation. One of the tasks of a writer is to move between thinking about content and form, in order to heighten the "what" of the story by selecting the best genre for the piece. An author who writes of migration faces the twin task of addressing alienation and form.

Imagine you are a migrant who had been a member of the main ethnic, cultural and linguistic group in your old country. Then after migrating, you are suddenly part of a minority in a new country. There is no shared cultural context between you and the majority of the people around you. Perhaps the only thing that most people know about where you came from is the name of a distant war. Little else outside of that frame is understood by the people in your street, at your school or workplace. As though overnight, you find yourself viewed through a small frame that is not of your choosing. This limited view amputates you: it narrows how you are understood, and therefore what you can communicate.

And vice versa.

II

My family arrived in our new country in the middle of winter, 1979. In the morning, steam came out of our mouths and there was dew on the grass. We spent the first days settling into the migrant hostel in Maribyrnong, in the western suburbs of Melbourne. All food was served at the canteen as cooking was not allowed in our living quarters. Breakfast was cereal and milk and lunch consisted of prepackaged sandwiches, which I quickly got used to. But dinner was always a big adjustment: you would collect your own plastic tray, put a plate on it and get served a large hunk of meat flavored with salt and pepper—no other flavors. The vegetables had been boiled and came without any dipping sauces. No matter how much salt you added, the food did not become more flavorsome; it merely became saltier.

After several days we ventured out of the hostel to explore this new world. We were waiting for a bus when we saw a sign that read: NO STANDING ANY TIME. My father must have read it several times, perplexed, before he called my oldest sister over. She was considered the authority as she had actually applied herself to learn English from the private tutor while we were still in Vietnam, while the rest of us kids had only followed her around making foreign-sounding, silly noises at each other. My sixteen-year-old sister stepped forward and read it carefully. Then she turned around and confirmed: "Yes, it's true—it says we're not allowed to stand here—at any time." My father's mouth turned grim and his whole bearing seemed to drop, for perhaps we'd made a terrible mistake. Could it be that we had risked our lives on the open seas to arrive at an even more repressive regime than the one we had just escaped from? The bus stop was right here, and yet we were not permitted to stand. In this impossible predicament, we each then tried to find some pose that could be interpreted, if it came down to an unfair prosecution, that was not in fact standing: slouching, leaning against a pole, poised about to dash away; I think one or two of us children may have even squatted by the side of the road, Vietnamese-style.

Before the end of the day, we realized that everyone ignored these signs, and in fact stood shamelessly, blatantly, next to or in front of the NO STANDING ANY TIME sign. I made a mental note: the word "standing" had been used in a peculiar way and only applied to cars, which could neither stand not sit nor squat.

As we settled in, we needed to find a way to taste our own food again. One of my parents, probably my mother, took things in her own hands and discovered a Chinese grocery somewhere in the city. She came home with provisions: jars of fermented pastes and sauces that warmed our nostrils. We bought a little electric cooker and began cooking food in our living quarters in the migrant hostel. I vaguely recall the boiling of vermicelli and the scent of a hot pot emanating from the electric cooker. Perhaps someone kept a lookout at the slightly open window for anyone official who might have been walking the grounds that evening, and to fan the plumes of pungent steam out the window.

We ate this delicious, welcoming food. It was like our innards unclenched and smiled for the first time in this new country. We are able to relax and take in our situation better. My mother and sisters started cleaning up, putting away our contraband cooking utensils. There was some stock spilt on the floor, which I slipped on as I went past. I fell, and hit my head on the pointy corner of the wall.

The next day at the migrant hostel school (a learning center to help us adjust) the female teacher was yelling at me, but I didn't want to answer her. She wanted to know what had happened, why did I have this big cut on my head, why was there dried blood sticking down my black hair where this lump had formed. I started to stammer and quiver. I told her in my best English, calling on all my efforts to make some sense.

"My mother cooking . . . water on the ground, I falling." Then I would have brought my hands up to my wound to indicate the impact with the pointy corner of the wall. The teacher's anger seemed to subside and she left me alone. I remained mortified at what I had revealed under pressure. I had to use the word "ground" instead of "floor," so now she probably thought we lived in a mud hut in Vietnam.

After my earliest chance, I ran back to our hostel and told my father what happened: how the teacher screamed at me about the cut on my head; how I told her that we had been cooking illegally in our rooms.

"We're going to be in so much trouble, aren't we?"

I started to think that they would send my family away to whatever this country's equivalent of the New Economic Zone was—to scratch out a life in dense virgin jungle, to die from dirty water, malnutrition and mosquito bites. I started to plan how we'd pack all our belongings, again, before they came to get us. Unbelievable, my father was smiling gently and looking above me, as though he was imagining the teacher who had shown this concern. "It's okay," he reassured, "you didn't say anything wrong. It's okay, my daughter."

III

From the time I knew any language at all, I had dreamt and thought and spoken in Vietnamese. The music of it all was like rain dropping on tropical leaves growing at different angles, making variously pitched staccatos and then tinkling down into rivulets. My first contact with English was exposure to the strange resonances it made inside my mouth; the adding of "s" on the end of everything, so it seemed at the time; the collapsing of all social relationships into the single pronoun "you" and its mirror "I."

Before we knew enough English to understand everything we were hearing, we learnt the shape of the words from television jingles—singing them loudly, with each of the words made up of similar-sounding Vietnamese words. The word *xe đạp* (bicycle) was close enough to "shut up" for us kids to use. Words like this became a tool of subversion, for if we were caught saying it, we would look nonchalant and say, "What? Bicycle . . ."

Less than a year after my family's arrival in Australia, I experienced that moment of unconsciously thinking in the adopted language. I was standing on the wooden steps in my public Primary School when this foreign thought arrived. The mind—*my* mind—had thought directly in English without my willing it, without having put any effort into my memory, for it was as surprising as suddenly growing a third arm and watching it wave back at me for the first time.

I was part of a wave of immigration fortunate enough not to have to amputate my "birth" limbs, as my host country took on a more pluralistic stance by the mid '70s. Those limbs remain under my jacket, weak and pale, yet ageing with the rest of me. I take them out now and again to grasp the texture of words and ideas, to finger-tap quiet rhythms with those tiny fingernails, to listen for the resonances within. They can also be useful when I need to reconnect with a time when my actions did not necessarily represent those of my entire race; they were just mine and my interlocutor's to answer for. My "alien" limbs are now strong through daily use, so that I can no longer imagine myself without them. After more than thirty years in Australia, my dominant language has become English. It shapes my conscious thoughts, while the Vietnamese still shapes my feelings. So how does this affect my approach to writing?

Given the double blow of cultural and linguistic displacement (both the "content" and "form" of one's life becomes unfamiliar as a result of migration), it then follows that the self is also experienced as uncanny. Who is the "I" in this exchange speaking this encountered language? How is one to approach the "I" to draw out its many-faceted secrets? How can this "I" be both familiar yet estranged from an original and undivided "I" (if such a person ever existed)?

I don't mean to be slippery or sly with my different aliases and identities; I cannot write about a self, using a single "I," when this self is fragmented.

IV

When I was in grade three my parents were able to send me to a Catholic school. They had the impression from the French colonial period in Vietnam that Catholic schools offered greater opportunities and provided a more formal and therefore stricter education. They were not to know that the Irish Catholics had been an oppressed minority in Australia's early settlement, and perhaps held more firmly to their beliefs as a result.

It was at my new school that I was introduced to the idea of an all-powerful, omniscient God. Until then I had been without this knowledge, but now that I had it I felt my world changing. During recess I went to the loo, and still heard the strident voice warning us: God watches us always. Always. I had a moment that could be considered a parallel with Adam and Eve's after they had eaten from the fruit of knowledge—they suddenly realized their nakedness, became ashamed and hid from God. Except I was thinking why would a powerful god watch a little kid in the toilet? Why? I couldn't understand the teaching I'd been given. Rather than feeling shame, I felt a vague sense of dismay.

My teachers were caring and attentive. I learnt to say the Lord's Prayer. I settled in with a group of Vietnamese girls like myself, and we played a

high-jump game called "elastics"—all day, every day—using rubber bands
that we'd hand-braided together into a thick cord. I was happy.

Living in a new country is a series of conscious and unconscious deci-
sions about what you hold onto and what you let go of. Many are super-
ficial choices, or are minor in their consequences. Some have long-lasting
effects on how others view you, on which doors will be open or closed to
you. And which doors do you try to keep open, despite the price?

In grade four, the children in my class were to go through First Com-
munion. My homeroom teacher asked me whether I wanted to take part
in this ceremony as well, and I guess if I had truly wanted to do it, my
parents would have supported me. After all, I was the one who had intro-
duced the idea of Santa Claus and the Tooth Fairy to them, and they
went along with it.

In religion class, we had started learning about the woman who had
spent her whole life in pleasure, wearing perfume and make-up, never lift-
ing a hand to help the poor, being carried up some mountain by her slaves.
But then she became sick and was going to die, even though she was still
young and beautiful. Just before she died, she renounced her sinful life-
style, and accepted Jesus Christ as the savior. So she was accepted into
the kingdom of heaven.

"What? She gets to go to heaven?"

"Yes."

"Because she said that she accepted that Jesus was the Son of God?"

"That's right."

"And there's no other way to get into heaven?"

"You don't have to wait until you're about to die—you can accept Jesus
now . . ."

"Even if you were, like, Ghandi, you wouldn't be able to go to heaven?"
We must have just learnt about Ghandi in history class.

"Not unless he accepted that Jesus Christ is the Son of God."

"But he was a man of peace, while that woman spent her life selfishly.
She gets to go to heaven, but Ghandi goes to hell?"

"If she accepts Jesus, she can go to heaven."

I thought about all my uncles, aunties, their children (dispersed across
the globe after the war), and my parents and siblings who would all burn

in hell. And if I accepted this First Communion, I would go to heaven where it would be nice, but there would be no one I knew. And in talking about heaven, if you were genuinely a saint like Ghandi—who although he was Hindu, was a man of peace—wouldn't you feel so upset that you were in this nice place while all these other people were being tortured in hell? If you were a saint that would upset you, and you would probably give up your place in heaven to save someone else.

I told my homeroom teacher and the assistant principal that I didn't want to undergo First Communion with the other kids. They looked at me, at each other, and then back to me. Something in my teacher's eyes dimmed when she looked at me after that, as though she had done her best to save my soul, but it was ultimately up to me.

The day arrived. My fellow classmates, who had been so nervous before the ceremony, came streaming out of the school church, so proud and confident. The boys looked dapper in their suits, shirts and polished shoes, and the girls beamed with joy in their white dresses and white veils (white being the color of death in Vietnam when worn on the head). I waited in the shadows with the other kids, who did not undergo First Communion as they held even stricter religious beliefs than Christianity, and imagined the crackling flames of damnation licking at our feet.

V

The task here is actually to untangle which consequences are due to being a migrant, and which are specifically due to having fled as a refugee. The impact of the latter comes down to this: that when things get really difficult, as they do once in a while, I remember that my family and I could have all easily died at sea, no problem, no trace, unable to be found, as was the fate of up to half a million of our contemporaries. Anything from that time onwards is to be considered "bonus points." In writing the above, it seems that some small part of me (and I assume for each member of my family as well) did die on our journey over. For a consciousness of the truth of our deaths is itself a form of death, even though our bodies are safe and sound. For the miracle of land and birdcall and halcyon dawn afterwards is now bled with the passage of time. For when we next face the abyss again, we already know its fathomless darkness, its ceaseless horror.

VUONG QUOC VU was born in Saigon. His family emigrated to the United States and settled in San Jose where he grew up. He has an MFA degree in Creative Writing from Fresno State University. He is the founder and editor of Tourane Poetry Press and *Perfume River Poetry Review*.

TWENTY TWO

Old men from my father's village
still speak of him and the night
he led a group of men across a river
to their freedom, he, himself,
carrying on his shoulder
a young man who could not swim.

At twenty-three, I am barely the man
my father was; I'm barely his shadow.
At my age, he had already made
a home with the timid farm girl
who would become my strong mother,
had fathered a son, the first of thirteen children,
and he had fought in a war
he was too poor to understand.

At twenty-two, my father was held
in a prisoner-of-war camp; he led
a group of men to climb over
the sharpened ends of bamboo poles

that lined the prison walls. They hid
in the mud of rice fields until night
to cross that river,
to return home to their villages.

My father told me this story one summer,
the summer my mother lived away,
the summer she told him if he missed her
to water her flowers, and so he drowned the garden,
the summer I was twenty-two and felt crushed
by the weight of life that lay before me,

the summer I sat with my father
in the still-bright evening
in the heat of the kitchen
and he became my friend.

THE YEAR OF THE PIG

In the Year of the Pig, the city burned,
and it was supposed to bring full bowls
the lucky year of the lucky pig.
How it always fed, even in war.
One pig can feed a whole village.

People had been in prayer all year—
incense and red candles glowing
in temples like kiln fire,
but now the temples burned.

In the marketplace, the meat of pigs,
butchered for the New Year,
lay with the bodies of the dead.
Charred flesh all the same—
Who now would eat the pigs?

FLOWER BOMB

> The bomb / also / is a flower.

> —*William Carlos Williams, "Asphodel, That*
> *Greeny Flower"*

My brother, come home from war,
sits now for hours in the garden.
I see now, he says, everything
as flowers, the tendency of all things
to bloom—the way blood spills and splatters
like asters, the fire from guns, the sun unfurling
after the longest night. Everything blooms.

Brother, he says, I saw so many dead
I've realized that the body is, after all,
a flowery thing—soft tissues, clustered petals
of cells. Despite the marble column of its spine,
the great architecture of how it stands,
the arches and taut ropes of muscle,
it is easily torn apart, gunned down,
drowned, and plowed under,
how it withers and wilts with hunger

When I saw the dead, I didn't look
at faces and never, never into the eyes.
I avoided all implications of a soul, a name.
I looked at hands—those miracles of sinew
and veins—and imagined them to be leaves.
I have seen severed hands
as if they'd fallen from a tree,
hands crushed and burned crisp like autumn leaves.
I have seen wounds like purple trillium
forced through the skin.
I have seen the plum colors of viscera.

Brother, I have come home from Hell.
How now shall I tell the story
of Man—the wars, wars, wars
until the end of time?
How now shall I tell—my mind
already a shattering lake of glass,
my heart bullet-holed—
to write in blood or with red rose petals?

OCEAN VUONG is a poet and essayist and is the author of *Night Sky with Exit Wounds* (Copper Canyon Press, 2016). His grandfather served from 1967–1969 as a member of the US Armed Forces during the American War in Vietnam. Born in Saigon, Vietnam, Ocean currently lives in the Pioneer Valley, Massachusetts.

THE WEIGHT OF OUR LIVING: ON HOPE, FIRE ESCAPES, & VISIBLE DESPERATION

> Surely it is a privilege to approach the end
> still believing in something.
>
> —*Louise Glück*

There should be tears. There should be a reason. It's 7:34PM on New Year's Eve. I am lying in my kitchen in Astoria, New York, my cheek pressed to the cold tiles. My mother has just called. *My child*, she says in Vietnamese, her voice barely a gasp, *your uncle has killed himself*. It was not until she heard herself say those words did she start wailing into the phone. I open my eyes and see only the blue and yellow tiles on the kitchen floor. Little blue flowers on tiny sun-lit fields. When did I fall? Is that my voice? I didn't know it could sound like that: like an animal that just learned the word for God. The cell phone lies open beside me.

I can hear my mother—now hysterical—sobbing through the crackling receiver. I reach for it. She is pleading for me to come home. And I can. I can take the bus or the train from Penn Station and be in Hartford before midnight—but I won't. I can't. Instead, I tell her the trains aren't working. That I will find a way home in the morning. In my shock I am selfish. I hang up. I go for a walk. And I keep walking, passing people decked in glitter, plastic top-hats, and glasses with "2013" across their eyes, shuffling to the myriad bars or parties to drink and welcome the new year. I walk until I end up in Brooklyn—near midnight, by the East River. My fingers and snot-brightened lips numb from cold and grief. Fireworks unravel across the New York skyline, coloring the black water with shredded light as I stand in the sharp, freshly anointed January air— slowly forgetting my hands.

———

I love going on walks by myself. No pressure to keep up conversation. And there is something about movement that helps me think. To charge an idea with the body's inertia. To carry a feeling through the distance and watch it grow. When I first arrived in New York City I spent most of my time wandering. I was seventeen and wanted to write poems. With a red notebook and a slim volume of Lorca's verses tucked under my arm, I walked the bright and liquid avenues, not ever bothering to look at street names or even where I was heading. I would start at my friend's illegal basement-sublet (where I was sleeping on a couch salvaged from the back of a local Salvation Army) in Jamaica, Queens and trek until I ended up in Park Slope, Red Hook, Richmond Hill, or Gowanus, and once—even an abandoned shipyard near Far Rockaway.

During these aimless forays, I kept finding myself looking up— particularly on residential streets lined with anything from monolithic tenements to luxury brownstones. But I also saw, attached to nearly every building, a skeletal structure of architectural finesse equal, in my eyes, to any of the city's glittering towers. Fire escapes. Not buildings exactly— but accessories. Iron rods fused into vessels of descent—and departure. Some were painted blue or yellow or green, but most were black. Black staircases. I could spend a whole hour sitting across the street from a six-floor walk-up studying the zig-zags that clung to a building filled with so many hidden lives. All that richness and drama sealed away in a fortress whose walls echoed with communication of elemental or exquisite language—and yet only the fire escape, a clinging extremity, inanimate and often rusting, spoke—in its hardened, exiled silence, with the most visible human honesty: We are capable of disaster. And we are scared.

———

It's New Year's Day. I'm standing in my uncle's home in Hartford. The front door is propped open to air out the small one-bedroom apartment. It's snowing. Sharp flakes flicker through the doorway and turn to rain on my face. A portion of yellow police tape flaps from the mailbox. I walk into the hallway where my uncle's body was just removed the night before. For some reason, I thought the police, during their investigation and collection of evidence, would make things *presentable* for the family. I don't know why I expected this. Maybe I've seen too many crime shows where a seasoned detective would prepare the grieving loved ones with a little speech before ushering the mourners into ground zero, forensics officers stepping gingerly across the rooms. But the police are long gone. And the first thing I see is the chair—sitting right beneath the attic opening where he placed a weight bar across and tied the rope. Next are the belts. Three of them—littered around the chair, all snapped at the buckle and coiled on the hardwood like decapitated snakes. He was determined. My legs grow loose, liquid. My jaw throbbing. I rush into the bathroom and vomit into the sink. As my sixth cup of coffee swirls down the drain I start to feel a wave of incredible sadness fill my bones. In his house, my uncle's absence is sharpened. The running faucet. The silent rooms. My arms heavy, I kneel at the sink, listening to the water, letting it drown the dull ache in my temples. I open my mouth to speak—but no one's here to listen. I open my mouth to pray, in earnest, but quickly abandon the endeavor when I hear my mother's voice outside the house, calling my name. She's walking up the driveway with a tray of food and a small folding table in her arms. I quickly grab the belts and toss them up into the attic's dark, opened mouth. I never want to see them again.

My mother comes in and starts placing hot dishes of vegetarian food on the small table. Her hands are shaking. The sound of utensils and glasses knocking into each other. This food is for my uncle. We Vietnamese believe the dead can still be nourished by our offerings and goodwill—even long after their death. She lights a bundle of incense and places a photo of him on the table between a steaming plate of rice and tofu braised in soy sauce and green beans. The picture is the yearbook photo from his senior year in high school. Taken almost ten years ago, it's still true to his late features. He isn't smiling, but his lips are parted slightly, as if on the verge of speaking. My mother and I kneel before the makeshift altar and raise the incense to our foreheads. We prostrate. We bow as if the dead, through their growing absence, have suddenly become larger than life. *Tell your uncle to eat,* she says, looking down at the floor. *Uncle,* I say, to no one, *please eat . . . We miss you. Please . . . eat.*

———

> *A hole is nothing*
> *but what remains around it.*
> —Matt Rasmussen

———

The first fire escape was developed in 1784 by Englishman Daniel Maseres and was designed for personal use. This early model was simple: a rope, attached to a window, was anchored to the ground with a heavy wooden platform from which one could climb down and flee from a burning ledge. However, by the early 20th century, traditional iron fire escapes began to appear in America on the side of residential buildings, reducing the personal fire escape to obsolescence. In its place, a more collective means of escape was issued.

I don't know why I am thinking of fire escapes after my uncle's death. Part of me feels suddenly closer to them, that sense of urgency and danger that fire escapes, in their essence, embody. Maybe this is why the collective fire escape has become so popular. Maybe I prefer such visible desperation to exist *outside* of my home, out of view, out of mind—but always there. While I go on with my daily life, as I sit with friends in front of the TV, our faces blue-washed, or as I place the birthday cake before my little brother's delighted face, the candles flickering on the teeth of all the smiling guests, while I make love, while I pray, the fire escape lies just a few feet away, dormant, conveniently hidden—but never completely. I gather my notions of terror and push it out the window, where it calcifies into a structure so utilitarian as to be a direct by-product of fear itself.

And yet, as I walked through the neighborhoods of New York, there were always at least one or two fire escapes on each street adorned with flowers, tin bird feeders, herb gardens, pink lanterns, bike racks, even cafe-style chairs and tables. I admired and envied this act of domestication. Imagine a pair of hands reaching between those cold black bars and placing a pot of lucent April tulips into the sun. Life touching the possibility of its extinguishment. It almost makes me forget what those black bars were intended for. And maybe that's for the better. Maybe we live easier decorating danger until it becomes an extension of our homes.

———

Ocean, get on.
I don't wanna.
Don't be a pussy.
Why does it have to be pink?
Cuz that's the cheapest color. Grandma didn't have enough for a boy bike. Are you getting on or not?
But you took off the training wheels.
I know—so we can go faster.
Okay.
Come up and sit here, in front . . . can you fit?
Yeah.
Ok here we go. Put your feet up. Are you ready soldier?
Siryesir!
Here we go. We're going! We're heading into enemy territory!
Ahhhh! . . . .Will they shoot us?
I don't know! Hang on! Don't let go of my arms! Don't let go ok? Your mom will kill me.
Don't worry! I won't.

———

My grandmother gave birth to my uncle, Le Duy Phuong, in 1984 when she was nearly 43 years old. The father is unknown, disappeared into the night after leaving a tin of jasmine tea and a few crumpled bills on my grandmother's nightstand, Ho Chi Minh's benevolent-rendered face gazing out of the creased currency. Three years after my uncle's birth, I would come into the world at the height of Vietnam's post-war reconstruction era. Food was scarce. Many families, including ours, were cutting their rice rations with sawdust. But we would survive, my uncle and I—growing up together, playing together and, eventually, immigrating to America together. I was his shadow in those early days, often accompanying him even into the bathroom, where we would continue our conversations and games as he sat on the toilet. Because even the door, as thin as it was, was for me an unbearable border. A week before his death, we would share one last conversation with each other.

I was in Hartford for the holidays, and we decided to catch up, as we always do when I'm home, over coffee. We drove to a nearby Barnes & Noble and sat in the cafe. Beneath the bright lights I could tell he looked distraught, gaunt, his eyes dark at the edges. *I can only manage to eat an apple and drink a bit of water these days,* he said. He was "tired of this world" he explained, albeit cryptically. He kept distressing about his failed relationships, his bills, his job at the nail salon. Despite being fluent in English and a high-school graduate, customers often assumed, perhaps because of his quiet demeanor, that he was a new immigrant, often speaking about him amongst each other as if he couldn't understand. *Why would he waste his time in college? It's better to keep doing manicures. He has such strong hands for an Asian.* I tried comforting him, fumbling with a quote from James Baldwin but abandoned it mid-sentence when I saw his distant, sunken gaze, as if he was watching a field burning behind me. I reached out to touch his elbow. *Hey . . . Hey, what's wrong?* He kept staring at the field.

> [. . .] *The thinking*
> *Of you where you are a blank*
> *To be filled*
> —Mary Jo Bang

When someone dies their silence becomes a sort of held note, a key on the piano pressed down for so long it becomes an ache in the ear, a new sonic register from which we start to measure our new, ruptured lives. A white noise. Maybe this is why there is so much *music* in dying: the funerals, the singing, the hymns, the eulogies. All those sounds crowding the air with what the dead can't say.

There is the sound of hard drumming now: a wooden mallet knocking against a wooden bowl, a small sharp gong pounded at a rate equal to the heart. A monk in a mustard-colored robe, accompanied by her two white-haired assistants, opens a page of scripture and chants along to the dissonant instruments thrumming through my uncle's tiny apartment. Everyone's here. My mother, my aunts, cousins, my uncle's friends and co-workers. About 20 people crammed into the living room. The couches and various furniture pushed flush against the walls, or stacked on top of one another. We are all kneeling before the makeshift altar. It's been 7 days. A soft, silken mound of ash from hundreds of incense sticks has accumulated in front of my uncle's photo. More food. Plates of rice and vegetables. More incense. More chanting. We bow when the monk directs us to. We bow in unison, the items of my uncle's life still scattered all about us: socks, single shoes, green packs of Wrigley's gum, cigarettes, DVDs fallen from their cases, receipts, bars of chocolate, Levi's, dress shirts, underwear—much of it disheveled by us, the mourners, trying to make room for ourselves in an empty house. With my finger coiled around the wire of my uncle's Xbox video game console, I lower my head and listen to the sounds of the Lotus Sutra, my favorite. Its deep droning rising from our collective despair. I let it enter me: a warm constant vibration crowding out that silent note on the piano of the dead. I close my eyes.

In Buddhism, it is believed that when one dies a tragic, emotional, or sudden death, the spirit might not realize it has died at all—and so it's imperative to remind that person of their present, bodiless state. It is also believed that when the body perishes, one's hearing ability is heightened, since the spirit becomes more air-like and can therefore hear with its entire being. The monk encourages us to speak to my uncle. My mother, who has been kneeling beside me, now stands, her hands look like knotted roots. *Little brother,* her voice quickly cracks into a sort of wail, *please listen to big sister. I know you are scared but you must be brave and leave this place. There is nothing left here.* Through her tears and strained voice, the

Vietnamese language, a language so dependent on subtle inflections and intonations, now sounds otherworldly, warping in her throat from low guttural groans to high, fluctuating whines. *Please don't stay in this house, little brother. Soon, people will move in and you won't recognize them. Sister will come see you every week at the temple. Sister loves you. Please go and find a way to your next birth. I will see you again in another life.* She looks around the room, as if trying to locate him. My hands are numb. I take the hood from my sweatshirt and cover my head, shadowing my face.

We finally start to leave in single file, the monk leading the way, still chanting, her assistants knocking on their instruments. They will head into a van and drive the 35 minutes to the temple where my uncle's urn will be laid to rest. It will be kept inside a cupboard with other urns until they can be scattered into the Connecticut river on an auspicious day in the Buddhist calendar. I stand behind the procession and am the last to leave. I blow out the candles, snuff the remaining incense and hurry out, not looking back. I tear off the scrap of police tape fluttering on the mail box and close the door.

———

Ocean, get on.
I don't wanna.
Don't be a pussy.
Why does it have to be pink?
Cuz that's the cheapest color. Grandma didn't have enough after groceries for a boy bike. Are you getting on or not?
But you took off the training wheels.
I know—so we can go faster.
Okay.
Come up and sit here, in front . . . can you fit?
Yeah . . . How come we're not moving?
We can't. We're not supposed to go yet.
What do you mean?
. . . .
Uncle?
You didn't save me. You were supposed to save me.
But how—

Where is my face? Who took my face? There's just a black hole now.
Uncle, please.
It's like God's thumbprint. Right on my face. Here—put your hand to it . . .
it feels like sand.

––––––

My arms swing wildly through the dark. As if the dark was something to be torn away. The room suddenly a cage. Everything smaller, everything pressed against my skin. My arms and legs tangled in a web of blankets and sheets, knocking into bedposts, a night stand, chairs, cups of water, clocks, phone cords. I'm on the hardwood. Bare-chested. Wet. Cold. Shuddering. My hands covering my face, fearing he is still there, staring down at me from his pink bicycle—a black oval in his face, sucking in all the light. I look through a crack between my fingers. I see the violet window, a few dull stars over Queens, New York. I get up, walk toward it and press my forehead to the pane. I look out into the quiet, blue-lit city, my face vanishing in the reflection as the glass steams beneath my breath, softening the orange light that has just come on in an apartment across the courtyard. The sky starting to recede into the grainy grey of another morning. There should be tears.

––––––

It's winter in New York. It's January 8, 2014. It's been a year. The temperature has been dipping lately and today has plunged to a debilitating 4 degrees. Too cold for a walk. I stand at my window and look across the courtyard. It's been foggy all morning; the milky whiteness descending so low one of the buildings across the way has vanished completely, leaving only its fire escape—suspended in the air. Like the black bones of some mythical creature fossilized on its way to touch the sky.

I wonder what would happen if I were to bring the fire escape back inside. In fact, what would the fire escape look like if I were to wear it on my person, personality—in public? What would a fire escape sound like if it was imbedded into my daily language—and not have to apologize for it? Could this be one reason we create art—one reason we make poems? To say the unsayable? I don't know—but I'd like to think so. After all, the poem never needs to clear its throat or talk of the weather or

explain why it's here, what it's looking for. It doesn't even need its creator
to speak. Its importance springs from its willingness to exist outside of
practical speech. It possesses no capital yet still insists on being worthy. I
come to the poem and it offers me immediate communication with some-
one's secret self, self-preserved from the mainstream and its hunger for
order through emotional sterilization. "Why, as poets," says Carl Phillips,
"[should we] strip and, thereby make visible, difficulty instead of satisfy-
ing the majority of people by veiling it? Because poetry is not only what
reminds us that we are human, but helps ensure that we don't forget what
it means to be so." In this way, the poem is more than paper and words,
more than the obscure fiddlings of the high-brow, it is an invitation to a
more private, necessary dialogue. I approach it as if climbing the rungs
of someone's fire escape—whether I go up or down—is between me, the
reader, and the poet. And maybe nothing is burning at all. Maybe we
are only up here for the view. But it's up here that I wonder, at the risk of
asking for too much, *what if a fire escape can be made into a bridge?*

Ocean, what do you think you want to be when you grow up?
I want to be a car.
What?! You can't be a car, you have to be a human.
Ok. I want to be you. You go fast. Like a car.

Boston. July 22, 1975. A large tenement fire breaks out on Marlbor-
ough Street. Standing on the building's fifth floor fire escape, awaiting the
fire truck's rescue ladders, is 19-year-old Diana Bryant and her 2-year-old
daughter, Tiare Jones. Before the ladders could reach them, the fire escape
collapses. At this moment, Stanley Forman, a photojournalist covering
Boston fires, raises his camera from the street, and captures the mother
and daughter mid-fall. Bryant would die from her injuries—while Jones,
having fallen on top of her mother's body, would survive. Forman's photo
would go on to win the 1976 Pulitzer Prize for best News Photography
and the title of World Press Photo of the Year.

In the photo, Bryant is seen falling headfirst. Her daughter, upright,
is behind her. Their limbs akimbo and blurred from the pull of gravity.

There are potted plants falling alongside them. The iron shards of the collapsed fire escape can be seen hanging jaggedly from the building. It is a photograph of wrenching urgency and terror, one that shows a woman the moment before her death. And I wonder whether the fascination is of death alone—or could it also be the failure of a device meant to prevent death. That one can indeed, escape the fire, and still perish through the means of that escape. That our last notion of safety, the plan-B, the just-in-case, has literally fallen apart when we need it most. The picture makes palpable, in a way, what we can't always say to one another without the risk of "dampening the mood": *I am vulnerable even when I should be safe.*

I think of the plotted plants. I think of Diana placing the green lives into fresh soil and putting them out on her fire escape. How happy she must have felt to make her own space a little more beautiful. How I, too, do what I can to make things a little more beautiful—(bearable?). I think of the difficulty of talking about collapse in person, face to face. I think of my uncle in the cafe. How blurred he must have felt—free falling like that and not being able to say it. How did we come to live in a culture in which it's taboo to speak of the unpleasant? *Let's talk about something else,* we say, *something cheerful. Let's save this for later,* we say, *Please, not now, not at the dinner table.*

The limits of my language mean the limits of my world, says Wittgenstein. And if we continue to censor my most vital dialogues, our world can only grow smaller. And here, the poem does not necessitate admittance to anyone's dinner table. It speaks to whomever chooses to listen, whom ever needs it. But mostly, it avoids the easy answers, the limited and stunted, convenient closures. And maybe all a poem can really do is remind us that we are not alone—in our feelings. And maybe that's nothing. And maybe that's more than enough. Still, there's no way of knowing if an engagement with poetry would have saved my uncle's life. Perhaps. And perhaps not. But I wish I could've found a way to share it with him more often, to have the courage to communicate on that urgent and open bandwidth. That we could trust each other with our frailties knowing that, as humans, we are, at our best, partially broken. I was never able to explain to him what I really do—with poems and words. My family calls me a scholar because scholars are revered in Vietnam. Having lost so much, they wanted, desperately, for something to be proud of. How can I tell them that I spend hours, months, writing poems very few people will read—and with barely any money to show for it? I hesitate to elucidate on my writing, fearing I would taint any esteemed image they have of me in the process. *Other families sacrifice everything for lawyers!* my uncle would say at family gatherings, a Heineken in his hand and his face flushed with delight, *But we, we did it for a scholar. We might be poor but we'll live forever in books!*

———

> There is another world
> but it is inside this one.
> —*Eluard*

———

I speak of poetry only because it is the medium that I am most intimate with. But what I mean to say is that all art, if willing, can create the space for our most necessary communications. The character in the novel, the brush strokes in the painting, its tactile urgency, the statue of the Madonna made from birdseed, partly devoured and narrowed into a yellowed sliver in the rain. I want to believe there are things we can say without language. And I think this is the space the fire escape occupies, a space unbounded by genre or the physical limitations of the artist's tools. A space of pure potential, of possibility, where our desires, our strange and myriad ecstasies can, however brief, remain amorphous and resist the decay actualized by the rational world.

And yet, in a time where the mainstream seems to continually question the power and validity of art, and especially of poetry, its need, its purpose, in a generation obsessed with appearances, of status updates and smiling selfies bathed (corrected?) in the golden light of filters, in which it has become more and more difficult for us to say aloud, to one another: *I am hurt. I am scared. What happens now?* the poem, like the fire escape, as feeble and thin as it is, has become my most concentrated architecture of resistance. A place where I can be as honest as I need to—because the fire has already begun in my home, swallowing my most valuable possessions—and even my loved ones. My uncle is gone. I will never know exactly why. But I still have my body and with it these words, hammered into a structure just wide enough to hold the weight of my living. I want to use it to talk about my obsessions and fears, my odd and idiosyncratic joys. I want to leave the party through the window and find my uncle standing on a piece of iron shaped into visible desperation, which must also be (how can it not?) the beginning of visible hope. I want to stay there until the building burns down. I want to love more than death can harm. And I want to tell you this often. That despite being so human and so terrified, here, standing on this unfinished staircase to nowhere and everywhere, surrounded by the cold and starless night—we can live.

ZACHARY WATTERSON's stepfather, Ronald Sitts, served as a lieutenant in the United States Navy, was attached to the USS *Intrepid* in 1967, and piloted helicopters on rescue missions over the Gulf of Tonkin. Watterson's short stories and essays appear in *The Massachusetts Review*, *The Stranger*, *Post Road*, *River Styx*, and *Commentary*. His work has received several awards, including a Pushcart Prize nomination.

A SOUNDTRACK OF THE WAR

"I hated being over there," Ron Sitts said. He looked at his hands. Freckles and blond hairs circled his knuckles. On his index finger a scarred-over, decades-old gash. Over six feet tall, he had a thin nose, large ears, deeply tanned skin, and a shock of silver-white hair. A man who was once a Kansas boy plowing his father's fields; planting, cultivating and harvesting barley, wheat, corn and sorghum; mowing and baling alfalfa. He rocked gently, his slippers on the tiled floor. We were sitting in the house he had built in a small town in south-central Colorado. "The massive destruction and human suffering caused a depression in me. I felt guilt that I was unharmed." From the time I was eight years old until I left home at eighteen, I lived with Ron and my mother in New Jersey. At twelve I was the best man at their wedding. They separated shortly after I left home but I have kept in close touch with Ron. His stories of flying a rescue helicopter over the Gulf of Tonkin in the late 1960s had kept me rapt at the dinner table when I'd lived with him, but this was the first time in years that he had spoken to me about the war.

"I felt guilt," he went on, "that my job was to rescue, not to kill. I was prepared to do whatever I was ordered to do. Even if it was against my principles. Later I began to feel glad it wasn't my job to kill."

"I try to imagine," I said, but I had other impressions of the war drumming in my brain—the Rolling Stones' percussion in "Paint It Black" as fires burned in Stanley Kubrick's *Full Metal Jacket*, his film about Marine recruits who endure basic training and later face the Vietcong during the 1968 Tet Offensive. Sergeant Hartman tells his recruits the "free world *will* conquer communism." And here comes Nancy Sinatra singing "These Boots Were Made for Walking." Private Joker, played by a bespectacled Matthew Modine, wears a helmet bearing the words BORN TO KILL and a peace-symbol button on his uniform. He attempts to explain the contradictory emblems by saying he's "trying to suggest something about the duality of man, the Jungian thing." I try to forget Hollywood.

Outside Ron's living-room window, the San Luis Valley sloped gradually south to San Antonio Mountain a hundred miles away in New Mexico. The dry earth received a little over a foot of rainfall a year. In my twenties I'd planted yucca and cottonwoods in the Highlands near the Sandia Mountains in Albuquerque. Here in south-central Colorado the high desert spanned a horizontal sweep of sand and rock eight thousand feet above sea level.

"I admired those who had the courage to stand behind their principles in the face of ridicule from many of their fellow citizens."

"You mean people who fled to Canada?"

"Them, and the ones burned their draft cards."

"I don't know what I would've done."

"And I admired the courage of those who went to war because they believed they were doing the right thing."

———

As a rescue-helicopter pilot in the United States Navy, Ron knew a world of water and fire and air. He flew helicopters called UH-2s that were commonly referred to as Angels. In 1965 he had joined the Navy and entered flight training at Pensacola, Florida. Two years later he boarded the USS *Intrepid*, a ship commissioned in 1942, the year he was born. Aboard the aircraft carrier in the Gulf of Tonkin, Ron spent long hours not in the air but on the ship. Sometimes he sat on a catwalk near the bow and watched flying fish soaring and diving into the spray. In the distance hovered the port of Haiphong and the serpentine islands off-shore from the city of Hong Gai. Navy cooks dumped garbage into the water and Ron saw hammerhead sharks trailing the ship. Hazardous as his rescue missions were at times, nothing compared to the landings he executed when swells made the USS *Intrepid* rise and fall and the sun glimmered off the glass on the tower of the superstructure and blinded him as he maneuvered his UH-2 down to the deck.

Thirty years after the war, his second marriage—to my mother—ended and he drove home to the American West. For Ron, the small Colorado town where he lives in a house pushed against the base of the Sangre de Cristo Mountains is home. The San Luis Valley held the sharp and agreeable smell of piñon and sage, the white sand, the cold winters, the elk, the snowdrifts, and the house Ron had built in the Baca Grande. The valley reminded me of standing on the shore and gazing out over the Pacific Ocean, which I had done at nineteen after driving across country from New York. I'd found a job washing dishes in a diner in Arcata, California, and in the afternoons I'd step onto the back patio, a dishrag over my shoulder, rubber gloves dripping soap, and look out over the sea.

In southern Colorado, I found the San Luis Valley resembled in magnitude nothing so much as the ocean. Ron mentioned the solidity of his house. He had "used fifty pounds of mortar for every sixteen tiles," since he was building it "to last for three hundred years." He had told me he would leave the house to me when he died, and so I joked that my daughter's great-great-great-grandchildren would have the place by then. "That's right," Ron said, a smile loosening the corners of his mouth. "The tiles should still be here, under their little feet."

———

The summer Ron's marriage with my mother ended, we spoke on the phone about the breakup. He was still in New Jersey and I had gone to live in Ann Arbor for the summer after receiving a grant to teach a writing workshop at a prison in Detroit. "If I had to do it all over again," Ron said about his marriage, "if I could go back a dozen years and know what I know now, I'd do it the same."

I said something hackneyed, an effort to console him, and knew my words were empty things. I held the phone to my ear and there passed between us a silence, the sort of silence that does not set things right but gives each person a chance to be alone.

"When I think about dying," he said, "about when it comes my time to die, I don't want it to be in New Jersey."

"You said so."

"I told you that?"

"You did but I don't mind hearing it again. I don't want to die in New Jersey either."

On the other end Ron laughed. It was good to hear him laugh, as if something inside him had been fixed for the moment. Not many months later he drove from New Jersey and the densely habited cities of the East to the open spaces of the West. Behind him was not only the war but also the two-story wood-and-brick house at the corner of Patton Avenue and Markham Road in Princeton. He had gutted the old floor and replaced it with new hardwood, staged his woodshop in the garage, and I remember coming home from school and hearing his table saw go quiet.

We sat together on the screened-in porch, the air fragrant with honeysuckle, rotting crabapples, butterfly bush blooms. On the scrub grass just beyond the porch, shadows of clouds moved swiftly and lightly. The light thinned as dusk drew near and in the cooler evening air, lightning bugs' luminous wings flared and vanished, specks of incandescence in the new dark. One afternoon I got in Ron's truck and we drove to the Delaware River. We sat in folding chairs on the shore and watched the flowing water and talked about the universe, exploding planets, galaxies near and far, the time-space continuum, the similarities between insects and airplanes, the durability of different woods, and the farm where he was raised outside McPherson, Kansas. In those years, he rarely spoke of the war, and when he did I listened until he had run out of stories.

———

When I visited him in Colorado, I traveled more than a thousand miles to see him. He spoke about the war. How in the Gulf of Tonkin he had loved the salty air, the ever-changing skies. How he had always respected and feared the sea. How in the Philippines, the morning before arriving at Subic Bay, then-Ensign Ron Sitts flew copilot alongside a senior pilot and Lieutenant Commander Charlie. They flew in the Angel pattern on the starboard side of the ship a hundred and eighty feet off the water. Ron heard the rotor winding down. The engine had just failed and soon they would plummet into the sea. Charlie grabbed the flight controls, disconnected the rotor from the engine and flattened the pitch of the blades while simultaneously pushing the nose forward and pointing the UH-2 down. They gained airspeed. About ten feet off the water, Charlie pulled the nose up and slowed airspeed and descent, and the helicopter sat down almost gently on the sea.

As soon as it touched the water, the chopper rolled. Ron unhooked his harness, tumbled over Charlie, scrambled and clambered but could not swim down through Charlie's open door. The life pack raft around his waist had caught on something. He wriggled out of the belt and swam free and when he reached the top of the water he gasped and wheezed and took oxygen into his lungs.

He could see the helicopter was upside down and sinking and he watched as Charlie and one crewman surfaced, inflated their rafts and crawled aboard. For a moment, Ron thought the fourth crewman was trapped inside the sinking Angel but then he appeared paddling in a raft on the other side of the disappearing helicopter. The wheels receded from view under a swell. Ten minutes later a UH-2 lifted the other two crewmen into the air. While Charlie and Ron waited for another chopper to come for them, Charlie paddled in his raft, and Ron treaded water in the South China Sea.

A giant shadow came up from below.

"Shark," Charlie whispered, and then shouted.

Ron saw his raft pack floating nearby, grabbed it, pulled its cord, and when the raft ballooned with air, he got in and scanned the foamy breakers. "Where is it?"

"I don't know."

The shadow shrank and disappeared. An Angel arrived and lifted them into the sky.

Angels had no armored plating. They flew over water, never land. One of Ron's jobs was to transport people and mail to cruisers, destroyers, escorts, and tankers. Late one afternoon, just before twilight, Ron and another of his copilots, a fellow named Billy, finished making their deliveries and had turned their UH-2 back toward the ship.

They flew low over the water and began to climb. When homeward bound, the usual procedure was to grab the *Intrepid's* tacan signal—an electronic high-frequency navigational aid system that measured bearing and distance from the ship—and it would lead them back to her. This time, however, there was only silence and darkness. There was no signal.

An electrical failure. No instruments, no radio contact, no ships in sight, and less than thirty minutes of fuel. They could see no lights. Nothing. Just a field of air and water. He and Billy gained altitude in order to see farther and flew in the general direction of where they thought their ship had been when they left her. At last she came into view: steel and fire and power, a dot the size of a dime on the gulf. They flew by the tower and signaled the need for an emergency landing and with about five minutes of fuel remaining they touched down.

When I think of the war apart from what I know of Ron's days in the Gulf of Tonkin, I think of the doorgunner in *Full Metal Jacket* firing at Vietnamese in the rice paddies below the chopper. The doorgunner, played by Tim Colceri, laughs and fires his machine gun. "Get some," he shouts, "yeah, yeah, yeah. Ha, ha. Anyone who runs is a VC. Anyone who stands still is a well-disciplined VC." He laughs some more. The camera shifts to human figures running in a rice paddy. One falls, and another falls. Blue water curves through brown and green land. "You guys ought to do a story about me sometime," the doorgunner says to the two stringers for *Stars and Stripes*, Private Joker and Rafterman.

"Why should we do a story about you?" shouts Private Joker.

"'Cause I'm so fucking good! That ain't no shit, neither. I done got me one hundred and fifty-seven dead," he says.

"Any women or children?"

"Sometimes."

"How could you shoot women, children?"

"Easy." The doorgunner coughs. "Just don't lead 'em so much." He laughs wickedly. "Ain't war hell?"

———

After two periods of Chinese occupation—111 B.C. to A.D. 938, and then, later, from 1406 to 1428—and a long French colonial campaign, the Vietnamese watched American troops snap open their parachutes and float to the ground. John Kennedy started the Vietnam War. Villages were bombed and covered in napalm, which burns everything and clings to human flesh. Our military dropped bombs on civilian targets in Hanoi and Namdinh. Women and children died from napalm, bombs, small weapons fire. Lyndon Johnson escalated the war. Richard Nixon carried on the war, and Gerald Ford was president when the last American soldiers, ten Marines from the embassy, departed Saigon on April 30, 1975. Having spanned four American presidencies, the war in Vietnam came to an end.

In the next president's—Jimmy Carter's—first year of office, I was born. That was two-and-a-half years after the final withdrawal of American troops from Vietnam. Home from the war, Ron went back to Kansas, married, earned his living as a carpenter, and on weekends he snapped photographs of the farmhouse where he lived with a dog he called Cheyenne and the woman who was his first wife. Now Ron says he'll never leave Colorado. When I think of him rocking in his chair, gazing out over the high alpine desert dotted with piñons and prairie dogs burrowing in the sand, I often wonder what he's thinking. At dusk, when the light is fading and the shadows are just so, the sand appears to be rippling like water. It can feel like you're stranded in the middle of an ocean, treading water in the colossal rollers of the South China Sea.

ADAM WIEDEWITSCH is poetry editor and columnist at *The Prague Revue* and a founding editor of *Tongue: A Journal of Writing & Art*. His poems have appeared in *Azul* (Holland), *Carapace* (South Africa), *New Contrast (*South Africa), and most recently in *Salamander* and *Paris Lit Up*. He has received fellowships from DAAD, the Eva Tas Foundation, The Millay Colony, and The Ledig House International Writers Residency. He teaches middle school in the south Bronx.

FISHERMAN'S HANG

    Your n-shaped rope
needs plenty of slack to coil
from the bottom   Four GI's
   drank ration beer
   as another wound
   around & around
   the rope—up the length—
   8 or 9 times   Remember tying hooks
leaders & lures—
same knot   He tucked the end
   through the top eye,
   & to the bottom eye—
   he formed the choke   Each of us took a turn
with the hangman's noose
around our neck—
we took pictures
& mustered up a bit more
laughter   The noose
   a goal for drinking
   games, tossed quarters
   rolled socks—
    In the picture
the skin still covers his trachea—
    it looks so soft

SAINT MICHAEL, WITH AGENT ORANGE

Whoever opens his chest
bound like an orange crypt
above standard-issue holsters
fatigues, badges & blouses
will be met by a boy.
A boy who's been scarred
by nails & falling off pigs;
a rural-type who knows sacrifice
is part of good work, honest
as stone; a trooper from
choked farms turned factory;
a VFW before his first tour.
No matter his station
another in a Florsheim box
develops in a fraudulent lens.
A two-dimensional private
& an expansive Princeton
confined to Hanoi silhouette—
the wry-smile of a potluck
on his thin, pursed lips.

2

On step, he rests uneasy
before One Pillar Pagoda
where, according to court record,
childless Ly Thai Tong dreamt
he met the Bodhisattva
who gave him a baby son
seated on petals of a lotus
flower. It is May. 1971.
There is a chemical sting
in the air. This is his tour
& with few echoes beside

the emerald pond-water
from which the pagoda springs,
a pregnant letter from home
amidst spells of fire-fight
is nothing like his dream.
Neither is this floral temple
designed to resemble the lotus
the same landmine Vietnam
he read about as a recruit.

HANH NGUYEN WILLBOND was born in Vietnam and adopted by the American poet and Vietnam war veteran Bruce Weigl. She is a mother and works as a Registered Nurse on a neurology ward. She is also at work on a memoir, which will be published by the Women's Publishing House in Hanoi, Viet Nam.

WAR MUSIC AWAKENING FOR
SOLDIER'S DAUGHTER

> *Among the musical pieces that premiered at the Los Angeles New International Music Festival in May was "Song of Napalm" by composer Vu Nhat Tan. The piece was inspired by Viet Nam war veteran and poet Bruce Weigl's famous poem "Song of Napalm," which was itself inspired by Nick Ut's photograph of Kim Phuc, the so-called "Napalm Girl." From America, Hanh Weigl (Bruce Weigl's adopted Vietnamese daughter) writes the following about her special experience reading the Vietnamese version of the poem on stage.*
>
> *—VNS*

I had never met composer Vu Nhat Tan. Honestly, I didn't much care for that genre of music, so I didn't pay much attention to his work. But last year, my father came home from one of his many trips to Viet Nam waving a CD in my face with great enthusiasm. "You must listen to this right away," he said. "It's Viet Nam's newest music." Of course, when I learned that the album didn't contain the newest Vietnamese pop songs, I didn't care to listen to it.

But one day in the car, when we couldn't decide what to listen to, my father rolled down all the windows and cranked up Tan's music.

"Are you kidding me, Dad?" I asked. "What kind of music is this? Could you please turn it down? Everyone is staring at us."

My father didn't pay attention. He had his hands up in the air, eyes closed, and was dancing in the car. When he saw my face, he said: "You don't know how to understand art. I am going to collaborate with him."

Six months later, my father had news for me about his "collaboration" with Tan. He said Tan would write a piece of music to go with his poem "Song of Napalm," and that the composition would be performed by the Southwest Chamber Orchestra, accompanied by Vanessa Van Anh Vo on two Vietnamese traditional instruments, dan tranh and dan bau. In addition, my father would read his poem in English and I would read the translated version by Nguyen Phan Que Mai in Vietnamese.

I stood frozen. For the first time in my life I would have to read a poem in public—in Vietnamese—in front of an audience in a big city. What if I got so nervous that I read the wrong word in the poem? What if, all of a sudden, I forgot my Vietnamese?

"Just find a Vietnamese professional reader to fill in for me," I said.

But in the end, because my father has this special power to persuade me, and because I love him, I agreed to participate.

Only a month before my flight to Los Angeles did I begin to read the poem "Song of Napalm" in Vietnamese. I had tried to read it years ago when my father had first written it, but because I was so young and it was so complicated, I never understood it.

I read the poem again and again, in English and in Vietnamese, but I still couldn't understand. I only knew that the poem alluded to a famous photograph by Nick Ut, *Napalm Girl*. I wondered why my father alluded to that particular photograph, why he dedicated the poem to my mom, and why the poem included such intimate moments between my mother and my father.

After speaking to my father, I understood what the poem was actually about: the consequences of war. More specifically, post-traumatic stress disorder, or PTSD. Currently, my father suffers from seizures so bad he couldn't go to Los Angeles to read the poem with me as originally planned. Recently, a neurologist told him that his seizures are a symptom of PTSD.

After speaking to my father, I gained a renewed relationship to the poem that was more personal and more intimate. I imagined my father living on a pitch-black deserted island after a long war. His hand reaches for someone, anyone, like the small and fragile hands of the napalm girl, reaching out, praying for someone to come to her, to ease her burns and her overwhelming pain.

Then my mother appears. She paints the sky blue, cuts out a bright yellow sun to glue onto the blue sky, plants trees and grass, and builds a warm nest for him. No matter how bright and colourful the island becomes, however, my mother still cannot change the truth about the war and its consequences.

I was very nervous on the night of the performance because we had only rehearsed three times. I was worried that I would read the poem wrong and waste everyone's hard work.

I think I stopped breathing for a long time. My heart beat rapidly, as though I was going to pass out. But when Vanessa began playing her dan bau, all of my fears disappeared. The musical notes were clear and pure and deep, and the sky was very blue. I even heard the birds chirping.

Then I heard footsteps, running, gunshots, and the sound of thunder roaring, and then a loud scream. I saw the girl running from her village, screaming in agony. I saw my father as a young soldier holding a mortar, aiming in her direction. I saw Vanessa plucking out human screams and cries from the dan bau string. I even saw Nick Ut preparing to snap a photograph, and I saw the orchestra and the conductor in the near distance, and then I saw composer Tan standing in silence, alone, watching.

When I read the last verse of the poem and Vanessa plucked the final musical note on the dan bau, I exhaled a breath of relief. I couldn't believe that the song was over. I wanted to run up to my father and Tan to tell them what I saw and felt.

Only then did I dare to look down at the audience. They were all standing. Their applause was so loud and long that I thought it would never end. I saw some of them crying. I knew that they saw what I saw, and I wanted to believe that they felt what I felt. Finally, I could see the real power of "Song of Napalm."

I began to understand our relationships and why we came to meet each other; me, my father, Nick Ut, and Tan. We are all living proof of the consequences of war.

And now in my dreams there is a world in peace, a world without war and without the sounds of bombs or gunshots. In that world, we walk together to the song of the Napalm Girl, singing to Tan's music about the beauty of peace.

SONG OF NAPALM
for my wife

After the storm, after the rain stopped pounding,
we stood in the doorway watching horses
walk off lazily across the pasture's hill.
We stared through the black screen,
our vision altered by the distance
so I thought I saw a mist
kicked up around their hooves when they faded
like cut-out horses
away from us.
The grass was never more blue in that light, more
scarlet; beyond the pasture
trees scraped their voices into the wind, branches
crisscrossed the sky like barbed wire
but you said they were only branches.

Okay. The storm stopped pounding.
I am trying to say this straight: for once
I was sane enough to pause and breathe
outside my wild plans and after the hard rain
I turned my back on the old curses. I believed
they swung finally away from me . . .

But still the branches are wire
and thunder is the pounding mortar,
still I close my eyes and see the girl
running from her village, napalm
stuck to her dress like jelly,
her hands reaching for the no one
who waits in waves of heat before her.

So I can keep on living,
so I can stay here beside you,
I try to imagine she runs down the road and wings
beat inside her until she rises
above the stinking jungle and her pain
eases, and your pain, and mine.

But the lie swings back again.
The lie works only as long as it takes to speak
and the girl runs only as far
as the napalm allows
until her burning tendons and crackling
muscles draw her up
into that final position
burning bodies so perfectly assume. Nothing
can change that, she is burned behind my eyes
and not your good love and not the rain-swept air
and not the jungle green
pasture unfolding before us can deny it.
          —Bruce Weigl

MATTHEW WIMBERLEY grew up in the Blue Ridge Mountains. His stepfather served in the air force, where he was stationed in U-Tapao Thailand during the Vietnam War. Wimberley is the author of the chapbook "Snake Mountain Almanac" selected by Eduardo C. Corral as the winner of the 2014 Rane Arroyo Chapbook Contest from Seven Kitchens Press, and winner of the 2015 William Matthews Prize from the *Asheville Poetry Review*. He was selected for the 2016 Best New Poets Anthology. Wimberley was a finalist for the 2016 Crab Orchard Series in Poetry First Book Award. He lives in Richmond, Virginia.

TWO DAYS HOME

Put out those cigarettes, boys.
Inhale the flames
all the burning we don't see.
No sleep as wind pushes
against weeds. Are men
out there who move closer
with each eye blink? Or
just monkeys and their racket
cried toward the ocean?
The body learns not to rest—
to tuck bed corners, clean weapons
slow and calm as if at any moment
a bullet couldn't reach inside
the safety of a chain link fence
a few spools of barbed wire
and undo everything.

Put out those cigarettes, boys.
Back state-side and alive
air thick as a cloth bandage—
blood-heavy mosquitos hum
peppered spots over the glades
among fireflies which relight.
Two days home at dinner

he finds himself in one quick move
dropping his fork into a bread basket
taking cover under a table as a police siren
whorls in the parking lot. At night
the ocean rolls onto the shore
the faint echo of bombers
somewhere above the clouds.
A mouse in the kitchen
boot steps on the tarmac.

IN MY FATHER'S WORDS, 1969

In the rain we smell wood-fires
from villages just outside the base—
odors of teak and mahogany
white flowers and moth-larva
consumed. We sleep on ammo
in the beds of deuce and a halves,
and when clouds break,
night settles on the ocean
snipers make us work by starlight.
From the flight-deck bombers take off
and return. Each plane lifted by eight engines
we hear them roar over mountains and gulf.

In the rain mongoose infiltrate
the base, come from the jungle
to steal food. We write letters home
send our uniforms to the river
to be washed clean of rain-water.
and polish the raw-metal of machinery.
Listen to birds, to the silence
between missions.

In the rain planes come back
ghost-makers. Bombs flatten the jungle
and we load more bombs. The air
is jet-fuel and blurred vision. Groans
sound from idle engines ready to burn
until we don't hear the sound anymore.

In the rain we forget the rain
even as it drums on our hooches
clanks off metal and soaks our boots
until we don't wear boots.

Neil Armstrong comes back
to lift our spirits. All day the sun is out
over the Gulf. While he speaks
we load bombs behind his back,
planes take off over his voice.

In the rain there is death.
Some die without knowing
they have died, on fire
in cratered earth,
from the force of the blast.
We load bombs sixty hours
a week.

But after the rain
we close our eyes
and load bombs
in our sleep.

KAREN SPEARS ZACHARIAS is an author/journalist and guest lecturer at Central Washington University, Ellensburg, Washington. Her work has been featured on CNN, National Public Radio, and in the *New York Times*. A vocal advocate for military families, Karen is a Gold Star daughter and author of the memoir *After the Flag Has Been Folded* (William Morrow). She served on the advisory board for the Vietnam Veterans Memorial Fund Education Center and for the Vietnam Women's Memorial Fund. She blogs at karenzach.com.

THE MAN IN THE JEEP

At first I never even noticed the jeep, what with trying to tie up the bulldog pup. Grandpa Harve was sitting in a mesh lawn chair nearby, his dead arm slung down between his legs. His good hand flicked a cigarette stub.

"Karen you hold her," Mama instructed over my shoulder. "Frankie, tie that in a double knot." Daddy's best buddy had given us a prize bulldog as a gift that day. We were all gathered outside the trailer house trying to figure out where to keep such a creature in a yard that had no grass or fence.

We hadn't lived at Slaughters Trailer Court in Rogersville, Tennessee, very long. It was just a dirt hill with six trailers slapped upside it. One was ours, and one belonged to Uncle Woody, Mama's oldest brother. I'm sure given the situation Mama would have rather not lived any place named Slaughters.

Folks often laugh when I tell them I grew up a trailer park victim. But when I drive through places like Slaughters, like Lake Forest or Crystal Valley, or any of the other trailer courts I once called home, I ache for the children who live there, and for the circumstances that led their mamas and daddies to make homes between cinder block foundations and dirt yards.

This was late July 1966. Just like any Southern summer, the days steamed and the nights stewed. I found myself missing the ocean breezes of Oahu, where we had last lived with Daddy. We'd left the island just a month before, shortly after I finished third grade. We had family in Rogersville, where both my parents had grown up.

"I knew the minute I saw that jeep," Mama told me later. "There aren't any military bases in East Tennessee."

I don't remember having any premonitions myself. I was used to seeing jeeps. We had lived near military bases all my life. Fort Benning. Fort Campbell. Schofield.

"Shelby Spears?" the soldier asked. He was clutching a white envelope. His fingers trembled.

"Yes?" Mama replied. Her whole face went taut as she clenched her jaw. She turned and handed the pup over to Brother Frankie. Little Linda hid behind Mama, rubbing her bare toes in the dirt. "Finish tying him up," Mama instructed.

Then, pulling down the silver handle of the trailer door, she stepped inside. The soldier followed.

I looked over at Grandpa Harve. His eyes were hidden behind dark sunglasses. A white straw hat shielded his drooping head. Sister Linda followed the soldier. I followed her. Frankie followed me.

For years now, I've tried to remember what happened next, but it's as if somebody threw me up against a concrete wall so violently that my brain refuses to let any of it come back to me. I suppose the pain was so intense my body just can't endure it.

I recall only bits. Crying. Screaming. Hollering like a dog does when a chain is twisted too tightly about its neck.

Frankie was sitting cross-legged on the blue foam cushion that served as the trailer's built-in couch. He pounded the wall with his fists. "Those Charlies killed my Daddy!" he screamed. "Those Charlies killed my Daddy!"

Grasping Mama's hand, Linda buried her face in her thigh.

I was confused. Who was Charlie? Who was this soldier? Why was Mama crying? "What is it?" I asked. "What's happened?"

"Daddy's dead!" Frankie yelled back at me, punching the wall again. "They've kilt our daddy! I'm gonna kill them Charlies!"

I had never seen Mama cry before.

Not even that December night in Hawaii when Daddy left us.

Sister Linda was six years old and was already asleep when Daddy and Mama asked Frankie and me to come into the living room. "We need to talk," Daddy said.

He'd never asked us to talk before. Not officially, like he was calling together his troops or something. Mama sat real quiet beside him on the red vinyl couch. Frankie and I sat on the hardwood floor, dressed in our pajamas, ready for bed.

"Frank, Karen," Daddy said, "I believe you both are old enough now to understand some things."

I was thankful he recognized my maturity. After turning over a whole can of cooking oil on top of my head earlier that evening while helping Mama in the kitchen, I was feeling a bit insecure about my status as the family's oldest daughter. I was nine years old.

"You both know who President Johnson is?"

We nodded in unison.

Daddy continued, "There's a country that needs our help, South Vietnam. President Johnson has asked me to go."

"Where's Vietnam?" Frankie asked.

"Whadda you gonna do there?" I asked.

"It's in Southeast Asia. We'll be helping protect the country from communism."

Tears stung. Not because I understood what communism was, or that Daddy would be in any danger. Simply because my daddy would be leaving me.

"Frank, you're the man of the house now," Daddy said. "I need you to take care of your mama and sisters."

"Yes, sir," Frankie replied, his voice too steady for a boy of just eleven.

"Karen," Daddy said, looking directly at me, "you need to help Mama take care of Linda. Okay?"

I nodded.

I held my tears until after I hugged Mama and Daddy and climbed into bed. Scrunching myself between the cold wall and the edge of the mattress, I began to cry.

A few minutes later Daddy flipped on the light. On the bed next to mine, curled into a ball like a kitten, a sleeping Linda didn't even twitch. "Karen?"

"Yes, sir?" I said as I wiped my nose on the back of my forearm.

"Are you crying?"

"Yes, sir," I replied.

"Why are you crying, honey?"

"I'm scared," I answered.

"Scared of what?" Daddy walked over and sat down on the edge of my bed.

"That you won't come home!" I wailed. Like monsoon rains, powerful tears rushed forth.

"Karen," Daddy said, smoothing matted hair back from my wet cheeks. "I'll come back. I promise."

Picking me up, he let me cry into his shoulder. He smelled of Old Spice and sweat. "But I need for you to stop your crying, okay? It upsets Mama."

"Okay," I said, sucking back the last sob. I didn't want to upset anyone.

"G'night, Karen."

"G'night, Daddy. I love you."

"I love you too, honey."

He flipped off the light. Grabbing my pillow, I sought to muffle the crying that grown-ups can control but children never can.

Daddy left early the next day, before the sun tiptoed over the horizon. He kissed me good-bye, but I barely woke in the predawn darkness.

From Vietnam, Daddy sent pictures of barefoot children in tattered clothing. He sent Linda a Vietnamese doll wearing a red satin dress, and me one wearing yellow. Vietnamese colors for happiness and luck. And he wrote letters, promising he'd be home soon.

Daddy did return for a short visit. His orders called it an R&R, a rest-and-recuperation trip. The order is dated May 8, 1966. The papers issue Daddy a leave for Manila in the Philippines, effective May 10. Skip a couple of spaces over from "Philippines," and in another type and ink are the words "and Hawii." Daddy swore to Mama he'd gotten a hold of a typewriter and changed his orders so he could come home to us. He laughed when he told Mama about that.

It was pitch-dark outside when Mama locked us inside the house and left to go pick up Daddy. Frankie, Linda, and I sat on the vinyl couch waiting for them to return. I was having a hard time staying awake. Earlier that week Frankie had dared me to stick my hand in a wasp hive in a banana tree. I'd done it, trusting, as Frankie claimed, that all the wasps were long gone.

Liar. Liar. Liar. I got stung countless times. My hand swoll up till it looked like a brand-new baseball mitt. The doctor had given me sleeping pills and told Mama that I needed to keep my hand elevated. I'd taken the pills off and on all day long. After a half hour or so of waiting for Daddy, I gave up the struggle and returned to Mama's bed. I was there, asleep, when I heard Daddy's playful voice and Linda's giggles.

"Hey there, Sleepy-head," he said when I stepped into the room.

"Hey, Daddy," I replied, climbing onto his right knee. Linda was sitting on his left one.

"Couldn't wait up for me?" he asked.

"I tried."

"Let me see that hand," he said, taking my right hand into his. He studied the swollen hand. "That must've hurt."

I glared at Frankie. "Yes, sir. It did."

"Guess you won't be sticking your hand into hives again anytime soon."

"No, sir. I sure won't."

Frankie grinned. Mama and Daddy laughed. Linda snuggled closer to Daddy and giggled some more. I continued to glare at Frankie. I couldn't see what everybody thought was so funny.

Daddy had changed since he first left us in December. He was thinner. Malaria, he told Mama. I asked her what malaria was.

"A mosquito disease," she said.

We'd had plenty of mosquitoes in Tennessee. They could leave big welts on a girl's ankles and belly. But I never knew bites could make a person lose weight. Daddy looked awfully thin to me. Like he hadn't had a hot biscuit or a plate of gravy in a month of Sundays. Even his hair looked thinner. He had a worrisome look in his eyes, too. Like somebody who spent too much time reading and studying and still couldn't figure out the sum.

I was in the kitchen one afternoon when Daddy told Mama about a little girl he'd seen get blown up by a bomb. That troubled him. It troubled me too, after I heard about it.

Daddy said the girl would come to the camp, and he and the other soldiers gave her C rations, pennies, gum, or candy, whatever they had. Frankie and I liked to get into Daddy's C rations, too. Not because the food tasted good. Most of it smelled and looked like cat food. We just liked the cans because they were painted army green. When we ate from them, we pretended to be soldiers in the jungles.

Daddy leaned his chair back on two legs as he took a draw from his cigarette. A little bit of the Pet milk he'd poured over his bowl of cobbler earlier had turned the color of peaches.

"The Viet Cong strapped a bomb around her," Daddy said, recalling the moment he'd seen the little girl explode. Mama stood by the kitchen sink, drying a plate, listening to Daddy. She didn't say a word. "She was just a little girl, about Linda's size," Daddy said. "She was always asking me for pennies, for gum. They strap these kids with bombs and send them into our camps. There's nothing we can do."

Daddy took another drag from his cigarette and mashed the end of it into his plate. Mama kept drying dishes. I studied the sadness on my daddy's face. He looked defeated. Tired. Plumb worn-out. I walked over and wrapped my arms around his neck from behind. He patted my hands. "Hey there, Sissy," he said.

"Hey, Daddy," I replied.

"Wanna go for a ride?" he asked.

"Yes, sir," I said.

"Run go get Linda," he instructed. "She can come with us."

Daddy loved to take Linda and me riding on his moped in between the rows of pineapple fields near our house. He'd found the moped in a ditch one day and brought it home and fixed it up. If something had an engine, Daddy could get it to run. He'd spend hours lying on his back underneath a car, tinkering with its parts. I don't ever remember any car we ever owned breaking down. But Daddy always found some sort of reason to spend his Saturday afternoons underneath the car's hood. The only thing he seemed to love more than fixing car engines was driving cars. Fast. He and Mama shared that, too. Their lead-footed ways.

One day, back in 1957, it had gotten him into a mess of trouble and practically killed Granny Ruth. He had her in the passenger seat beside him when he was broadsided on a highway outside Knoxville. Granny

Ruth was hurt real bad. She spent weeks lying in the hospital bed. Mama says Granny Ruth never did fully recover from that wreck. She died from a stroke in 1962, shortly before we left for Hawaii.

Mama didn't like Daddy taking us girls out on the moped. She wouldn't ride it with him except for a time or two, down to the end of the street. And she wouldn't watch as we whizzed in and out of the red dirt roads of Wahiawa's pineapple fields. But Linda and I loved it. We squealed with delight, especially when Daddy revved up the engine.

"Faster, faster!" Linda would scream.

"Yeah, faster, faster!" I'd chime in.

Our hair, hers dark, mine blond, would whip every which way about our heads. Daddy would yell at us, "Hang on tight!"

Linda sat in front between his legs and gripped the bike's handles. Daddy kept one arm around her. I sat on the back, grasping his waist. Sometimes, when he wanted to go really fast, he'd have one of us wait in the fields while he took the other out. "Safer that way," he said.

He wouldn't go far, but he'd go as fast as the bike would take him. It was probably only zero to thirty in five minutes, but Linda and I felt like we were going at the speed of light. It was better than a Scrambler ride at the fair. Plus, we got the extra kick of having Daddy all to ourselves.

During that time he was home in May 1966, Daddy took Linda and me for several rides in the pineapple fields. He took Mama fishing along Oahu's North Shore. And he tossed balls with Frankie in the driveway. He ate hot biscuits and milk gravy that Mama made.

Daddy didn't talk much of war or of Vietnam. Other than the story of the little girl, I never heard him mention it again. He cleaned his gear, shined his boots, and grew sadly quiet as it got closer to the time when he had to return. He didn't make me any more promises. But this time I wasn't worried about his leaving. He'd come home just like he'd said. I figured he'd be home again soon enough. So on May 20, 1966, I barely woke at all when Daddy came in to kiss me good-bye.

"I love you, Karen."

"I love you too, Daddy," I said. I sat up and gave him a hug. He flipped off the overhead light, and I fell back to sleep, confident that there would be plenty of time for more hugs from Daddy.

In June our family returned to Rogersville in anticipation of that promise. Daddy said he'd be home in time for my tenth birthday on November 12. Perhaps even on Veterans Day.

Daddy kept his promise, in a way. He did come back. Via airmail, in a cargo plane full of caskets.

T he tears streaming down Mama's face frightened me.

Grandpa Harve didn't rise from his lawn chair until the man in the jeep pulled away. And if he ever hugged or comforted his daughter in any way, I never witnessed it. But tears trickled from beneath his dark glasses throughout the rest of the day. Grandpa Harve loved Daddy as much as any of us.

As I tried to sleep that first night, fear blanketed me. Never warm, it at least wrapped me up real tight. I took refuge in fear's cocoon. Sometimes I still do.

I could hear Mama's cries through the thin panel boards that separated our bedrooms. She had cried all day long. Loud, wailing cries. Bitter water. That day I'd seen Mama raise her head and plead with God Almighty Himself. She kept asking Him the same question over and over. "Why me, God? Why me?"

If God gave her an answer, I never heard it.

I wasn't bold enough to ask God why myself. I figured you had to know Him well enough to ask such a personal question. Still, I prayed each night. Clasping my throat, I prayed the only prayer I knew: "Our Father, who art in Heaven, hallow'd be thy name."

Sometimes I fell asleep before I got to the part about "Forgive us our trespasses, as we forgive those who trespass against us." But not usually. Getting to sleep is hard when you're worried about having your head cut off. It was a notion I obsessed over after I overheard some kinfolk discuss whether somebody had tried to cut off Daddy's head. From that moment on, for years to come, decapitation haunted my slumber. Avoiding dismemberment became my focus early in life.

Prior to Daddy's death, I had never even thought much about my neck before. The only times I ever noticed I had a neck were when Mama told me there was enough dirt in its creases to grow cotton. But nearly every night hence, I fell into a fitful sleep with my hands resting on my throat. I figured being asleep was too much like being dead. No telling what people do to you when you're dead or asleep.

Perhaps it's different for the dead. Perhaps the dead know what's going on in a way the sleeping don't. But can they really offer any help? Or is it just like those dreams where an intruder climbs into your bedroom window and he's stealthily coming toward you, and you begin to scream for help? Then you wake up and your mouth is open, but there is no sound at all. Just the clock ticking, the refrigerator humming, and dark silence.

I suspect if Daddy really saw how hurt we all were, he would have done something to help us. But he didn't. I hope it's because he couldn't—not because he was so busy rejoicing up in heaven that he didn't care about the hell he'd left us in.

It's hard to explain what losing a father does to a family. Daddy's death is the road marker we kids use to measure our life's journey. Before his death, ours was a home filled with intimacy and devotion. After his death, it was filled with chaos and destruction.

I thought about our family's loss decades later while reading an article published in *The Oregonian*. It was the police account of a young man whose body had surfaced in the Columbia River. Hoping that somebody could help identify the boy, the newspaper ran a photo of the shirt he was wearing. It was a custom-made T-shirt with the picture of a skull on it. Law enforcement officials couldn't identify the boy because his head was missing.

That shirt was his only legacy. And unless someone recognized it, his headless body would be buried in a grave marked "John Doe." Whatever thoughts or memories his soul would carry into the afterlife would literally be cut off forever.

I think that's what losing Daddy did to us. With him gone, we were headless. It was as if somebody came into our home with a machete and in one swift slice decapitated our entire family.

ACKNOWLEDGMENTS

Inheriting the War is the culmination of 10 years of research and conversations. I am indebted to the many writers, veterans, family, friends, colleagues, and mentors who have spoken with me over the years, pointed me in the right direction, and in so many ways guided and nurtured this anthology. I'm especially grateful to Cathy Linh Che and Ocean Vuong for their friendship, many conversations and role as contributing editors, and to the writers in this collection whose work has inspired me and provided a sense of community. With gratitude to the institutions that have offered encouragement and hospitality, especially the William Joiner Institute for the Study of War and Social Consequences—Boston, UMass, and to New York University for their generous support of this collection. Special thanks to Angelo Nikolopoulos at the Creative Writing Program at New York University. And to W. W. Norton, especially to Jill Bialosky for her commitment to this anthology, and to Maria Rogers, Drew Weitman, Nancy Palmquist, Will Scarlett, and all of the staff for their support.

PERMISSIONS

Grateful acknowledgment is made to the following authors, publishers, translators, and agents for their permission to reprint poems in Inheriting the War: Poetry and Prose by Descendants of Vietnam Veterans and Refugees.

MARY JO BANG: Excerpt from "You Were You Are Elegy" © 2007 by Mary Jo Bang, originally published in *Elegy* by Mary Jo Bang, Graywolf Press 2007. Printed with permission of Graywolf Press.

QUAN BARRY: Excerpt from "child of the enemy" from *Asylum*, by Quan Barry, © 2001. Reprinted by permission of the University of Pittsburgh Press.

TOM BISSELL: "Part 2: Chapter 1" from *The Father of All Things: A Marine, His Son, and the Legacy of Vietnam* by Tom Bissell, copyright © 2007 by Thomas Carlisle Bissell. Used by permission of Pantheon Books, an imprint of the Knopf Doubleday Publishing Group, a division of Penguin Random House LLC. All rights reserved.

STAR BLACK: "To A War Correspondent" and "Recollection" from *Balefire* by Star Black © 1999 by Painted Leaf Press. Reprinted with permission of the author.

LILY KATHERINE BOWEN: "Lanterns" and "Falling" © 2016 by Lily Katherine Bowen. Printed with permission of the author.

EMILY BRANDT: "Petroleum," "Kapok," "Cork," "Ash," and "Silk" © 2016 by Emily Brandt. "Cork" and "Silk" both appeared in *Epiphany's* War Issue, and "Kapok" appeared both at *Podium* and in *BluePrintReview*. Printed with permission of the author.

CATHY LINH CHE: "Los Angeles, Manila, Đà Nẵng" © 2016 Cathy Linh Che, originally published in *Poem-a-Day* on April 21, 2016 by the Academy of American Poets. Printed with permission of the author. "Split" from *Split*. Copyright © 2014 by Cathy Linh Che. Reprinted with the permission of The Permissions Company, Inc., on behalf of Alice James Books, www.alicejamesbooks.org.

LAREN McCLUNG is the author of *Between Here and Monkey Mountain* (Sheep Meadow Press 2012), a collection of poetry that addresses the aftermaths of war. Her father served one tour in Vietnam (1968–1969) deployed with the 173rd Airborne. Poet Afaa Michael Weaver writes of her collection: "The troubles of a nation's wars come to bear on a child who grows into a poet who must lift these nightmares into her hands and remember." Her poetry has appeared in journals and reviews including *Harvard Review, Poetry, Massachusetts Review, War, Literature & the Arts*, and elsewhere. She has been the recipient of a Teachers & Writers Collaborative Van Lier Fellowship, an Iraq and Afghanistan Veteran Workshop Teaching Fellowship, and has led workshops in poetry at Goldwater Hospital on Roosevelt Island and in the Creative Writing Program at New York University. She currently teaches at New York University.